About the Peace and Security i⁞

Until recently, security was defined mostly in geopolitical terms with the assumption that it could only be achieved through at least the threat of military force. Today, however, people from as different backgrounds as planners in the Pentagon and veteran peace activists think in terms of human or global security, where no one is secure unless everyone is secure in all areas of their lives. This means that it is impossible nowadays to separate issues of war and peace, the environment, sustainability, identity, global health, and the like.

The books in the series aim to make sense of this changing world of peace and security by investigating security issues and peace efforts that involve cooperation at several levels. By looking at how security and peace interrelate at various stages of conflict, the series explore new ideas for a fast-changing world and seeks to redefine and rethink what peace and security mean in the first decades of the new century.

Multidisciplinary in approach and authorship, the books cover a variety of topics, focusing on the overarching theme that students, scholars, practitioners, and policymakers have to find new models and theories to account for, diagnose, and respond to the difficulties of a more complex world. Authors are established scholars and practitioners in their fields of expertise.

In addition, it is hoped that the series will contribute to bringing together authors and readers in concrete, applied projects, and thus help create, under the sponsorship of Alliance for Peacebuilding (AfP), a community of practice.

The series is sponsored by the Alliance for Peacebuilding, http://www.allianceforpeacebuilding.org/, and edited by Charles Hauss, Senior Fellow for Innovation.

For a list of all books in the series, please visit https://rowman.com/Action/SERIES/RL/RLPS21 or scan the QR code below.

Civil Society, Peace, and Power

Civil Society, Peace, and Power

Edited by
David Cortright, Melanie Greenberg,
and Laurel Stone

ROWMAN & LITTLEFIELD
Lanham • Boulder • New York • London

Published by Rowman & Littlefield
A wholly owned subsidiary of The Rowman & Littlefield Publishing Group, Inc.
4501 Forbes Boulevard, Suite 200, Lanham, Maryland 20706
www.rowman.com

Unit A, Whitacre Mews, 26–34 Stannary Street, London SE11 4AB

Copyright © 2016 by Rowman & Littlefield

British Library Cataloguing in Publication Information Available

Library of Congress Cataloging-in-Publication Data Available

ISBN 978-1-4422-5855-6 (cloth : alk. paper)
ISBN 978-1-4422-5856-3 (pbk. : alk. paper)
ISBN 978-1-4422-5857-0 (electronic)

♾ ™ The paper used in this publication meets the minimum requirements of American National Standard for Information Sciences—Permanence of Paper for Printed Library Materials, ANSI/NISO Z39.48-1992.

Printed in the United States of America

To Karen, for patient and loving support throughout the writing and editing process.

—David

To Anna Rose and Jed, in the hope that they will inherit a more peaceful world.

—Melanie

To Mom and Dad, for exemplifying how to love, encourage, and inspire.

—Laurel

Contents

Acknowledgments

This volume was made possible by a generous grant from the Rockefeller Brothers Fund to a consortium of the Alliance for Peacebuilding, the Global Partnership for the Prevention of Armed Conflict, and the Kroc Institute for International Peace Studies at the University of Notre Dame. Our collaborative work focused on the creative ways in which civil society engages with key policy actors in a range of conflict settings, and how these partnerships can be strengthened during a turbulent time for peace and security in the world. The editors and authors are very grateful to the Rockefeller Brothers Fund for supporting such a significant peacebuilding project.

As part of the learning outcomes from the grant, we held a conference in October, 2015, at Notre Dame, bringing together the book authors, editors, and experts from around the world—together, some of the best minds working on issues of civil society participation. The editors would like to thank all of the experts who joined in these conversations, and the Kroc Institute for hosting the conference.

We are deeply grateful to Anna Milovanovic and Ryne Clos for their invaluable editing support, and the deep substantive knowledge and fresh thinking they brought to the chapters in this volume. We also thank Charles (Chip) Hauss, the series editor, for his encouragement of this book from the beginning.

Preface

At a time when power is shifting between governments and non-state actors at all levels of society, in every country, the very nature of the social contract is transforming. Some countries are becoming more repressive, and others more open, yet in all states the power of civil society voices, amplified through the technology revolution, cannot be ignored. Citizens are able to communicate with governments, and with each other, in ways never before possible, allowing for creative peacebuilding, shared governance, and new approaches to fragility and human security. While very powerful counter-trends exist—witness the closing of civil society space in countries like Russia, South Sudan, Venezuela, and a host of authoritarian imitators—civil society engagement continues to shape the global landscape in new and vital ways. This book explores a special aspect of civil society empowerment: the new ways in which civil society engages with policymakers to create structures for sustainable peace, development, and human security.

This volume arose out of a remarkable collaboration between the Kroc Institute for International Peace Studies at the University of Notre Dame, the Alliance for Peacebuilding (AfP), and the Global Partnership for the Prevention of Armed Conflict (GPPAC). All three organizations have worked closely for years with civil society in peacebuilding, conflict prevention, and human security and have engaged in programs linking civil society with policymakers in the areas of sustainable development, human security, and cooperation with Regional Inter-Governmental Organizations (RIGOs). In 2012, the three organizations joined as a consortium, under the auspices of a generous grant from the Rockefeller Brothers Fund, to explore more rigorously the roles that civil society can play in shaping policy, building new institutions, and linking peace, development, and security during this tumultuous period of world history.

This volume is a reflection of the consortium's work over three years together. The chapters offer new conceptual lenses for understanding emerging forms of civil society power and human security, as well as case studies highlighting creative ways in which civil society has engaged with policymakers to build more sustainable peace in areas riven by deadly violence. All of the chapter authors came together in October 2015, at a conference held at the University of Notre Dame, to solidify our understanding of how the themes in the volume link together, and how the individual cases add up to a more comprehensive whole.

The volume is divided into four sections. The introductory section, with chapters by John Paul Lederach and Peter van Tuijl, sets forth a framework for understanding the power of civil society to make transformative change and to build peaceful, inclusive societies.

Section 1, Shaping the Sustainable Development Agenda, "Amplifying the voices of civil society in fragile states through the International Dialogue on Peacebuilding and Statebuilding (IDPS) and the New Deal," focuses on civil society action in fragile states. It pays particular attention to the New Deal as a bold experiment in linking peacebuilding with statebuilding, as embodied now in Goal 16 of the 2030 Agenda for Sustainable Development.

Section 2, Partnering with Regional Organizations, "Strengthening the role of civil society engagement in Regional Inter-Governmental Organizations (RIGOs) for peace and security," focuses on the understudied, yet potentially powerful, relationship between civil society groups and regional organizations such as the Economic Community of West African States and the Pacific Islands Forum.

Section 3, Engaging the Military for Human Security, "Increasing civil society participation in security sector reform to enhance human security," focuses on transformative peace processes between civil society and security sector actors, redefining human security in challenging contexts such as Guatemala and the Philippines.

In the conclusion, we tie together the central themes of the book, while discussing the development of more effective peacebuilding architecture and how to make progress in the delivery of human security as a global public good.

David Cortright, Melanie Greenberg, and Laurel Stone

Introduction

John Paul Lederach

The invitation to write for this volume offers an opportunity for me to reflect upon questions of where our field of peacebuilding and conflict transformation has come in these past decades and the challenges that lie ahead. I want to begin by telling a mostly unknown story about the publication of one of my books, a volume that quite a few in the peacebuilding community have read, *Building Peace: Sustainable Reconciliation in Divided Societies*. The book emerged around experiences in the 1980s and early 1990s. It reflected many workshops and intense on-the-ground engagements primarily in Latin America and Africa. I was invited to develop a small book, based on those experiences, that was submitted to one of the publishing arms of the United Nations. I wrote the manuscript and sent it off to the publisher. After the usual back-and-forth editing process, my copy of the published book arrived one day in the mail. I opened the package and pulled the book out. On the front cover I read the bold type heading, then did a double, and triple take. The title was not the one I had given the book. It had been changed. The title read: *Building Peace: Sustainable Development in Divided Societies*. The word *reconciliation* had been replaced with the word *development*. I sent off an email and was soon on the phone with the publishers reminding them that I had used the subtitle "Sustainable Reconciliation in Divided Societies." Within hours all the copies of the book were called back from wherever they had been sent in the world. Sometime later a second edition came out with the original title as I had intended, though it was not widely distributed. Two years later with an additional chapter, the book came out from USIP Press in the form that most now know it.

Only very recently did I reflect back on that "bump" in the publishing world almost thirty years ago. My reflection is this: Shifting the title from *Sustainable Reconciliation* to *Sustainable Development* probably happened because the category for the concept of reconciliation did not exist in the mainstream at that time. The category that did exist, particularly when attached with sustainability was the concept of development. My guess is that someone probably just typed it in without a second thought.

That brought me back to reflect on the original impulse of why I chose to use the word reconciliation within a book that was focused on peacebuilding. Two initial thoughts on that purpose provide a launching pad for several observations about the role of civil society in peacebuilding.

First, the phrase *sustainable reconciliation* was intended to provoke a conversation and critical reflection in our wider field of peace and conflict studies. My grounded experiences of peacebuilding during the decade of the 1980s led to a deep appreciation for how much more was happening than what commonly was referred to as a *peace process*. The term reconciliation lifted elements of that complexity forward and provoked the imagination. The core elements had to do with a profound respect I was gaining around the deeper meaning and dynamics of *identity, power, and exclusion*. This probes toward the challenge of what fear for survival means, an experience that comes with the cyclical reality for many people who are facing yet another decade of open violence and structural injustices. And these deeper themes—fear, threat to identity, exclusion—bubble into demands for justice, truth, and more direct participation. I suggested that if we orient ourselves toward reconciliation as central to peacebuilding, we invoke these deeper questions and the drivers underpinning protracted violence. Who am I? Who are you? And how are we going to choose to be *we*? Four decades later these inquiries still present themselves in every context where I have worked, and they require us to think carefully about complexity and relational spaces. They demand serious attention to the very nature of how we think constructive and sustainable change happens. So for me, including the word reconciliation as part of the title was to lift forward the notion of the relational complexity of what's happening at any given situation.

The second thought parallels the first concern. The closer I got to the work that had me navigating day by day from grassroots community engagements to higher level political negotiations and back again, the more I realized the gap between the local and the national body politic was profound. However, in much of the peacebuilding literature any fundamental understanding of the interdependence between levels did not exist. I had come to the deep conclusion that reconciliation among other things requires us to ask questions about the quality of relationships and the quality of relational spaces that coexist when multiple types and levels of change unfold simultaneously in settings of really deep-rooted conflict.

These perspectives brought me to look beyond the narrow approach of seeking conflict resolution through a particular political set of negotiations that required an orientation toward the questions of how wider transformation of whole societies emerges. Reconciliation evokes the notion of how we move from deep harm to flourishing communities.

My hope was to provoke the notion that there is something more than an exclusively high-level negotiation underway in these settings. In the years that have transpired I remain absolutely convinced that relationships and relational spaces really do matter. But I also know that I am probably as perplexed as ever about the challenges that remain before us and that we have to creatively face over and again in any given context. For me those contexts most recently have been long-term work in Colombia and Nepal. And these lead to three relentlessly persistent challenges that face peacebuilding. I once learned that the Brazilian term for nonviolence is relentless persistence. I think these are relentlessly persistent challenges that affect not only the wider endeavors of peacebuilding but in particular the topic of how civil society empowerment emerges with capacity to influence and connect to decisions that really affect the whole body politic and provide people the capacity to engage meaningfully in the changes that affect their lives.

INTERDEPENDENCE

I have become increasingly respectful of how challenging interdependence really is. I think it has much to do with an increased understanding of the nature of complexity and complex systems. I have always come with and from a tradition in my own scholarship that has been systems-oriented. I had the privilege of studying with pioneers who very much engaged in this kind of thinking, from Elise and Kenneth Boulding across to the Quaker conciliator, Adam Curle. They were always thinking about much bigger systems-related issues. In the last decade or so I think the field of peacebuilding has begun to engage more concretely in systems orientations, how the dynamics within a system function to repeat certain cycles and patterns, and how we have to think creatively about those patterns and the way that we engage them.

Systems engagement will always lift out the significance of interdependence. The challenge we face is bringing a more holistic understanding of interdependence to the change processes we seek to sustain. A recent example emerges with research from the Peace Accords Matrix at Notre Dame's Kroc Institute. This investigation looks systematically at the implementation record of comprehensive peace agreements over the past thirty years. We know from this work that the quality of an agreement is only proximate to the quality of its implementation. Whereas many understand an agreement to represent the end point of a process, I see a peace accord as the door that opens up into a whole new range of challenges about to unfold.

In peace accords the interdependence of provisions within an agreement are dynamically related. However, our operationalization of accords tends to push provisions into specialized units and projects. Essentially we break down agreements into program areas and provisions as if they are separate from each other. We soon come to understand that when one set of provisions slows down or fails to meet its designated time frame, these can cascade and create effects on other provisions and the whole of the process. This reaffirms how much peacebuilding really is about interdependent *processes* of change.

Over the past four decades I rather consistently find that we have improved our capacity to *give recognition* to interdependence. If I were writing this years earlier I would say that the biggest challenge we have between grassroots and higher-level negotiations, it still remains the case to some degree, is insufficient recognition that other levels of society need each other in very concrete and meaningful ways. Grassroots communities—due to experiences of corruption, state institutions that fail them, and direct harm from state structures under the control of certain mechanisms that do not permit delivery of basic services—have a cynical view of cooperation with the state. At the same time the conflict history has left a residue of dysfunctional competition within the civil society movements. At the higher level, we find that local communities rarely appear on national radar screens until a politician makes a speech and appeals to their constituencies. And then it's usually called consultation: coming in and out quickly but not with a sense of deep context-related understanding. That would have been my view thirty years ago. While many of these same challenges endure, I do see a significant shift that has resulted in much greater recognition that sustainable, constructive, and peaceful change requires *participation* of more than one level of politics. However, practical interdependency of levels requires a great deal of creativity and change in both formal and informal behavior. We remain in our infancy. We are still learning what dynamic interdependency requires of people, social movements, institutions, and the whole body politic.

Just recently in Colombia this was illustrated for me in a very concrete way in a meeting of community leaders from eight regions. Hardest hit in the history of the sixty-year war in Colombia, these regions have initiated work to understand what the successful implementation of the hoped-for peace agreement will need in order to build sustainable transformation. Alongside those nearly thirty leaders from the eight regions were representatives of twelve government institutions tasked with delivering services that would pertain to particular provisions of the future agreement. These included representatives for example of a special unit on victims, a department that focuses on national prosperity and peace, and the newly formed

Ministry of Post Conflict. Those twelve people each made a ten-minute presentation of their work and approach, how and why it contributes to a peaceful transition. Across the twelve they had never heard each other make those speeches, not to say anything about the communities' interaction with those particular institutions. Several dynamics were illustrated in a two-hour session.

First, very few had anything close to a robust understanding of interdependence, of how one set of initiatives and services affects another, or how public services and politics work in ways that improve the capacity to really respond to the deep patterns of harm that a half-century war has produced. With these twelve institutions and the thirty community leaders I made a summary conclusion for the days' work and shared the following. *Listening today I was reminded of Eduardo Galeano, the famous Uruguayan poet, who once said, likely with his hands thrown in the air: "Who will make peace among the peacemakers?" In Spanish, it has a wonderful resonance "Quien pacifica a los pacificadores?" Building off Galeano, in Columbia right now I would ask "who will coordinate the coordinators?"*

THE GREAT GAP OF STRATEGIC COORDINATION

Our second challenge requires us to face more directly the great gap of coordination. We have attended to this by making "networking" more central to peacebuilding. I think this has oriented itself toward meetings and talk, but not always into targeted coordination for the purpose of social change. Readers of my books will see two very specific shifts in my language from the book *Building Peace* (1994) to the book *The Moral Imagination* (2005). On the one hand, I shifted from the *middle out* description of networking to what I called the *web approach* in *The Moral Imagination*. I left the architecture of sociology, and I went to the brilliance of spiders. I made an argument that spiders are the closest thing that we have to spatial and relational geniuses. They help us understand how change is embedded in and unfolds across particular spaces. On the other hand, I shifted from a focus on institutions toward an understanding of platforms, inclusive of formal institutional spaces but not bound by those. Both merit further comment.

On networking and the challenge of coordination, I have been struck rather consistently that we are increasingly interested in networking. In fact, networking to some degree has become almost the fallback position of every proposal anybody anywhere writes. This is evident in Colombia, where the combination of two rather extraordinary things sit side by side: the site of the world's longest armed conflict and the country with the most peace proposals. Within Colombia, while I haven't done the study myself, I would wager there are probably at least a dozen if not two dozen groups that use the word *network* in their alliance or in their particular organization. There are people across the board who make the case that what they are doing is linking up people. And yet they and society at large remain deeply divided. Using the terminology does not mean that we have evolved our imagination of practice. The two are quite different, and it is where I think some of the perplexing aspects come into play.

Networking rarely contributes to social change when done just for sake of networking. This becomes particularly challenging, I think, as we begin to look in very concrete ways at the dynamics and deep patterns addressed in settings of protracted conflict. While we need to draw lessons from places where networking has made a significant difference, I am highly cognizant that some of the greatest genius of when and how networking works emerges in the specific context from which it initiated and to which it responds. To some degree we understand that networking is necessary, but we haven't always developed the strategies by which it becomes effective or by which it finds the ways to make an impact at particular times and places. If I had a small formula for that, and I am always a bit shy of anything too formulaic, it would seem to me that networking happens, not because the like-minded have gotten together, but rather when it really builds spaces that are highly improbable with a focus on system change. It requires you to be in relationships with people that you may not understand or like. This has been particularly hard, I think, for the peacebuilding community. We would rather all gather around folks that have a similar vision of peace. Effective networking places us in that hard arena of looking for the improbable, of developing relationships that cut across what is already known. The key to this in many regards is finding improbable connections coupled with actionable proposals, ideas, and ways that create meaningful influence and cooperation.

When I find these elements in place it has required a long series of relation-ships to be built in order to act opportunistically—at any given moment—when things emerge that make the unthinkable possible. How we can be in a place where the unthinkable that is now possible may have some chance of surviving? It is the odd paradox of time and commitment in peacebuild-ing that requires long, slow relationship cultivation and the capacity to seize that moment where something significant can actually enter a conversation and make a difference in a set of decisions. That to me has been a significant challenge. I call it a relentless and persistent challenge because I do not think that it can happen by way of a single recipe. It has to find creativity continu-ously throughout the context in which it is being done and throughout the time periods that are in place. It requires that we remain long-term strategic and short-term responsive.

CREATIVITY

The third reflection takes up the challenge of creativity. I have been increasingly of the view that social change is less about the technical formula of delivery and more about the artistic, creative process. When we couple these two, good things happen. If we rely exclusively on our technical capacities, we will find them insufficient for the nature and the depth of the challenges we face.

I return for a moment to the notion that peacebuilding requires *generative platforms*. I understand these as seeking the source and capacity to continuously generate innovations that respond to highly dynamic and adaptive systems within which we are working. More commonly we try to house this in the form of organizations, networks, and institutions. When these become formal more attention is focused on their structure than on the generative process of critical and creative response. This requires a constant orientation toward learning about how the complexity of dynamic contexts built for years around division and violence will offer up new forms of old patterns and that we, in turn, must continue to have a capacity to bring forward innovation to possibilities that were not completely understood or known that emerged from our learning. This requires an ability to be deeply grounded so that we remain critically capable of understanding patterns and dynamics while seeking to nurture and lift forward authentic voices of change. As our Colombian friend Ricardo Esquivia always says, to be grassroots means you have to be close enough to the ground to *hear the roots grow*. I fear that a lot of our professional work assumes that we already have the answers, that we don't need to listen in quite the same way anymore. I think that is a huge mistake because creativity comes from that place where you are hearing the grass grow. You are close enough that you know something concrete is presenting itself, but it has to be brought forward in a way that it is never quite been formulated or sculpted before. Though the patterns of exclusion, threat to identity, and fear persist they will take on new and adaptive forms. Our challenge as artists of social change places us at the liminal edge of bringing into existence something that responds with creativity to old, newly clothed patterns. This will always require the creative act every time we do it. That is a platform that is both ongoing and generative.

If I have learned anything over the last twelve years of accompanying a foundation in Nepal and of now landing with my colleagues in Humanity United, I would leave three very simple provocations to ponder.

One, I remain convinced that our time frames around social change are far too short. We have not been willing to look seriously at the nature of what really significant change means in deep-rooted, long-lasting, durable conflict areas, especially in contexts of armed and structural violence. At a minimum

I think we should orient ourselves toward decade-thinking. I have written a small memoir on my experiences in Nepal, and one of the chapters is on the meaning of decade-thinking. I wrote the chapter because it is not easy to think in decades. I have only had one foundation ever say they would agree to a decade pledge, and then they asked, "So how do we think in decades?" And I said, "I don't know. We'll have to figure it out now." It was really amazing. After nearly forty years of work, this was the first time I ever had a foundation that took seriously the notion that it may require a decade, minimally, to engage in peacebuilding in places that have had four and five decades of structural and open violence.

So I think our time frames are too short and, by virtue of that, they are weak in taking advantage of opportunity for deeper transformation. That's the paradox. We do not have a long enough time frame to understand what has to be built and held in place, and we do not have the capacity to move in the ways that opportunity presents. It is a real dilemma mixed in this.

Two, I place myself squarely in the camp of raising my hand and saying, yes, I have sinned, please forgive me. It is this: the dissemination of knowledge and tools is not the same as fostering creativity, cultivating relational genius, and nurturing healthy activists. I think we have attended more to the development of tools and the dissemination of knowledge than building the deepest capacities and generative platforms to make fuller use of the tools. Healthy people in healthy organizations are what foster the capacity to really understand what relationships mean in a given context and to engage in sustained and critical creativity. Health and creativity sit at the far edges of what we do in the mainstay of our work and not at the center. I think it should be inverted.

Three, and this comes from a number of locations, I have learned to *never confuse a project with a social movement.* I think we confuse the two all the time. We have accepted that social change happens by way of the agency of projects. I have never understood why we have been unwilling to actually face one of the hardest and deepest questions in the whole of our field: Why do we accept the *projectization of human relationships* engaged in complex social change? Projects and social movements are very, very different. What we're after is the deeper transformation, and that requires a form of *accompaniment* that goes well beyond and is not defined by a project. We need to develop the fundamental concept of patient capital. The project can be contributive, but my fear is that we've actually taken this to another level: our lives and our relationships are defined by the parameters of projects. This is a confusion that we need to address as one of the most resilient of the complex challenges we face.

Civil society empowerment in my view will always require innovation. It will always require being close enough to the ground that you can hear the grass grow. It will always require the improbable connection across people and levels that has to be built and rebuilt time and again because it must live in settings that are dynamic and adaptive. This challenge of maintaining creativity, developing empathetic understanding, and building improbably long-term relationships are precisely what the authors in this volume develop. The chapters that follow explore peacebuilding practice and the value of creative partnerships in the fields of development, cooperation with regional organizations, and the complex interaction of civil-military relations. This volume identifies key lessons and approaches to the challenges of constructive change in the pursuit of reconciliation in settings of protracted, deep-rooted conflict.

Chapter 1

Civil Society and the Power to Build Peaceful and Inclusive Societies

Peter van Tuijl

In September 2015, the United Nations General Assembly agreed upon 17 Sustainable Development Goals (SDGs) for 2016–2030. The new development agenda is framed in "Five Ps": people, planet, prosperity, peace, and partnership; and includes Goal 16: "Promote peaceful and inclusive societies for sustainable development, provide access to justice for all and build effective, accountable and inclusive institutions at all levels."[1]

The acknowledgment of the importance of "peace" and the inclusion of Goal 16 in the SDGs is a significant step forward for Civil Society Organizations (CSOs) working on peacebuilding and conflict prevention. The predecessor of the SDGs, the Millennium Development Goals (MDGs), did not include any reference to armed violence, peace, or security. This left an omission in the main consensus on the global development agenda during 2000–2015.[2] Civil society lobbied intensively to ensure a "peace goal" in the SDGs. This effort to shape and influence policy at the highest levels is further examined by Erin McCandless in chapter 2 of this volume.

The prominence of peace and the importance of Goal 16 in the SDGs as a political commitment supported by all UN member states is an unprecedented opportunity for civil society to revisit its role and constitute a longer-term vision on what it aims to achieve in building peaceful and inclusive societies. Current discourse on civil society and peacebuilding takes a predominantly functional approach to the role of civil society. This volume focuses more on the agency and opportunity of civil society in relation to building peace and creating effective, accountable, and inclusive institutions. It perceives civil society as having greater leverage within a framework of power relations. In fact, without the impactful voice of civil society, it is unlikely that Goal 16 in the SDGs would have been there.

The international community is facing an increasing number of crises in different countries and regions of the world. How does civil society challenge and transform power relations and institutions at different levels and foster action to address the disparities in access to power and resources that are often at the root of armed conflict? How can this capability help to solve the widely acknowledged problem that the international system lacks mechanisms for linking local realities to global, regional, and national policy processes? If the assumption is true that peacebuilding policy will be stronger when civil society is empowered, we need to better understand how civil society is able to navigate the complexity of violent conflict in order to assert its potential in institutionalizing mutually accountable relationships that contribute to building peaceful and inclusive societies. As McCandless observes, the act of influencing policy for peace is a challenging and complex endeavor in and of itself.

Civil society needs to address how it defines and expands its role in shifting balances of power in state relations in international organizations and regional arrangements, in order to determine how civil society may contribute to long-term and institutionalized solutions supporting peace. Asserting such a role comes with greater responsibilities and risks. Yet the alternative is a civil society that fails to prioritize the long-term solutions focusing on conflict prevention and human security while instead going along with the tendency of governments and international organizations to resort to short-term crisis management and providing humanitarian assistance.

APPROACHES TO CIVIL SOCIETY AND PEACEBUILDING

Civil society and peacebuilding are both widely debated concepts. Our discussion is limited to some of the most significant approaches. As for peacebuilding, we follow the definition proposed by Paffenholz: *peacebuilding* aims at preventing and managing armed conflict and at creating sustainable peace after large-scale organized violence has ended.[3]

Peacebuilding is related to, but distinguishable from, the broader and deeper concept of conflict transformation, briefly described by Lederach as "changing conflict into something constructive."[4] Conflict transformation requires changes in structures of interaction or institutions, as well as changes in human relationships, in order to achieve substantive change.[5] Our main focus is on the structural component of conflict transformation and how the role of civil society in peacebuilding may foster institutions that meet human needs. This supports the emphasis in conflict transformation on the importance of bottom-up approaches and the elicitive method of conflict analysis, which seeks information from those in society who are closest to and most affected by conflict but who are often not consulted or included in conventional considerations of causes and solutions to conflict.[6]

We do not address other elements of conflict transformation, such as changes in individuals, in personal relationships, or in culture, with the exception of touching upon gender relations. Overwhelming evidence supports the need to change gender relations to build peace. The effort to change gender relations accordingly is situated in significant ways in the civil society sphere.[7]

Definitions of civil society usually start with identifying a realm of voluntary associations in between the family and the state where people freely organize and produce a colorful variety of actors, such as nongovernmental organizations (NGOs), faith-based groups, community associations, women's groups, organized not-for-profit efforts, and professional collectives. Different ways to further identify the role of civil society in public life can be categorized in three groupings: as a set of nonstate actors; as a public sphere or arena of interactions; or as a set of norms and values, promoting a good society.[8]

The actor approach to civil society emphasizes the countervailing power that civil society leverages versus state or market actors. In this view, organized civil society is an important part of the checks and balances in the political community and thus contributes to democracy and social justice. The perception of civil society as a public sphere or arena of interaction puts less emphasis on civil society as a totality of actors but rather analyzes the nature and quality of the dialogue between individual citizens and social groups on issues of common concern. This includes, for example, the role of the media. Finally, to consider civil society foremost in a normative sense focuses on civil society as a holder and manifestation of positive values, such as solidarity, trust, cooperation, tolerance, and social capital.

The immediate critique is that civil society cannot always be perceived in a positive light. Civil society is not necessarily a force for good but can also be the home of intolerance, sectarianism, the cultivation of gender inequity and female oppression, violent ideologies, and other forms of organized mischief. The Hells Angels or Al-Qaida can also be seen as manifestations of civil society. In recent years, the notion of "uncivil society" has taken on a higher profile particularly in relation to the spread of violent extremism. The term uncivil society can also be worn as a badge of honor by activists who wish to distinguish themselves from a violent, oppressive government.[9]

Taking a normative approach, we define civil society in this and the following chapters as principally and practically nonviolent[10] and gender-sensitive. To make this distinction explicit, and after adding these elements to the definition provided in the *Oxford Handbook of Civil Society*, we come to the following description of civil society as "the un-coerced association between the individual and the state in which people undertake collective, [*non-violent and gender sensitive*] action for normative and substantive purposes relatively independent from government and the market."[11]

This normative definition of civil society incorporates a qualified, relative independence from government and the market. For some this is a point of profound critique. In this view, civil society is rarely, truly free and instead quite dependent upon the political space granted by governments while often financially supported by Western donor governments who promote particular values of liberal democracy. Rather than a vehicle of positive social change, the role of civil society is more likely to be embedded in a neoliberal project that at best only softens the impact of state oppression and corporate interests.[12] We will return to this critique.

Paffenholz has developed a prominent approach connecting the concept of civil society with peacebuilding. In an extensive study, based on eleven country cases, she presents a framework with seven functions that civil society may have in contributing to peacebuilding and conflict transformation. These functions are: (a) the protection of citizens against violence from all parties; (b) monitoring the accountability of state actors; (c) advocacy of articulate interests—especially of marginalized groups—and public communication about these interests; (d) socialization of values and the development of in-group identity, especially of marginalized groups; (e) building social cohesion, positive social capital, and bridges between different groups; (f) intermediation and facilitation of dialogue between citizens, but also between citizens and the state; and (g) service delivery to create entry points for peacebuilding.[13]

The seven functions proposed by Paffenholz comprehensively embrace the role of civil society as actor-associational life, as public sphere of interaction, and as good society promoting positive norms and values. The assumption is that this functional approach absorbs each of the three principal roles of civil society that alone cannot achieve effective social change but can instead balance the weakness of each role with the strength of the others. The seven functions are also analyzed in different stages of conflict.[14]

Applying this framework across different country studies, Paffenholz presents a relatively positive assessment of the civil society contribution to peacebuilding, although she sees this contribution as secondary to political forces. Civil society can play an important and often effective role in peacebuilding in all stages of conflict. However, this role is mainly supportive when compared to the role of political actors, such as the conflict parties themselves. The timing of the civil society contribution is also an important determinant of its effectiveness.[15]

The functional approach to the role of civil society in peacebuilding is supported by a growing volume of quantitative research. An investigation of the process leading to eighty-three peace agreements from 1989 to 2004 concluded that civil society was involved in about one-third of these agreements, and, where it was involved, the durability of peace increased. According to the study, "The inclusion of civil society actors in peace accords can be of critical importance in anchoring the peace."[16] Similar research into twenty-five peace agreements concluded between 1996 and 2006 found a "strong correlation between active civil society participation in peace negotiations and the durability of peace during the peacebuilding phase."[17]

Research on the participation of women in peace processes shows similar indications of the specific importance of women for peace.[18] Paffenholz's recent work has built on and contributed to this kind of quantitative research while further elaborating how and under what circumstances the contributions of civil society and particularly of women can make peace negotiations most effective.[19]

While rich in scope and useful in understanding different aspects of the conduct of civil society in peacebuilding, the functional approach developed by Paffenholz describes the role of civil society predominantly as a complement to state power but falls short of describing its role in contesting such power at different levels—local, national, regional, and international. Advocacy is identified as the most important and effective among the seven functions, but it is defined merely as "communication" of particular interests.[20] This understates the function of advocacy in promoting principled ideas, norms, and structural changes in institutional relationships and fails to acknowledge the power that advocacy can harness.[21] We define civil society advocacy as "an act of organizing the strategic use of information to democratize unequal power relations."[22]

In her review of Paffenholz's book *Civil Society and Peacebuilding: A Critical Assessment*, Dudouet argues that the various activities clustered under "advocacy" are radically different in essence and in their relation to the state, varying from opposition to collaboration. Dudouet also points to the relevance of social movement literature, with its extensive descriptions of the repertoire of contention tactics as "reactions from below" to their macropolitical context.[23]

Civil society advocacy may take a soft "insider" approach that entrenches the status quo, thereby confirming the critique of civil society as a neoliberal project. But the articulation of the interests of marginalized groups may also lead to clashes with the state and fuel discord rather than consensus. Marchetti and Tocci go so far as to describe civil society organizations as "conflict society organizations."[24] On the basis of research in Cambodia, Christie observes that

> if civil society and the state are constructed in a way that places them in opposition to one another, in a context where what is and is not on their respective

purview is being struggled over, then the perpetuation of civil society in environments of conflict should not be expected to resolve conflict. Rather, it transforms its character, addressing some aspects of conflict, but opening up new dynamics at the same time.[25]

The difficulty in describing the role of civil society in peacebuilding is that civil society organizations are both manifestations and possible solutions to violent conflict. The functional approach identifies a great number of positive roles for civil society to contribute to peacebuilding. Quantitative research and empirical studies substantiate this approach and validate the importance of the civil society contribution. This provides justification for focusing on the role of civil society in policy discourse on peacebuilding. Yet, the functional approach to the role of civil society needs to be complemented with a better understanding of the advocacy-oriented activities of civil society and how they may influence or contest the status quo and challenge power relations relevant for peacebuilding and transformative change.

CIVIL SOCIETY POWER AND THE FEATURES OF ADVOCACY FOR PEACE

The nature of violent conflict has changed dramatically over the past three decades. The good news is that there has been a significant decrease in wars between states.[26] The bad news is that violence has fragmented and become dispersed across nations, regions, and transnationally. Levels of conflict within states and violence by nonstate actors have increased. Although there is less violence, it has become more difficult to manage its cross-border impacts. Violence is sometimes intractable within a greatly increased complexity of different actors, causes, and effects. It is able to move across different geographic spaces. Deciphering the complexity of armed violence and designing effective public responses have become some of the most important problems of our time.

Traditionally, state power has been the force to constrain violence, and state sovereignty is the building block for the international supply of order and the regulation of conflicts without resorting to war. The monopoly on the coercive power of the state, shaped by the police and the military, has been at the heart of perceiving security conceptually, legally, politically, and practically. Current security challenges diminish this power.

Following Naím in his recent book *The End of Power*, we define power as "the ability to direct or prevent the current or future actions of other groups and individuals."[27] In addition, we apply the distinction coined by Nye between "hard" and "soft" power, as it is useful to identify the realm of civil society power.[28] Hard power essentially stands for physical, military, or police force, exercised in conflict and by means of deterrence (the threat of using physical power). Nye also defines economic power as hard power. Soft power is constituted in the compelling nature of norms and cultures, the power of reputation, goodwill, and reciprocity. Boulding has elaborated the importance of the reciprocity of power relationships between different actors in his concept of "integrative power": we do what the other wants because we trust and respect each other and value our mutual relationship.[29]

Naím argues convincingly that barriers to power have weakened. Revolutionary transformations in the scope and potential of human lives—including changes in information technologies, education, medicine, and health care—are making power easier to get and harder to keep. People have more choices and identities and greater mobility, and their perceptions and thinking are changing accordingly. This results in the rise of many micro powers, smaller players and even individuals that can make their mark without many resources. The ability of smaller forces to challenge mega players illustrates an emerging capacity to shape power relations rather than merely witnessing their competition. As an example, one could contend that Edward Snowden's decision to reveal massive amounts of information about the US National Security Agency is affecting US power more than the rivalry between the United States and China. The rise of micro powers is also greatly affecting the power of states to constrain violence, aptly summarized by Naím in paraphrasing Churchill: "Never in the field of human conflict have so few had the potential to do so much damage to so many at so little cost."[30]

Understanding this context of changing power relations, how can we perceive the potential challenging of state power by civil society advocacy for the sake of building peaceful and inclusive societies? Before reviewing this question, we will first elaborate the features of civil society power.

To the extent civil society has power, it is soft power. Civil society power is grounded in the quality of information it articulates, which is the foundation of its legitimacy. We can think of legitimacy either as a normative or as a sociological concept.[31] Normatively, an institution is legitimate when its practices meet a set of standards that have been stated and defended. Sociologically, legitimacy is a matter of fact. An institution is legitimate when it is accepted as appropriate and worthy of being taken into consideration or followed by relevant audiences. Despite a myriad of attempts to increase the self-regulation of the civil society sector by means of more and improved business and reporting standards, civil society legitimacy is mostly of a sociological rather than normative nature.

Three elements in particular stand out in the quality of knowledge and information as foundational for the legitimacy, and thus the power, of civil society organizations working on peace and security. They are to a large extent also the cornerstone for the effectiveness of "advocacy" in the functional framework outlined above.

The first is the knowledge about and connection to local communities. There is a widespread acknowledgment that all conflict is local and that the involvement of local stakeholders is vital in preventing and defining solutions to violence. Individuals or local communities need to have a sense of "agency" to play an effective role in changing conflict dynamics. Civil society organizations are assumed to have greater access and understanding of those local realities with active linkages to local communities, including women. Whether this is always true or not can be debated across specific contexts.[32] Regardless, the assumption of a local connection is important in establishing a framework of civil society power and is illustrated across the case studies presented in this volume.

Second, technical knowledge about the issues being raised and a nuanced understanding about the relevant political processes in a conflict setting are equally important sources of legitimacy and crucial for the effectiveness of civil society advocacy. It is one thing to know a lot about a local community in a conflict zone. It is quite another thing to understand a specific government bureaucracy, a parliamentary process, or the way a military officer thinks. The advantage of longer-term civil society engagement is also that knowledge and specialization can be built up over time, whereas government representatives on particular issues frequently change and lack localized knowledge and institutional memory.

Third, civil society networking is able to link and connect information about local realities to national, regional, and international policy processes and vice versa. This allows civil society networks to creatively maneuver between the different layers of state power. Civil society power is exercised because opportunities for influencing the behavior of state actors can be created by delivering information from one level to another and vice versa. Keck and Sikkink have called this the "boomerang effect." For example, when local-level channels of communication between the state and local actors are blocked, civil society collaboration or networks across national borders may utilize regional or international platforms to raise a concern and identify allies to put pressure on the government that initially is unwilling to listen.[33]

On a note of caution, the role of civil society in articulating information, especially from local communities, should not be confused with political representation. The question "who do you represent?" is often asked when civil society organizations present information that is not liked. It can be a sign of contestation not based on any principle or disposition of civil society.[34] Or, as Michael Edwards puts it, "Civil society has a voice, not a vote."[35]

One can reverse the "representation" argument further. Civil society advocacy for peaceful and inclusive societies entails an enactment of citizenship.

That is, advocacy can provide a practice through which people claim rights and fulfill responsibilities as members of a given polity. Civil society organizations may recognize that representative government at the national level is not a sufficiently effective arrangement to address domestic or cross-border threats to human security. They also may recognize that representative governance does not naturally extend to the global arena, and in order to prevent or resolve local conflict, people may need to organize globally.[36]

NEW SECURITY CHALLENGES AND OPPORTUNITIES FOR CIVIL SOCIETY

In this time of diminishing state power, asking how civil society may use its power to support building peaceful and inclusive societies, while facing important new security challenges, is critical. Three major observations require consideration. First, even though state power is increasingly challenged, it is not in the process of disappearing. It is important to hold on to the principal protective function of state power, certainly as long as no viable alternatives are in sight. Second, civil society has to respond to the rise of nonstate armed actors—the most significant new security threat—and the ambiguities this brings out in the application of state power. Government responses to this new threat have reduced the political space for civil society in many countries, but meeting the challenge of violent nonstate actors also creates new opportunities for civil society to engage in reforming and shaping the state security sector. Third, civil society has greater opportunities to seek new ways of contributing to the international order.

Despite profound changes in how violence and war are manifest, the protection and deterrence of state-coercive power remains important to establish human security. Nye argues, "People want three things from their political institutions: physical security, economic well-being, and communal identity."[37] There are plenty of people or groups—micro powers as Naím would call them—who are prepared to intentionally use armed violence as a means to an end, be they terrorists, pirates, criminals, or freedom fighters. Even in the best of circumstances, that is, in situations with minimal threats and with optimal room for nonviolent approaches of conflict resolution, a form of publically conceived and controlled coercion is a necessary bottom line for the security of women, children, the poor, and marginalized groups.[38]

Intrastate and civil war has become the dominant form of armed violence.[39] In many places in the world, we see organized nonstate armed groups challenging state-coercive authority. Nonstate armed actors are defined as "actors who are willing and able to use violence to pursue their objectives; are not integrated into formal state institutions; possess a certain degree of autonomy with regard to politics, military operations, resources, and infrastructure; and have an organizational structure (i.e., unlike spontaneous riots)."[40] These actors are usually not bound to state territory and are an important manifestation of the dispersal of violence across borders. They can be politically or criminally motivated, or both, which compounds the confusion in formulating a response strategy from the perspective of building peaceful and inclusive societies.

The rise of nonstate armed actors has a double effect on the power configuration for civil society. On the one hand, civil society is forced to demonstrate its loyalty to state authority that is struggling with nonstate armed actors, at the risk of being accused of complicity with violent extremism, terrorism, or criminals. Yet, civil society must demonstrate that it has a different approach to violent extremism than the state, with a greater emphasis on nonviolent approaches. Civil society also has to acknowledge and appreciate the real power as well as the at times real legitimacy of grievances represented by nonstate armed actors. Relating to and even negotiating with such actors is often a necessary part of building peaceful and inclusive societies.[41]

While civil society can play a meaningful role in encouraging and supporting state and nonstate actors to come to a negotiating table, it may have to do so in a distorted and risky power equation between state and nonstate armed groups.[42] An example is the situation in Mali, where the government elected in 2013 has consistently paid lip service to a process of reconciliation but in fact has put little energy into it. The government gambled on international support by the United Nations, France, and Algeria to control and subdue nonstate actors in the North. It left civil society efforts to promote peacebuilding and human security for the country as a whole in a weakly supported and uncertain middle ground.[43]

More sharply, state power is ambivalent in its application; it can support and protect people, but it can also neglect, attack, and abuse them. State responses to civil society power are equally caught in this dichotomy. The space, scope, and opportunities for civil society to play a positive role in promoting peace, human security, and inclusive societies—all of the different roles defined in the functional approach—are to a large extent configured in how state power responds to the way it is challenged by civil society. This brings us to the issue of civil society space and how it relates to the three entry points reviewed in the following chapters—development policy, regional organizations, and civil-military interaction for human security.

Just as civil society may contest state power, state power often contests or restricts the political space for civil society. This is a dynamic at all times. What is relevant in the context of this volume is that the dominant frame to justify attacks on civil society space at the moment is related to terrorism, countering violent extremism (CVE), and state security. Counterterrorism measures are examples of the vulnerability of state power in the face of small groups and individuals. In response to terrorism, governments are inclined to go too far in exercising control on their populations in order to "protect" them.

As for civil society, the tendency among states to resort to control in response to terrorism manifests itself in different ways. There is a focus on the finances of civil society organizations via the Financial Action Task Force (FATF). Even though there is minimal evidence that civil society organizations are used as a conduit to finance terrorism, the FATF has established a global regime to prevent it. This makes it difficult, for example, to transfer money to civil society organizations in the Middle East.[44] There is even greater pressure on civil society organizations to interact with representatives of armed groups, especially when they have been listed as "terrorists."[45]

For regimes that are politically repressive in nature, the counterterrorism frame is a convenient excuse to label any sort of civil protest as "terrorism" and limit the organizational and operational space for civil society organizations, whether they are domestic or international in nature. Ample research and documentation show how legal and practical measures restricting the space for civil society have grown in many countries. CIVICUS has established a "Civil Society Watch" and publishes an annual "State of Civil Society" report that contains much information in this regard.[46] The International Center for Not-for-Profit Law provides reports on many of the legal restrictions for civil society.[47] Since 2010, the United Nations has designated a Special Rapporteur on the Rights to Peaceful Assembly and Association. His reports to the UN Human Rights Council are a constant reminder of the shrinking space for civil society.[48] Global freedom and human rights as measured by Freedom House have declined in parallel with the rise of restrictive measures for civil society. The 2015 *Freedom in the World* report has the telling subtitle *Discarding Democracy: Return to the Iron Fist.*[49]

POLITICAL SPACE AND CIVIL SOCIETY POWER

There is much evidence indicating an alarming attack on the space for civil society worldwide. But is that all there is to say about the role and the power of civil society? While the legal and practical freedom of civil society is indeed contingent on government behavior, from the angle of peacebuilding, the contestation over civil society space is an endemic part of conflict transformation. Referring back to our question on power relations, we contend that a limitation in political space for civil society should not be confused with a limitation in power. One could equally argue that the attack on civil society space is a sign of the growth of civil society power, or at least the perception of its power. By the same token, and in line with Naím's analysis, attacks on the space for civil society can also be seen as signs of a relative weakening of state power. The brute force of political oppression can be shocking and is a very good reason to protest and hold governments to account for violations of human rights. But this does not necessarily indicate that such oppression is effective in redressing the state-civil society power relationship in favor of the state.

The analysis of the role and opportunity for civil society to contribute to building peaceful and inclusive societies requires an approach that includes thinking about power relations. If such analysis stops at applying the framework of human rights only, the conclusion would be that freedoms of association, assembly, and expression are violated more than ever, and that civil society is at the point of being knocked out. However, states are weaker, certainly when it comes to issues of peace and security, which presents a problem for governments in an area of their primary responsibility. This calls for scrutinizing the relative power of civil society versus state power to respond to these challenges and build greater civil society leverage in support of building inclusive societies and human security.

The situation in fragile states provides a good illustration of this, where weak state structures and emerging governments—in terms of legitimacy and capacity—often operate in a more or less equal playing field with civil society. The absence or weakness of government may spur civil society to take on a more political role as it may have to assert a greater responsibility to provide services and security for local communities and shape the beginning of a public domain. A stronger state will be enabled to emerge if people begin to understand that they need shared structures to provide stability and security. In supporting and making first steps in this direction, civil society can help strengthen the necessary ownership of the process of state formation by building or rebuilding inclusive societies where they are most needed.

The discourse on statebuilding in fragile states often uses the term "ownership" but rarely explains who "owns" what. The word "ownership" is commonly used in donor language as a proxy for indicating how citizens should relate to political processes in the absence of functioning institutions. Strengthening local ownership of the development process in fragile states is essential to give meaning to state sovereignty. Civil society organizations are often the only channels for creating such "ownership."

The shift in civil-military relations provides another illustration of a power balance that is coming toward rather than moving away from civil society. There is a growing realization that even considerable coercive force means little if it lacks social capacity and legitimacy. Civil society is strong in these latter dimensions of soft power. The reshaping of the civil society-security sector relationship is still a daunting task since it requires fundamental shifts in conceptual thinking, practical approaches, and, perhaps above all, language and cultures of work. Yet the power equation is favorable for these changes.[50]

The opportunity for civil society in power relations in the international sphere is also shifting in a positive manner.[51] International cooperation is essential to avoid conflict, and systemic international cooperation is facilitated by multilateral institutions with established rules and practices. However, there is a contradiction at the heart of contemporary multilateralism. Intervention in the domestic affairs of states, undermining sovereignty, is justified on the basis of democratic principles such as the defense of human rights. But the structures of multilateralism are profoundly undemocratic. The UN is based on sovereign equality, but it does not operate according to democratic principles.

In recent years, demands for multilateral organizations to become more accountable to their "civil society" rather than simply to states have proliferated.[52] The sociological legitimacy of states is declining, which in turn affects the legitimacy of multilateral organizations. As states are increasingly being forced to collaborate more in multilateral settings in order to provide for their security, an important opportunity is manifested for civil society to contribute to building peaceful and inclusive societies. The effort to build structured relationships between civil society and regional organizations is a response to this opportunity. As the great majority of new security threats are playing out beyond national borders, it is important to note that "peaceful societies" should not necessarily be equated with "societies" within the borders of nation states only.

CHALLENGES TO THE CIVIL SOCIETY POWER FRAMEWORK

Looking at civil society in conflict prevention and peacebuilding within a framework of power relations provides an additional lens to the functional approach describing its role. It is a necessary approach to address the role of civil society in conflict prevention and to assess the potential of the civil society idea in building peaceful and inclusive societies. The civil society role is not limited to service delivery or a watchdog function only, but can help to transform conflict and support changes in institutional and social relationships. Yet we do not mean to suggest that all is well with civil society. There is still considerable work to do in changing power relations more fundamentally. The added value that civil society potentially has in contributing to building peaceful and inclusive societies can be brought to the table only if presented in a more equal and level playing field. This is consistently problematic.

The participation of civil society in policy and decision-making processes is not enshrined in any form of international standard. As a result, contending issues around civil society participation in international policy processes have become unfortunately common. Information is either not shared or provided too late. Invitations to civil society are ad hoc, and the selection of civil society representatives is often not done by civil society itself but by officials who want to ensure only "friendly" voices. As a result, the number of civil society organizations included, and their speaking time in decision-making processes, is limited. In sum, significant obstacles that minimize the benefit of the civil society contribution remain.

Several issues beyond the scope of this volume exist, and these necessitate further research, exploration, and advocacy. The first is the importance to strive for institutionalized, structured relationships between civil society and governments and international organizations in various policy processes. Second is the importance of developing new repertoires in different aspects of the civil society-security sector relationship. The security sector needs civil society to help it protect civilians.

This brings us to the third issue, which is the need for a deep conversation between different parts of civil society—notably the peacebuilding organizations on the one hand, and the humanitarian and human rights organizations on the other—about roles, responsibilities, principles, and effectiveness. The imperative to save lives and diminish human suffering in a crisis situation, enshrined in principles of neutrality and impartiality, creates a particular set of issues in the relationship with governments, the military, and the police as well as nonstate actors in conflict zones. The human rights movement has made important progress in challenging state sovereignty and establishing the right to intervene in the face of serious crimes against humanity. Both approaches deserve scrutiny in relation to changing power relations, the role of civil society, and how they contribute to conflict transformation and substantive change.[53]

The point is to be more forthcoming about the important differences within the approaches of different civil society groups and some of the practical dilemmas in a difficult operational context. In the face of oppressive governments there is a tradition of not speaking out about differences within civil society, at the risk of exposing "dirty laundry," but in the long run this does not create healthy relationships among different civil society groups and impairs progress.

A fourth point is that more thinking and debate are necessary on the implications of acknowledging the role of civil society in power relations. Further discussion should concentrate on the accompanying need to design the mechanisms for accountability that should come with civil society's greater responsibility in the public domain. This starts with a discussion of the civil society role in substituting for the state in service delivery in fragile states, and extends to more elaborate engagement in shaping and influencing the role of the military and police in providing human security.

OUTLINE OF THE BOOK

Building upon the themes discussed in this chapter, the three main sections of this book present different entry points for a discussion of civil society within a framework of power relations. The gender dimension, intimately related to structures and distribution of power, is a fourth entry point discussed across all sections.

The first section in the book starts with a detailed account of the important role of civil society in shaping the new 2030 Agenda for Sustainable Development, in particular, Goal 16 on building peaceful and inclusive societies. The chapters refer to the experiences of the civil society platform generated by the International Dialogue on Statebuilding and Peacebuilding (IDPS) and the "New Deal." They examine the participation of civil society in different countries that were expected to benefit from the New Deal process.

Weak state power in fragile states or conflict-affected countries makes the capacity and social capital-building functions of civil society much needed in order to promote inclusion and development. But at the same time, how does a relatively strong civil society deal with a weak state, and vice versa, how does a weak state cope with a strong civil society? How in such situations can civil society contribute to a process of statebuilding that ensures a revitalized state that is capable of being a home for peace by superseding previous lines of conflict that have caused fragility? To apply a principle of the subordination of civil society to state authority does not work well in such situations and creates tensions and dilemmas at different levels. The chapter on Afghanistan in particular highlights the gender perspective, which entails a challenge to power at all levels of society.

The second section reviews the opportunity for civil society to build relationships with regional organizations. The increasing acknowledgment of the importance of regional organizations as a means to reinforce state power for peace, security, and development is a relatively recent phenomena. It is a response strategy foremost based on three factors: the weakness of global institutions in delivering peace and security, the capacity of regional arrangements to benefit from regional knowledge and respond to a multipolar world, and the increasingly transborder nature of violent conflict which causes spillover effects across regions.[54] To perceive and address violent conflict within a regional scope makes sense, analytically and politically. It helps to create a new space for civil society in which empowerment and inclusivity can be construed in parallel with regional organizations building their role and legitimacy.

The third section looks at the relationship of civil society with the security sector, the embodiment of state-coercive power. The security sector faces difficulty coping with changes in the nature and dispersal of violence across national borders. A number of failures in building peace and development on the basis of an external intervention (Iraq, Afghanistan, various UN missions) have initiated discourse in the military and created incentives to seek collaboration with civil society in an attempt to find the right combination of hard and soft power in a comprehensive approach to new security challenges.

Responding to similar challenges, police forces in a number of countries have resorted to the use of hard power, leading to a militarization of law enforcement.[55] In other cases, police forces have collapsed as a public entity in the face of urbanization, transnational crime, and violent extremism, and instead have become a threat to public security itself. On a positive note, there is increasing support for the concept of community policing, where an engagement with civil society seeks to find the balance between hard power and increasing soft power capabilities.[56] The needs of humanitarian assistance organizations and the desire for rigorous implementation of humanitarian principles have long dominated the debate on civil-military relations. This is too narrow a focus and does not support developing a broader approach to how civil society can deepen its understanding of, and relationship with, the security sector. A greater role for civil society in shaping, collaborating with, and monitoring the security sector will not only require greater accountability from the security sector, but it will also require a deeper accountability of civil society itself.

We turn now to the first section of the volume, beginning with an in-depth examination of the significant role played by civil society in shaping the 2030 Agenda for Sustainable Development—a process that illustrates the power of civil society to advocate for peacebuilding in global development policy through the dissemination of expert analysis and information and through persistent engagement with international organizations.

NOTES

1. The goals may be found at https://sustainabledevelopment.un.org/sdgs. United Nations, "Transforming Our World: The 2030 Agenda for Global Action," A/RES/70/1, https://sustainabledevelopment.un.org/content/documents/21252030%20Agenda%20for%20Sustainable%20Development%20web.pdf.

2. The United Nations Development Program and the Swiss Government initiated an effort to repair this omission to some extent by means of the *Geneva Declaration on Armed Violence and Development*. Though the Declaration was signed by 113

countries and provided a useful platform for work on small arms reduction, it did not become as central in global governance discourse as the Millennium Development Goals. *The Geneva Declaration on Armed Violence and Development*, 2006, http://www.genevadeclaration.org/fileadmin/docs/GD-Declaration-091020-EN.pdf.

3. Thania Paffenholz, ed., "Preface," in *Civil Society and Peacebuilding: A Critical Assessment* (Boulder: Lynne Riener, 2010), viii.

4. John Paul Lederach, *The Little Book of Conflict Transformation* (Intercourse, PA: Good Books, 2003).

5. Erin McCandless, *Polarization and Transformation in Zimbabwe: Social Movements, Strategy Dilemmas and Change* (Lanham, MD: Lexington Books, 2011), 190–191.

6. John Paul Lederach, *Preparing for Peace: Conflict Transformation across Cultures* (Syracuse: Syracuse University Press, 1995).

7. For a concise overview of the evidence, refer to Valerie M. Hudson et al., *Sex and World Peace* (New York: Columbia University Press, 2012). For an overview of the obstacles to women's participation in peace processes, see Karen McMinn, "Candid Voices from the Field: Obstacles to a Transformative Women, Peace and Security Agenda and to Women's Meaningful Participation in Building Peace and Security," Action Research Report sponsored by Cordaid, Global Partnership for the Prevention of Armed Conflict, and Women Peacemakers Program, 2015, https://www.women-peacemakersprogram.org/assets/CMS/Action-Research/WPP-15-01-WPP-publicatie-LRPages.pdf.

8. The distinction is based on Michael Edwards, *Civil Society*, 2nd edn. (Cambridge, MA: Polity Press, 2009); Raffaele Marchetti and Nathalie Tocci, eds., *Conflict Society and Peacebuilding: Comparative Perspectives* (New Delhi: Routledge, 2011); and John Gaventa, "Civil Society and Power," in *The Oxford Handbook of Civil Society*, ed. Michael Edwards (Oxford: Oxford University Press, 2011). This section draws in particular on the latter.

9. McCandless, *Polarization and Transformation in Zimbabwe*, 18–19.

10. This does not imply that all civil society rejects the use of force under all circumstances, but there is a permanent bias toward nonviolent solutions to conflict.

11. Michael Edwards, "Introduction: Civil Society and the Geometry of Human Relations," in *The Oxford Handbook of Civil Society*, ed. Michael Edwards (Oxford: Oxford University Press, 2011), 13.

12. Raffaele Marchetti and Nathalie Tocci, eds., "Conflict Society in Conflict and Peace," in *Conflict Society and Peacebuilding: Comparative Perspectives* (New Delhi: Routledge, 2011).

13. Thania Paffenholz, ed., *Civil Society and Peacebuilding*, Part 1.

14. Christoph Spurk, "Understanding Civil Society," in *Civil Society and Peacebuilding: A Critical Assessment*, ed. Thania Paffenholz (Boulder: Lynne Riener, 2010), 23.

15. Thania Paffenholz, "Conclusion," in *Civil Society and Peacebuilding: A Critical Assessment*, ed. Thania Paffenholz (Boulder: Lynne Riener, 2010), 425.

16. Desirée Nilsson, "Anchoring the Peace: Civil Society Actors in Peace Accords and Durable Peace," *International Relations* 38, no. 2 (2012).

17. Anthony Wanis-St. John and Darren Kew, "Civil Society and Peace Negotiations: Confronting Exclusion," *International Negotiation* 13, no. 1 (2008).

18. Marie O'Reilly, Andrea Ó Súilleabháin, and Thania Paffenholz, *Reimagining Peacemaking: Women's Roles in Peace Processes* (New York: International Peace Institute, 2015), https://www.ipinst.org/wp-content/uploads/2015/06/IPI-E-pub-Reimagining-Peacemaking-rev.pdf; McMinn, "Candid Voices from the Field."

19. Thania Paffenholz, "Civil Society and Peace Negotiations: Beyond the Inclusion-Exclusion Dichotomy," *Negotiation Journal* 30, no. 1 (2014).

20. Thania Paffenholz and Christoph Spurk, "A Comprehensive Analytical Framework," in *Civil Society and Peacebuilding: A Critical Assessment*, ed. Thania Paffenholz (Boulder: Lynne Riener, 2010), 68–69. In a recent publication, Paffenholz rephrased her conception of this to "agenda-setting and the application of pressures by civil society organizations." See Thania Paffenholz, "Civil Society and Peacebuilding," *Development Dialogue* no. 63 (December 2015), 111.

21. Margaret Keck and Kathryn Sikkink, *Activists beyond Borders: Advocacy Networks in International Politics* (Ithaca, NY: Cornell University Press, 1998), 8–9.

22. Lisa Jordan and Peter van Tuijl, "Political Responsibility in Transnational NGO Advocacy," *World Development* 28, no. 12 (2000): 2052.

23. Veronique Dudouet, "Rezensionen," *Die Friedens-Warte* 85, no. 4 (2010): 114.

24. Raffaele Marchetti and Nathalie Tocci, eds., "Conflict Society in Conflict and Peace."

25. Ryerson Christie, *Peacebuilding and NGOs: State-Civil Society Interactions* (New York: Routledge, 2013), 200.

26. Joshua S. Goldstein, *Winning the War on War: The Decline of Armed Conflict Worldwide* (London: Penguin, 2011).

27. Moisés Naím, *The End of Power: From Boardrooms to Battlefields and Churches to States, Why Being in Charge Isn't What It Used to Be* (New York: Basic Books, 2013), 23.

28. Joseph S. Nye, *Soft Power: The Means to Success in World Politics* (New York: Public Affairs, 2004).

29. Kenneth Boulding, *Three Faces of Power* (Newbury Park, CA: Sage Publications, 1989), 24–25.

30. Naím, *The End of Power,* especially 107.

31. This paragraph draws from Robert O. Keohane, "The Contingent Legitimacy of Multilateralism," GARNET Working Paper No. 09/06, University of Warwick, September 2006, http://www2.warwick.ac.uk/fac/soc/pais/research/researchcentres/csgr/garnet/workingpapers/0906.pdf.

32. Thania Paffenholz, "Unpacking the Local Turn in Peacebuilding: A Critical Assessment towards an Agenda for Future Research," *Third World Quarterly* 36, no.5 (2015): 857–874.

33. Margaret Keck and Kathryn Sikkink, *Activists beyond Borders*, 12–13. For civil society networking, see Steve Waddell, *Global Action Networks: Creating Our Future Together* (Basingstoke, England: Palgrave MacMillan, 2011).

34. Enrique Peruzzotti, "Civil Society, Representation and Accountability: Restating Current Debates on the Representativeness and Accountability of Civic Associations," in *NGO Accountability: Politics, Principles and Innovations*, eds., Lisa Jordan and Peter van Tuijl (London: Earthscan, 2006).

35. Michael Edwards, *NGO Rights and Responsibilities: A New Deal for Global Governance* (London: The Foreign Policy Centre, 2000), 29.

36. Lisa Jordan, "Global Civil Society," in *The Oxford Handbook of Civil Society*, ed. Michael Edwards (Oxford: Oxford University Press, 2011).

37. Joseph S. Nye, *Understanding International Conflicts: An Introduction to Theory and History*, 4th edn. (New York: Longman, 2003), 241.

38. For an eloquent plea supporting the non-violent approach, see Diana Francis, "New Thoughts on Power: Closing the Gaps between Theory and Action," in *Advancing Conflict Transformation. The Berghof Handbook II*, eds., Beatrix Austin, Martina Fischer, Hans-Joachim Giessmann (Farmington Hills, MI: Barbara Budrich Publishers, 2011).

39. The Uppsala Conflict Data Programme (UCDP) records forty armed conflicts in 2014, of which only one is an interstate conflict. The remaining thirty-nine conflicts were fought within states, but thirteen of them—or 33%—were internationalized in the sense that one or more states contributed troops to one or both sides. Therése Petterson and Peter Wallensteen, "Armed Conflicts, 1946–2014," *Journal of Peace Research* 52, no. 4 (2015): 537.

40. Claudia Hofmann and Ulrich Schneckener, "NGOs and Nonstate Armed Actors, Improving Compliance with International Norms," Special Report 284 (Washington, DC: United States Institute for Peace, 2011).

41. David Cortright et al., "Friend Not Foe: Opening Spaces for Civil Society Engagement to Prevent Violent Extremism," Report to Cordaid from the Fourth Freedom Forum and the Kroc Institute for International Peace Studies at the University of Notre Dame, 2nd edn. May 2011, http://www.hscollective.org/wp-content/uploads/2013/09/Friend-not-Foe-2.pdf.

42. Sophie Haspeslagh and Zahbia Yousuf, eds., "Local Engagement with Armed Groups in the Midst of Violence," *ACCORD: An International Review of Peace Initiatives* Insights 2 (May 2015), http://www.c-r.org/downloads/CONJ2670_Accord_new_paper_for_January_06.05.15_WEB_2.pdf.

43. See the series of op-eds by WANEP and GPPAC in the International Peace Institute (IPI) Global Observatory 2013–2015: http://theglobalobservatory.org/by/peter-van-tuijl/.

44. Ben Hayes, "Counter-Terrorism, 'Policy Laundering,' and the FATF: Legalizing Surveillance, Regulating Civil Society," *The International Journal of Not-for-Profit Law* 14, nos. 1–2 (April 2012). See also the civil society online platform on the Financial Action Task Force (FATF) at http://fatfplatform.org.

45. Ben Hayes, "Terrorising the Rule of Law: The Policy and Practice of Proscription," Statewatch Analysis and the Policy Laundering Project, 2005, http://www.statewatch.org/terrorlists/terrorlists.pdf.

46. See: CIVICUS.org.

47. See: http://www.icnl.org.

48. See: http://www.ohchr.org/EN/Issues/AssemblyAssociation/Pages/SRFreedomAssemblyAssociationIndex.aspx.

49. See: https://freedomhouse.org/report/freedom-world/freedom-world-2015#.VhpzDFTtlHw.

50. Lisa Schirch, ed., *Handbook on Human Security: A Civil-Military-Police Curriculum* (The Hague: Alliance for Peacebuilding, GPPAC, Kroc Institute, 2015), https://www.peaceportal.org/documents/130617663/0/FINAL+HANDBOOK+November+30+1154.pdf/25025a3b-3247-4714-b1b4-d1530d84b0f1.

51. Keohane, "The Contingent Legitimacy of Multilateralism," 2006.

52. The current 1 for 7 Billion Campaign asking for a transparent process to select a new UN Secretary-General is a good example. See http://www.1for7billion.org for more details.

53. There is an emerging discourse with a profound critique of the human rights approach and the human rights movement. Stephen Hopgood, *The Endtimes of Human Rights* (Ithaca, NY: Cornell University Press, 2013).

54. Peter Wallensteen and Anders Bjurner, eds., *Regional Organizations and Peacemaking: Challengers to the UN?* (London: Routledge, 2015).

55. Michael Shank and Elizabeth Beavers, "The Militarization of U.S. Police Forces," *Chicago Tribune*, October 22, 2013.

56. Community policing aims at partnerships between the police and the community with the goal to achieve public safety by enhancing trust. For more, see Nicholas Turner, "Testimony to President's Task Force on 21st Century Policing" (Written testimony on behalf of Vera Institute of Justice, New York, January 9, 2015), http://www.vera.org/sites/default/files/resources/downloads/nick-turner-testimony-presidents-task-force-21st-century-policing.pdf.

Section 1

SHAPING THE SUSTAINABLE DEVELOPMENT AGENDA

Chapter 2

Civil Society and the 2030 Agenda

Forging a Path to Universal Sustainable
Peace through Policy Formulation

Erin McCandless

On September 25, 2015, the United Nations General Assembly (UNGA) formally adopted the 2030 Agenda for Sustainable Development, including a set of SDGs aimed at wiping out poverty, fighting inequality, promoting sustainability, building peaceful and inclusive societies, and tackling climate change. The new goals are universal in their application and far broader in vision and intent than their predecessors, the MDGs. Unlike the MDGs' framework, peace-related issues are strongly featured. This achievement came with robust participation of civil society, engaging and interacting in new ways in a more open and inclusive policy formulation context.

In the new framework, peace is named as one of the five areas of critical importance identified in the Preamble, and it is defined in broad and universal terms: "We are determined to foster *peaceful, just and inclusive societies.*" The centerpiece of this approach is Goal 16, to "promote peaceful and inclusive societies for sustainable development, provide access to justice for all and build effective, accountable and inclusive institutions at all levels." A number of other goals and targets—such as Goal 10 on reducing inequalities, and Goal 5 on gender equality and empowerment—ensure that peace is seen as more than an enabler of development but as a core aspirational goal relevant to all countries, not just those considered fragile and conflict-affected.

Several broad currents of research, practice, and policy built a foundation for this shift. Centrally, there was a rising commitment to do development differently in countries affected by conflict and fragility, both to pay far greater attention to context in shaping aid approaches and to respect and foster the need for robust institutions as a starting point for development to take root. Such arguments drove the creation of the IDPS, which forged the "New Deal for Engagement in Conflict-affected and Fragile States" led by members states affected by conflict and fragility who felt that the MDG framework did not speak to their country's realities and priorities. By the time the SDG process started in 2012, the IDPS initiative had already begun the challenging process of building a deep dialogue among these countries (now organized as the "g7+"),[1] Northern partners, and civil society around what was needed to guide both national and international policies in conflict-affected and fragile states.

Other informative processes included: the increasing awareness of the impact of violence, especially armed violence, for all societies and across all levels of development; the growing acknowledgment of the role of inequality and exclusion, particularly horizontal inequality, as significant contributors to violence, instability and conflict; the growing policy movement to ensure gender equality and empowerment as a key driver of peaceful and prosperous societies; a longtime concern with the role of good governance and increasing awareness of the need for effective institutions, including informal ones; and a strengthening debate about the role of international drivers of injustice and instability, from transnational crime to trade agreements, alongside more inclusive global governance structures and processes to create an international context supportive of national peace and development efforts.

Despite these powerful converging trends, the inclusion of peace issues so prominently within the 2030 Agenda was not a foregone conclusion. Issues relating to violent conflict, good governance, human rights, reconciliation, and rule of law had been notably missing from the MDGs. As discussions began on the SDGs, these issues were not solidly a part of the mainstream development discussion and were little-known to generalist diplomats and government negotiators. Additionally, the topic found resistance from a number of member states, and in some cases from parts of the UN system itself. In short, there was considerable work to do for those keen to see these issues meaningfully included in the framework, and uncertainty remained until the final days of negotiation.

Understanding civil society's role and impact is complicated since the process overall was exceedingly complex, with myriad governmental, intergovernmental, and nongovernmental actors engaging at all levels and in different ways. It can be viewed as an embodiment of the "transnational advocacy network" where actors working internationally on an issue—be they from civil society, international organizations, or governments—are "bound together by shared values, a common discourse, and dense exchanges of information and services."[2] In this case however, there were several such transnational networks at play around core issues that eventually fell under a single umbrella to bring peace into the 2030 Agenda. While a broad set of civil society groups was engaged, this analysis centers around peacebuilding-oriented actors, drawing particularly on the experience of peacebuilding CSOs, including think tanks, nongovernmental organizations (NGOs) from both the Global North and the Global South, NGO coalitions focused on peace issues, academics and their institutions. Many other civil society actors were involved in one or more aspects of this discussion including those focused on issues such as: governance and accountability, justice, human rights, and gender issues; and those with other mandates, such as faith-based organizations.

As part of a project examining civil society's role in building peaceful, just, and inclusive societies, this chapter focuses on civil society efforts to influence and shape policy at the highest levels and to infuse peace concerns into a breathtakingly ambitious global agenda. The analysis focuses on the strategies that civil society employed, reflecting upon how they used their agency to maneuver within the existing power structures and capitalize on entry points to become a serious player in the process. The research draws upon published literature related to civil society and social movements, transformative change, and peacebuilding. It also relies on the unpublished literature produced within civil society during this process and a number of interviews with key informants who were centrally positioned in the process.[3] The analysis is also informed by my own engagement in the process[4] that brings both advantages (insider awareness) and limitations (the bias of my experiences), common for a "participant-observer."

An examination of relevant literature to frame the discussion is followed by a historical narrative of what took place—the "story" of how the process unfolded with the engagement of civil society. Four key questions that have challenged civil society are then examined from different vantage points. In closing, I reflect on how both the processes and outcomes of the 2030 Agenda move us collectively toward the realization of a more universal, sustainable peace.

CONTEXT, STRATEGIES, AND DILEMMAS
FOR CIVIL SOCIETY ACTION

Strategic choices around how to influence change are shaped by context. Social movement scholars have underscored the importance of the "political opportunity structure," or those features of the political system that create the overall abilities and capacities for civil society groups to organize.[5] At the same time, while context and culture shape civic action, civil society movements are sources of innovation and actions that expand the forms of contention available to succeeding generations of activists.[6] This certainly helps to explain the rise of transnational advocacy networks, in an era of rising global public challenges, and the central role of civil society actors across borders in fueling these networks.

Reflecting on strategies that civil society actors face, it can be helpful to distinguish between process- and substance-oriented choices. In 2011, I described two primary strategy dilemmas that civil society faces in seeking transformative change. The first was whether to prioritize political or economic rights (rights or redistribution). The second was whether and how to work with government and/or donors given their political, economic, and social agendas (participation or resistance).[7]

Issues surrounding the meaning and politics of participation gained traction through civic action in the 1990s and 2000s around relieving or cancelling debt, and participating in international financial institutions (IFIs) and promoting poverty reduction strategy papers (PRSPs) where deep concerns around the quality of participation arose.[8] African scholars have argued that capacity development is often required for people to participate effectively, and that participation of the poor will be futile unless power structures that perpetuate poverty are simultaneously addressed.[9]

Others have suggested that the quality of participation relies on the influence of political context, societal expectations of the process, and the method and organ of participation.[10] Questions of participation are now reappearing in the discourse around *inclusion* and the norm of *inclusivity*. A burgeoning literature and matched policy interest in this area are focused on the need for more inclusive political settlements. A new large comparative study has found that the quality of inclusion matters; when included actors can influence quality of agreements or implementation or push for negotiations, influence is correlated with a higher rate of sustained agreements.[11] Core questions for civil society, however, are whether a critical, autonomous voice can be maintained and efforts to foment structural, transformative change can be sustained when working as partners in processes that are controlled by governments and/or international actors.

Other dilemmas for civil society emerge around substantive issues, especially the framing of policy advocacy. While discourses and priorities will shift over time and undoubtedly play out differently in different contexts, the substantive differences in emphasis by civil society actors always constitute challenges and dilemmas. Additionally, it is clear that there is complex interaction between questions of who participates, who is included and excluded, and what substantive issues are represented on behalf of civil society. These undoubtedly have important impacts on the results.

Assessing the outcomes and impacts of civil society action, particularly at higher-than-project levels, is a complex task with inherent causality challenges. Scholars and practitioners in the peacebuilding field have increasingly turned their attention to how one can understand and strategically influence change that supports peace, in particular "peace writ large," while social movement scholars have discussed questions of what certain actions/tactics achieved, and what accounts for the "success" of an action.[12] Peace writ large (PWL) is concerned with the "bigger picture" of a conflict, both focusing on terminating violence and supporting a just and sustainable peace by addressing factors that drive conflict.[13]

Understanding how particular outcomes translate into higher-level impacts is widely acknowledged as rife with methodological challenges, especially if linking to contested and normative concepts of transformative change and peace. Social movement literature assumes that public policy outcomes will influence the way the political system as a whole functions. Most agree that translation of grievances into political impact involves structural change,[14] that is, changes *of* rather than changes *in* society.[15]

According to eminent peace theorists (i.e., Curle and Galtung), transformative strategies for peace and change often require the use of confrontational strategies to raise the profile of latent conflict and bring the existence of structural violence into public awareness. Peacebuilding scholars are also conceptualizing the need for vertical integration in peacebuilding, in part to address the challenge of a variety of peacebuilding activities or "peace writ little" (pwl) not adding up to PWL.[16] Vertical integration can be viewed as "a strategy to link actors, ideas and efforts vertically for peacebuilding and development impact."[17] Published studies evaluating civil society or social movement action on peace outcomes at the national level have been few and far between.[18]

Studies attribute success to a variety of factors that concern, among other things, the nature of the strategies employed, who is involved, the diversity and depth of their social base, and the length of time such strategies are sustained.[19] Keck and Sikkink argue that networks are effective in various ways: (1) by framing debates and getting issues on the agenda; (2) by encouraging discursive commitments from states and other policy actors; (3) by causing procedural change at the international and domestic level; (4) by affecting policy; and (5) by influencing behavior changes in target actors.[20] While peacebuilding evaluation importantly raises the importance of factoring considerations of context into evaluation processes to ensure peacebuilding outcomes, social movement theorists link movement success to favorable political opportunities or operating environments.[21]

Both the new 2030 Agenda for Sustainable Development and the recent reviews of the UN's peacebuilding and peacekeeping work strongly point to a renewed energetic focus on peace sustainability, departing from the more limited and problematic focus, as some scholars argued, on the immediate aftermath of conflict without attention to longer, deeper drivers of peace.[22] Undoubtedly much new attention among scholars and practitioners will be placed on the question of how to achieve sustainable peace. There is no magic solution that can ensure sustainable peace, but there is a growing body of

evidence to suggest that the process must be nationally owned with increasing
levels of state and society ownership. Clear and growing processes must be in
place to address drivers of conflict and fragility.

FROM OUTSIDE TO MAINSTREAM: CIVIL SOCIETY
ENGAGEMENT IN THE POST-2015 PROCESS

The process leading up to the agreement of the 2030 Agenda for Sustainable Development in September 2015 was one of the most complex and
wide-ranging negotiations the international community has ever attempted.
In addition to civil society actors,[23] member states and their intergovernmental bodies were extremely active,[24] as well as a wide array of actors more
broadly from within the United Nations system.[25]

At the end of 2011, the UN process began with the formation of the UN
Task Team. Some civil society peacebuilding organizations launched discussions on peace and the post-2015 framework in Washington, DC, and New
York in the early part of the year. Many of these early discussions drew in
actors and issues from the New Deal for Engagement in Fragile States, which
offered a broader framing for development in fragile and conflict-affected
environments and had been wrestling with issues of goals applicable to their
countries and how to measure them.

The announcement of the leadership of the High Level Panel (HLP) in May
2012 drew further attention, and by the opening weeks of the UNGA session in September 2012 in New York, the issues were gaining traction. One
informal peacebuilding civil society network involving CSOs from North and
South[26] issued a statement on September 21, the International Day of Peace,
entitled "Bringing Peace into the Post-2015 Development Framework."
This was followed by a well-attended event (that included representatives
of African civil society) on "Mainstreaming Peacebuilding and Prevention
in the Post-2015 Agenda" hosted by a group of peacebuilding NGOs. Civil
society also participated in the Global Thematic Consultations that launched
in the fall of 2012. In Monrovia, Liberia, a meeting hosted by Finland and a
number of UN agencies was held on the topic of "Conflict and Fragility and
the Post-2015 Development Agenda," bringing together many of the peacebuilding policy CSOs that would be part of the discussion for the next several
years, along with many local CSOs.[27]

At this stage, the issues were being moved forward primarily by CSOs
with sufficient flexibility in their existing mandates and funding to be able to
engage in an emerging policy discussion without extensive preliminary conversations with their donors and constituents. These were mostly established
peacebuilding CSOs from the Global North, although the early involvement

of regional CSOs such as Igarapé and Africa Center for the Constructive Resolution of Disputes (ACCORD) was important. The participation of focused coalitions such as the Civil Society Platform on Peacebuilding and Statebuilding (CSPPS) and the Alliance for Peacebuilding (AfP) at this stage was also helpful in providing mechanisms for coordination and collaboration, raising general public awareness and enabling the involvement of Southern civil society participants who might not otherwise have been able to engage.

The Rio+20 conference in 2012 established a process for ongoing member state discussion of sustainable development through the Open Working Group (OWG), which met for the first time in March 2013. Other processes underway at the time were eleven global thematic consultations and the deliberations of the HLP. Civil society advocacy efforts over this period were focused on the HLP process and on the thematic consultations. Much of this activity took place beyond New York, involving engagement with the panel members in their home countries or at the global consultations of the panel and the thematic groups. The year also saw peacebuilding CSOs becoming more involved in some of the broader civil society coalitions engaged in the post-2015 process, as well as important convenings on the issues of how to measure progress against peace-related goals and targets, such as the session in Glen Cove in the summer of 2013.[28] In April 2013 a group of New York-based CSOs hosted a full day workshop for senior UN officials entitled "Conflict, Violence, and Instability in the Post-2015 Development Agenda: Workshop for the United Nations System,"[29] which helped establish a broader consensus on the merits of this approach.

The report of the HLP in May 2013 reflected many of these civil society efforts to ensure that peace issues became a core part of the ongoing discussion on the SDGs. Peace and good governance were identified as among five "transformative shifts" and were detailed in two of the preliminary twelve proposed goals (#10 and #11). These goal candidates also included proposed national targets that were manageable in number, well focused and coherent. While the HLP's report was greeted with relief by peacebuilding CSOs, important issues failed to make it into the final document (notably conflict prevention and resolution, as well as reconciliation). This no doubt had much to do with the fact that for many member states, a more traditional development focus was the starting point, with meaningful and legitimate precedents to those of prior official UN processes, such as the Millennium Declaration, the 2015 World Summit Outcome, and the Rio+20 agreement. There was however enough included to form a solid basis for advocacy work.

The epicenter of advocacy shifted to the UN in New York and a series of sessions of the OWG in the General Assembly from March 2013 to July 2014. Peacebuilding CSOs increased their activities around the opening weeks of the General Assembly session in September 2013, putting together a number of side events and making their voices heard behind the scenes. A highlight was a well-attended event on September 23rd at Scandinavia House on "Stability and Peace: Finding the Heart of Sustainable Development."[30] Civil society engagement with member states increased, particularly among member states of the g7+, but also more influential "emerging powers" that brought different views on how to handle peace and stability. Additionally, the 8th Open Working Group session in February 2014, "Conflict Prevention, Post-conflict Peacebuilding and the Promotion of Durable Peace, Rule of Law and Governance," provided an important space for discussion of peace-related issues.

African member states have a central role in these processes, both in the broader development conversation and as home to the majority of least developed countries (LDCs) and fragile and conflict-affected states. Many non-African countries also follow a strong lead from African countries, including Northern donor countries that are investing in Africa's development. Perhaps the most important impact of the work of African peacebuilding civil society representatives was in advocating for, and supporting, the inclusion of peace issues within the Common African Position on the post-2015 development agenda, finalized in March 2014. This included peace and security as one of six priorities for Africa's development. The establishment of a unified African position came at a critical stage in the OWG negotiation process and was particularly important in shifting the center of gravity of member state views on peace issues, with some who had been negative now moderating their positions.

The final session of the OWG took place in July 2014, with eight days of intense debate culminating in a marathon twenty-nine-hour session. By this time, the governance, rule of law, and security issues had become conflated into one "peace" goal, Goal 16, including a list of ten targets which covered everything from reducing death rates to improving global governance. The survival of Goal 16 was a significant political achievement, albeit at the cost of a meaningful reduction in its coherence. Peacebuilding CSOs remained relieved that their concerns had been taken up by many member states.

The next major milestone was the publication of the Secretary-General's synthesis report in early December 2014, *The Road to Dignity by 2030*. This did not make changes to the OWG's list of goals but added a new framing that stressed the transformative and universal nature of the project, pulled together the current state of thinking on implementation issues, and brought in the findings from some of the technical advisory discussions that had been ongoing in parallel to the OWG sessions.

By early 2015 it was becoming increasingly likely that Goal 16 would be included in the new SDGs, but it was also important to include the new approach of treating peaceful, just, and inclusive societies as a core part of the development agenda in the Preamble and Declaration of the document. These challenges required continuing work with member states. At the same time, discussions on sustainable development targets and indicators were beginning, and the civil society peacebuilding community was keen to ensure that a decade's work of designing and working with peace indicators was included. The United Nations Development Programme (UNDP), playing a lead role for the UN in this process, put together a Virtual Network of stakeholders for the development of indicators for sustainable development goal 16, which created space for civil society expertise to feed into higher-level UN channels. This became an important clearinghouse for brainstorming and collating input for indicators across Goal 16, bringing together both the justice and the peacebuilding communities.

The critical issue of financing the development goals also came into focus at this time with the July 2015, 3rd International Conference on Financing for Development in Addis Ababa. The new agenda needed funding and the financing conversation had been taking place separately from the mainstream of the SDG discussions. It did not reflect the more transformative parts of that agenda—in particular the new emphasis on fostering peaceful, just, and inclusive societies. The release of the States of Fragility 2015 report by the Organisation for Economic Co-operation and Development (OECD) drew attention to the failures of the international system to provide adequate funding for fragile and conflict-affected countries.[31] A small group of CSOs reinforced this messaging in the weeks before Addis Ababa with some focused convening of member state actors.[32]

With concerns on the political front over the inclusion of peace issues in the SDG document—whether they would be reflected in financing decisions, as well as the need to ensure that the peace goal was supported by a strong set of indicators and measures—CSOs remained actively engaged right up to the final meeting of member state negotiators in August 2015. It was here that, after three years of continuous consultation and hard work, 193 governments united behind a shared vision and plan for humanity's future and approved for adoption during the September General Assembly Summit the final SDG outcome document, *Transforming Our World: the 2030 Agenda for Sustainable Development*.

ISSUES, STRATEGIES, AND DILEMMAS FOR CIVIL SOCIETY

The role of civil society as reflected in the post-2015 process now extends beyond shouting and criticizing from the sidelines to critical advocacy and providing pragmatic alternatives. While the former remains important, civil society needs to be well positioned to provide solutions that work when called to. (Showers Matowa)

As the MDGs became the priority of national governments, donors, and international financial institutions, money flowed into MDG-related projects. It was reasonable to assume that the SDG framework would be similarly influential, and the stakes for civil society in the 2030 Agenda were high. Yet, the environment of the post-2015 policy conversation was unique in a number of ways that presented distinct challenges to civil society engagement. The degree of civil society access at the UN headquarters was unprecedented, with a variety of formal and informal routes through which to provide input and engage actively in the discussion. However, the complexity, uncertainty, and constant flux of the underlying processes reduced the effectiveness of many traditional civil society approaches. Ensuring that civil society engagement was itself inclusive, reflecting the perspectives and insights of those impacted by violence and fragility—with Southern as well as Northern voices—was a struggle. Additionally, the fundamental puzzle of how to articulate peace issues most effectively was underlying these processes. These key strategic challenges for civil society are examined in more detail below.

How to Adapt to Unprecedented Access?

The post-2015 process offered greater openness to civil society engagement, more than any previous large UN negotiation. In an environment of this complexity, traditional civil society dilemmas and approaches were not always effective. Issues of whether, for example, to resist the process from the outside given limited access, or to participate in narrow, perhaps compromised and limited ways from the inside, were transcended by this new approach.

A broad range of formal opportunities were available. The major group system had been affirmed at the Rio+20 meeting and continued through the OWG process and the member state negotiating phase that followed, including venues for: NGOs, women, indigenous peoples, children, and youth, among others. These social groups were able to participate in formal hearings and informal meetings to make their views known and provide input into the process. The UN Non-Governmental Liaison Service worked with the office of the president of the General Assembly to develop an approach to civil society participation in major events, such as thematic debates, by soliciting nominations for a selection committee for civil society speakers. The cochairs of the OWG also frequently held hearings for civil society on particular topics, and many of the major processes included opportunities to contribute research and commentary online.

One notable new feature was that many UN agencies had set aside budgets specifically for civil society consultations and engagement to a degree that was new in the UN system. A variety of internet-based platforms were created for outreach and analysis. The *World We Want: Visualizing People's Voice*[33] project reached out directly to get the views of individuals from around the world and was met with an enthusiastic response.

This greater degree of access also created new challenges for civil society engagement. One significant side effect was that the sheer volume of papers, reports, and advocacy pieces was very high. Messaging had to be carefully targeted to the needs of the specific audience, designed to be relevant to the process underway and crafted to be heard. It was not enough to publish a report or advocacy piece: to be noticed required follow-up and direct outreach to decision-makers. This required understanding the dynamics of the process in detail, and an appreciation for the concerns and objectives of the negotiators, as well as for the constraints they faced.

This process was also exceptionally political. It was not enough for civil society to simply produce quality research and set out strong arguments. Technical approaches that worked in Washington, DC, or Brussels were less effective at the UN in New York. These negotiations were taking place against a backdrop of wary relationships between developed and developing countries (as evidenced by the heated discussions over "common but differentiated responsibilities"), deteriorating big-power interactions over peace and security issues (in the Middle East and beyond), and a growing voice from emerging powers. A greater degree of access for civil society required a greater appreciation of the political complexities of the negotiating environment.

Some CSOs were faster to adapt to this new context than others. On occasion the cochairs of the OWG process felt the need to directly request civil society groups to make their contributions more concrete and relevant to the discussions at hand. At the same time, some civil society groups were less able to take advantage of the new openness. CSOs from the Global South were constrained by geography, resources, and capacity (as described below). Those who were able to get funding to come to New York, however, often found they had better access than the larger international nongovernmental organizations (INGOs), particularly with developing country delegates. In this context, inside strategies could backfire to the extent that a CSO became associated with a particular political or geographic point of view. For example, Northern CSOs were often viewed by Southern member states and civil society as being in the pocket of Western governments.

How to Navigate the Complexity of the Operating Environment?

From an advocacy perspective, the level of complexity was unprecedented. The SDG process had enormous scope, with consultations taking place all around the world at national, regional, and global levels, revolving around a series of arcane negotiations at the UN in New York. During the four plus years of the post-2015 process, there was often a considerable lack of clarity around issues such as the next steps in the process or the relevant importance of particular actors, events, and points of entry and engagement. There were also countless, often overlapping meetings that might have potentially been relevant to a particular thread of discussion, but it was unclear which was the most significant.

The process was also very fluid. Negotiating teams in New York were operating in the absence of clear instructions from their capitals on key issues, including those related to the peace agenda. Individual delegations might therefore take their cues from first principles, or from statements made by regional bodies. Member state positions also shifted over time, quite noticeably in some cases, as countries came to more clearly think through which issues within the SDGs concerned them the most. This fluidity was accentuated by the changing dynamics of the negotiating formats themselves. The structure of the OWG process, with small groups of (in some cases unrelated) member states sharing a seat, was quite different from the intergovernmental negotiations that followed. Additionally, although principal groups of actors (member states, UN officials, civil society, etc.) had distinct rights and responsibilities and fields of action, it was possible to see a significant new initiative arise from a member state representative one day or another new initiative arise from a think tank report the next.

The key quality that separated one actor from another was less their formal categorization and more their functional efficacy—their ability to contribute to the discussion and add value in real time. Many links were developed between different types of actors based on practical interdependence; for example, some member state delegations might rely on civil society support and backup, while CSOs might rely on the endorsement of a key UN agency.

In this complex and fluid environment, with low barriers to participation, civil society actors—especially those that were well placed geographically with resources to take advantage of the context—no longer needed to focus so much of their energy on simply getting a seat at the table. An effective civil society strategy now involved developing collaborative partnerships; working in ad hoc coalitions with member states, UN officials, and others based on mutual interests; and sharing information and acting in concert to identify new, jointly owned ways to move the SDG agenda forward.

How to Foster Inclusion and Ownership of Southern Actors and Perspectives?

A core challenge for CSOs, throughout the policy-formation process, was the tension around centrally including and positioning Global South perspectives, especially from conflict-affected countries. This included perspectives from local, grassroots organizations and addressed the logistical, financial, capacity, and political obstacles of doing so. Inclusion is a core peacebuilding tenet and an evolving international norm. But achieving this in practice in the complex, high-level global policy process centered in New York presented profound challenges.

A small number of Southern regional CSOs were active and able to engage locally, regionally, and internationally, such as Igarapé in Brazil and ACCORD in South Africa. Some partnership organizations (e.g., the Global Partnership for the Prevention of Armed Conflict [GPPAC] and the CSPPS) canvassed their local members and networks, and brought representatives to engage on high-level platforms at different stages in the process.[34] Some INGOs and coalitions were also able to find funding for individuals to participate in policy dialogues in New York and globally, but a sustained and well-resourced engagement from the Global South was not achieved.

Resource constraints were part of the problem. Funding was available for INGOs from their customary donors (typically Northern governments and government agencies), but it was very hard to get new funding for efforts outside those traditional relationships, particularly for Global South organizations who might not have a history of working in global policy centers or a network of contacts among potential grant providers. As one Southern activist shared:

> Northern NGOs tend to be dominant and by far more active, either directly engaging with the process in their own right, or as representing the broader civil society. This is not surprising considering that Northern NGOs tend to be better resourced. There is a perception that with the tightening fiscal space Western donors more and more fund their own civil society to do work in the south as opposed to supporting southern NGOs. There are some concerns about big NGOs speaking for the smaller ones, a difficult dynamic to disentangle given the need for civil society to create a common voice.[35]

There was also a significant difference between organizations that focused on governance and justice issues, who were able to leverage significant new funding for SDG engagement, and peacebuilding organizations, who largely continued to depend upon existing donor relationships. When direct engagement from Global South organizations did occur, it generated good access and opportunities for hearing the concerns of people in the affected regions; an example was the work of the Africa Platform, formerly the Africa CSO Platform on Principled Partnership (ACP).

How to Frame Peace Substantively in the Agenda

Framing and defining the issues central to achieving peace has historically been a widely contested field[36] and there are innumerable lists of what activities peacebuilding can include.[37] In this case, the challenge was even greater, as the problem was about how to articulate a peace perspective in a universal, aspirational set of broadly based development goals and targets that were designed to be relevant to all societies.

The restrictions of a policy document based on goals and targets required that those engaging in this area make choices as to what they would consider to be the most important issues to address in building sustainable peace. This was contrary to some of the key lessons learned by peacebuilders in recent decades, namely that peacebuilding is context-specific and needs to be approached holistically with a concerted, context-driven strategy, rather than implementation of generic, prioritized lists. Civil society had to think both in terms of what will work *politically*, forging broad acceptance of an overall peace perspective, and technically, articulating evidence-based areas of focus that would lead to sustainable peace in a wide range of different societies.

A core part of this framing already existed. Publications such as the Global Burden of Armed Violence reports[38] and the *World Development Report (WDR) 2011: Conflict, Security, and Development* have provided ample evidence for the development community of the harmful impacts of violent conflict.[39] These and other reports demonstrated that the eradication of extreme poverty required attention to the particular needs of fragile and conflict-affected societies. While the WDR proposed strengthening national institutions and improving governance in three priority areas—citizen security, justice, and jobs—Peacebuilding and Statebuilding Goals (PSGs) focused on: inclusive politics, people's security, access to justice, economic livelihoods, and accountable service delivery.[40] While both approaches provided an existing body of research in support of policy advocacy, they sparked substantive debates over certain concepts.

The concept of state fragility, for example, was not universally accepted, and the category of "fragile and conflict-affected states"—well established among donor countries and the development community—had never been formally taken up by UN member states. Civil society groups noted that the PSGs focused primarily on internal factors (at the national and local levels) and were largely silent on external drivers of instability and violence. Furthermore, they did not speak to issues of equity and inclusion in global governance and decision-making.

Several competing camps of discourse emerged: justice and governance on the one hand, and those rooted in peacebuilding and human security approaches on the other. The first group, led by Western governments and large CSOs such as the Open Society Institute, lobbied for a cluster of issues related to criminal justice, rule of law, accountable and transparent government, and human rights at a country level. The second group, led by New Deal stakeholders, especially g7+ governments, as well as CSOs involved in peacebuilding and conflict prevention, focused on issues related to peace, freedom from violence, political inclusion and dialogue, human and citizen security, conflict resolution, and social cohesion. There were also historic North-South debates within these camps. For example, for many Northern countries, rule of law is about justice and governance issues within states, whereas for many of the G77,[41] rule of law is about global governance and Security Council reform.[42] The g7+ sought to engage both positions.

Peacebuilding CSOs generally sought to engage with member states by listening, providing platforms for dialogue and reflection, and building bridges between the different perspectives. Many g7+ governments had capable representatives at the UN, but they had limited resources. CSOs provided technical and moral support and bolstered the broader argument by demonstrating that there was solid civil society and research support for the inclusion of peace issues. They also engaged with the emerging powers, such as Brazil and South Africa, who had been largely sidelined in the IDPS/New Deal discussions, yet had firm ideas about the inclusion of peace and stability issues in the SDG process.

The broadening of the approach toward thinking of peace in universal terms occurred over time through the course of member state negotiations and with the strong engagement of civil society actors in New York and other capitals in many parts of the world. The International Dialogue and g7+ countries (Timor-Leste in particular) were pivotal in establishing the political credibility of this agenda, with the listing of "conflict and conflict-affected countries" as a group of states deserving special attention in precursor agreements in the General Assembly. A number of African delegations were successful at including language addressing root causes of conflict in Africa in General Assembly agreements.

CSOs worked diligently to broaden the acceptance of the peace agenda in the SDGs by promoting the acknowledgment that violence was a fundamental dimension of human suffering, as much part of the human experience as poverty and hunger.[43] CSOs also played a key role in ensuring that additional items were included, such as the naming of certain external root causes (such as illicit financial and arms flows) and explicit recognition of the need for more inclusive global governance (important to the emerging powers in particular). The impact of these efforts by states and CSOs was evident in the Secretary-General's synthesis report at the end of 2014, and took its final shape in the Preamble of the 2030 Agenda document that highlighted a determination to "foster peaceful, just and inclusive societies that are free from fear and violence."[44]

ASSESSING OUTCOMES AND IMPLICATIONS
FOR SUSTAINABLE PEACE

Given the nature of deeply interactive engagements among many different actors, it is difficult to draw definitive conclusions on the role of civil society in these developments. Assessing the impacts of peacebuilding policy-level work is always challenging. Nonetheless, interviews with well-placed sources and from my own experience in the process suggest that civil society played a deeply influential role in key ways. These included:

* providing robust analysis throughout, especially at crucial moments in the process;
* influencing politics at multiple levels and breaking obstacles through persistent negotiations;
* providing influential ideas without needing to take credit;
* lobbying persistently, and at the highest levels;
* supporting the wider inclusion of civil society actors around the world in consultative processes.

This last point is key, for as one CSO representative has suggested, "People are ahead of their leaders, demanding moral leadership and change."[45]

As highlighted above, understanding impact is complicated by many factors. In addition to causality issues common with social science research, the timescale over which changes may be felt can be decades or even generations. For example, the impacts of the 1995 Fourth World Conference on Women in Beijing are still being felt twenty years later, and will continue to be felt for some time to come. The impact is not just in the implementation of a particular agreement, but must be viewed through all the other international, regional, and national agreements and policies that it affects. Like ripples in a lake, the effects of a major change in international norms and standards can be felt in myriad ways in shifts in policies, standards, attitudes, and actions across the world.

The challenges are very clear in the case of the peaceful, just, and inclusive societies dimension of the 2030 Agenda. The broad scope of the SDG agreement encompasses a wide range of issues that are often cited as being among the root causes of conflict. This breadth provides a stage for the articulation of a comprehensive vision of peaceful societies and takes critical steps in addressing issues that lay a foundation for sustainable peace, across societies and universally, that is in many ways unprecedented in its compass.

The outcomes of the combined efforts of different actors to infuse peace within the post-2015 framework include the following:

- Policy directly referencing peace and how to achieve it in place at the highest level, to be applied universally;
- Mainstreaming discussions of peace in development thinking and practice;
- Exposing large numbers of diplomats, other policymakers, and influencers to the broader ideas of peacebuilding;
- Setting a precedent for more inclusive policymaking, including better pathways for the involvement of civil society;
- Providing a framework for greater participation and inclusion of civil societies in the SDG framework and its implementation; and,
- Setting a precedent for coordination among peacebuilding policy organizations to support a major policy achievement.

Building upon these outcomes and the critical insights of literature and practice, the following three priorities are suggested as fundamental starting points to support the transformative efforts required to bring about sustainable peace within *and across* societies:

1. Address or hold promise of addressing common drivers of conflict and violence on the one hand, and peace and resilience on the other—globally, within, and across member states;
2. Offer ongoing pathways for meaningful inclusion of societal actors; and
3. Provide clear implementation and financing mechanisms.

Regarding the first point, the peaceful, just, and inclusive societies dimension of the 2030 Agenda is much greater than just Goal 16. It is a package, including several goals and targets that together encompass the potential for significant change at national and international levels. It is unprecedented in the way it brings together a broad range of structural issues that often underlie or contribute to violent conflict and fragility, alongside and embedded within traditional development objectives, and in the way it puts forth an expansive range of targets (169) covering political, economic, and social realms, to affect them.

Goal 16 addresses both internal drivers of violent conflict (lack of access to justice, corruption, unaccountable institutions, exclusive decision-making at national and subnational levels) and external ones (illicit financial and arms flows, organized crime, exclusive global governance). Other goals and targets, including Goal 10 (on reducing inequalities), and Goal 2 (gender), are also highly relevant for transforming structures and institutions, and ultimately shifting power relations at multiple levels—a foundation for achieving genuine, just, and sustainable peace.

At the same time, some argue that the framework could go further in addressing structural drivers of conflict and fragility. On the economic side, as one Indian government representative suggested, the framework "is a floor, not a ceiling," because substantive drivers of injustice issues are not addressed.[46] Some Global South activists argue that the framework is not sufficiently transformative because it does not fundamentally shift the macro-economic framework and reposition country economies so that they are not so vulnerable to global economic volatility–processes that create poverty and inequality in the first place.[47] Neither does it provide pathways for addressing contexts where there are serious disparities of land and resources that fuel conflict. These are important issues for ongoing attention and debate, both at national and international levels. The critiques are driven by the experience of scholars, policymakers, and activists across the Global South, who have been at the receiving end of global frameworks and internationally prescribed policies that have often resulted in adverse effects within their countries.

Crucially, the framework is weak on mechanisms to foster reconciliation, conflict resolution, peacemaking, and more generally the social and relational side of social cohesion, at all levels within society. This was consistently advocated by civil society, and featured in the New Deal Common Indicators.[48] While Goal 16 was by all accounts a magnanimous achievement, it came with some expense at a concerted effort to mainstream a peace and conflict "lens" throughout the framework. Some efforts were made in this regard,[49] but ultimately this agenda lost ground to the wider push for one inclusive goal. The other fallout of this goal is a concerning perception that "peace" is associated with primarily security, governance, and rule-of-law activities, despite decades of evolutionary thought to ensure it is perceived as an integrated concept, with development also at its core.[50]

The second area concerns the ways in which the framework and its implementation offer ongoing pathways for inclusive participation. This is crucial for addressing power asymmetries and exclusionary policies that fuel violence and violent conflict. The substantive content of the 2030 Agenda addresses these issues in myriad ways, notably by effectively mainstreaming the concept of inclusivity through many of its goals: education (Goal 4), economic growth and full employment (Goal 8), infrastructure (Goal 9), cities (Goal 11), and societies and institutions (Goal 16). By emphasizing participation and inclusion in a range of issues that are often interactive and interdependent, the 2030 Agenda addresses power asymmetries in a way that most official peacebuilding agreements do not. Central to realizing results in this area will be how the pathways for participation are actively forged, in particular at national levels.

The third area is focused on implementation, and the financing needed to ensure this. While it is still too early to assess the provision of clear implementation and financing mechanisms, civil society has expressed concerns. To date, despite the space created for civil society in forging the 2030 Agenda, governments are in the driver's seat on almost all discussions around implementation, measurement and review processes, and financing. The discussions are being forged within narrow, high-level spaces with limited engagement for meaningful civil society participation.

On each of these areas the New Deal, its processes, and instruments can and should be engaged. The three New Deal constituencies are committed to this after years of investment in forging this international social compact. Civil society is playing a leadership role in thinking through how to guarantee alignment across the two frameworks to ensure that (1) the New Deal processes support conflict-affected states to work toward and strengthen the 2030 Agenda outcomes, supporting prioritization and the shaping, relevance, and building of ownership of the goals in relevant countries; and (2) the SDGs support New Deal implementation—the overarching goal of the three IDPS constituencies in the New Deal process.

Saferworld argues that 17 goals and 169 targets "risk making implementation so challenging that the agenda is either very selectively implemented or, worse, quietly ignored by decision-makers who already feel over-burdened." Further, it suggests, many of the global targets are not quantified, which will make it difficult to ascertain whether they have been achieved by 2030. Nor is there a commitment by member states to set quantified benchmarks for success at a national level. This will also make it harder to hold leaders accountable. None of this is helped by an agreement on a weak follow-up and review process.[51]

Building upon many of the insights that have come through the New Deal process, Saferworld argues that meaningful implementation will involve identifying national indicators for the SDG targets and collecting data to track and uphold the ambitions set out in Goal 16. In addition, as priorities to fit each context are defined, inclusive consultations at the national level need to be held in order to put people's needs at the forefront of development. Global processes will also need to be leveraged to enable and support national-level action and to address transnational drivers of conflict such as illicit financial flows and strengthening nonofficial and official data collection capacities.[52]

In the final analysis, the success of the 2030 Agenda will be measured not only in the specific implementation of the goals, but by its impacts. The quality and degree to which it will be implemented will depend upon how successor agreements, standards, and practices engage and build upon and support the implementation of these goals and targets. Crucially, a transformative impact relies upon the uptake by national governments, and how they align their national policies and practices.

CONCLUSIONS FOR SCHOLARSHIP AND ACTION

The 2030 agenda is one of the most progressive international agreements to date and offers promising entry points for civil society participation in advancing development and peace. The atmosphere at the time of its adoption in 2015 was celebratory. Peacebuilding advocates and their allies, among member states and UN officials, congratulated each other in getting peace issues onto the negotiating table and keeping them there through years of sustained effort. This was a significant achievement, although only time will tell if the SDG goals and targets force a rethink of policy at national and global levels and whether they create space for bringing about requisite structural changes.

The following lessons highlight takeaways from the role of civil society in forging the 2030 Agenda. First, as scholars have long argued, it continues to be vital to understanding the context within which civil society engagement occurs. The context here—and one that will no doubt continue—is complex, dynamic, chaotic, and rapidly changing but also accessible to civil society engagement. CSOs are compelled to play new types of roles that involve much more direct collaboration with governmental and intergovernmental actors to achieve results. Scholars can further reflect upon these issues, and how these new contexts affect civil society strategizing, dilemmas, and impact.

This context of complexity and direct engagement creates challenges to traditional ways of organizing. A special concern is ensuring that Global South actors are meaningfully included in the process. Many new entry points and opportunities exist for civil society engagement, but civil society actors need to think carefully about how to take advantage of these openings to bring meaningful results for all. Deeper reflection is also needed on how to conceptualize and capitalize on the phenomena of transnational advocacy networks in ways that are transformative and build inclusion. In this context, maintaining a focus on peace issues within a development framework is vital, as they can easily get drowned out in a movement to infuse SDGs in national development frameworks. Further, we need to better understand how the diffusion of actors across multiple issue networks can be meaningfully managed in interactive ways to ensure that the implementation of the SDG agenda truly addresses the root causes of conflict and fragility, engages national capacities of resilience, and brings transformative results. Utilizing the New Deal framework in IDPS countries can support this, notably, by ensuring that country-driven analysis of what drives conflict and fragility is engaged, and the commitment to political dialogue that engages national actors remains central to informing how the prioritization and sequencing of SDG implementation is undertaken.

Steadfast attention by peacebuilding-oriented CSOs is particularly needed to ensure that international attention is maintained on core priorities likely to guarantee the success of the sustainable peace agenda in the three areas discussed above, around: (1) addressing common drivers of conflict and violence and building support for the conditions of peace globally and within and across member states; (2) forging pathways for meaningful inclusion of societal actors in all aspects of the implementation of the 2030 Agenda; and (3) working for the implementation and financing of this agenda.

By targeting the UN, civil society actors can impact global norms and standards and influence the way the international community prevents and responds to outbreaks of violence. At the same time, because the UN is a body of member states, it remains necessary to target these member states and national institutions in support of the development-as-peace agenda. Most importantly, civil society must ensure ever-stronger attention and action to deepen its engagement with people at all levels, in all countries. This is what will pivotally guarantee that this universal project fosters a people-driven and owned agenda for sustainable peace.

NOTES

1. Which now include: Afghanistan, Burundi, Central African Republic, Chad, Comoros, Côte d'Ivoire, Democratic Republic of the Congo, Guinea, Guinea-Bissau, Haiti, Liberia, Papua New Guinea, São Tomé and Príncipe, Sierra Leone, Somalia, Solomon Islands, South Sudan, Timor-Leste, Togo, and Yemen.

2. Margaret Keck and Kathryn Sikkink, "Transnational Advocacy Networks in International and Regional Politics," *International Social Science Journal* 51, no. 159 (1999): 89.

3. A key contributor to this article in laying out the detailed story of civil society participation, with deep insider knowledge of the process at the UN headquarters in New York, is Andrew Tomlinson, director of the Quaker UN Office. Other key informants interviewed: Paul Okumu, Rob Muggah, Showers Mawowa, and Henk-Jan Brinkman.

4. Erin McCandless participated in the 2030 Agenda process on behalf of civil society engaged in the New Deal process, through the Civil Society Platform on Peacebuilding and Statebuilding (CSPPS), while she served as a representative to the Executive Committee of this body.

5. Anders Uhlin, "The Transnational Dimension of Civil Society: Migration and Independence Movements in Southeast Asia," in *Civil Society and Authoritarianism in the Third World*, eds., B. Beckman, E. Hansson and A. Sjögren (Stockholm: PODSU, Stockholm University, 2001).

6. Doug McAdam and David Snow, eds., *Social Movements: Reader on Their Emergence, Mobilization, and Dynamics* (Los Angeles: Roxbury, 1997).

7. The first dilemma concerns whether a rights-based approach, often assumed by many in the Global South to be associated with civil and political rights and individual liberties or an approach, focused on the redistribution of wealth, land, and other natural resources, will more readily achieve the desired change. In the second dilemma, participation refers to the strategy of partnering with, or working within, processes set up by government or donors, and resistance to the strategy of fomenting change by working outside the system, challenging and transforming existing structures of authority or processes that visibly reinforce the status quo, or creating entirely new, parallel structures and processes. The former reflects contemporary discourse and evolving practices around the nature of civil society relations with the state and international donors in particular, while the latter—often used in leftist, nationalist, and social movement discourse and practice—implies radical, and even confrontational strategies and anticipated radical outcomes, that is, structural, transformative change. These were developed as heuristic devices to understand Zimbabwe's polarization, but are argued to have much wider relevance for civic actors. Erin McCandless, *Polarization and Transformation in Zimbabwe: Social Movements, Strategy Dilemmas and Change* (Maryland: Lexington Books, 2011).

8. McCandless, *Polarization and Transformation in Zimbabwe*.

9. The African Charter for Popular Participation in Development suggests that people must be empowered to effectively participate (Arusha 1990). Gumah argues that empowerment means the provision of space and institutional frameworks for consensus building, and equipping people with the requisite knowledge and skills to participate effectively and meaningfully in the national policy dialogue process. Awudu Ahmed Gumah, "Prospects for Poverty Reduction in Ghana: A Critical Analysis of the PRSP Process and Outcomes" (Harare: *AFRODAD PRSP Series*, 2003).

10. Genevieve Painter, *Quality Participation in Poverty Reduction Strategies: Experiences from Malawi, Bolivia, and Rwanda* (London: Eurodad, 2002).

11. Thania Paffenholz, "Results on Women and Gender from the 'Broader Participation' and 'Civil Society and Peacebuilding' Projects," Briefing Paper, Centre on Conflict, Development, and Peacebuilding Geneva: The Graduate Institute of International and Development Studies, 2015, http://graduateinstitute.ch/files/live/sites/iheid/files/sites/ccdp/shared/Docs/Publications/briefingpaperwomen%20gender.pdf.

12. See, for example, McAdam and Snow, *Social Movements*, 461 for insights into social movements and http://dmeforpeace.org/ to gain insight into the peacebuilding evaluation community of practice.

13. Mary B. Anderson and Lara Olson, *Confronting War: Critical Lessons for Peace Practitioners* (Cambridge, MA: CDA, 2003).

14. Björn Beckman, Eva Hannson, and Anders Sjögren, eds., *Civil Society and Authoritarianism in the Third World: A Conference Book* (Stockholm: Department of Political Science, Stockholm University, 2001).

15. Piotr Sztompka, *The Sociology of Social Change* (Oxford: Blackwell, 1993).

16. Anita Ernstorfer, Diana Chigas, and Hannah Vaughan-Lee, "From Little to Large: When Does Peacebuilding Add Up?" in "Vertical Integration in Peacebuilding," special issue, *Journal for Peacebuilding and Development* 10, no. 1 (2015).

17. Erin McCandless, Tim Donais, and Eric Abitbol, "Vertical Integration: A Dynamic Practice Promoting Transformative Peacebuilding," in "Vertical Integration in Peacebuilding," special issue, *Journal for Peacebuilding and Development* 10, no. 1 (2015): 1–9.

18. Collaborative for Development Action's (CDA's) Reflecting on Peace Practice (RPP) program has delved into this area for over a decade, while McCandless has developed a framework for evaluating social movement impacts on transformative change and peace at the national level. Refer to McCandless, *Polarization and Transformation in Zimbabwe.*

19. For example, refer to Doug McAdam, "Freedom Summer Project, Mississippi, 1964," in *Protest, Power, and Change: An Encyclopedia of Nonviolent Action from ACT-UP to Women's Suffrage*, eds., Roger S. Powers and William B. Voegele (New York: Garland Publishing, 1997), 192–194; and Lloyd M. Sachikonye, "Civil Society, Social Movements, and Democracy in Southern Africa," *Innovation: The European Journal of Social Science Research* 8, no. 4 (1995): 399–411.

20. Margaret Keck and Kathryn Sikkink, "Transnational Advocacy Networks in International and Regional Politics," 201.

21. See for example, Jack A. Goldstone, "Introduction: Bridging Institutionalized and Noninstitutionalized Politics," in *States, Parties, and Social Movements*, ed., Jack A. Goldstone (Cambridge: Cambridge University Press, 2003), 20. Some also elevate explanations based on resource mobilization or collective action over the role of political context; for example, see William A. Gamson, *The Strategy of Social Protest*, 2nd edn. (Belmont, CA: Wadsworth Publishing, 1990).

22. Erin McCandless, "In Pursuit of Peacebuilding for Perpetual Peace: Where the UN's Peacebuilding Architecture Needs to Go," Working Paper for the Future of the Peacebuilding Architecture Project, Center for International Policy Studies, University of Ottawa and the Norwegian Institute of International Affairs, 2010, http://www.cips-cepi.ca/wp-content/uploads/2015/01/McCandless.pdf.

23. The Major Group process alone identifies nine sectors (from business to local authorities and women). Traditional NGOs (North, Global South, large and small, policy and grassroots, and multi- and single-mandate) were all present, but academics and think tanks and the media all had key roles. Coalitions of civil society groups were also notable for their important role in this discussion.

24. These included national government ministries and departments, UN mission diplomats, and national negotiating teams. Governments also acted through regional organizations, such as the African Union, and through UN-based voting blocks, such as the "G77" (nonaligned nations) or the "LDCs," and through the General Assembly, United Nations Economic and Social Council (ECOSOC), and the Security Council, as well as the governing boards of the International Financial Institutions (IFIs).

25. Including actors from all programmatic departments of the secretariat and most of the agencies, funds, and programs, including voices both from headquarters and the field. Also, officials from the World Bank and other international institutions.

26. "Bringing Peace into the Post-2015 Development Framework: A Joint Statement by Civil Society Organizations," September 2012, http://www.cspps.org/

documents/130616042/130626578/2012_09_28_CSO_Joint_Statement_Post-2015_
ENG.pdf/a187d69f-3a87-46b1-82d1-90e24768424d.

27. International NGOs participating included ACCORD, Igarapé, the Institute for Economics and Peace, International Alert, Saferworld, and the Quaker UN Office, along with academics and think tanks such as the NYU Center on International Cooperation.

28. UNICEF, PBSO, UNDP, *Report of the Expert Meeting on an Accountability Framework for Conflict, Violence, Governance and Disaster in the Post-2015 Development Agenda* (Glen Cove, NY: June 18–19, 2013).

29. International Peace Institute, "Conflict, Violence, and Instability in the Post-2015 Development Agenda," Meeting Note, October 2013, https://www.ipinst.org/wp-content/uploads/publications/ipi_e_pub_post_2015.pdf.

30. Quaker United Nations Office, "QUNO Co-Hosts a High Level Side Event in the Opening Week of the 68th General Assembly on Stability and Peace," September 2013, http://quno.org/timeline/2013/9/quno-co-hosts-high-level-side-event-opening-week-68th-general-assembly-stability-and.

31. OECD-DAC, *States of Fragility 2015: Meeting Post-2015 Ambitions*, Revised edition (Paris: OECD, 2015), http://www.keepeek.com/Digital-Asset-Management/oecd/development/states-of-fragility-2015_9789264227699-en#page1.

32. QUNO, "Funding for Peace: Lessons Learned," Meeting Note, June 2015, http://cic.nyu.edu/sites/default/files/quno_cic_ffd_meeting_note_final_june_2_2015.pdf.

33. The World We Want, "Visualizing People's Voices," http://millionvoices-data.worldwewant2015.org/

34. Rob Muggah of Igarapé, interview with author, January 2016.

35. Showers Matowa of SAPES, interview with author, December 2015.

36. The Alliance for Peacebuilding lists many of them: http://www.allianceforpeacebuilding.org/2013/08/selected-definitions-of-peacebuilding/.

37. United Nations Peacebuilding Fund, "What is Peacebuilding?" http://www.unpbf.org/application-guidelines/what-is-peacebuilding/.

38. Anna Alvazzi del Frate, Keith Krause, and Matthias Nowak, eds., *The Global Burden of Armed Violence 2015* (Geneva: Small Arms Survey of Geneva Declaration on Armed Violence and Development, 2015).

39. World Bank, *World Development Report 2011: Conflict, Security, and Development* (Washington, DC: World Bank, 2011), http://web.worldbank.org/WBSITE/EXTERNAL/EXTDEC/EXTRESEARCH/EXTWDRS/0,,contentMDK:23256432~pagePK:478093~piPK:477627~theSitePK:477624,00.html.

40. International Dialogue on Peacebuilding and Statebuilding, "New Deal Principles," published online, http://www.pbsbdialogue.org/en/new-deal/new-deal-principles/.

41. The G77, an intergovernmental organization of developing countries in the UN, was established in 1964 to articulate and promote their collective economic interests.

42. Rob Muggah, interview with author, December 2015.

43. For example, the statement by the Quaker UN Office at the 8th session of the OWG makes this point clearly. Refer to QUNO, "QUNO Participated in Open Working Group 8

on the Sustainable Development Goals," March 2014, http://quno.org/timeline/2014/3/quno-participated-open-working-group-8-sustainable-development-goals.

44. United Nations, *Transforming Our World: The 2030 Agenda for Sustainable Development* (New York: UN, 2015), http://www.un.org/ga/search/view_doc.asp?symbol=A/RES/70/1&Lang=E.

45. Peter van Tuijl, statement during "Strengthening Peacebuilding Policy through Civil Society Empowerment" conference, University of Notre Dame, October 25–27, 2015.

46. Remarks during the "Delivering on the Promise of Goal 16" event during the UN General Assembly debate, September 24, 2015.

47. Patrick Bond, interview with author, October 2015.

48. IDPS, "Peacebuilding and Statebuilding Indicators: Progress, Interim List and Next Steps" (IDPS Global Meeting, Washington, DC, April 19, 2013).

49. CSPPS brought analysis to bear, building upon its years of central participation in the New Deal process developing the PSGs, targets, and indicators; see: "Putting Sustainable Peace and Safe Societies at the Heart of the Development Agenda: Priorities for Post-2015," CSPPS and QUNO, September 2013, http://tinyurl.com/j2l86ar.

50. Erin McCandless, "Wicked Problems in Peacebuilding and Statebuilding: Making Progress in Measuring Progress in Peacebuilding and Statebuilding," *Global Governance* 19, no. 2 (2013): 227–248.

51. Thomas Wheeler, "Peace Finds Its Place at the Heart of the New Global Development Framework," Saferworld, August 3, 2015, http://www.saferworld.org.uk/news-and-views/comment/182-peace-finds-its-place-at-the-heart-of-the-new-global-development-framework.

52. Ibid.

Chapter 3

The Politics of Inclusion

Civil Society Engagement in the New Deal

Kristen Wall and Rachel Fairhurst

As detailed by Erin McCandless in chapter 2, the New Deal was the precursor to, and formative framework for, the SDGs. With an eye toward drawing lessons for the 2030 Agenda, this chapter analyzes the challenges and successes of the New Deal's ambitions to offer a new path out of fragility from the perspective of the civil society leaders engaged in its implementation. The New Deal attempted to change both the process of development and its content. Changes in process concern who is participating, how, and with what degree of influence. As such, they are inherently political and contested. The New Deal's genesis lay in a reaction by a self-identified group of fragile states, the g7+,[1] against international development practices in which fragile countries had little role in shaping donor development priorities and strategies. Civil society actors similarly advocated for a greater role in the development process, asserting that development outcomes must ultimately be informed by and accountable to citizens.

The core promise and challenge of the New Deal lies in shifting spheres of leadership, inclusion, and power in setting the development agenda in fragile states. Civil society has encountered numerous obstacles to greater engagement in New Deal implementation. As demonstrated by the views shared below, civil society actors have struggled for meaningful inclusion in the New Deal's implementation during its pilot phase, and have sought to ensure the framework's accountability to citizens of such states.

Many governments of the g7+ are hesitant to empower civil society as full partners in decision-making, seeing them interchangeably as implementers of their policies or as political threats. They are wary of civil society's efforts to hold them accountable to New Deal commitments. A lack of political will from donors and fragile state governments, whether due to low capacity or competing interests, also remains disappointing to some civil society activists. Despite these substantial challenges, civil society actors at national and international levels continue to advocate inclusion in the New Deal implementation process.

We argue that increasing civil society's participation in the New Deal's negotiation and implementation is central to creating statebuilding and peacebuilding processes that foster inclusive societies capable of overcoming fragility. Through persistent advocacy, capacity building, negotiation, and outreach to governments, civil society groups have used the opportunity afforded by the New Deal to increase their inclusion in policymaking—and in so doing increase the accountability of both donors and fragile states to citizens of fragile countries. The growth in civil society's capacity and influencing power marks a modest but important shift in power and inclusion dynamics at national and international levels. Sustaining and deepening this shift can help to build more participatory, accountable, and peaceful societies.

In this chapter we draw upon semi structured interviews with twenty-two civil society leaders from eight fragile states, including Central African Republic, Liberia, Sierra Leone, South Sudan, and Togo and from international nongovernmental organizations based in the United States, the United Kingdom, and the Netherlands.[2] We trace civil society's engagement with the New Deal process: through advocacy, monitoring, contributions of technical expertise, and strengthening relationships among civil society groups as well as with governments. We also examine how civil society's involvement is changing political dynamics by improving state-society relations, broadening societal ownership of the New Deal, and bringing citizen perspectives into technical discussions.

A NEW VISION: THE PROMISE OF THE NEW DEAL

Building on more than a decade of advocacy in international development policymaking circles, civil society helped to elevate state-society relations as a central concept around which to design approaches to bring states out of fragility. The New Deal, adopted in 2011 at the Fourth High Level Forum on Aid Effectiveness under the aegis of the IDPS,[3] is a joint initiative of the g7+, CSOs, and donor states working on conflict and fragility. The New Deal focuses development efforts around the following five PSGs as an approach to foster peace and development:

1. Legitimate politics—fostering inclusive political settlements and conflict resolution;
2. Security—establishing and strengthening people's security;
3. Justice—addressing injustices and increasing people's access to justice;

4. Economic foundations—generating employment and improving livelihoods; and
5. Revenues and services—managing revenue and building capacity for accountable and fair service delivery.[4]

To achieve the PSGs, the framework envisions a three-step technical process within each participating state for: (1) conducting an assessment of fragility factors affecting each PSG, (2) developing indicators for each PSG to define and track progress, and (3) negotiating new aid compacts between donors and g7+ governments based on the assessment and indicators.

The PSGs recognize that state legitimacy depends on government responsiveness to the needs of local communities and vulnerable populations. Four of the PSGs focus governments on delivering tangible results to society: economic livelihood, security, justice, and public services. These are the foundation and basis of governance and development. The New Deal commits both donors and fragile states to improving government relationships with society. The New Deal document states that "constructive state-society relations ... are at the heart of successful peacebuilding and statebuilding. They are essential to deliver the New Deal."[5]

In addition to shifting development priorities toward peacebuilding and statebuilding, New Deal principles also seek to change the process by which international actors work with donor states and civil society to set and implement the development agenda. The New Deal envisions new partnerships between donor states, fragile states, and civil society to create "country-led and country-owned transitions out of fragility."[6] This inclusive approach acknowledges that affected countries, rather than donor states, must lead peacebuilding and statebuilding processes.

However, government-led efforts are insufficient: building peace requires a whole-of-society approach, with the robust participation of civil society.[7] Soon after development actors signed the New Deal agreement, civil society argued that:

> strengthening the state sector is not enough to build effective and legitimate institutions. Effective, legitimate and resilient governance requires not only a broad spectrum of capacities in the state but also in society at large. There is no "state" without "people" who benefit from the right of "citizenship", and no state that is viable and resilient in the long term, without a strong and active citizenry.[8]

The New Deal's focus on state-society relations illustrates an evolution in international policy recognizing that addressing fragility is as much a political task as a technical one. By aspiring to "inclusive and participatory political dialogue,"[9] the New Deal departs from technocratic state-centric models of development that focus exclusively on building government institutions and neglect the importance of the political process. State-society relations, defined by the British Department for International Development (DFID) as "interactions between state institutions and societal groups to negotiate how public authority is exercised and how it can be influenced by people,"[10] are inherently political and frequently contested.

The outcome of these negotiations determines whose needs and interests are represented by the state, and defines how power is distributed within a society. As an early OECD paper on statebuilding and fragility points out, "state building is not a technical process of creating new government institutions or strengthening existing ones. ... Formal institutions need to be rooted in society otherwise they risk becoming mere shells or being captured by private or patrimonial interests."[11]

Attempts to improve state-society relations from an exclusively top-down or technical approach are often derailed by the self-interest of those governing, a lack of understanding of local perspectives, and a gap in trust between citizens and the government. Citizens must engage in political processes to inform and monitor policymaking through bottom-up efforts to spur or complement government-led reforms. Civil society can aggregate the voices and priorities of groups of citizens and organize them to influence policy; it can also serve as a check on political power by monitoring government action and disclosing abuses of power and resources.

By acknowledging the role of civil society in shaping state-society relations, the New Deal opened up the possibility for more inclusive political processes to negotiate development outcomes and statebuilding reforms. Such an opening was an intentional result of bottom-up efforts by civil society over more than a decade advocating its inclusion in a new approach to development.

Getting to the Table

Increasing civil society's inclusion in development policymaking has been a political process since transnational civil society networks began mobilizing in response to civil society's marginalization in global discussions on aid effectiveness in the early 2000s. The OECD initiated these discussions—a series of High Level Forums (HLFs) on aid effectiveness in Rome (2003), Paris (2005), Accra (2008), and Busan (2011)—to increase development effectiveness in service of the ambitious agenda set forth by the MDGs.

The Paris Declaration of 2005, the first output of the HLF process, articulated a state-centric model of development that was negotiated with low civil society participation. In response, a transnational network of civil society organizations—the International Civil Society Steering Group—was organized ahead of the Accra HLF in 2008. Through advocacy, it achieved several priorities in the resulting Accra Agenda for Action, including recognizing civil society as a development actor in its own right, the inclusion of civil society in HLF dialogues, and moving discussions on aid effectiveness beyond technical processes of aid delivery to focus on inclusive, rights-based development.[12] By the Fourth HLF in Busan, South Korea, in 2011, at which time the international community endorsed the New Deal, civil society, through its advocacy efforts, had become an officially recognized stakeholder in aid effectiveness negotiations.[13]

As it became apparent that conflict-affected countries were falling short on achieving development goals,[14] the IDPS emerged out of the HLF at Accra. Through the IDPS, donor and fragile states pledged to engage in a dialogue to develop "realistic peacebuilding and statebuilding objectives that address the root causes of conflict and fragility and help ensure the protection and participation of women."[15] Civil society was not an initial partner in the dialogue. In response, Interpeace, an international peacebuilding organization, conducted a round of consultations with more than fifty civil society groups, most of them from fragile states, to bring key recommendations to the IDPS. This included the subsequently adopted recommendation that civil society be an official IDPS member and be included in working groups.[16] Through effective advocacy and collaboration between organizations from the North and South, civil society won greater institutional inclusion in global processes to address fragility and development, a modus operandi that continues in current activities around the New Deal.

CONTRIBUTIONS OF CIVIL SOCIETY IN IMPLEMENTING THE NEW DEAL

The process of negotiating the New Deal framework demonstrated that, in order to influence international development policy, civil society actors had to mobilize, coordinate, and develop their capacity to work together and advocate within political policymaking processes at the international level. This required leveraging international and national perspectives, forging alliances, and coordinating as transnational networks. Once the negotiations secured key tenets of participatory political dialogue and a focus on state-society relations in the New Deal framework, civil society turned to the task of defending the political space won in the agreement and putting the agreement principles into meaningful practice.

In the pilot phase of the New Deal from 2012 through 2015, civil society expanded and institutionalized its networks—galvanizing new and existing networks of hundreds of CSOs in diverse sectors around the issues of peacebuilding and statebuilding. Institutionally, the IDPS now recognizes a civil society secretariat, the CSPPS or "the Platform," a diverse group of CSOs working on issues of peacebuilding, statebuilding, conflict, and fragility at local, national, regional, and global levels. Originally coordinated by Interpeace and now hosted by the Dutch relief organization Cordaid in The Hague, the CSPPS operates as a central convening platform for the participation of civil society actors in international IDPS meetings and processes.

The majority of the CSPSS executive committee is comprised of members from fragile states. This reflects the emphasis within the Platform on including the voices of fragile countries in the decisions that affect them. The Platform has enabled civil society to defend and expand political space for its inclusion nationally and internationally, and to marshal technical expertise across a range of fields to contribute to citizen-centered implementation of the New Deal. Civil society networks at the national level have also facilitated relationship- and trust-building across some societal divisions, an essential process in conflict-torn countries in which social cohesion must be repaired to reduce risks of conflict relapse and to foster inclusive societies.

Bridging Social Capital

Civil society groups in fragile contexts face unique challenges. Armed conflict damages the enabling environment for civil society by limiting political space and human rights and eroding trust and social capital. As Frauke de Weijer and Ulrike Kilnes note, "Civil society in fragile states often itself suffers from the legacy of fragility or conflict, which weakens its capacity to perform its role. Civil society in fragile states is often polarized, reflecting existing fault lines in society that often contributed to the history of conflict, or widened because of it." Civil society also faces security threats and dangers as political space closes. Critics of government policy may be targeted as political opponents, and in many contexts governments have passed legislation that limits legal space for registration and operation. Despite, or perhaps due to, these challenges, civil society actors in fragile contexts are on the front lines of mediating deeply strained state-society relations and mending the social fabric.

The CSPPS's priority was catalyzing the formation of new national platforms and civil society coalitions on the New Deal in pilot countries. Initially, after identifying local focal points, the CSPPS funded awareness-raising meetings that invited a broad array of CSOs to learn about the tenets of the New Deal. Most focal points were able to gain legitimacy by promoting inclusive dialogues with multiple stakeholders and assisting a broad range of civil society in organizing domestic platforms or core teams. These were structured in working groups parallel to the IDPS process, or organized around the PSGs, to coordinate New Deal activities. However, some focal points struggled to unify civil society platforms, resulting in weak coalitions and limited impact.

The networks galvanized by the New Deal brought together new social groupings that increased social capital and created bridges to resolve societal conflict. In some contexts, like Sierra Leone, the government initially excluded CSPPS focal points and associated coalitions in favor of organizations closer to itself; however, CSPPS organizations reached out to these organizations in an attempt to work together. In Somalia, the formation of the Somali Civil Society Alliance brought together CSOs from three previously warring states.[17] In Togo, civil society mobilized national Muslim, Christian, and secular networks to advocate peace under the framework of the New Deal, facilitating an interfaith endorsement of the process.

The CSPPS also connected International NGO members, such as Interpeace, Saferworld, and the Alliance for Peacebuilding with national coalitions, building a global civil society network working together to advance inclusive peacebuilding and statebuilding in international and national forums. The CSPPS forum has served as a vehicle for civil society leaders from fragile states to engage in international dialogue with donor states, elevating national civil society perspectives within the IDPS process. Additionally, civil society has strengthened regional networks in West Africa through the New Deal by sharing lessons learned across pilot countries in Sierra Leone, Togo, and Liberia.

According to civil society leaders, the growth of these networks has created new relationships and linkages among peacebuilding and development actors and has broken down silos in development and peacebuilding communities. Increased collaboration across sectors supports the development of more holistic and integrated analysis of conflict and development imperatives, which are complex and interlinked, though too often treated separately in practice. In some instances, civil society engagement in the New Deal process has normalized the practice of including civil society and peacebuilding in development planning. The growth in civil society networks has strengthened civil society's capacity to access and inform policymaking processes, advocate greater inclusion and political space, and contribute relevant technical expertise to ensure New Deal processes reflect citizen voices and perspectives.

Improving State-Society Relations

Similarly, civil society networks have been able to begin to build more constructive state-society relations. Mistrust between the state and citizens often characterizes fragile contexts, and civil society activists involved in implementing the New Deal express a common sentiment that g7+ governments often view independent CSOs as adversaries or threats. A member of Liberian civil society described the often difficult relationship with government: "Mistrust is rife, as for the past fifteen years governmental institutions have viewed civil society as a group trying to undermine them, with a subsequent breakdown in the working relationship." If long-term conflict and a return to violence are to be prevented, "a system of continuous engagement between government and society must develop," another respondent emphasized.

Civil society through the New Deal process has in some cases been able to overcome the trust gap and improve relationships between itself, the g7+, and donor governments. In order to have a voice in the process, civil society has persistently reached out to government actors, building bridges between the state and society. The New Deal provides a shared agenda and focus for all of the stakeholders involved, coordinating tripartite governance on peacebuilding and statebuilding in a way that "civil society, governments and donors will all be 'pulling the same oar,'" as one CSPPS participant remarked. Even in contexts where civil society has struggled to access high-level discussions, such as Somalia, government working groups have invited civil society to participate on specific issues at lower levels of the process. This has allowed civil society to engage with government counterparts in technical forums on specific development policy issues. Opportunities for collaboration have enabled new relationships and increased communication between civil society and government.

As the New Deal provides a platform for discussing politically sensitive issues, it has created an "unprecedented political space" for CSOs to engage with their governments. Having these discussions on conflict and fragility increases mutual understanding of the different challenges each stakeholder faces and provides opportunities for new collaboration. In some countries, civil society representatives described shifting from an adversarial stance in order to develop more constructive relationships with the government. "As civil society, we are cognizant that we can't remain on the periphery, unleashing accusations on the government—we are trying to work alongside them," one Liberian civil society advocate acknowledged. Civil society actors from several pilot countries professed a belief that their constructive advocacy and technical contributions had been instrumental in ameliorating relations, even in settings where antagonism had previously dominated interaction.

Where some respondents lauded the New Deal for providing a safe space for civil society to engage with governments on sensitive political issues, others urged caution and suggested that this sense of safety is something of an illusion created by international attention to the process. The New Deal, while promoted by the g7+, also opens them to criticism and difficult reforms. One interviewee noted that with growing pressure on the Somali government to honor New Deal commitments from both civil society and donors, the government has become "very afraid of how powerful we are or perceived to be." Over the course of the New Deal there have been increasing threats about restrictive NGO legislation and limitations on what NGOs can and cannot do.

This underscores the importance of ensuring a coordinated approach by international and national CSOs. One civil society actor from the Democratic Republic of Congo (DRC) called for greater support at the international level, saying "if you want to critique the government about the organization of the elections, it's very difficult, you have to tread carefully, and you need courage. You have to be courageous to be critical." Because strengthening state-society relations is inherently a political process, civil society is often on the front lines of negotiating for greater political space and advocating the inclusion of a wider set of interests. These efforts can be challenging or even dangerous in closed societies.

While civil society has actively pursued New Deal implementation in some contexts, in other pilot countries it has remained passive, whether due to low capacity, high barriers to relationship-building with governments, or lack of will to drive the process forward. Civil society efforts, often poorly resourced, have at times lacked sufficiently coordinated strategic action to hold governments accountable. These and other challenges described in more detail below have limited civil society's impact in several pilot countries.

Promoting People-Centered Development

Through the CSPPS, civil society leaders have provided technical expertise and contextual understanding that has brought citizen voices and perspectives into the process to inform New Deal outputs. The diversity of national coalitions has meant that CSOs working in human rights, development, education, religion, women's rights, and peacebuilding are available to contribute their expertise within a unified framework. Operating as a coalition ensures that a diverse range of experts from multiple fields are available to address the complex causes of conflict and fragility, and allows members to leverage their combined influence. CSOs provide analysis and conduct advocacy work to influence New Deal policies at the national level. Their work is also elevated to the global advocacy stage, where the CSPPS works through thematic working groups on technical and political processes related to New Deal implementation—such as the fragility assessments, indicator design, and compacts.[18]

Civil society has helped formulate inclusive country fragility assessments, which act as diagnostic tools intended to identify drivers of fragility. Fragility assessments identify sources of fragility and resilience in the five peacebuilding and statebuilding goal areas, providing a conflict-informed analysis upon which to design development efforts. In several pilot countries, including the DRC and South Sudan, civil society leaders organized broad-based, participatory workshops with other civil society actors to identify key drivers of conflict and fragility, and governments largely integrated these findings in their official assessments. In other cases where civil society's input was not originally solicited, such as Liberia, it offered community-based perspectives on regional drivers of conflict that were subsequently included in the revised assessment.

As part of a working group on IDPS indicators, civil society was actively involved in the global process of developing universal indicators to measure g7+ progress toward reaching the PSGs, working alongside government ministers and IDPS stakeholders for more than a year. The inclusion of indicators on reconciliation processes and more informal mechanisms is due in part to civil society's contributions. Civil society representatives helped formulate and advocate sex-disaggregated data that will allow pilot countries to track progress on key indicators for women and girls, such as girls' educational levels, and identify disparities in women's access to resources and services. At national levels, civil society across several countries, including South Sudan, DRC, and Liberia, played an active role in helping design and evaluate national indicators and bring in additional civil society actors to contribute to the process.

Civil society has promoted societal, not just government, priorities during New Deal processes. At the international level, civil society leaders successfully advocated the adoption of perception-based indicators to ensure citizen experiences are represented when assessing country progress toward peacebuilding and statebuilding goals. This occurred despite initial reservations expressed by some g7+ governments that such indicators could be politically manipulated domestically.

Similarly, CSOs have been instrumental in ensuring that gender awareness is incorporated into the New Deal, as Mahbouba Seraj and her colleagues explore in greater depth in their chapter on the subject and the New Deal experience in Afghanistan. Cordaid, for example, has published policy documents outlining measures to incorporate gender perspectives into the New Deal process,[19] and has engaged in international advocacy to promote gender mainstreaming. With Cordaid's support, national gender equality groups in South Sudan and Afghanistan mobilized to apply a gender lens in fragility assessment processes and promoting gender equality through the New Deal. Civil society groups in Togo and Liberia have also promoted gender mainstreaming as an important dimension of New Deal implementation, holding conferences with government officials and other civil society groups on the issue.

OVERCOMING EXCLUSION: DEFENDING
AND EXPANDING POLITICAL SPACE

A Brookings Institution paper assessing New Deal implementation found that donor and g7+ interlocutors considered civil society inclusion important, at least in principle, with the recognition that civil society can convey citizens' concerns, hold the government accountable, and "act as a bridge between diverse and often conflicting communities at the local level."[20] There is also recognition within the IDPS that the New Deal process can be strengthened by "bringing in civil society and the public into the process and creating a sense of 'country' rather than state ownership."[21]

In order to advocate more citizen-centered implementation of the New Deal, civil society actors have had to establish and maintain their inclusion in policymaking and implementation decision-making. Civil society has worked continually to overcome its marginalization and the numerous barriers to its participation in global and national discussions on the New Deal's implementation. The CSPPS had to negotiate its presence at every international IDPS meeting, and the Platform held many side events at international conferences to raise the visibility of its efforts and build awareness of the importance of civil society's inclusion. In pilot countries, focal points and coalitions have consistently promoted the message of including civil society with government authorities.

Meaningful civil society inclusion in New Deal implementation requires donors and governments to recognize the role of civil society in voicing citizen interests, and to open decision-making processes to civil society input. As Thania Paffenholz asserts, inclusive peacebuilding processes depend on the quality of participation—"inclusion for the sake of inclusion (even if large numbers of actors are involved) does not add to the quality of processes. What matters is meaningful inclusion, where included actors are able to make substantive contributions to political agreements and their implementation."[22] In many cases, civil society has, through its own mobilization efforts, succeeded in breaking through barriers to its meaningful inclusion in decision-making. However, there are many instances in which hostile political environments, exclusionary practices, and inadequate resources have prevented civil society from playing as large a role as its members would hope.

Co-Optation

Despite the New Deal's emphasis on inclusivity, some believe the g7+ has interpreted its "country-led and country-owned" characteristics as "government-led and government-owned," with civil society viewed as government implementing partners. Some governments have partnered with "GoNGOs," or government-sponsored NGOs, excluding more independent CSOs from

New Deal processes. "They tell you they're engaging with civil society, but the question is, 'What kind of civil society and what kind of engagement?'" warned one civil society actor.

A respondent from Sierra Leone remarked that early in the process, "When we looked at the fragility assessment, those that were consulted were mainly organizations that are very close to the powers that be." The CSPPS has, in certain instances, been successful in preventing governments from resorting to GoNGOs as their point of contact in the New Deal. The CSPPS asserts its rights under the IDPS to select representative partners, emphasizing that the New Deal empowers civil society on the basis of legitimacy and inclusiveness. This approach has been effective in ensuring the independence and authenticity of civil society representation, although government attempts to work with a parallel network of GoNGO partners is a recurring issue.

Civil society can also be fragmented among those more or less supportive of the government. A respondent in the Central African Republic (CAR) noted, "Many CSOs can be turned. Many are used in peace marches set up by the government or actual support marches for the government." One interviewee discussing Somalia noted that the government has at times used the fractured nature of civil society as a reason not to engage with the sector, with the message that "civil society can engage but only once you're all singing the same song, united, and one person to represent."

When governments select GoNGOs as partners in the New Deal, they create obstacles to civil society engagement at the international level. One CSPPS representative shared that government-backed civil society groups defer to their governments more at international meetings, and it can be difficult for civil society to jointly strategize across national boundaries as a civil society coalition. Furthermore GoNGOs are predominantly sourced from the elite, and are thus often out of touch with community perspectives.

As an Afghan civil society actor emphasized, "even though elites might be the point of contact and listened to, they're not representing the grassroots." This is a particularly pressing fact for international engagement with civil society on the New Deal, as there needs to be a strong contextual understanding of the contours of the society and the different groups operating within it, to ensure that traditionally marginalized groups are not excluded, and that an artificial civil society is not presented as a voice representing all citizens.

Narrow Conception of Civil Society

Inclusion of representative groups is also a challenge due to donor practices. Some scholars have argued that in fragile states, "the current international policy framework inhibits donor engagement with a full range of nonstate actors, thus restricting civil society engagement in state building."[23] One barrier is the tendency within the donor community to privilege INGOs, which are disproportionately based in the North. Even when funding national civil society, donor organizations often favor NGOs, which are formally constituted and appear to present a lower risk for project delivery and funding; but in doing so, they may exclude less formal bodies that might have greater local membership, legitimacy, and relevance for political transitions. NGO-based engagement can also foster accountability toward donors rather than local priorities and may exclude important functions that less formal civil society actors play.[24] It is important that all members of the IDPS recognize the diversity of actors involved in civil society and create spaces for genuinely broad inclusion.

Overall, national CSOs have been the loudest voices for including more informal forms of civil society, including traditional leaders and faith-based groups. However, in official IDPS processes, NGOs and, occasionally, faith-based organizations have led civil society participation. The CSPPS has undergone internal reforms to achieve a greater balance of national Southern voices, and INGOs see one of their primary roles as elevating Southern perspectives within the global policy and advocacy arena, as well as at national levels.

State-Centric Processes

The nature of international institutions and processes poses structural barriers to civil society's inclusion. Though many donors profess support for civil society, challenges emerge when civil society engages at the international level, in part because of the state-centric design and structure of the multilateral process. As one international NGO representative said:

> the Dialogue itself, in terms of the discursive and regulatory and political systems, was never designed to include this civil society input ... there is a good deal of catch-up to be done simply convincing those systems that there is another leg of this structure that should be included. There are neither formalized seats nor formalized channels.

The heterogeneity of civil society again poses challenges in such settings, where governments expect points of contact to represent certain constituencies. Civil society groups must establish legitimacy with government counterparts as well as their peers and constituents.

At the September 2013 Brussels conference to endorse a Compact for Somalia between donors and government officials, three GoNGO delegates were invited, and INGOs were only invited, at short notice, to attend as observational members. While official IDPS international meetings include CSOs, the number of invitations and viewing passes has expanded and the format of civil society participation is renegotiated at every meeting. "Civil society has always managed to ensure [our] presence [at international meetings] but at the cost of a very long negotiating process about how many can we be and how much talking time we are allowed during the meeting."

Additionally, civil society actors believe that donor and g7+ governments are particularly disinclined to include civil society members in policy discussions on national security issues, which are deemed matters for governments exclusively. A respondent from South Sudan remarked that although the government included civil society in many areas of discussion, it viewed topics such as tribal-related drivers of conflict as matters of national security and therefore falling under the exclusive mandate of the government, without the involvement of civil society. In Somalia, the New Deal working group on security, which is co-led by donor and Somali officials, is closed to civil society. Opening these and other policy conversations to citizen input is an ongoing challenge.

A STALLED PROCESS: THE NEED FOR POLITICAL DIALOGUE

By advocating for greater inclusion, civil society is attempting to bridge the gap between the ambitious vision of the New Deal for inclusive, participatory political dialogue, and the reality of closed decision-making that characterizes development processes. By far the greatest obstacle to the New Deal's implementation is the lack of robust political support from donor and fragile state governments. Delays from within the IDPS toward New Deal processes in the first years of the pilot phase contributed to a belief that the New Deal was "not really put on the front burner," according to one international civil society correspondent. Most civil society representatives are unsatisfied with the level of government engagement, and local CSOs find that the New Deal progress reports "on paper" do not match government efforts.

Ensuring a commitment to implementation has been a key civil society advocacy priority. CSOs have called attention to slow progress in some contexts where donor or government implementation has lagged. As one interlocutor shared, "We have been trying to push the government so that we have a work plan to see results over time." In the absence of local accountability, some CSOs and donor states are applying multisided pressure on g7+ governments so that governments remain accountable to their commitments. In Liberia, for example, civil society brought the slow pace of implementation of the New Deal and lack of civil society inclusion in the process to the attention of the ambassador of Sweden, one of Liberia's New Deal donors, after efforts to hold the government directly accountable failed.

There is also widespread perception among many members of the CSPPS that donor country governments do not fully understand the New Deal process and are often reluctant to step back to enable greater country ownership. CSOs have sought to build greater donor support; for instance in the United States AfP has secured the support of the US Agency for International Development's Office of Conflict Management and Mitigation to raise awareness of the New Deal and promote US engagement. Such outreach has led international development missions to open previously closed doors to civil society in contexts such as Somalia. More can be done to achieve broader intragovernmental understanding of New Deal commitments in donor countries, including broadening awareness within legislative and executive branches.

Insufficient Political Will

Despite the New Deal's stated commitment to inclusive political dialogue, the political challenges of the PSGs and inertia of traditional development approaches have often meant that the reform promised by the agreement has proved elusive and is translated into merely a technical exercise. Civil society actors critique an overemphasis on technical processes—completing fragility assessments, indicators, and compacts—to the detriment of political dialogue. Technocrats and program officers dominate participation in meetings. Although highly skilled in the issues at hand, these individuals often lack the requisite political authority to ensure governmental commitment and buy-in to the process. "They're participating with only experts of government but not the leaders of government," objected one respondent from the DRC. Conversely, seemingly technical decisions can have highly political implications that must be resolved to move the process forward.

In several contexts, donor insistence on speed and completion of technical aspects of the process precluded time and space for broad-based deliberation among government and civil society actors. Civil society actors see this emphasis as a short-term gain in the technical process at the expense of a long-term political loss. Building trust and broad buy-in to implement a new national program often requires more time and patience than donors may be accustomed to.

Most civil society actors believe that the promise of the New Deal lies in its potential to change the process by which development decisions are made, by sharing power more equally between fragile states, donors, and civil society, and fostering more political dialogue. Urgent deadlines can undermine the slow process of building new consensus on difficult political issues. As CSPPS wrote as early as 2012, "We hold that process is as important as output, and recommend a better balance between both post-Busan."[25] While completion of technical processes is important, political support is necessary to ensure that policies have sufficient resources and backing to be meaningfully implemented.

The ongoing tension between technical responses to what is viewed as a highly political process is frequently raised by civil society actors, particularly by representatives of g7+ CSOs. One respondent remarked:

> as long as civil society follows the technical process of the IDPS it will go nowhere. The IDPS was set up as a political platform and a political space for dialogue. It was never intended to be a technical team. The technical work of the IDPS was supposed to help inform the political dialogue. What we have right now is a technical dialogue, not backed at all with any political situation or engagement. This is actually killing the process.

An overly technical approach will not advance real political progress in the New Deal. At the same time, a representative from the CSPPS pointed to a tendency among many to consider peacebuilding as an exclusively political process, which can be legitimately separated from development issues. There must be an attempt to find a balance of the political and the technical, as each supports the other in ensuring sustainable implementation and results.

In most of the pilot countries only one government ministry is tasked with implementing the New Deal and awareness of the New Deal outside of the focal point office is often low or nonexistent. Such narrow political buy-in from the governments of the g7+ precludes genuine progress in the implementation of the New Deal—a point that was frequently raised by interviewees. A Sierra Leonean civil society leader said, "The government ... should also have a kind of a cross-sectoral engagement on the process. Even within government I assure you that information is very limited. The way in which the focal points or the taskforce share information with the other ministries is weak." The isolation of the New Deal within one ministry makes the process more vulnerable to delays due to capacity and organizational challenges within that ministry. It also precludes the widespread buy-in that may be needed to counter political interests opposed to the New Deal agenda, as civil society groups in South Sudan have found.[26]

The limited capacity of many g7+ governments also affects their ability to drive implementation. The complexity of the New Deal process and copious amounts of required communications put further strain on overstretched departments. The international g7+ secretariat within the IDPS has suffered from low capacity and limited ability to provide support to pilot states. Recent OECD and UNDP investments to support the capacity of the international g7+ secretariat through an OECD "help desk" providing policy support and a UNDP Support Facility may contribute to greater progress. These new offices provide general information about the New Deal, technical advice, and logistical and financial support to government ministers for attending major events; all of these functions have been well utilized by g7+ governments.[27]

Building National Ownership

Partially in reaction to perceived stagnation at the government level, national civil society groups view local ownership of the New Deal as essential to its success. They fully support the "country-led and country-owned" principles of the New Deal and seek to involve and represent broad constituencies and diverse perspectives in its implementation. As one interlocutor said, "The wider public must be engaged in understanding the issues of their own fragility and where they are. For me, this requires a lot of political buy-in and broader citizen engagement and in the absence of doing that, all the work [to implement the New Deal] won't accomplish much."

Civil society actors see one of their primary roles as building public awareness and facilitating national ownership of the process through engagement with grassroots communities. Local ownership is the foundation of public accountability for government implementation of the New Deal. While governments are often more accountable to the international community than their own citizens, civil society within pilot countries believe that their governments must first and foremost be accountable to local populations. CSOs are well placed to track actual in-country implementation activities, and stress the importance of having independent verification of government reports.

International donors also lack accountability to local populations, and civil society representatives emphasize the need to hold donors equally accountable for their commitments to the New Deal as well. Many embrace indicators as a tool for leverage in tracking government and donor performance and commitment to the goals of the New Deal. According to one Liberian civil society actor, the New Deal

is a huge opportunity to hold the donor and the government accountable in terms of those developments that have been made, how those development commitments are realized and who is responsible for the development plan working or not working. The indicators present a very clear opportunity and a good benchmark in terms of being able to see concretely that yes there has been progress or no there is no progress.

Building the political will to make the difficult reforms required by the New Deal may be the most challenging task facing New Deal proponents. In addition to challenges of coordination and low capacity, reforms encounter entrenched political interests that will need to be confronted. A long time civil society activist from West Africa noted, "The government seems to be afraid. ... It's not about the aid money. It's about the peacebuilding and statebuilding goals. Those goals seem to be simple but they are tough for some African governments." Likewise, donors, long accustomed to leading decisions about development policy, often find it difficult to forge genuine partnerships that require sharing power and decision-making with g7+ and civil society. Realistic fears of corruption and heightened risk from country-led development processes have slowed donor support for genuine reform. These competing interests will need to be confronted and negotiated if the New Deal is to deliver on its promise to change the way development is conducted in fragile states.

THE NEW DEAL, CIVIL SOCIETY, AND PEACEBUILDING: LOOKING AHEAD

The New Deal is beset by many problems familiar to the development field: unequal power relationships, the marginalization of local voices in policy processes, and an emphasis on technical processes to the detriment of genuine political dialogue. However, it is one of the only forums in which some of these issues can be addressed. As South Sudanese civil society respondents state, "The New Deal is the only framework South Sudan has that secures the space for civil society as key players in development."[28] While the pace and success of New Deal implementation has disappointed some, civil society representatives nonetheless share a general consensus on the opportunities the framework offers, despite setbacks in its implementation.

In the majority of contexts, civil society representatives see the New Deal as an unprecedented opportunity to bring issues of peacebuilding, development, and government accountability to the fore of national and international agendas. They believe the principles of the New Deal are sound and that the fragility assessments and indicators developed to date offer leverage to promote accountable development and peacebuilding efforts in fragile countries. Many feel that the framework provides entry points for constructive engagement with governments on previously unaddressed drivers of conflict. As one civil society actor from Sierra Leone expressed, "We consider the fragility assessment as a springboard—it's the launching pad for us and we will now use that to see how we can make our voices heard and to make our own input."

Seeing these opportunities, civil society plays multiple roles in the New Deal implementation process. It protects and attempts to enlarge political space by organizing new, broad-based political dialogues about the causes and paths out of fragility. It facilitates *rapprochement* within the civil society sector and between civil society and government actors, incrementally strengthening social cohesion. It also presents the interests of marginalized communities, including women and youth, within policy debates. Civil society groups in many pilot states are capitalizing upon the New Deal's integrated framework to bring diverse stakeholders together to develop a unified and integrated vision to achieve a peaceful future.

At the beginning of the pilot period in 2012, merely 9 percent of all overseas development assistance (ODA) to fragile states and economies was allocated to the PSGs for legitimate politics, security, and justice combined.[29] A shift to New Deal priorities will require significant changes. A review of the New Deal's implementation suggests that greater political commitment is needed on all sides to build momentum and effect real change.

The IDPS New Deal Monitoring Report of 2014 assessing the progress of the New Deal, found that, "there is little evidence that the New Deal has played a formative role in shaping political priorities around the PSGs, or informing the political vision for country-led transformation from fragility to resilience."[30] While it commended the New Deal for increasing opportunities for dialogue among stakeholders and greater transparency in some forms of donor aid, it concluded that, "The results are mixed ... progress on the ground has to intensify if there is to be a 'paradigm shift' in the way development cooperation is conducted in fragile and conflict-affected states."[31]

Civil society members in a few pilot stages have expressed frustration with a lack of meaningful change. One interviewee, speaking about Somalia, reflected pessimistically that the New Deal "has not altered [donor] priorities, the way they choose their priorities, the way they deliver money, the way they monitor and evaluate. Nothing about the way donors engage in Somalia has changed because of the New Deal." In South Sudan, civil society leaders say that donors engaged in many of the same practices that go against New Deal principles, including creating aid conditionalities, outsourcing analyses, and rushing consultative processes.[32]

While civil society has essential contributions to make to the process, the future of the New Deal will depend on matching commitments from the g7+ and donors. For the g7+, interest in the New Deal will wane if it does not deliver on its promise to give governments of fragile countries greater decision-making and agenda-setting power on development. Donor support for the New Deal is contingent on the acceptance of greater risk as fragile states assume more ownership of development processes. All actors, including civil society, must find strategies to address stakeholders' core interests and concerns in order to ensure the viability of frameworks such as the New Deal. Civil society can mitigate the risk of greater country ownership of development by taking a more prominent role in monitoring government activity and expenditures. National civil society is well placed to assess actual progress, inclusiveness, and quality of the process and could, for instance, publish parallel monitoring reports to track implementation and verify progress reports.

Stakeholders must also consider how to evaluate country ownership of in-country processes to ensure that this central concept is meaningfully practiced and avoid what some civil society members fear—a New Deal Compact that is new in name only, but that represents little change from previous development practices. There may be a need for more defined assessments of the degree of inclusiveness of New Deal processes, measuring both the depth and breadth of inclusion. Such evaluations could assess the extent of civil society engagement, civil society's access to decision-making in the process, and the number and type of constituencies engaged. It could also evaluate the quality of partnership between donors and fragile societies, noting whether national governments and civil society have a greater role vis-à-vis donors on setting the development agenda. The New Deal offers an opportunity to change power relations between donors and g7+, as well as between governments and civil society. However, this takes time, dialogue, and genuine commitment. An evaluation process would highlight the degree to which the New Deal is enacting the principles that make it unique.

Adapting to Crises in Fragile States

New Deal stakeholders are also taking stock of crises that have set back implementation and seeking ways to make the agreement more relevant and responsive to the challenges that face fragile states. Since the beginning of the pilot phase in 2012, crises in five implementing countries—CAR, South Sudan, Liberia, Sierra Leone, and Guinea—have delayed or suspended New Deal implementation. An interviewee from CAR noted that, "our country is constantly in conflict. We need a sound implementation of the New Deal process but emergencies always keep us back and in consequence implementation remains superficial ... all institutions are weakened by the crisis and conflicts."

Despite these unexpected derailments in the process, civil society has found utility in applying the principles of the New Deal to address complex crises. For example, South Sudanese civil society groups have advocated the inclusion of the New Deal framework as the basis for a peace agreement.[33] In West Africa, civil society groups have used New Deal principles to evaluate and critique responses to the Ebola crisis. Civil society representatives have made the case at international forums, including the World Bank Fragility, Conflict, and Violence Forum in 2015, that the Ebola crisis was due in part to still fragile state-society relations that facilitated a collapse of the health care system.

Key principles of the New Deal such as country ownership of development aid, using country systems, and participatory dialogue with local populations were not followed in the international response to the Ebola crisis, which further contributed to a lack of trust and cooperation in affected populations. CSPPS research teams in Ebola-affected countries found that Liberians, for example, perceived a reliance on international intervention as reminiscent of historical patterns and "fostered Liberians' distrust of the international humanitarian community." The government's militarized response to the crisis also fed mistrust. Sierra Leone and Guinea initially excluded civil society in disaster response, only rectifying this upon lobbying from civil society actors themselves, which significantly slowed effective responses.[34]

Rather than see the New Deal as irrelevant to unforeseen crises, civil society groups have reaffirmed the utility of the New Deal framework and called for greater application of its principles to guide postcrisis interventions. Developments such as the Ebola outbreak and renewed conflict in some pilot countries also demonstrate the need for the New Deal to have a crisis response strategy to stay relevant to emerging events. Such a strategy could include the development of early warning mechanisms using the fragility assessment and indicators process, perhaps linking with those developed by such civil society groups as the West Africa Network for Peacebuilding, as described in Emmanuel Bombande's chapter in this volume. Others in civil society have suggested the importance of dynamic, ongoing fragility assessments that include identification of drivers of conflict in order to identify and respond to emerging crises.[35]

CONCLUSION: PEACEBUILDING IN THE POST-2015 FRAMEWORK

The New Deal is increasingly relevant in the current global environment of insecurity and polarization, where an uptick in violent conflict has resulted in "development in reverse" for many regions. The proportion of people living in extreme poverty is increasingly concentrated in fragile and conflict-affected states, with some projections that 62 percent of the world's poor will live in fragile states by 2030.[36] Making progress on the 2030 Agenda will require a shift in priorities, reflected in the United Kingdom's recent commitment of 50 percent of aid to fragile states.[37]

While the New Deal's pilot phase had flaws, it nonetheless helped to ensure that peace and governance were integrated into the 2030 Agenda Goal 16, which aims to "promote peaceful and inclusive societies for sustainable development, provide access to justice for all and build effective, accountable and inclusive institutions at all levels."[38] CSPPS members suggest that the New Deal PSGs "shaped [the 2030 Agenda's] thinking on how issues like justice and legitimate politics underpin peaceful societies and needed to be addressed."[39]

Throughout the pilot phase of the New Deal, civil society was actively advocating the inclusion of peace in the post-2015 agenda, using the PSGs as examples.[40] Drawing from lessons learned during the New Deal indicators process, CSPPS was able to demonstrate why and how peace can be measured, for example, stressing the importance of achieving a balance between universal indicators and country-level indicators, disaggregating data across all SDGs to monitor horizontal inequalities, which are drivers of violent conflict, and using a diverse set of indicators to measure progress.[41] Members sought to build relationships and organize meetings with emerging donor states such as China to build consensus on Goal 16.[42]

With the conclusion of the New Deal pilot phase in December 2015, the OECD has conducted an independent review of the process to shape its future application in the context of the 2030 Agenda. The values underpinning the New Deal, the ongoing lessons it offers, and the key successes and obstacles the process has faced should be harnessed and absorbed in the implementation of the 2030 Agenda and SDG 16. With the passage of the 2030 Agenda, civil society actors are continuing to underscore that conflict and insecurity are the largest obstacles to eradicating poverty and are advocating the alignment of the SDGs and PSGs to build upon progress. Civil society continues to promote an inclusive vision of society-owned reforms and development policymaking processes that enable broad citizen participation. Additionally, the 2030 Agenda offers new opportunities to address some of the obstacles encountered during the New Deal pilot phase. The high profile of the SDGs may help to broaden political and social buy-in to future New Deal efforts in order to overcome the lack of political will that has slowed its progress to date.[43]

Civil society's assessment that the New Deal framework is still relevant for the post-2015 framework is echoed by other analyses. A recent Overseas Development Institute paper concludes that the New Deal's influence has been significant and is "on the right track" regarding present day challenges:

> The importance of the first three PSGs—inclusive political settlements, security for all and justice for all—is now encapsulated in SDG 16. The importance of the fourth—economic foundations—is now reflected in SDGs 7 to 9 that cover energy, growth and infrastructure. And the fifth—domestic revenues—was the foremost issue at the recent third Financing for Development conference in Addis. The recent high level reports commissioned for the forthcoming reviews of UN Peace Operations and Peace Architecture echo many of the New Deal concerns. The reports stress the need to bring conflict prevention back to the fore and to focus more on politics, especially "inclusive national owned" political settlements (the first PSG). At a country level the two conflicts that have reignited in g7+ countries have both been about lack of progress on inclusive political settlement, the first PSG. And the Ebola crisis that hit three g7+ countries

so severely has reminded us all of the vital importance of building and using countries' health systems.[44]

The inclusion of a global goal on peaceful societies is a significant achievement for those working to bring fragile states out of cycles of conflict. As the pilot phase of the New Deal demonstrates, however, it is the implementation stage that will determine to what degree progress is made in building peaceful, resilient societies. Civil society's efforts to open political space and promote inclusive policymaking will continue to challenge the status quo and are likely to be met by ongoing obstacles. However, over time, civil society will continue its progress in making international and national development processes more inclusive and reflective of citizen priorities. The international momentum surrounding the SDGs provides a new opportunity to further advance these efforts.

NOTES

1. Since the inception of the g7+ in 2010, it has expanded from seven to twenty member countries spanning four continents. Seven pilot countries originally volunteered to implement the New Deal: Afghanistan, the Central African Republic, the Democratic Republic of Congo, Liberia, South Sudan, Sierra Leone, and Timor-Leste. As of 2014, twelve countries have participated in the New Deal process on a formal and informal basis. Additional countries were Chad, Comoros, Guinea-Bissau, Somalia, and Yemen.

2. Comprehensive findings are included in Kristen Wall and Rachel Fairhurst, *Assessing Civil Society Engagement in the New Deal: Opportunities and Challenges*, Kroc Institute for International Peace Studies, March 2014, http://kroc.nd.edu/sites/default/files/Assessing_Civil_Society_1.pdf.

3. The International Dialogue on Peacebuilding and Statebuilding is a forum comprising the g7+, donors from the OECD, the UN, the World Bank, the African Union, the African Development Bank, and civil society representatives. It is the first forum for political dialogue to bring together conflict-affected and fragile countries, international partners, and civil society to catalyze successful transitions from conflict and fragility. For further information on the IDPS, see http://www.pbsbdialogue.org/about/.

4. International Dialogue on Peacebuilding and Statebuilding, "A New Deal for Engagement in Fragile States," December 2011, http://www.pbsbdialogue.org/media/filer_public/07/69/07692de0-3557-494e-918e-18df00e9ef73/the_new_deal.pdf/.

5. Ibid.

6. Ibid.

7. Frauke de Weijer and Ulrike Kilnes, "Strengthening Civil Society? Reflections on International Engagement in Fragile States," *European Centre for Development*

Policy Management (ECDPM) Discussion Paper 135, October 2012, 5, www.ecdpm.org/dp135.

8. Interpeace, "CSOs and the IDPS," Policy Brief 4: Core Civil Society Messages to the International Dialogue on Peacebuilding and Statebuilding, August 2011, 2, http://www.interpeace.org/wp-content/uploads/2011/08/2011_08_CSOs_And_IDPS_Policy_Brief_4_en_v2.pdf.

9. de Weijer and Kilnes, "Strengthening Civil Society?" 5.

10. Department for International Development (DFID), "Building Peaceful States and Societies," DFID Practice Paper, 2010, 15, https://www.gov.uk/government/publications/building-peaceful-states-and-societies-a-dfid-practice-paper.

11. OECD-DAC Fragile States Group, "Statebuilding in Situations of Fragility," April 2008, 4, http://www.oecd.org/dac/governance-peace/conflictandfragility/docs/41212290.pdf.

12. CIVICUS, "CIVICUS' 2013 Enabling Environment Index," 2013, 6, http://www.civicus.org/downloads/2013EEI%20REPORT.pdf.

13. Voluntary Action Network India, "Civil Society Engagement in Aid Effectiveness Discourse," 2013, 4–5, http://www.vaniindia.org/publicationpdf/Primer%20Inside%20-Civil%20Society%20Engagement.pdf.

14. World Bank, *World Development Report 2011: Conflict, Security and Development*, 2011, http://siteresources.worldbank.org/INTWDRS/Resources/WDR2011_Full_Text.pdf.

15. Interpeace, "CSOs and the IDPS," Policy Brief 1, August 2011, http://www.interpeace.org/index.php/documents/international-dialogue/168-policy-brief-1-an-introduction-to-the-international-dialogue-on-peacebuilding-and-statebuilding/file.

16. Interpeace, "Peacebuilding and Statebuilding—Interpeace Brings the Voices of 50 Civil Society Organizations," April 12, 2010, http://www.interpeace.org/2010/04/peacebuilding-and-statebuilding-interpeace-brings-the-voices-of-50-civil-society-organizations/.

17. Paul Okumu, "State-Society Relations: The Prospects for the New Deal Engagement in Addressing an Enabling Environment in Conflict-affected and Fragile States," in *State of Civil Society 2013*, ed., CIVICUS, 204, http://socs.civicus.org/?page_id=4289.

18. Civil Society Platform for Peacebuilding and Statebuilding, "About the CSPPS," http://www.cspps.org/about-us.

19. Karen Barnes Robinson on behalf of Cordaid, "Integrating Gender into the New Deal for Engagement in Fragile States," Policy Paper, September 2012, https://www.cordaid.org/media/publications/Cordaid-7247-02-PP-Gender_into_the_New_Deal-DEFHR-web.pdf.

20. Jacob Hughes et al., "Implementing the New Deal for Fragile States," Brookings Institution, July 2014, 7–8, http://www.brookings.edu/research/papers/2014/07/implementing-new-deal-fragile-states.

21. International Dialogue on Peacebuilding and Statebuilding, Working Group on New Deal Implementation, *New Deal Monitoring Report 2014*, November 2014, 28.

22. Thania Paffenholz, "Inclusive Politics: Lessons from and for the New Deal," *Journal of Peacebuilding and Development* 10, no. 1 (2015): 88.

23. Rosan Smits and Deborah Wright, "Engagement with Non-State Actors in Fragile States: Narrowing Definitions, Broadening Scope," Clingendael Netherlands Institute of International Relations, CRU Report, 2012, 8, http://www.clingendael.nl/sites/default/files/20121200_cru_engagement_with_nsa_in_fragile_states.pdf.

24. Ibid.,12–14.

25. Interpeace, "Recommendations to the Co-Chairs and the Steering Committee of the International Dialogue on Peacebuilding and Statebuilding," February 10, 2012, 3.

26. CSPPS CSO Working Group, "The New Deal Implementation in South Sudan: A South Sudanese Civil Society Perspective Paper," March 2015, 16, http://www.cspps.org/documents/130616042/130793247/New+Deal+Perspective+Paper++Final+2015.pdf/449c693d-61de-4d67-b3ef-4de932d6d788.

27. United Nations Development Program, "UNDP Support Facility Implementation Overview," 2014.

28. CSPPS CSO Working Group, "The New Deal Implementation in South Sudan," 6.

29. OECD, *States of Fragility 2015: Meeting Post-2015 Ambitions* (Paris: OECD Publishing, 2015), 16.

30. International Dialogue on Peacebuilding and Statebuilding, Working Group on New Deal Implementation, *New Deal Monitoring Report 2014*, 14.

31. Ibid., 3.

32. CSPPS CSO Working Group, "The New Deal Implementation in South Sudan," 8–9.

33. Ibid., 19.

34. Erin McCandless and Nicholas Bouchet, "Tackling and Preventing Ebola while Building Peace and Societal Resilience: Lessons and Priorities for Action from Civil Society in Ebola-Affected New Deal Countries," CSPPS Policy Report, May 2015, 13, http://www.cspps.org/news/-/asset_publisher/2nEICmeFS2z2/content/tackling-and-preventing-ebola-while-building-peace-and-societal-resilience-lessons-and-priorities-for-action-from-civil-society-in-ebola-affected-new-/.

35. CSPPS CSO Working Group, "The New Deal Implementation in South Sudan," 12.

36. OECD, *States of Fragility 2015*, Highlights, http://www.oecd.org/dac/governance-peace/conflictfragilityandresilience/docs/FINAL%20States%20of%20Fragility%20Highlights%20document.pdf.

37. Department for International Development, "UK Aid: Tackling Global Challenges in the National Interest," November 2015.

38. United Nations General Assembly 68th session, "Report of the Open Working Group of the General Assembly on Sustainable Development Goals," A/68/970, August 12, 2014, 10, http://www.un.org/ga/search/view_doc.asp?symbol=A/68/970.

39. Civil Society Platform for Peacebuilding and Statebuilding, "2030 Agenda and the New Deal—Where Next," November 2015, http://www.cspps.org/documents/130616042/130793247/From+New+Deal+to+the+2030+Agenda+FINAL-3-2.pdf/2146ea87-5f55-4c41-bf04-08fb8b80a91d.

40. "Bringing Peace into the Post-2015 Development Framework: A Joint Statement by Civil Society Organisations," September 21, 2012, http://www.cspps.org/

documents/130616042/130626578/2012_09_28_CSO_Joint_Statement_Post-2015_
ENG.pdf/a187d69f-3a87-46b1-82d1-90e24768424d.

41. Civil Society Platform for Peacebuilding and Statebuilding, "Post 2015, Goal 16
and Lessons on Indicators: Civil Society Perspectives from the New Deal Work on Indicators," February 25, 2015, http://www.cspps.org/documents/130616042/130793247/
CSPPS+statement+post-2015+indicators+and+New+Deal+Lessons+-+25+Feb+2015.
pdf.

42. Global Partnership for the Prevention of Armed Conflict, "Promoting
Peaceful and Inclusive Societies for Sustainable Development in the New
Global Development Agenda: Beijing Seminar Report," March 24, 2015,
http://www.gppac.net/news/-/asset_publisher/fHv91YcOz0CI/content/
promoting-peaceful-and-inclusive-societies-in-new-post-2015-goals/.

43. Civil Society Platform for Peacebuilding and Statebuilding, "2030 Agenda and
the New Deal—Where Next."

44. Marcus Manuel, "Implementing the New Development Framework in Countries Affected by Conflict and Fragility," Overseas Development Institute Briefing
Note, September 28, 2015, http://www.pbsbdialogue.org/media/filer_public/c4/6d/
c46dc18d-52bb-4635-9ea5-dfb2d5ecced7/odi_briefing_paper_idps_side_event.pdf.

Chapter 4

Integrating Gender into the New Deal Process

Mahbouba Seraj, Karen Robinson, and Dewi Suralaga

A key linchpin of success for the New Deal is how effectively the commitments around inclusion, participation, and equality are integrated into its three main components. Gender equality and women's participation in political processes are critical to the realization of some of the New Deal's central aims of country leadership, local ownership, multistakeholder collaboration, and constructive state-society dialogues. As the New Deal evolves, gender analysis could be a valuable tool for unpacking some of the key concepts, particularly the power dynamics that are present in these contexts. Implementation of the New Deal could further be a mechanism through which to advance the implementation of United Nations Security Council Resolution 1325 (UNSCR 1325) on Women, Peace, and Security (WPS) and other commitments on gender equality set forth in the New Deal's "One Vision, One Plan" principle. Despite this, the New Deal itself and the processes that developed from it are largely gender-blind, and opportunities to integrate a gender-sensitive approach to peacebuilding and statebuilding are being missed. The growing body of evidence and policy commitments around the need and significant benefits of integrating gender equality are often ignored, and the New Deal has failed to offer guidance or new ideas in this area, representing a major gap between the vision and the implementation of this important new framework.

This chapter explores how issues relating to gender could be better incorporated into the New Deal process to strengthen peacebuilding and statebuilding, with a particular focus on Afghanistan. It first presents the rationale for integrating gender into these processes and what would be required to make the key elements of the New Deal process more gender-sensitive. It then sketches the role of broader civil society engagement, reflecting on the experiences of members of the CSPPS in their quest to integrate gender into

75

the New Deal as well as the peacebuilding and statebuilding processes within their respective countries. Finally, it turns to the example of Afghanistan, focusing in particular on the contribution that women's organizations have tried to make to rebuilding and restoring peace and stability to the country.

GENDER IN PEACEBUILDING AND STATEBUILDING

Conflict, peacebuilding, and statebuilding are all gendered processes, and there is an extensive and growing body of literature on the different impacts conflict and its aftermath have on men and women, and the roles they play.[1] Despite the adoption of several resolutions on WPS at the UN Security Council since 2000 and a plethora of international, regional, and national policies, these issues are often under-resourced, neglected, or deliberately marginalized in statebuilding and peacebuilding programs. As Castillejo notes:

> While donors support a range of gender initiatives in these contexts, these are mostly not linked up to the broader statebuilding agenda; have a technical rather than political focus; and are discrete "gender" projects rather than genuine mainstreaming. Moreover, donor approaches to gender often de-link gender power relations from broader patterns of power and resource distribution.[2]

There are many explanations for this, such as the inherent tension between the normative goals of gender equality and women's rights embodied in international commitments and the social, political, cultural, and institutional reality in many fragile and conflict-affected states. Additionally, those involved in peacebuilding and statebuilding often face an overloaded agenda and can be resistant to adding other priorities. Actors with limited time and resources and a crowded policy agenda can also dismiss gender issues as a less immediate concern in the early stages of peacebuilding and statebuilding, leading to it fall off the agenda. There has also been a failure to understand the link between gender issues and political contestation over power and resource distribution in fragile and conflict-affected states. Finally, there is a dearth of relevant research and examples of good practices in integrating a gender perspective into peacebuilding and statebuilding.

While evidence is incomplete and there is still significant resistance to advancing gender equality, there are a number of compelling reasons for integrating these issues into the New Deal and other frameworks.[3] First, gender equality and women's human rights are important goals in their own right, most recently articulated in Goal 5 of the SDGs. Peacebuilding and statebuilding processes are opportunities to advance this agenda, as linked to Goal 16, given the fluid nature of postconflict spaces and the possibilities they present to renegotiate and reshape gender and power relations. Secondly, there is instrumental value in integrating gender into peacebuilding and statebuilding, attested to by the growing body of evidence linking gender equality to improved development outcomes.[4] While there is no clear consensus on the impact that gender-sensitive approaches have on peacebuilding and statebuilding processes, recent findings illustrate specific examples of how they can strengthen efforts to build sustainable peace and strong states and societies.[5] Cross-country analysis shows that higher levels of economic growth and poverty reduction can be found in countries where women report greater empowerment. UN Women found that conflict-affected communities that experienced the most rapid economic recovery and poverty reduction were those that had more women reporting higher levels of empowerment.[6]

Finally, gender sensitivity can also greatly enhance accountability, inclusion, and legitimacy, which are the key underlying principles of peacebuilding and statebuilding. If women and girls are given space to engage and have their voices heard, it is more likely that these processes will address a broader range of issues and be better designed and targeted to meet the needs of all members of society. Women's organizations have also been shown to play a vital watchdog role in monitoring government actions and holding leaders to account for their actions across a range of sectors.[7] This is particularly important in fragile and conflict-affected contexts where there is competition over limited resources, weak or reduced institutional capacities, and governance challenges such as corruption and lack of accountability that can result in failures to meet the needs and priorities of all citizens.

Despite the growing acceptance of the need for gender sensitivity, a brief review of the key documents and outputs of the IDPS reveals that gender issues do not feature strongly, despite some token mentions in the Dili Declaration, Monrovia Roadmap, and the New Deal itself.[8] This reflects previous findings in this area, such as an overview assessment from the gender equality module of the 2011 Monitoring Survey of the Paris Declaration revealing that donors and recipient countries were failing to allocate sufficient resources to enable implementation of their policies and commitments on gender equality, despite the many gender-related commitments that bilateral donors have adopted.[9] A thematic review on gender for the UN Peacebuilding Support Office carried out in 2014 similarly found that a huge gap remains in operationalizing existing policy commitments for integrating gender into peacebuilding. One such example is the UN Secretary-General's Seven Point Action Plan (7PAP) to increase women's participation and channel at least 15 percent of UN-managed peacebuilding funds to projects that support gender equality.[10]

Despite the failures to date, there are several possible entry points and strategies that could be used or applied more systematically when implementing the three pillars of the New Deal (PSGs, FOCUS, and TRUST) that would contribute to greater gender sensitivity of peacebuilding and statebuilding efforts. These are each explored in more detail below.

THE NEW DEAL'S PEACEBUILDING AND STATEBUILDING GOALS (PSGs)

As explained in chapters 2 and 3, the PSGs are intended to enable progress toward achieving the MDGs (replaced by the SDGs) and provide a framework for prioritizing the needs of fragile and conflict-affected states. The issues outlined in the PSGs are similar to those that women's organizations have been advocating over the past decade, and they are also important in the context of the WPS agenda. Yet the current PSGs do not adequately reflect a gender perspective, thereby undermining efforts to build secure and sustainable states and societies.

For example, researchers and women's organizations have emphasized that including women at the negotiating table is critical to the success of peace talks and ensures that gender-related issues are raised and can inform strategic decisions made during negotiations. Yet this important finding and perspective is not reflected in PSG 1 (legitimate politics). The record shows that the numbers of women leading or participating in the peace processes remains extremely low, with UN Women reporting that only 4 percent of signatories and 2.4 percent of chief mediators across thirty-one peace talks between 1992 and 2011 were women.[11] The impact of this oversight cannot be overestimated, with new research demonstrating that quality participation of women's groups in peace agreements in fact increases the likelihood that they will be implemented.[12] Table 4.1 illustrates what the PSGs look like from a gender perspective.

The PSGs are important for full implementation of the New Deal, but specific indicators to measure change and progress at both the national and international levels are needed. A set of fifty indicators was proposed by the Steering Committee of the IDPS in 2012 and has now been used by various countries as they develop their fragility spectrums and assessments. These indicators are also relevant for measuring global trends in conflict and fragility and evaluating progress and areas for future investment. While some of the indicators call for the collection of sex-disaggregated data, only two indicators, incidence of rape and sexual violence and access to service delivery for marginalized and vulnerable groups, can be considered gender-specific. Even where guidelines require that indicators be sex-disaggregated, few countries have effective systems established or the political will to collect this data. It will be essential for civil society groups to monitor this closely. Where the information needed to measure progress against the indicators

Table 4.1 A gender perspective on the peacebuilding and statebuilding goals

PSG	Key Issues to Consider
Legitimate politics: Foster inclusive political settlements and conflict resolution	The political settlement is broadened beyond an elite settlement to become a societal compact, including women and strategically and adequately addressing gender issues. Institutions uphold women's rights and both women and men are able to participate in decision-making at all levels, including through holding public office. Civil society proactively includes women's organizations as engaged and active members. Broad-based processes for conflict resolution and reconciliation build on women's grassroots peacebuilding efforts and address gender-related inequalities and insecurities. Women leaders representing a range of backgrounds and identities (urban, rural, wealthy, poor, etc.) are included in all negotiations.
Security: Establish and strengthen people's security	Improved behavior, effectiveness, and accountability of formal and informal security actors, particularly in relation to the protection of women. Particular attention to the gender-specific security needs and to the specific vulnerabilities of women and girls. Support for the full and meaningful participation of communities, including women leaders and networks, in shaping security priorities and their provision. Physical security is understood as a necessity for women's economic security as well as their access to and opportunities for political participation, education, health care, and other services.
Justice: Address injustices and increase people's access to justice	All grievances, injustices, and violations, including sexual and gender-based violence, are addressed by peace and reconciliation processes. Formal justice mechanisms are accessible, affordable, and protect women's rights. Traditional, nonstate, and informal means for dispute resolution and adjudication are strengthened and aligned with international human rights standards, particularly in relation to women's human rights.
Economic foundations: Generate employment and improve livelihoods	Job opportunities are created and reduce incentives to engage in violence and conflict, and the barriers to women's access to formal employment are actively addressed. Funding is allocated to income-generating projects including some quick wins, particularly for youth and marginalized groups. Women are prioritized and targeted for involvement in labor intensive public and community works. Increased agricultural productivity and domestic private sector development benefit women farmers and entrepreneurs.

(Continued)

PSG	Key Issues to Consider
Revenues and services: Manage revenue and build capacity for accountable and fair service delivery	Resources are raised, prioritized, and managed in a way that contributes to more equitable service delivery, ensuring that the vulnerable and marginalized have access to these services.
	The specific barriers that affect women's and girls' ability to access services are addressed.
	There is sound and transparent public financial management, including through the use of gender budgeting.
	Natural resources are managed in a transparent way that benefits all members of society.

Source: This table has been adapted from Cordaid 2012. *Integrating Gender into the New Deal for Engagement in Fragile States.* The Hague: Cordaid. https://www.cordaid.org/media/publications/Cordaid-7247-02-PP-Gender_into_the_New_Deal-DEFHR-web.pdf, 13.

does not exist at the national level, guidelines or templates should refer to the need for investing greater resources into the collection and analysis of sex-disaggregated data.

In defining gender-sensitive indicators, it is important to recognize that consensus on what to measure and how to quantify the results, as well as defining what counts as a violation of women's rights or a priority gender issue, can vary from context to context. There are already several international proposals for indicators on WPS issues, and these could be a starting point for gender-sensitive indicators of peacebuilding and statebuilding. In 2009, UNSCR 1889 called on the UN Secretary-General to deliver a set of indicators for use at the global level to track implementation of UNSCR 1325.[13] The Technical Working Group on Global Indicators for UNSCR 1325 developed twenty-six indicators in 2010, and these are now used in some settings to measure progress.[14]

The Global Network of Women Peacebuilders (GNWP) has also developed a set of indicators based on extensive consultations with partner organizations across a range of fragile and conflict-affected states to monitor the implementation of UNSCR 1325 at the national level. Both sets of indicators overlap with different elements of the PSGs and offer useful options that could be adopted to identify country-specific and global-level indicators. The indicators within individual countries' National Action Plans (NAPs) on UNSCR 1325 can also be used to measure progress against the PSGs, as emphasized in the case study below on Afghanistan.

Given the challenges in generating the political will and resources needed for monitoring UNSCR 1325, folding these indicators into the New Deal process could be an effective way to leverage support for collecting data that would aid the implementation of both policy agendas. It is important to recognize that developing indicators for the PSGs is not merely a technical exercise but also a political process.[15] This can make it even more difficult to ensure that gender issues are reflected in the final set of indicators. It also makes it more important to resist the political trade-offs that may force gender issues to the bottom of the priorities list.

As argued above, women's rights and gender equality are important measures of successful peacebuilding and statebuilding, and they must be integrated into PSG indicators as they are developed. If this is not done, it is unlikely they will be taken into account in the coming years or be reflected in national development plans and strategies. There is also a risk that gender issues are simply mentioned as a crosscutting theme across all dimensions of peacebuilding and statebuilding, rather than falling under any specific funding or political priority. Monitoring and accountability can be challenging where gender issues are not the responsibility of a specific group of actors. The issues are more likely to be left unaddressed, or not engaged in a meaningful way. The process of articulating the goals and indicators for the new SDGs, particularly Goal 5 on achieving gender equality and empowering women, as well as Goal 16, represents another opportunity to bring the gender, peacebuilding, and statebuilding debates together.

FOCUS

Given that gender issues remain marginalized from donors' statebuilding and peacebuilding agendas despite a certain degree of rhetorical commitment, there is a need for a new approach to ensuring that they are taken into account. "FOCUS," the second pillar of the New Deal, emphasizes developing new ways of engaging and supporting transitions that are country-led and country-owned rather than imposed by donor countries' own development agendas.[16] One of the seminal elements of FOCUS is the fragility assessment (FA), a tool that the g7+[17] and the OECD's Inter-agency Network on Conflict and Fragility (INCAF) have been jointly developing that will assist governments in identifying the drivers of conflict and fragility and sources of resilience. These assessments are intended to lead into the development of a one-country vision and plan that will be implemented through a compact to enhance harmonization and help to align donor resources to country priorities.

Initially, five countries undertook FAs (DRC, Liberia, Sierra Leone, South Sudan, and Timor-Leste), and since then, several other g7+ countries have either undergone or are planning an FA or similar process.[18] As noted below, Afghanistan presented its initial assessment in March 2016. Despite a few guiding questions that relate to women's needs and vulnerabilities, it is not clear whether gender dynamics are recognized by the fragility assessment framework as one of the drivers of conflict, fragility, or resilience.[19] If gender dynamics were recognized, it would lead to a different assessment of fragility and, more importantly, offer new avenues toward resilience. Such gender-sensitive assessments could take into account the extent of women's political participation and their security vulnerabilities; gender-differentiated barriers to justice; and obstacles to women's access to land, credit, and services. By explicitly identifying the different needs of men and women and their capacities for resilience and contributing to peacebuilding, inclusive fragility assessments would ensure that these gender-related priorities are taken up in subsequent national planning processes.

There is also a need to integrate a gender perspective into fragility spectrums, a planning tool through which governments, in consultation with national stakeholders, rank their countries on a scale of one to five according to the different subdimensions of the PSGs. Ideally these are based on inclusive analysis of fragility using a mix of qualitative and quantitative methodologies. While not intended to be a blueprint with fixed criteria that can be applied across all contexts, the spectrum tool can help countries track their progress toward more sustainable peacebuilding and development.

According to recent research, an important predictor of state instability is how its women are treated, and in particular the level of violence against women in those societies. This supports the need for these factors to be included in any measure of fragility that is developed as part of the New Deal.[20] Steps toward gender equality could be used as important milestones for measuring progress in each of the PSGs. For example, the drafting and then implementation of laws relating to women's land or inheritance rights, or the increased capacity of the security services to respond to sexual violence, could be indications that a government is moving away from the fragile end of the governance spectrum toward greater resilience.

Another key part of FOCUS is supporting inclusive political processes such as country dialogues, where all members of society, including government and civil society, are able to have a voice and play a role in leading national peacebuilding and statebuilding efforts. The exclusion of women from participation means that even where processes are "country-led and country-owned," elite men typically lead and own the processes, and only a narrow group of actors are able to influence the agenda. Transforming peacebuilding and statebuilding spaces to make them more inclusive is a long-term and challenging process directly linked to the full implementation of UNSCR 1325, and it is an area in which women's organizations and advocates have been active for some time. As part of the process to develop NAPs on WPS, for example, many countries have held wide consultations and carried out scoping exercises to identify key priorities. These could be

Table 4.2

Entry points for integrating a gender perspective into FOCUS include:

- Ensuring that all fragility assessments are informed by gender analysis and done in consultation with civil society, including women's organizations, while supporting the collection of sex-disaggregated statistical and survey data.
- Ensuring that gender-related priorities inform any national plan and vision.
- Fostering legitimate and inclusive spaces for peaceful dialogue, as well as creating opportunities for women to share ideas and discuss priorities for feeding into these spaces at the local and national levels.
- Building conflict-sensitivity and conflict management capacity among women's organizations.
- Building and strengthening inclusive, transparent, and legitimate institutions for governance.
- Ensuring that civil society, including women's groups, is able to engage in, and monitor, formal country dialogues and informal political dialogue methods.

Source: This table has been adapted from Cordaid 2012. *Integrating Gender into the New Deal for Engagement in Fragile States.* The Hague: Cordaid. https://www.cordaid.org/media/publications/Cordaid-7247-02-PP-Gender_into_the_New_Deal-DEFHR-web.pdf.

a potential resource for identifying national and regional peacebuilding and statebuilding priorities in the context of national implementation of the New Deal. Table 4.2 offers possible entry points for a gender perspective to be included in FOCUS.

The New Deal emphasizes the importance of having one vision and one plan, so the work that has already been done in the area of WPS to create strategic plans and foster networks and partnerships of key stakeholders should serve as a basis upon which to expand. Furthermore, existing UNSCR 1325-related monitoring mechanisms, indicators, and data collection processes could readily be incorporated into the activities that constitute the FOCUS pillar of the New Deal. Donors therefore do not need to replicate the process of dialogue or develop key national priorities to ensure the successful integration of a gender perspective.

TRUST

Supporting peacebuilding and statebuilding can be of high risk for the international community given governance and security challenges, and the weak capacity and unpredictability of political and economic reforms that characterize these contexts. The New Deal recognizes that specific management systems and a reduction in aid volatility are essential to mitigate these risks, and, at the same time, that building the capacities of both government and civil society is also critical to strengthening the transparency, accountability, and responsiveness of state structures.[21] The final pillar of the New Deal, TRUST, outlines how resources and aid will be managed more effectively and transparently and how funding will be streamlined. Peacebuilding compacts in particular are one of the New Deal's key mechanisms for financing postconflict recovery.[22] These compacts are intended to enhance the identification of realistic priorities, mutual accountability, and more effective management of pooled funding.

UN Women has carried out detailed research that confirms that most planning and results frameworks fail to include indicators and activities that include women or gender issues, and where they are included they are not matched with adequate budget allocations.[23] Issues such as fiduciary risk, limited infrastructure, or weak governance structures may create an even more difficult operating environment for women's organizations than in peaceful contexts. Recent findings from an OECD study confirm that while donor support for gender equality and women's rights in fragile and conflict-affected states has increased 10 percent annually since 2008, funding is still insufficient, with only 6 percent of aid targeting gender equality as the principal objective.[24] Sustained and reliable core funding is needed not only for special programs but also for overhead and staffing costs so that women's organizations and community-level or grassroots groups can play an effective role in working for women's empowerment and gender equality.[25]

Integrating gender equality and women's rights issues into the transition compacts could help to address some of the identified funding gaps and ensure that financing of these issues is included at the earliest stages of post-conflict recovery financial planning. The GNWP and the Dutch development agency Cordaid have advocated for an innovative multistakeholder financing mechanism, based on a model that aims to increase sustainable financing as well as encourage domestic resource mobilization for the implementation of UNSCR 1325-related commitments.[26] As a result of these efforts, the Global Acceleration Instrument for Women, Peace and Security and Humanitarian Action was launched in February 2016, and is intended to mobilize more flexible, timely and robust funding to governments and civil society organizations. These types of initiatives could be linked to New Deal compacts to further leverage resources for gender-related programs. They are highly relevant for the case of Afghanistan, as noted below. However, while new compacts are an important step, it is important to note that much of the burden of gender-related planning, analysis, and programming falls on under-resourced and marginalized national women's machineries (NWMs) in fragile and conflict-affected states.

The implementation of the New Deal and decisions around aid funding and programming are led by ministries of finance in conflict-affected countries. These ministries wield significant power and financial resources

Table 4.3

Entry points for integrating a gender perspective into TRUST include:

• Allocating aid transparently and aligning it with country priorities.
• Using a gender budgeting approach to ensure that resources are allocated to and reach men and women.
• Managing the risks associated with aid delivery in fragile states, and ensuring joint oversight of funds so aid addresses women's needs.
• Supporting country-level mechanisms, including partnerships with women's organizations in order to strengthen mutual accountability and alignment of resources.
• Strengthening the capacity of all national actors, including women's organizations and national women's machineries.
• Allocating adequate resources to women-focused and gender-related activities and indicators in national planning frameworks.
• Strengthening gender budgeting capacities.

Source: This table has been adapted from Cordaid 2012. *Integrating Gender into the New Deal for Engagement in Fragile States.* The Hague: Cordaid. https://www.cordaid.org/media/publications/Cordaid-7247-02-PP-Gender_into_the_New_Deal-DEFHR-web.pdf.

in contrast to the NWMs, which remain marginalized from development and broader peacebuilding policy planning processes. It is important that both finance or economic planning ministries *and* women or gender affairs ministries engage in dialogue around aid allocation, management, and delivery and jointly address capacity gaps. Governments should also commit to ensuring that the minster for gender or women's affairs is represented at discussions relating to the implementation of the New Deal. Finally, compacts and donors rely disproportionately on women's organizations to fill the gaps left by state services. Therefore, sufficient financial, human resources, and technical support should be allocated to national women's organizations. Table 4.3 offers possible entry points for including gender perspectives in TRUST.

CONTINUING CHALLENGES FOR CIVIL SOCIETY

Cordaid's policy paper on gender in the New Deal in September 2012 was the first time these issues had been linked and marked a significant contribution to civil society engagement in the New Deal process.[27] Building on that research, together with the CSPPS and the IDPS Secretariat, Cordaid organized a discussion about the issue during the IDPS Steering Committee meeting in Juba in December 2012. Since then, the CSPPS platform and its members have embarked on a challenging endeavor to promote the integration of gender into the New Deal process, particularly in their respective countries.

At the global level, civil society has echoed the call for more inclusive PSGs. The CSPPS has proposed that the PSG indicators "should incorporate a more direct focus on women's empowerment and access to security, justice and services. The IDPS Indicator's working group should explore how the shared indicators on PSGs could be linked to or incorporate results from ongoing efforts to monitor implementation of UNSCR 1325."[28] However, as described above, the approved PSG indicators would need to be strengthened with more specific gender components to yield meaningful progress on gender equality.

Although the idea to integrate gender in New Deal implementation has gained support at global- and national-level policy dialogues, the survey conducted by Cordaid in 2015 with the CSPPS country focal points revealed many challenges.[29] A CSPPS member from South Sudan argued that "gender priorities raised during the negotiations more often fall into the cracks when the final document comes out." Representatives from a number of other countries offered similar assessments.

During a side event on gender issues and New Deal implementation during the IDPS Steering Group meeting in November 2015, some of the trends that emerged from the CSPPS country focal points experience were presented in a document based on the Cordaid survey. The results confirm several of the key points raised in the analysis above.[30] One result is that with some exceptions, such as in Togo where gender-based organizations were consulted, FAs and indicators covering the PSGs in national development plans have tended to be gender-blind. FAs have fallen short of fully addressing gender-related issues, particularly violence against women and women's participation in decision-making. More generally, women have tended to be excluded from processes to define key priorities in national strategies, including those linked to the New Deal. This is particularly common in the case of high-level meetings and forums. As the figures cited above indicate, the vast majority of those who participate in these discussions are men.

Another finding is that women's organizations and networks have mobilized in many countries to participate in, and support, New Deal implementation, but a lack of technical expertise, financial resources, and discriminatory practices prevent them from playing a constructive role. Funding challenges remain a particularly serious problem for women's groups focusing on gender issues. Meanwhile, examples of effective approaches to promoting the inclusion of gender issues within the New Deal, cited by the CSPPS focal points, include training and sensitizing women's rights advocates in New Deal-related issues, and linking the New Deal with parallel national processes such as the development of UNSCR 1325 NAPs. These are among the concrete steps that civil society groups and official government bodies could undertake together in realizing gender empowerment objectives.

Despite difficulties in actively participating in formal processes, many CSPPS members report that they have undertaken studies, participated in consultations, carried out targeted advocacy with key government ministries, and promoted dialogue with a range of stakeholders around the New Deal and gender issues. Some of the priority needs identified by CSPPS members to improve New Deal implementation include: increasing access to flexible funding for women's organizations; increasing political will and government support to implement gender-sensitive laws and policies as part of peacebuilding compacts; and building capacity support for CSOs so that they can meaningfully engage in consultations around FAs and defining PSG indicators.

These opportunities and challenges for integrating gender priorities into the New Deal process have not received much attention in many of the g7+ countries. However, Afghanistan's strong network of women peacebuilders has created a context where gender discussions are occurring in the development of peacebuilding and statebuilding policy. While many challenges remain, Afghan women's pursuit of a gender-inclusive society illustrates a hopeful example for how women's equality could acquire greater recognition within the New Deal process.

DISPATCH FROM THE FIELD: AFGHANISTAN AND THE NEW DEAL

After a decade of conflict, Afghanistan endorsed the New Deal for Engagement in Fragile States in 2011 and nominated itself as a pilot country of the g7+ group in order to accelerate its recovery.[31] Despite its volatile security context and complex development challenges, Afghanistan provides an important case study for the New Deal. Its vibrant civil society, in particular its women's organizations, have shown how these actors can work with government processes to strengthen the New Deal and empower local stakeholders even in a very difficult setting. The position of women's organizations in Afghanistan and the role that they have played in peacebuilding draws attention to the need for a deeper engagement around gender issues in Afghanistan's postconflict future. The pages below offer a glimpse of the activities of women's organizations in the country and present suggestions for how the New Deal process can be strengthened to prioritize the needs of women during its reconstruction.

Historically in Afghanistan, peace and transition negotiations have been exclusive processes involving elite state political and military actors. Afghan women have struggled persistently over the past fifteen years to be included in Afghanistan's political process and in discussions on peace and security issues. They have represented their constituents in the parliament and played their part in the country's defense and police forces, but unfortunately they have been largely ignored by their government as well as international societies and donors on major political and development issues. Much remains to be done to integrate gender into Afghanistan's national development and security policy.

Afghanistan consists of an old civil society that was born in exile (mainly in Pakistan), and a new civil society that appeared post-2002. The Afghan Women's Network (AWN) began in the new era of civil society as an umbrella network. It now comprises 118 organizations, with offices in five zones across the country. The AWN works as a consultancy while advocating for women's rights and acting as a watchdog for the implementation of government policies. As funding for CSOs in Afghanistan increased, the organization's goals have migrated from being project-oriented to issue-oriented, allowing for longer-term change.

The role of a free media in Afghanistan is one of the biggest achievements of the country next to its strong, women-led CSOs. The media has proven vital to many CSO successes and provides a connection between the AWN's work and the public. It has become actively involved in Afghanistan's development, social, and political spheres, becoming the voice and conscience of civil society and the people of Afghanistan. The media continues to raise gendered voices and highlight women's concerns. Because of this, it has been targeted by insurgents, and many brave journalists in the country have lost their lives.

CSOs have been included in some government processes. In one such case, the AWN was appointed by the government to participate in a fact-finding mission alongside religious scholars and members of other CSOs to investigate the 2015 murder of Farkhunda Malikzada, a 27-year-old Afghan woman accused of burning a copy of the Qur'an. The AWN found the police and authorities cooperative in providing information about the case to those on the fact-finding mission. The mission found that Farkhunda had not burned the holy book and that even if she had, Islamic law does not provide for the death sentence as punishment for a woman in such a case, only for a man. Although the findings of the mission were not reflected in the final disposition of the case, the AWN continues to raise this incident in the media and urges that those who committed the murder be punished according to the law.

Aside from engagement with the government, CSOs are also in discussions with those who threaten security. The Taliban claims not to want to work with corrupt government officials. Corruption in Afghanistan is now on a grand scale (unlike before 2002, when it was more petty) and has hindered the rule of law in the country. Since women's groups are not known for their corruption in Afghanistan, this has allowed for the AWN to be in talks with the Taliban. The AWN aims to have logical and productive discussions that will build peace and women's rights in the country. This inclusive dialogue process may be able to bring about change that the government of Afghanistan has not been able to achieve.

Gender and the New Deal in Afghanistan

While some INGOs and donor countries have shown interest in integrating gender into their action plans and development funding, gender equality in Afghanistan has generally been an afterthought in development programs. The New Deal and its processes have been largely gender-blind, and issues of women's empowerment have not received adequate attention. Difficulties have emerged in integrating the New Deal process and building ownership within the Afghan government, as well as for the parallel implementation of competing gender-related initiatives such as the National Action Plan for the Women of Afghanistan (NAPWA) and Afghanistan's NAP on UNSCR 1325 (NAP 1325).

Afghanistan established a New Deal coordinating structure based within its Ministry of Finance, and also assigned a staff member for the g7+ secretariat based in Timor-Leste. The country began a fragility assessment, "Afghanistan's Pathway toward Resilience and Stability," but faced many extended delays caused by a lack of proper coordination between Afghanistan's government and the UNDP. The former president of Afghanistan, Hamid Karzai, deferred the country's assessment to 2015. Major obstacles delaying implementation of the New Deal pilot program have included postponed national election processes that lacked legitimacy in the eyes of the Afghan people, a lack of cooperation between the two main political party leaders, the withdrawal of coalition military forces, and thousands of continuing Taliban attacks that have further undermined the country's security. Throughout the tumult and despite the enormous obstacles, Afghanistan's women's organizations have made important contributions to peacebuilding and statebuilding principles, making the country a critical case study from which to understand gender sensitivity in the New Deal.

For many in Afghanistan there is stigma attached to the New Deal and being labeled a fragile state. It has been hard for potential implementers to accept that Afghanistan is a fragile state, so there has not been effective progress in implementing the New Deal in the country. Although some elements have been taken from it and implemented, there is fatigue on the part of many key players. The many meetings and identification of action items have not led to widespread change.

Gender and the Tokyo Mutual Accountability Framework (TMAF)

Afghanistan established the Tokyo Mutual Accountability Framework in July 2012. The TMAF has served as Afghanistan's New Deal because it builds on the New Deal's TRUST and FOCUS pillars even though it does not explicitly recognize the New Deal process itself. The five thematic areas of the TMAF are (1) representation, democracy, and equitable elections; (2) governance, rule of law, and human rights; (3) integrity of public finance and commercial banking; (4) government revenues, budget execution, and subnational governance; and (5) inclusive and sustainable growth and development. These overlap with some of the New Deal PSGs but do not include security and justice. Afghanistan has also created a government Aid Management Policy (AMP), which is in line with the TRUST principles, in order to encompass these components. Afghanistan's CSOs were involved in developing the content of both the TMAF and the new AMP, but the process was not all-inclusive. Only selected NGOs were involved and gender integration was not a priority, as is the case with most agreements and policies of the government.

The only area where gender or women's issues are specifically mentioned is under the pillar of governance, rule of law, and human rights, where there is reference to implementation of the law calling for the elimination of violence against women. While this is a meaningful step, since violence against women has become endemic in Afghanistan, the lack of the reference to gender in the rest of the TMAF's four pillars is concerning. Despite extensive recommendations made by the AWN, civil society organizations, and INGOs for gender to be included in all of the five goals in the New Deal, they have not been incorporated.

Major gaps in gender equality in Afghanistan are not being addressed. These include the lack of access to basic services such as education, the judicial system (in order to obtain ownership and inheritance rights), and health care facilities. Additionally, women's mobility and access to their surroundings, including going outside of their homes to shop or visit family members, remain difficult. Political will to support and monitor the performance of government entities in addressing the gender gap is lacking. The government of Afghanistan does not implement a gendered budgeting approach, therefore failing to allocate adequate resources to the implementation of its gender-related commitments. As a result, the majority of women's programs are not implemented on time. One of the AWN's recommendations, with support of other women's organizations and INGOs at the Tokyo Conference, was to make aid for the government of Afghanistan conditional on gender equality and women's participation. Some European countries, such as Finland and Italy, have made a point to implement this conditionality in their future assistance to Afghanistan.

CSOs need financial support to strengthen their work in promoting a gender agenda in peacebuilding efforts within the New Deal process. This does not necessarily entail new donor commitments of money for the Afghan government, but instead could be in the form of a gender liaison official. This official would work closely with the Ministry of Finance, particularly in the early stages of the process, to ensure that gender action plans are properly resourced for implementation. International donors can play an important role in applying pressure on the ministry to ensure resources are distributed equally and allocated to implementing gender action plans.

The AWN, other CSOs, members of parliament, and human rights activists in Afghanistan have produced many documents, studies, and recommendations on integrating gender into the implementation of each goal of the New Deal process.[32] Additionally, two reports by the International Development Association (IDA) of the World Bank and UN Women provided thorough recommendations to the government of Afghanistan and international donors. Unfortunately, none of these recommendations have played a role in integrating gender into the New Deal to date. The government only began its fragility assessment in 2015, however, so there will be many opportunities for gender to be integrated into the New Deal process in Afghanistan in the future.

1325 and the National Action Plan

These challenges related to integrating gender into the New Deal should not overshadow the important achievement of Afghan women's CSOs and the government in launching the UNSCR 1325 WPS National Action Plan (NAP 1325). The Ministry of Foreign Affairs initiated the plan in the presence of President Ashraf Ghani, who spoke about the situation of women of Afghanistan, their place in the Afghan constitution, and the political commitment of the government to focus on gender-related issues. Ghani's speech offered a renewed focus on the complementary implementation of the New Deal in Afghanistan in parallel with the TMAF. This was illustrated in part by the government's appointment of four female ministers, two female governors, and the planned appointments of female ambassadors.

Due to early and constant engagement of women's organizations like the AWN, and the presence of some women from other CSOs as members of the NAP 1325 technical committees, gender is included in every section of the plan, with monitoring and evaluation by women's organizations and CSOs built in. Presently, the ministries of foreign affairs and finance appear committed to securing the budget needed to implement NAP 1325, which was previously overlooked by the government. The NAP 1325, the TMAF and the New Deal have created positive movements in the area of gender integration in all aspects of peacebuilding and statebuilding. CSOs and donor nations now have the opportunity to make a proactive effort to take the ideas mentioned in these frameworks and move them toward implementation. The AWN has positioned itself to monitor the implementation of the NAP 1325, writing a shadow report with the Swedish International Development Cooperation Agency (SIDA) to assess progress and call the government to account. This work is also linked to and supportive of the New Deal.

Afghan women can capitalize on the overlap between UNSCR 1325 and the New Deal by identifying entry points that intersect between the NAP 1325 and New Deal process. The results of the fragility assessment provide an opportunity for informing revisions to NAP 1325 and the government's AMP. Finance Minister Ahmad Eklil Hakimi presented the government's fragility assessment at the Fourth Ministerial Meeting of the g7+ in Kabul in March 2016. The study looks at drivers of fragility and conflict and makes recommendations for priority actions for Afghanistan's transition toward a resilient and peaceful state. As part of the assessment, a framework for ongoing monitoring and evaluation of the New Deal will be developed. The Aid Management Directorate will be primarily responsible for developing this framework, supported by other government ministries. Additionally, the fragility assessment will be revised on a periodic basis. An advisory board has already been established and is chaired by the Ministry of Finance. The board includes representatives from the Office of the President, the government ministries covering each of the five PSGs, the donor community, and civil society groups including women's organizations.

There appears to have been a shift in the government of Afghanistan's policy toward a more gender-friendly approach to the New Deal. This has been due mainly to the presence of strong women's CSOs and the potential of the policy framework articulated in the NAPWA and NAP 1325 to bring a more gender-sensitive approach to peacebuilding and statebuilding. Progress in achieving these goals will be extremely difficult, however, as long as there is a worsening security situation and a failure to come to agreement with the Taliban. A general shift in the direction of Afghanistan's policies and its security condition will be necessary to realize the country's potential for gender inclusion.

CONCLUSION

Members of CSPPS, particularly those in the New Deal pilot countries, have strongly and actively pursued efforts to support the inclusion of gender in the New Deal. The key components of the PSGs, TRUST, and FOCUS provide a strategic and practical entry point for enhancing gender equality in peacebuilding and statebuilding. Increased attention to gender is critical to strengthening efforts to build sustainable peace, states, and societies as well as for enhancing accountability, inclusivity, and legitimacy. There can also be no sustainable peace without meaningful inclusion of broader civil society. A particular focus is needed to ensure gender sensitivity and women's effective participation in peacebuilding and statebuilding.

Despite the efforts of CSPPS and others, there is little evidence of action to build a more inclusive and gender-sensitive peace in Afghanistan. AWN and other civil society groups have made efforts to incorporate gender issues into the New Deal process, risking their lives in some cases to speak publicly for women's equality. This work faces many obstacles in a society that remains riven by armed conflict and corruption, in a setting of widespread misogyny.

Nonetheless, there may be some cause for optimism in the future. Afghanistan has the essential ingredients of gender-related policies such as the gender goals within the TMAF, the NAPWA, and the NAP 1325. The Afghan government's latest commitments toward the New Deal and the president's direct participation in the launching of the NAP 1325 also suggest there is now the political will and possibility to bring the processes closer together. The development and articulation of strategies to implement the SDGs in Afghanistan, especially goals 5 and 16, will further enhance this opportunity in the years ahead. The meaningful participation of CSOs in the implementation and governance of the New Deal in Afghanistan will be crucial. Afghanistan has strong and capable women, such as members of the AWN, who are well placed to be active participants and leaders in this process. However, for their potential to be realized the Afghan government and international community must act to provide the necessary resources and political space to ensure inclusive, bottom-up integration of gender equality within the New Deal process.

NOTES

1. C. Moser and F. Clark, eds., *Victims, Perpetrators or Actors?: Gender, Armed Conflict and Political Violence* (London: Zed Books, 2001); UN Women, *Sourcebook on Women, Peace, and Security* (New York: UN Women, 2012); Funmi Olonisakin, Karen Barnes, and Eka Ikpe, *Women, Peace, and Security: Translating Policy into Practice* (London: Routledge, 2012); Haleh Afshar and Deborah Eade, eds., *Development, Women, and War: Feminist Perspectives* (Oxford: Oxfam GB, 2004).

2. Clare Castillejo, "Building a State That Works for Women: Integrating Gender into Post-Conflict State Building," Working Paper no. 107 (Madrid: FRIDE, 2011), 18, http://fride.org/download/WP107_Building_state.pdf.

3. For detailed analysis of the key reasons for integrating gender into peacebuilding and statebuilding processes, refer to UN Women, *Sourcebook on Women, Peace, and Security*.

4. Valerie M. Hudson et al., "The Heart of the Matter: The Security of Women and the Security of States," *International Security* 33, no. 3 (Winter 2008/09): 7–45; World Bank, *2012 World Development Report on Gender Equality and Development* (Washington DC: World Bank, 2012).

5. For an overview of recent research, refer to UN Women, *Preventing Conflict Transforming Justice Securing the Peace: A Global Study on the Implementation of United Nations Security Council Resolution 1325* (New York: UN Women, 2015), http://wps.unwomen.org/en.

6. Patricia Justino et al., "Quantifying the Impact of Women's Participation in Post-Conflict Economic Recovery," Households in Conflict Network Working Paper, November 2012.

7. For example, see Karen Barnes and Peter Albrecht, *Civil Society Oversight of the Security Sector and Gender* (Geneva: DCAF/OSCE, 2008); GNWP, *Security Council Resolution 1325: Civil Society Monitoring Report 2014* (New York: GNWP, 2014), http://www.gnwp.org/sites/default/files/resource-field_media/2014Global%20Report_Aug13_2015HiRes_Jim.pdf.

8. Cordaid, *Integrating Gender into the New Deal for Engagement in Fragile States* (The Hague: Cordaid, 2012), https://www.cordaid.org/media/publications/Cordaid-7247-02-PP-Gender_into_the_New_Deal-DEFHR-web.pdf.

9. Jenny Hedman with Patti O'Neill, and Catherine Gaynor, "Findings from the Gender Equality Module of the 2011 Paris Declaration Monitoring Survey," prepared on behalf of the OECD, Development Co-Operation Directorate, http://www.oecd.org/dac/gender-development/49014760.pdf.

10. Eleanor O'Gorman, "Independent Thematic Review on Gender for the UN Peacebuilding Support Office: Final Report," March 2014, http://www.un.org/en/peacebuilding/pbso/pdf/Final%20Report_Thematic%20Review%20on%20Gender%20&%20Peacebuilding.pdf; United Nations, "Tracking Progress: Seven Point Action Plan," A/65/354–S/2010/466, Report of the Secretary-General on Women's Participation in Peacebuilding, http://www.un.org/en/peacebuilding/pbso/pdf/seven_point_action_plan.pdf.

11. UN Women, *Women's Participation in Peace Negotiations: Connections between Presence and Influence* (New York: UN Women, 2012), 3. http://www.unwomen.org/~/media/headquarters/attachments/sections/library/publications/2012/10/wpssourcebook-03a-womenpeacenegotiations-en.pdf.

12. Thania Paffenholz, "Results on Women and Gender," Briefing Paper, Centre on Conflict, Development and Peacebuilding and University of Geneva, Graduate Institute of International and Development Studies, 2015, http://graduateinstitute.ch/files/live/sites/iheid/files/sites/ccdp/shared/Docs/Publications/briefingpaperbroader%20participation.pdf.

13. United Nations Security Council, Resolution 1889, "Women, Peace, and Security," S/RES/1889, October 5 2009, http://womenpeacesecurity.org/media/pdf-scr1889.pdf; see also United Nations Security Council, "Women, Peace and Security: Report of the Secretary-General," S/2010/173, 2010.

14. United Nations Security Council, "Women and Peace and Security: Report of the Secretary-General," S/2004/814, October 13, 2004, https://documents-dds-ny.un.org/doc/UNDOC/GEN/N04/534/14/PDF/N0453414.pdf?OpenElement.

15. Jamil Chade, "The Conflict and Fragility Agenda Post-Busan: Directions, Opportunities, Challenges," *Geneva Peacebuilding Platform*, Brief No. 2, 2012, 3.

16. The acronym FOCUS is derived from the five key elements of the country-led pathways out of fragility: fragility assessment; one vision, one plan; compact; use PSGs to monitor; and support political dialogue and leadership.

17. The g7+ is a group of fragile and conflict-affected states that are collectively working to transition toward peace and development. As of January 2016, the g7+ has twenty members from across all geographic regions.

18. International Dialogue on Peacebuilding and Statebuilding, "New Deal Implementation Progress Overview," Seventh International Dialogue Working Group Meeting on New Deal Implementation, 2015, http://www.pbsb dialogue.org/media/filer_public/00/52/00527062-ddc0-418a-9e55-eee78312ff4d/ rd_2_nd_implementation_progress_overview_feb_2015.pdf.

19. International Dialogue on Peacebuilding and Statebuilding, "Draft Concept Note for 'Road Testing' the Fragility Spectrum and Menu of Indicators," Room Document 8, June 2012, http://cso-effectiveness.org/IMG/pdf/ rd8_en_concept_note_roadtesting_fragility_spectrum_and_menu_of.pdf.

20. Valerie M. Hudson et al., *Sex and World Peace* (New York: Columbia University Press, 2012).

21. OECD, "Supporting Coherent and Sustainable Transition from Conflict to Peace," Draft Guidance, November 4, 2011, 41.

22. The acronym TRUST is derived from the five key elements of more effective aid management proposed under the New Deal: transparency; risk sharing; use and strengthen country systems; strengthen capacities; and timely and predictable aid.

23. Hanny Cueva-Beteta et al., *What Women Want: Planning and Financing for Gender-Responsive Peacebuilding* (New York: UN, 2010), 14.

24. OECD-DAC, *Financing UN Security Council Resolution 1325: Aid in Support of Gender Equality and Women's Rights in Fragile Contexts* (Paris: OECD, 2015).

25. Cindy Clark, Ellen Sprenger, and Lisa VeneKlasen, *Where Is the Money for Women's Rights?: Assessing Resources and the Role of Donors in the Promotion of Women's Rights and the Support of Women's Organizations* (Toronto: AWID, 2006).

26. Dewi Suralaga and Mavic Cabrera-Balleza, eds., *Financing for the Implementation of National Action Plans on UNSCR 1325: Critical for Advancing Women's Human Rights, Peace and Security* (The Hague: Cordaid and the Global Network of Women Peacebuilders, 2014), https://www.cordaid.org/media/medialibrary/2014/10/ FinancingUNSCR1325_2014_27oct.pdf.

27. Cordaid, *Integrating Gender into the New Deal for Engagement in Fragile States.*

28. "International Peacebuilding and Statebuilding Indicators: CSO Joint Submission," Saferworld, January 2013, summary and full article accessible at http://www. saferworld.org.uk/resources/view-resource/717-international-peacebuilding-and-statebuilding-indicators-a-cso-joint-statement.

29. Survey responses were received from CSPPS country team members in Burundi, Central African Republic, Chad, DRC, Guinea, Liberia, Nigeria, REPAOC (Network of West and Central African NGO National Platforms), South Sudan, and Togo.

30. International Dialogue on Peacebuilding and Statebuilding, "Integrating Gender into the Future of the International Dialogue and New Deal Implementation," International Dialogue Steering Group Meeting, November 2015, http://www.pbsbdialogue. org/media/filer_public/5e/54/5e542b5c-300d-4f22-af87-68a1567d2815/rd_9_ gender_and_the_new_deal.pdf.

31. The source of the information presented throughout this section comes from coauthor Mahbouba Seraj's personal experiences in Afghanistan, including several interviews with CSOs on the ground there.

32. Cordaid, *Integrating Gender into the New Deal for Engagement in Fragile States.*

Section 2

PARTNERING WITH REGIONAL ORGANIZATIONS

Chapter 5

From National Security to Human Security

Developing Effective Partnerships between the UN, Regional Organizations, and Civil Society

Darynell Rodriguez Torres

The complexity of global security threats and the fact that the drivers and effects of violence impact entire regions explain the growing trend toward regional approaches to security management. Regional organizations have distinct comparative advantages in addressing these challenges because they are often able to detect and respond to crisis faster, and their advice is more likely to be accepted by local actors and to result in positive outcomes.[1] As a result, Regional Inter-Governmental Organizations (RIGOs) are increasingly being called upon to take a more proactive role in the design and implementation of security policies in their regions.

While RIGOs are uniquely placed to play a relevant role in regional and global security management, they also face some important shortcomings. In many cases their financial and organizational capacities are not sufficient to enable them to play a meaningful role in conflict prevention and peacebuilding. RIGOs can also be prone to domination by a regional hegemon, something that can create suspicion and undermine their legitimacy and ability to act. Most importantly, the effectiveness of these organizations in conflict prevention and peacebuilding depends upon the will of member states and whether they want the organization to be active and effective in these areas. This decision depends on the level of political trust and cohesion existing among its members.[2]

As the nature of armed conflict changes and new security threats emerge, regional organizations need to reformulate their mandates to promote not only the security of the state (national security) but the security of the people who live in those states (human security). Managing collective risks from the perspective of both states' and people's interests requires a new type of multilateralism—more inclusive, flexible, innovative, and able to provide creative responses to increasingly complex challenges.

With the increasing importance of human security in the international agenda, CSOs are becoming more significant actors in peace and security governance. They can contribute to articulating a "people-centered—bottom-up" perspective that is often missing in state-centric security analysis. As regional organizations progressively take greater responsibilities for preventing and managing conflicts, the development of spaces for consultation and coordination with CSOs becomes critical.

This section of the book presents insights based on the experiences of CSOs in different regions of the world relating to RIGOs. This chapter examines the arguments in favor of a greater division of labor among the UN, RIGOs, and civil society and explores how to best achieve the potential of this cooperation in the areas of peace and security and the challenges to stronger international cooperation. The chapter then reviews concrete recommendations to improve coordination and cooperation between RIGOs and the UN—which could be operationalized under the framework of Chapter VIII of the UN Charter. It also looks at the role of CSOs and how the different levels of action (local, regional, and global) can be connected. Lastly, the chapter presents key insights drawn from the experience of practitioners and researchers that can be considered when designing mechanisms for regional engagement with CSOs.

WHY IS A DIVISION OF LABOR NECESSARY?

RIGOs are by their nature intergovernmental forums. Their mandates and limits are imposed by their member states and more precisely by the governments that represent those member states at a particular moment. Many of these organizations were created in the context of the Cold War, and their structures were designed to respond to Cold War security challenges. Forums such as the Organization of American States (OAS, 1948) and the League of Arab States (LAS, 1945) were established as spaces for political cooperation linked to regional military alliances. The process of decolonization brought forward a new wave of regionalism in Africa and Asia, which led to the creation of organizations like the Organization of African Unity (OAU, 1963), the Association of Southeast Asian Nations (ASEAN, 1967), and the South Asian Association for Regional Cooperation (SAARC, 1985).

The added value of these organizations was largely defined in terms of their ability to forge alliances to contain foreign threats and enhance the national security of their members. The structures of these organizations and the mechanisms developed to prevent and manage conflicts were, and in most cases still are, based on an analysis of risks and responses made from the perspective of the state. But the changing nature of conflict creates threats beyond the state that require multilateral and multidimensional responses.

Discussions about how to use the potential of regional organizations to manage armed conflicts are not new. During early negotiations on the configuration of the United Nations, the role of regional organizations in peace and security was already on the agenda.[3] Chapter VIII was included in the UN Charter as a way of leveraging these regional arrangements and providing a framework for the relationship between the UN and RIGOs in the field of peace and security. However, it can be argued that this instrument has been underutilized and that cooperation between the UN and RIGOs remains limited.[4]

The understanding of what constitutes international security has evolved in recent decades, reflecting the changes in security concerns and objectives.[5] The renewed interest in regional approaches to peace and security responds to the realization that many conflicts are essentially regional and therefore the analysis of the causes and the potential responses should also be approached from a regional perspective. According to Cedric de Coning, the trend toward a regional approach to peacebuilding can be explained by three main factors: (1) conflicts are rarely isolated within the borders of a state; (2) those who are closer to the problem are often in a better position to understand and influence it; and (3) their proximity ensures that they have a long-term interest in its outcomes. De Coning argues that the analysis of conflict dynamics and policy responses should take into consideration this regional dimension using a complex systems approach.[6]

While numerous policy documents and public statements recognize the importance of regional approaches to conflict prevention and peacebuilding, these recommendations are rarely acted on. Van Langenhove, Selzer, and Gartland identify six main factors that explain this.[7] First is the fear of divided responsibility. The UN Security Council fears an erosion of its authority if it delegates too much responsibility to regional organizations. This fear can be explained by the fact that the delegation of authority to RIGOs may strengthen the position of regional hegemons.

Second is the diversity in the objectives and mandate of RIGOs. While some organizations are explicitly geared toward peace and security issues, others are oriented more toward economic integration. Third, RIGOs possess different capacities. A discrepancy exists between the lofty ambitions and the more limited financial and human capacities of some RIGOs. The lack of budget and staff of the African Union (AU) often constrains its ability to act. On the other hand there is also an imbalance in the concrete capacities for conflict prevention and peacebuilding. While some organizations like the EU, the Economic Community of West African States (ECOWAS), the Intergovernmental Authority on Development (IGAD), and the Organization for Security and Co-operation in Europe (OSCE) have developed effective early warning systems for conflict prevention, others such as the LAS, the OAS, the Economic Community of Central African States (ECCAS), and the Southern African Development Community (SADC) do not have these systems in place. Even where those systems exist, capacity deficits mean that early warning is not translated into timely action.

Fourth, UN-RIGO cooperation in conflict prevention and peacebuilding can be subject to particular difficulties. In terms of operational conflict prevention, states may resist the involvement of the UN for fear of internationalizing the conflict. Conflict prevention and peacebuilding efforts are then left to regional organizations which may not have optimal operational capacities. Conflict prevention and peacebuilding are extremely sensitive areas where states' guardedness toward external intervention in their internal affairs constitutes a significant obstacle for increased UN-RIGO cooperation.

Fifth, shortcomings within the structure of the UN have presented an obstacle to past cooperative initiatives between the UN and RIGOs. The strategic direction of the UN Security Council is heavily affected by its rotating membership leading to inconsistent support to this process. At the same time different secretaries-general may assign different levels of priority to cooperation with regional organizations.

Finally, cooperation between the UN and RIGOs on the one hand, and CSOs on the other, is hampered by a number of obstacles. First, CSOs are not always granted access to policy meetings dealing with peace and security issues within RIGOs or the UN. To gain accreditation to a regional organization, CSOs are often required to be accredited by their own country government. If this government is under the sway of an authoritarian regime, accreditation can be problematic. Second, CSOs do not always have the resources to establish the liaison offices in New York and Geneva that are so crucial for gaining personal collaborative contacts with state officials and policymakers at the UN.

Despite the difficulties, many voices are calling for better coordination between the UN and RIGOs and a better articulation of their respective roles. These calls for cooperation have included suggestions for coordination in specific countries as well as more general recommendations for global cooperative action on such issues as controlling illicit arms trafficking to creating of a UN standby force.[8]

While the mandates and capacities of regional organizations to address peace and security issues vary greatly, a recent study identified at least twenty-nine RIGOs with potential capability to have an impact on issues of peace and war.[9] However, when looking at the effectiveness of these organizations one can see substantial differences. Organizations such as the EU rank high in terms of effectiveness, while others like SAARC, SADC, or IGAD are considered largely ineffectual. In the middle we can find organizations like ASEAN or the OSCE whose effectiveness has changed in different historical periods.[10]

Identifying the comparative advantage of each organization and the right balance between local, regional, and global initiatives is one of the key challenges to promoting a more effective division of labor. While there are strong arguments in favor of regional approaches, sometimes neighbors are not only part of the solution but also part of the problem. Member states may prevent the regional organization from acting effectively, or it could be perceived as favoring one of the parties in the conflict over another. In these cases the UN may have a comparative advantage, with more resources, experience, and distance from the local situation, and with a stronger legal standing for addressing problems related to peace and security.[11]

On the other hand, relying solely on continental or global organizations can create greater risk that other factors and interests, not necessarily at the core of the problem, come into consideration. For example, issues like the "global war on terror" can cloud the understanding of local or regional conflict dynamics.[12] Since international bodies are often more influential in setting global and regional agendas, efforts should avoid a top-down approach that may override the advantages a localized approach can offer.

De Coning proposes that as a general rule the most tactical and practical mediation and peacemaking roles should be assigned to those closest to the problem. This is an argument for giving greater priority to subregional organizations. Regional and international bodies could then provide operational support and ensure that strategic international efforts are aligned to regional and local initiatives.[13]

Favoring a regional approach to conflict prevention and peacebuilding could also contribute to a better articulation of the emerging roles of local and regional CSOs. While significant efforts have been made at the UN to reach out to CSOs, an important gap remains. RIGOs may find themselves in a better position to make these connections. The example of ECOWAS discussed in Chapter 6 of this book provides good insight into how a close collaboration with civil society organizations can help to create an effective early warning and early response system.

CIVIL SOCIETY AND PEOPLE-CENTERED SECURITY

Strong arguments can be made in favor of the role of civil society in conflict prevention and peacebuilding. CSOs tend to work in areas and with people directly affected by the conflict, which gives them a good understanding of the situation and even some access and influence over armed actors that official interlocutors often lack. This proximity to communities affected by the conflict gives them a unique perspective regarding the causes and effects of violence. Also, the fact that local CSOs do not need an "exit strategy" guarantees a long and sustained interest in finding a solution to the problem.

The number of CSOs working in the areas of peace and security has grown exponentially in recent decades. As a result, a greater need exists to strengthen cooperation between RIGOs and civil society, as noted in several UN reports. The Secretary-General's 2011 report on preventive diplomacy highlights the unique contribution that regional and subregional organizations can make in this area and calls for a better division of labor with CSOs that are involved in Track II and Track III diplomacy.[14] UN General Assembly Resolution 65/283 on strengthening the role of mediation in dispute settlement stresses the importance of partnerships at international, regional, and subregional levels, including partnerships with CSOs.[15]

UN reports acknowledge that CSOs have a comparative advantage in demonstrating that people can be active agents of security and not merely passive recipients. In this regard, collaboration with CSOs is one of the venues that RIGOs can use to enhance their capacities for conflict prevention and bring these intergovernmental organizations closer to the needs and expectation of the citizens of their member states.

CSOs can direct attention to the underlying causes of conflict that need to be addressed, providing a "reality check" for understanding the local context and contributing to the correct analysis and diagnosis of the conflict drivers. CSOs also have the potential to raise awareness about the costs of violence and promote regional solidarity. Furthermore, civil society actors have the potential to play an important role in raising awareness about the costs of continued conflict and the opportunities to solve it. Some of the key roles that CSOs can play at the different stages of the conflict cycle include: strengthening capacities to mediate conflict, making government structures more responsive through participation in political processes, early warning of emerging crises through monitoring, providing humanitarian relief, facilitating Track II dialogue processes, contributing to transitional justice processes, and many more.[16] The effectiveness of RIGOs as peacemakers and peacebuilders can be greatly enhanced through deeper cooperation with CSOs. Engaging large segments of the wider society in peacebuilding processes can give depth and durability to the changes needed to support sustainable peace.[17]

Despite the advantages of partnering with CSOs, engagement with these organizations in the work of RIGOs is limited and reveals broader tensions. For example, while the LAS established a Civil Society Secretariat in the wake of the Arab uprisings, resistance to civil society in certain member states remains strong. When the Union of South American Nations (UNASUR) drafted its constitutive treaty, the term "civil society" was avoided altogether as its members considered it implicitly a term developed in "the North." The organizational chart of the IGAD in Eastern Africa includes an "NGO and Civil Society Forum," but such a body is not yet operational.[18]

Some of the variables that explain this restricted engagement include funding shortages, personality differences, and varying priorities within RIGOs. CSOs also bear a share of responsibility for sometimes difficult relationships and inadequate partnerships with RIGOs. Common, generalized criticisms are that they can be "poorly organized, personality-centric, clientalistic, and at times fractious."[19]

Despite these obstacles, there are examples where trust has been established and good working relationships have emerged. The following two chapters provide evidence of this. Gender CSOs in the Pacific Islands, for example, led a successful campaign around UNSCR 1325 working closely with the Pacific Islands Forum. The West Africa Network for Peacebuilding (WANEP) developed a close working relationship with the ECOWAS in creating an early warning system to prevent armed conflict. Other cases not included in this volume are IGAD's own early warning system Conflict Early Warning and Response Mechanism (CEWARN), which draws upon local networks to collect information on cross-border and pastoral conflicts in the Horn of Africa, and the high-level policy discussions between civil society groups and the LAS on issues of human security and human rights, including discussions on the civil war in Syria. These and other examples demonstrate that despite the challenges, mutually beneficial partnerships can be formed between RIGOs and CSOs.

The question is not what approach to use (global, regional, or local through CSOs) but how to combine the different levels of action and find the appropriate forms of cooperation among these different actors. The following section will look at some of the challenges of operationalizing this cooperation. It also provides recommendations to move toward more effective coordination.

OPERATIONALIZING COOPERATION BETWEEN THE UN AND RIGOS

According to Luk Van Langenhove, the international system is currently transitioning from the traditional Westphalian conception of multilateralism based on the notions of territoriality, state sovereignty, and the national interest toward a new type of multilateralism where multiple actors beyond the state are claiming their own space and expect to see their own interests and concerns addressed.[20] This transition is developing more naturally in areas such as business, economics, and the protection of the environment—where the role and need for cooperation among multiple stakeholders is acknowledged. However, advancing multistakeholder approaches to multilateralism becomes more difficult in discussions about security policy.

Security is still widely considered an almost exclusive domain of the state. In this sense, the design of most security policies is usually accomplished through a top-down approach in which the state defines what is a security threat and which policies should be implemented to mitigate the threat. Security discussions within multilateral institutions are particularly sensitive because many states see them as potentially undermining their national sovereignty. Yet it is increasingly difficult to ignore the changing nature of global security challenges today. Threats to security have moved from being interstate to domestic, from international to transnational, with the majority of the victims in new challenges being civilians rather than combatants.[21]

The spillover effects of armed conflict increasingly spread to neighboring states and become a trigger for regional destabilization and a risk to global security. Therefore, the management of these multidimensional security challenges needs to incorporate a multidimensional conception of security, including the discussion of what constitutes a threat for an individual or a particular community. Multilateral forums are increasingly being asked to reconcile national security and human security concerns.

As mentioned in the previous section, while the UN has acknowledged the need to deepen collaboration with RIGOs in the area of peace and security, formalized cooperation and systematic coordination are limited. The different efforts undertaken to develop a closer relationship between the UN and RIGOs since Boutros Boutros-Ghali proposed the "Agenda for Peace" in 1992 have been primarily ad hoc meetings between the UN Secretary-General and his counterparts from regional organizations. Cooperation has developed more under the pressure of circumstances or as a result of practice rather than of strategy and principle.[22]

The discretionary nature of these interactions subordinates them to the interest, or lack of interest, of the UN Security Council or the UN Secretary-General. This noninstitutionalized approach limits the ability of RIGOs to develop more inclusive and effective frameworks for peacebuilding and conflict prevention.

The UN's High Level Meetings (HLMs) and "retreats" functioned for a time as a venue for coordination. The HLMs took place mainly between 1994 and 2006. The goal was to develop a strategic partnership between the UN and RIGOs. Rather than using a general model of cooperation, these meetings favored a flexible approach for cooperating in crisis management. The HLMs focused mainly on issues of peace and security, the role of regional organizations in conflict prevention and peacebuilding, and mechanisms to improve coordination in peacekeeping and peacebuilding.

For example, the HLM of 2003 discussed a new vision of global security based on a network of effective and mutually reinforcing multilateral mechanisms (regional and global). The 2005 HLM called for a greater partnership between the UN and RIGOs to build on the comparative strengths of these organizations. As interest in these meetings grew so did the number of participants, making them more difficult to manage.[23] The change in leadership at the UN and new directions within the UN Department of Political Affairs saw a decline in the interest in cooperating with RIGOs and led to the disappearance of this mechanism.[24] The last HLM between the UN and RIGOs took place in 2006. The HLMs have now been replaced by retreats. This is an even less institutionalized discussion forum and more subject to the discretion of the Secretary-General. There have been three retreats convened so far: one in 2010, another in 2012, and most recently in May 2015.

The relationship between RIGOs and the UN Security Council needs strengthening. From time to time the UN Security Council is briefed by the Secretary-General of a regional organization, but the interaction is ad hoc and far from being systematic. This is one of the areas where there is great potential for improvement. Currently, the Security Council is only briefed about potential trouble spots if the Secretariat chooses to do so or if a member state decides to raise the issue. As pointed out by Bertrand G. Ramcharan, the international community is entitled to expect that the Security Council and regional organizations collaborate to maintain a true global watch over threats to international peace and security and that the watch will be systematic.[25] This lack of regular interaction is a significant weakness in UN preventive diplomacy efforts.

It seems clear that the institutional relationship between the UN and RIGOs should be optimized and advanced toward a more structured and systematic approach. Van Langenhove, Selzer, and Gartland suggest updating the existing Memoranda of Understanding between the UN and RIGOs to act as flexible frameworks of cooperation. This would clarify roles and responsibilities in conflict prevention, mediation, and peacebuilding based on mutual trust and reliance. It would also make reporting by RIGOs and information sharing more regular and systematic. As part of this process, RIGOs should clarify their status in relation to Chapter VIII of the UN Charter in order to outline more clearly their rights and obligations in comparison to other UN bodies, particularly to the UN Security Council.[26]

Aside from the formal institutional mechanisms, one more intangible issue is that of establishing trust. As noted earlier, cooperation between the UN and RIGOs seems to be affected by a fear of divided responsibility. On the other hand, RIGOs may want to assert their role in the region rather than involve the United Nations for dealing with regional crises. Establishing a regular mechanism of interaction and cooperation would help to build trust, promote mutual understanding, and bolster mutual capacities. The revival of the HLMs may be one of the avenues to do this.

As part of this renewed HLM process, modalities of work in conflict prevention and peacebuilding could be further developed. These modalities could include consultations at the UN headquarters, development of shared indicators for early warning, the creation of a conflict prevention capabilities database, improved information flows, and better field coordination and joint missions. Cooperation could also grow with improved exchange of liaison officers, more mutual working-level meetings, joint trainings in conflict prevention, and enhanced collaboration with civil society. Ramcharan proposes the establishment of regional rapporteurs at the UN who could be regularly briefed by regional and subregional organizations in their particular areas of responsibility. This would deepen cooperation between the UN and RIGOs for preventive diplomacy.[27] An example of this proposal was suggested for the creation of permanent representations of the OSCE at the UN and vice-versa during the 2014 Security Days at the OSCE.

Cooperation is needed not only between the UN and RIGOs but among regional organizations themselves. Horizontal cooperation among RIGOs in different regions could make a significant contribution to strengthening the global peace and security architecture. Van Langenhove supports the idea of building trust and cooperation among RIGOs through a mechanism for learning and transferring knowledge from one organization to another and from one case to another. Each regional organization operates in a specific context, but they are all faced with similar challenges and issues, he writes. They therefore have an interest in exchanging information and sharing their respective experience and best practices in implementing their mandate.[28]

There are some examples of this kind of information sharing. International IDEA, a Stockholm-based intergovernmental organization that specializes in the promotion of democracy, runs the Inter-Regional Dialogue on Democracy. This is a platform for regional organizations to share experiences, exchange information, and further dialogue on democracy-building and related issues. GPPAC has also organized two global conferences (2011 and 2015) that brought together representatives of different RIGOs with representatives of civil society, the UN, and the business sector to discuss cooperation in conflict prevention and peacebuilding.[29] Much more coordination is needed for regional organizations to work together and with civil society representatives for conflict prevention and peacebuilding.[30]

The role of regional organizations in mediation, conflict prevention, and resolution could be strengthened by creating regular, interregional dialogues with representatives from the UN, regional organizations, and civil society. Such a process would allow for an exchange of experiences, a development of trust, and an empowerment of these actors to address today's complex security challenges.

Bringing in the CSOs

If it is difficult to outline cooperation between the UN and RIGOs, it is even more challenging to form cooperation among these actors and civil society. Because of their intergovernmental nature, the primary allegiance of global and regional multilateral organizations lies with their member states, some of which are often reluctant to open these forums to nonstate actors such as CSOs.

Human security and national security should not be understood as antagonistic concepts; rather they are mutually reinforcing. As the international community demands that RIGOs assume more responsibilities in enhancing regional and global security, it makes sense to incorporate a human security dimension into their work. Cooperation with CSOs that apply this approach to peace and security could become one of the avenues to bring a bottom-up approach to security into the work of RIGOs.

Some civil society organizations have developed valuable expertise in the field of conflict prevention and peacebuilding. These organizations are distinct from humanitarian, development, or human rights NGOs. They have developed significant capacities in conducting conflict assessments, recognizing the roles of religious actors in reconciliation, engaging polarized groups and armed actors, and developing collaborative relations and coordination with other stakeholders. The creation of greater synergies and institutional channels of cooperation between RIGOs and CSOs would constitute an important contribution to the global peace and security architecture.

One of the main obstacles to building this relationship is again the issue of trust. RIGOs and civil society groups are not always aware of their respective mandates, capacities, and roles in conflict prevention. The relationship between regional government officials and civil society actors has not always been easy. In fact, more often than not that relationship has been characterized by tensions and mutual suspiciousness. The development of cooperation does not start from a blank sheet but rather from an acknowledgment of these difficulties. The first contacts and engagements between these actors should be seen more as confidence-building opportunities rather than as output-oriented working meetings.

The relationship between CSOs and RIGOs must be built and nurtured through regular interactions. It cannot be suddenly activated when a crisis emerges. It needs to be developed and consolidated before the escalation of conflict. In this sense, the establishment of spaces that favor regular interaction, consultation, and joint analysis between CSOs and RIGOs must be encouraged and supported.

These spaces for interaction can contribute to developing a common understanding of the problems they face and a common language for dealing with them. Government actors and CSOs often speak different languages. When CSOs and multilateral organizations refer to an issue they do not necessarily share the same terminology or understanding. Recent research reveals differing perspectives between governments and civil society about the UN's peacebuilding architecture. The UN's understanding of peacebuilding in postconflict countries focuses on rebuilding infrastructures, good governance, and the rule of law, but local civil society actors view peacebuilding as a process of reconciliation and focus their work on reestablishing relationships that were broken during the war.[31]

The challenge for CSOs is how to create informal spaces for CSO-RIGO cooperation when official avenues are closed. This requires networking, strategic engagement, and investment. Crucially, CSOs need to show RIGOs how their work relates to regional policymaking and what added value they bring to the table.

This is true not only for the task of enhancing interactions between CSOs and RIGOs but also for the broader challenge of elevating the role of civil society in peacebuilding more generally. To strengthen civil society voices means designing strategies and programs to overcome the imbalance of power between state and society and the inertia of political actors and the policymaking process. The question is not so much about the existence of mechanisms to provide a voice to civil society actors, but whether or not these mechanisms can enable civil society to have some influence in the policymaking process.

Advocacy efforts from CSOs can contribute to influencing regional organizations and their key member states to deal more effectively with issues of peace and security. The advocacy of citizen groups depends upon gaining spaces for participation and adequate processes for engagement. There is a need to ensure that civil society actors included in a particular process are able to exercise influence. This is often difficult because when inclusive processes challenge established power structures, there can be a natural resistance toward the new actors. CSOs are often not well prepared to handle this resistance.[32] It is therefore important to work in developing the advocacy capacities of CSOs to enable them to balance some of the existing power relations and make them more influential in regional processes.

collaboration of EPLO, EU representatives would not know whom to invite or how to reach out to the relevant CSOs. Relying upon a platform of CSOs to figure out collaboration takes the burden away from RIGO officials, counters potential biases, and provides more legitimacy to the process. The EU model of creating an autonomously formed civil society platform is an approach that other regional organizations may wish to consider.

Investing in Inclusiveness

Systematic engagement with CSOs requires sustainable funding and designated staff capacities. EU officials and CSOs recognized this when designing the EU's CSDN. Each year the EU allocates a budget to develop a number of focused consultations and discussions with CSOs with expertise in conflict prevention and peacebuilding. The budget allocation is organized in cooperation with EPLO, which is responsible for managing a large part of that budget.

EPLO is then responsible for organizing civil society participation and gathering their input on key areas of Europe's external policy toward fragile and conflict-affected regions and countries. According to a former director of EPLO, the fact that the platform can focus on functional tasks such as proposing topics of discussion and selecting participants rather than having to worry about fundraising has been fundamental to the success of this program.

Sustainable civil society platforms such as this are unfortunately the exception, not the norm. Often RIGOs either lack the required financial resources or are less interested in obtaining systematic civil society input. CSOs therefore have to spend considerable time and effort in fundraising to support their engagements with RIGOs. Even when project funding is available, it often covers only one or two meetings a year. Without sustained funding it is difficult to maintain meaningful follow-up with RIGO officials and build more stable infrastructures for RIGO-civil society cooperation in times of crisis.

Investing in the development of in-house capacities to elicit civil society's perspectives is another track that can be developed in parallel to the support of CSO platforms. For example, regional organizations could consider the designation of some staff to serve as civil society liaison officers that would actively seek and coordinate civil society input in various countries. This can be done through the organization of town hall meetings, policy debates, and cross-learning exercises. These persons should also be tasked with tracking the inclusion of civil society actors, including women and youth, in different peacebuilding-related processes and their outcomes. This information can then be processed and distributed among the different decision-making bodies of the organization when particular policies are discussed in order to ensure collaboration.

Investing in inclusiveness is not only a task for governments, RIGOs, and the UN. CSOs must also invest to enhance their advocacy capacities to have meaningful participation and influence in policymaking. Inclusive processes challenge established power structures and there is a natural resistance toward new actors.[39] CSOs need to prepare to overcome this resistance, be more assertive about what they bring to the table, and claim their own space. It is therefore important to work in developing the advocacy capacities of CSOs to enable them to balance some of the existing power relations and make them more influential.

CONCLUSION

The international system is in transition, and the multilateral structures that were created to facilitate global governance are also going through a slow but profound transformation. Multilateral forums are moving from being closed systems of sovereign states, with little room for open debate and no space for the involvement of citizens, to becoming an "agora"—"a public realm in which institutional issues can be debated and perhaps decided."[40]

Van Langenhove describes this process as "multilateralism 2.0." It is characterized by three major trends: (1) the diversification in international organizations and a rise of transnational policy networks, (2) increasing interconnectivity between policy domains horizontally (e.g., the linkage of finance to trade and climate issues), and (3) the growing role of citizens, as evidenced by increased involvement of nongovernmental actors at all levels. The last is perhaps the most fundamental change as it challenges the state-centric approach of the international system. It is also the most difficult to institutionalize.[41]

The new multilateralism that is emerging must be able to incorporate the great variety of actors and interests to respond effectively to increasingly complex challenges. The international system in the twenty-first century is truly global and thus requires coordinated actions at multiple levels. Improving connections between the UN, RIGOs, and CSOs will become even more important in the creation of this more inclusive multilateralism.

Regional organizations are well positioned to lead this change. They should turn from being organizations of member states into organizations that also represent the interest of their citizens. RIGOs are often perceived as too far removed from day-to-day realities of the people who live in the region, and they need to make an effort to show their relevance to the people. This can be accomplished by empowering citizens to contribute toward improving their lives and working with civil society networks to provide greater economic security (freedom from want), physical security (freedom from fear), and uphold human rights (freedom from indignity). These are the three pillars of human security.

Harmonizing national security concerns, where the state is the focus, and human security concerns, where individuals are the focus, is the key point for this work. CSOs can become a valuable partner for RIGOs in fulfilling this mission. For this to occur, RIGOs must make efforts to reach out and open up more spaces for citizen participation, becoming more transparent and accountable not only to their member states but to the people living in their region.

NOTES

1. Craig Collins, Erik Friberg, and John Packer, *Overview of Conflict Prevention Capacities of Regional, Sub-Regional and Other Inter-Governmental Organizations* (The Hague: European Centre for Conflict Prevention, 2006), http://www.i4pinternational.org/files/203/8.+overview+of+conflict+prev+capacities.pdf.

2. Laurie Nathan, "The Peacemaking Effectiveness of Regional Organisations," Crisis States Working Papers Series No. 2, London School of Economics, Development Studies Institute, 2010, http://www.lse.ac.uk/internationalDevelopment/research/crisisStates/download/wp/wpSeries2/WP812.pdf.

3. Luk Van Langenhove, "The UN Security Council and Regional Organisations: A Difficult Partnership," in *Belgium in the UN Security Council: Reflections on the 2007–2008 Membership*, eds., Jan Wouters, Edith Drieskens, and Sven Biscop (Antwerp: Intersentia, 2009).

4. Van Langenhove, Anna Sophie Selzer, and Josh Gartland, 2015, "Strengthening the Global Peacebuilding Architecture through Chapter VIII" (working paper presented at the "Conference on Strengthening Peace and Security Cooperation towards Democracy and Development," Vienna, Austria, April 29–30, 2015).

5. Barry Buzan, Ole Wæver, and Jaap de Wilde, *Security: A New Framework for Analysis* (Boulder, CO: Lynne Rienner, 1997).

6. Cedric De Coning, "Regional Approaches to Peacebuilding," *United Nations University Centre for Policy Research*, 2015, http://i.unu.edu/media/cpr.unu.edu/attachment/1007/Regional-Approaches-to-Peacebuilding.pdf.

7. Van Langenhove, Selzer and Gartland, "Strengthening the Global Peacebuilding Architecture through Chapter VIII."

8. Katherine Konrad, "Appendix III: UN and Regional Arrangements since 1990: Doctrine, Developments, Current Thinking," in *Regional Organizations and Peacemaking, Challengers to the UN?* eds., Peter Wallensteen and Anders Bjurner (London: Routledge, 2015).

9. Peter Wallensteen and Anders Bjurner, eds., "The Challenge of Regional Organizations: An Introduction," in *Regional Organizations and Peacemaking, Challengers to the UN?* (London: Routledge, 2015).

10. Nathan, "The Peacemaking Effectiveness of Regional Organisations."

11. Peter Wallensteen, "International Conflict Resolution, UN and Regional Organizations: The Balance Sheet," in *Regional Organizations and Peacemaking,*

Challengers to the UN? eds., Peter Wallensteen and Anders Bjurner (London: Routledge, 2015).

12. De Coning, "Regional Approaches to Peacebuilding."

13. Ibid.

14. Ban Ki-moon, "Preventive Diplomacy: Delivering Results," Report of the Secretary-General (New York: United Nations, 2011), http://www.un.org/wcm/webdav/site/undpa/shared/undpa/pdf/SG%20Report%20on%20Preventive%20Diplomacy.pdf.

15. United Nations General Assembly, 65th session, Resolution 283, "Strengthening the Role of Mediation in the Peaceful Settlement of Disputes, Conflict Prevention and Resolution," June 22, 2011, http://www.un.org/en/ga/search/view_doc.asp?symbol=A/RES/65/283.

16. Catherine Barnes, "Agents for Change: Civil Society Roles in Preventing War and Building Peace," *Global Partnership for the Prevention of Armed Conflict*, 2006, http://www.operationspaix.net/DATA/DOCUMENT/5509~v~Agents_for_Change__Civil_Society_Roles_in_Preventing_War___Building_Peace.pdf, 28.

17. Catherine Barnes, "Agents for Change: Civil Society Roles in Preventing War and Building Peace."

18. Sarah Smiles Persinger, "Regional Organizations and Peacebuilding: The Role of Civil Society," *Kroc Institute for International Peace Studies Policy Brief*, October 2014, http://www.gppac.net/documents/130492842/131146243/Regional+Organizations+and+Peacebuilding+The+Role+of+Civil+Society+(1).pdf/9f716c8f-267c-4533-ae7d-6dd3a9a0f4e8.

19. Ibid., 3.

20. Van Langenhove, *Multilateralism 2.0.*, EU-GRASP Working Papers No. 21 (Bruges: UNU-CRIS, 2010).

21. Mary Kaldor, *New and Old Wars: Organised Violence in a Global Era*, 3rd edn. (Cambridge: Polity Press, 2012).

22. Nina Græger and Alexandra Novosseloff, "The Role of the OSCE and the EU," in *The United Nations and Regional Security: Europe and Beyond*, eds., Michael C. Pugh and W.P.S. Sidhu (Boulder: Lynne Rienner, 2003).

23. Rodrigo Tavarez, *Regional Security: The Capacity of International Organizations* (New York: Routledge, 2010).

24. Ibid.

25. Bertrand G. Ramcharan, *Preventive Diplomacy at the UN* (Bloomington: Indiana University Press, 2008).

26. Van Langenhove, Selzer, and Gartland, "Strengthening the Global Peacebuilding Architecture through Chapter VIII."

27. Ramcharan, *Preventive Diplomacy at the UN*.

28. Van Langenhove, "Chapter VIII of the UN Charter: What It Is and Why It Matters," published online by the United Nations University, August 26, 2014, http://unu.edu/publications/articles/chapter-viii-of-the-un-charter-what-it-is-and-why-it-matters.html.

29. The first conference took place in Madrid in November 2011 and was jointly organized by GPPAC and OAS. The conference report is available at https://www.peaceportal.org/c/document_library/

get_file?uuid=304651c1-23b5-415e-a49c-a16ba133ad29&groupId=125878116. The second conference was hosted by the OSCE in Vienna in April 2015. It was organized jointly between GPPAC, International IDEA and UNU-CRIS. More information about this event is available at http://www.gppac.net/news/-/asset_publisher/fHv91Y-cOz0CI/content/conference-on-strengthening-peace-and-security-cooperation-to-wards-democracy-and-development/.Documents from these conferences are available at http://www.idea.int/democracydialog/international-conference-on-strengthening-peace-and-security-cooperation.cfm.

30. An example of this is a meeting organized in Beirut with the League of Arab States to discuss collaboration with civil society in the aftermath of the Arab uprisings. For more on this meeting, refer to the "Conference Report," found at http://www.partners4peace.com/documents/125878116/0/MENA+Conference+Report+-+Final+(1).pdf.

31. Camila Campisi and Laura Ribeiro Rodrigues Pereira, *Filling the Gap: How Civil Society Engagement Can Help the UN's Peacebuilding Architecture Meet its Purpose* (The Hague: Global Partnership for the Prevention of Armed Conflict, 2015). http://www.peaceportal.org/documents/130492842/131164610/Filling+the+Gap.pdf/ebc53edd-5265-4b9a-806f-bd9d9786dd63.

32. Thania Paffenholz, "Can Inclusive Peace Processes Work? New Evidence from a Multi-Year Research Project," *University of Geneva Graduate Institute of International and Development Studies' Centre on Conflict, Development, and Peacebuilding Policy Brief*, April 2015, http://graduateinstitute.ch/files/live/sites/iheid/files/sites/ccdp/shared/Docs/Publications/Can%20Inclusive%20Peace%20Processes%20Work.pdf.

33. Ibid.

34. Erica Chenoweth and Maria Stephan, *Why Civil Resistance Works: The Strategic Logic of Nonviolent Conflict* (New York: Columbia University Press, 2011).

35. Campisi and Ribeiro Rodrigues Pereira, *Filling the Gap*.

36. Paffenholz, "Can Inclusive Peace Processes Work?"

37. *Constructive Engagement—Building a People-Oriented Community* (Jakarta: ASEAN Secretariat, 2010), https://www.peaceportal.org/documents/130225323/130275120/ConstructiveEngagement-Building+a+People-Oriented+Community.pdf.

38. Campisi and Ribeiro Rodrigues Pereira, *Filling the Gap*.

39. Paffenholz, "Can Inclusive Peace Processes Work?"

40. Jan Klabbers, "Two Concepts of International Organization," *International Organizations Law Review* 2, no. 2 (2005): 282.

41. Van Langenhove, *Multilateralism 2.0*.

Chapter 6

The Role of WANEP in Crafting Peace and Security Architecture in West Africa

Emmanuel Bombande

This chapter examines the West Africa Network for Peacebuilding (WANEP) and its relationships and partnerships with governments in the region to promote peace and security. The chapter shows how WANEP helped political leaders move away from misconceptions of adversarial relationships between civil society and government in the immediate postindependence years. It traces the early development of WANEP and the parallel evolution of a peace and security architecture in ECOWAS and in the AU. The chapter focuses on the WANEP program with ECOWAS for early warning to prevent violent conflicts in West Africa, thus bringing to the fore the unique expertise and strategic roles available to CSOs. The discussion underscores the complementary roles of civil society with governments, particularly in peacebuilding, conflict prevention, and promotion of human security. The WANEP-ECOWAS partnership in conflict prevention is offered as a good example of cooperation between CSOs, regional organizations, and the UN to achieve peace and security.

BACKGROUND ON CIVIL SOCIETY AND ARMED CONFLICT IN WEST AFRICA

The predominance of autonomous groups, traditional institutions, chiefdoms, and informal structures of society in West Africa predated the colonial era and swayed heavily on the organization of social relations.[1] These groups provided access to community mobilization for various initiatives and influenced cultural values and religious beliefs. These social organizations were often shaped by the political and social context of people in West Africa coexisting in kingdoms and states that were interdependent of one another, although over time these groups became better organized and represented various competing interest groups in the building of new African states.[2]

The first unique experiences in the narrative of civil society were in relation to colonial exploitation and the predation of natural resources, and internal feuding within society over access to resources and economic, political, social, and development rights. Some of the movements growing out of these struggles transformed into political parties and led the struggle for independence. The Aborigines Rights Protection Society (ARPS) was formed in the Gold Coast. It drew on the support of traditional chiefs and people in society with the specific purpose of opposing the Crown Lands Ordinance of 1896 and to act as guardians of Fanti customary rights and institutions.[3] Inspired by ARPS, the West African National Congress was established in March 1922 through the inspiration of Joseph Casely-Hayford. It had a social vision of pan-African nationalism and was the first interterritorial political movement to emerge in British West Africa.[4] It drew its support from the creole societies of the 19th century in West African cities.[5] These broad mass movements and civil society associations were the hinges on which political parties were founded. Such was the case for the Convention People's Party founded by Dr. Kwame Nkrumah, which led Ghana to independence on 6 March, 1957.[6]

Although societal development in West Africa anchored around civil society groups, their roles initially were wrongly perceived as controversial. West African states evolved from colonial domination and exploitation into emerging states with deep internal divisions, social exclusion, and state fragility. Significant changes resulted, however, from the contributions and roles of civil society in the postindependence period. In the independent new nations, the state became the center of contested political power around which intense antagonism reframed social relations.[7] CSOs were caught in between the tensions of these new social relations and the dynamics of political hegemony. Rather than embrace independent civil society organizations, national governments viewed them with suspicion. Statebuilding was misunderstood as only the function of the central government, a concept alien to traditional society that had coexisted interdependently while embracing diversity. In many West African countries statebuilding began with structural injustices and deep social fissures that sowed the seeds of social, economic, and political exclusion across society. Political power was concentrated in a hierarchy of a few political elites who controlled and distributed state resources only for a privileged few.

This narrative defined the relationships between early organized CSOs and governments. Civil society groups inspired the liberation struggles but became subjected to state control, resulting in antagonistic relationships. Some governments perceived CSOs as conduits for donor policy influences. They saw them as detractors with the potential of organizing people outside state structures. This misapprehension worsened when, in some instances, new state leaders took the mantle of leadership and rather than working toward economic and political liberation became oppressive of their own people. Against this background, the postindependence years witnessed unhealthy confrontation between some governments and CSOs. In the absence of credible political parties offering policy alternatives, CSOs stood up and demanded good governance, respect for human rights, and nonviolence and transparency in the management of the affairs of the state.

A critical challenge confronting new nation states in the immediate postindependence era was how to manage the enormous diversity of ethnic, religious, geographic, and various interest groups. The competition for political power was not grounded in political tolerance and good democratic practice. This sowed discord and generated social fissures along ethnic, geographic, and religious lines. Policies by some national governments, rather than mobilizing citizens for the common social project of development, were often skewed along ethnic lines and interests. This fueled suspicion, rivalry, discontent, mistrust, and enmity among various ethnic groups. In extreme cases these resulted in ethnic conflict and civil war.

The types of threats confronting the region were pervasive, creating an environment of insecurity with a high potential for widespread destabilization and risk of state failure in a number of countries. The politicization of ethnic differences heightened the perceived or real threat of ethnic conflict in Mali, Liberia, Sierra Leone, Guinea, Côte d'Ivoire, and Nigeria. The refusal by some governments to allow peaceful changes in leadership through free and fair elections compounded by poorly managed transitions inherent with power struggles denied some countries a sense of national identity.

In many countries in the region, there was a deep sense of frustration around the absence of social justice. Cronyism and nepotism rather than good credentials and competence determined who had public service employment. A burgeoning youth population felt excluded from weak democratic systems in which latent issues of conflict could not find expression. This led to deepened suspicions, increased negative rumors, and mutual mistrust across nations. These youths were vulnerable and many of them were easily recruited into armed insurgency groups.

Pervasive social discontent, economic inequalities, and endemic corruption created the conditions for the wars of the region. The emerging conflicts were fueled by the exploitation of natural resources and arms trafficking. These factors were exacerbated by the inability of states afflicted by these wars to stop the violence. This was particularly the case in the Mano Union region comprised of Guinea, Liberia, and Sierra Leone. The wars impoverished the entire region, and by 2004 the United Nations Human Development Report (UNHDR) categorized eleven of the fifteen countries in West Africa as part of the least developed nations in the world.[8] Research by the Sahel and West Africa Club showed concentric cycles of economic deprivation moving incrementally inward from the coastal belt to the forest regions, on to the savanna belt, the Sahel, and the Sahara. Compounding these social and economic issues were problems associated with drug trafficking, money laundering, and the proliferation of small arms and light weapons.

The Liberian civil war began in December 1989 and spread across the borders sustaining another war in Sierra Leone. These wars were unprecedented. Armed groups, particularly the Revolutionary United Front (RUF), abducted children and forced them to fight and witness war and its atrocities.[9] In Liberia, the war began in 1989 and raged in two phases for fourteen years and only ended with the Accra Comprehensive Peace Agreement in August 2003. This prompted the resignation of Charles Taylor, who was regarded as the architect of West Africa's civil wars. A two-year interim government led by Gyude Bryant focused on recovery and preparations for elections.

In Sierra Leone, as in Liberia, the colonial legacy had created two-class systems with weak bureaucracies, which sowed the seeds for popular discontent. In the immediate postindependence years, mismanagement exacerbated dysfunctional state institutions and encumbered economic growth. As a consequence, the young population both in cities and rural areas became ever more marginalized without access to proper education and employment. A grisly civil war persisted for eleven years from 1990 to 2001. On 7 July, 1999, President Ahmad Tejan Kabbah signed the Lomé peace accord in the Togolese capital Lomé, with Foday Sankoh, the leader of the RUF. The Lomé accord ended the war, but the country remained gripped in insecurity and recurring upsurges in violence. Guinea-Bissau also experienced military disruptions and political instability in 1997–1998 and 2004–2005.

In Côte d'Ivoire, an attempted military coup d'état escalated into civil war, dividing the country between north and south from 2002 to 2006. Ten peace agreements were signed during this period. After elections were postponed six times and finally held in November 2010, the political crisis continued. Even with the assertive roles and leadership of ECOWAS, strongly supported by the UN, sporadic violence ensued. The crisis only ended when the UN, upon request from ECOWAS, endorsed a military operation by French forces that captured and arrested President Gbagbo and his wife Simone Gbagbo on 11 April, 2011. As of this writing President Gbagbo is awaiting trial at the International Criminal Court in The Hague.[10]

A decade and a half after the end of the civil wars in Liberia and Sierra Leone, a repeat of this cycle is apparent in the Boko Haram insurgency and increasing violent extremism ravaging the northeastern federal states of Nigeria and spreading into Niger, Chad, and Cameroon. Boko Haram is a violent extremist insurgency group founded by Mohammed Yusuf in northeastern Nigeria and now led by Abubakar Shekau. Its literal meaning is "Western education is forbidden." Its official name is Jama'atu Ahlis Sunna. The group announced on 8 March, 2015, that it had pledged allegiance to the Islamic State of Iraq and Syria (ISIS). Thousands of young people from Cameroon are now fighting alongside Boko Haram. These are young people who lack access to school and employment.[11] This conflict illustrates the porosity of West Africa's borders and how plausible it is for insecurity to spread across borders into neighboring countries that lack the capacity to stop such incursions.

THE EMERGENCE OF THE WEST AFRICA NETWORK FOR PEACEBUILDING (WANEP)

This context of conflict and insecurity in the West Africa region provided the impulse for the establishment of WANEP. The initial inspiration for the founding of the network emerged from discussions in the 1990s of university students from the region attending the Center for Justice and Peacebuilding (CJP) at Eastern Mennonite University. The Winston Foundation for World Peace provided an initial grant for the first phase of exploring the establishment of a regional peacebuilding network. The foundation initially focused on nuclear disarmament initiatives, but in the 1990s it diversified to support start-ups and new initiatives in peacebuilding. The research grant has provided support for the Nairobi Peace Initiative to engage in research for long-term peacebuilding efforts in West Africa.

At the time there was no coordinated or collective response to the emergence of violent conflicts in the region. There was no full-time and dedicated credible institution in West Africa with requisite knowledge and expertise in peacebuilding and conflict prevention. The impetus for the first peacebuilding initiatives in the region came from CSOs outside the region. The London-based organization International Alert had engaged in peacebuilding training activities during the civil unrest in Liberia and Sierra Leone but these activities were short term and project based. They did not have national or regional ownership and did not have long-term prospects for institutional presence and sustainability.[12] The Centre for Conflict Resolution in Cape Town was already well established and actively involved in analysis, training, and capacity building in the Southern Africa region but without reach across the continent.[13] ACCORD, based in Durban, South Africa, was also in existence with the primary objective of influencing political developments in Africa by bringing conflict resolution, dialogue, and institutional development to the forefront as alternatives to armed violence and protracted conflict.[14] In the horn of East Africa, the Nairobi Peace Initiative-Africa (NPI-Africa) had been established in 1984. As a continental peace resource organization, NPI-Africa had engaged in a broad range of peacebuilding and conflict transformation initiatives in Africa, including mediation and dialogue facilitation, training and capacity building, healing and reconciliation.[15] African peacebuilding organizations thus existed in various parts of the continent, but the region that was most in need of peacebuilding efforts and where local capacities were weakest was West Africa.

In response to this need, a nascent community of peacebuilding practitioners and former students began to conceptualize the creation of a regional CSO. This initiative emerged from the cross-fertilization of ideas, learning, and knowledge sharing on the best approaches to peacebuilding and the prevention of conflict. This process was greatly influenced by the groundbreaking work on strategic peacebuilding by John Paul Lederach, who offered key operating principles for guiding peacebuilding practice.[16] The building of infrastructures for peace is a critical component of these principles. Sustaining peacebuilding in strategic ways requires an infrastructure that can provide institutional grounding, organizational capacity, and sustainability for the long term.[17]

After consultations in seven West African countries, with the support of the CJP at Eastern Mennonite University and NPI-Africa, a regional conference in Accra gathered in 1998 to establish WANEP. The regional secretariat of the new organization was created in Accra, while national coordinators and staff were established in seven states originally and soon afterward in all fifteen countries of the region. The thinking in the establishment of WANEP was that it would serve as an institutional base for strategic approaches to peacebuilding in West Africa. The pool of peacebuilding expertise available in the hub at the regional secretariat would provide the human resource support to catalyze and coordinate collective efforts both institutionally and in knowledge content both at national and regional levels. WANEP sought to support the implementation of programs at national levels. In each country a national secretariat took the lead in the implementation of peacebuilding activities, with support and backstopping from the regional secretariat. This was the concept of the hub and spider web.

The theory of change at that time was that conflict transformation for long-term peace and stability would happen simultaneously at national and regional levels with an institutional scope and expertise at both levels. The concept of a network for collaborative approaches to peacebuilding recognized first and foremost that peacebuilding had to be a locally owned effort but aided with external support. Second, it required attention to the particular West African context of porous borders where people across national boundaries are culturally and socially interconnected to one another but have been divided and set apart by the decisions of colonial authorities. The challenge is to increase the resilience and capacities of vulnerable people and countries through collective responses to security threats throughout the West Africa region.

The exigencies of trying to stem the raging wars within the region became the immediate priority. The first national network was established in Sierra Leone. The initial activities of the network involved the convening of capacity-building workshops and the facilitation of twelve national-level dialogues among different stakeholder groups. The objective of the dialogue sessions was to help each stakeholder group determine its own set of peacebuilding activities and to create spaces for healing and reconciliation.

These dialogues revealed the deep resentments and underlying issues of mistrust that propelled armed conflict. In one workshop in the Sierra Leonean northern town of Kenema, a young schoolteacher who had joined and fought with the RUF recounted his personal story. He had graduated as a schoolteacher from Training College, married, and had a child. He worked hard at teaching, but his salary never came at the end of the month. In order to take care of his family, he traveled to the capital Freetown every month to pursue and collect his salary. In that process, the monies he spent on transportation and paying off bribes in Freetown trimmed off 60 percent of his hard-earned salary. One day, Foday Sankoh, the leader of the RUF, came to the school where he was teaching and invited them to join the war effort with the promise that Sierra Leone would be liberated from chronic corruption and the burden of bad leadership. The young schoolteacher explained with a determined voice how he did not hesitate to join Foday Sankoh and the RUF. He later regretted that he became part of an armed group that inflicted cruelty and atrocities on the very people they were supposedly seeking to liberate.

Out of the stakeholder sessions in Sierra Leone emerged the idea of a specialized program for women leaders, which became the Women in Peacebuilding Network (WIPNET). There were very few women peacebuilding practitioners in the region at the time. Yet women constituted the majority of the victims of these wars. The absence of women facilitators in stakeholder dialogues posed unique challenges. It was difficult for women who were abducted and raped to talk openly about such personal ordeals in inappropriate gender environments. These concrete challenges on the ground informed the design of WANEP programs, leading in this case to the creation of a unique space for women peacebuilders in West Africa. Lisa Schirch, a professor of peacebuilding at Eastern Mennonite University, spent time with WANEP as a Fulbright scholar and contributed immensely to the design of a resource manual on women in peacebuilding. WIPNET emerged as an active and vibrant program that helped to train women with specialized skill sets and capacities for peacebuilding practice. Nobel Peace Prize laureate Leymah Gbowee was the first WANEP coordinator of WIPNET in Liberia.[18]

THE EVOLUTION OF ECOWAS

As WANEP emerged within civil society in response to regional armed conflict, the states of the region working through ECOWAS followed a similar trajectory in creating new regional mechanisms for addressing peace and security. Spurred on by the need to respond to the multiple armed conflicts in the region, West African leaders recognized the inadequacy of their existing security policies and structures and began to develop a new legal and policy framework. This was a significant change for the organization. The preoccupation of political leaders in the region in the initial postindependence years had been achieving stability and economic growth. ECOWAS was founded in 1975 among the sixteen countries of West Africa with the goal of forging integration and economic development. Mauritania was among the founding states but later withdrew from the organization. At the time of its establishment, ECOWAS did not give much attention to issues of peace and security in the region. This changed as instability and armed conflict spread in the region.

When Liberia imploded into civil war it became obvious that the peace and security of the region were threatened by intrastate conflict. Leaders in the region understood the urgency of addressing conflict prevention in the same way as they had prioritized economic development and integration. This required a revision of the treaty establishing ECOWAS. The revised treaty of 1993 committed the organization to supporting good democratic practices and, for the first time, specifically included reference to peace and security. Article 58 of the revised treaty specified that security would be an objective of the regional organization. In pursuit of that objective, the article empowered ECOWAS to "establish a regional peace and security observation system and peacekeeping forces where appropriate."[19]

A further significant shift for ECOWAS came in the 1999 protocol on mechanisms for conflict prevention, management, resolution, peacekeeping, and security. This protocol sought to implement Article 58 of the revised treaty and provided a framework for dealing with the immediate and proximate causes of armed conflict. It outlined the types of sanctions that could be applied on member states for violating the provisions of the protocol. It also created a mechanism for preserving peace through a regional early warning system. The result was the West Africa Early Warning Response Network (ECOWAS), designed for conflict prevention.[20] This ECOWAS mechanism was built and structured on the Warning and Response Network (WARN) program previously designed by WANEP. Thus began a distinct partnership between ECOWAS and WANEP in which ECOWARN evolved as a hybrid program of the two groups.

These developments within ECOWAS coincided with the transition of the OAU into the AU. This organizational change brought with it new principles, norms, and protocols for defining the role of the AU in issues of peace and security on the African continent. The Constitutive Act establishing the AU in 2000 recognized that "the scourge of conflicts in Africa constitutes a major impediment to the socio-economic development of the continent." It committed member states to promote peace, security, and stability as a prerequisite for the implementation of development and integration goals.[21]

The most significant departure of the AU from its predecessor was the inclusion of Article 4(h) in the Constitutive Act, which recognizes the right of the AU to "intervene in a Member State pursuant to a decision of the Assembly in respect of grave circumstances, mainly war, genocide and crimes against humanity."[22] Presently the AU is the only regional organization that unequivocally recognizes the right to intervene in a member state on the stated grounds. The inclusion of this principle into the Constitutive Act was reflective of the resolve by member states never again to be paralyzed and held back in stopping violent conflicts on the premise of noninterference in the face of gross atrocities such as the 1994 genocide in Rwanda.

To help implement these new commitments, the AU created the Africa Peace and Security Council with authority to make political decisions on these matters. It also created a new mediation and advisory capacity in the Panel of the Wise.[23] Other new mechanisms included a Continental Early Warning System (CEWS), the Peace Support Operations unit, the African Standby Force, and the Military Staff Committee, along with a special fund. This was a comprehensive set of tools for the prevention, management, and resolution of conflict on the continent.[24] A conference of African leaders in Durban, South Africa, in 2002 adopted a declaration urging each member state of the AU to establish its own national infrastructure for peace to build state capacity in the mediation of conflicts.[25] The AU's CEWS was implemented in West Africa through the ECOWARN program involving WANEP and ECOWAS. The implementation of the broader AU initiative thus depended on effective institutions for early warning at the regional level.

THE WANEP-ECOWAS PARTNERSHIP FOR EARLY WARNING

As ECOWAS created its early warning observation system it sought direct cooperation and assistance from civil society organizations and came to rely on the involvement and expertise of WANEP. This assistance consisted of data collection and analysis and the preparation of reports for use by ECOWAS and AU officials. In the past ECOWAS showed no interest in such cooperation, but as the organization broadened its policy mandate to peacebuilding, it began to seek civil society expertise and participation. In 1999 ECOWAS commissioned WANEP to conduct an assessment of regional

conflict prevention mechanisms and capacity. In 2000 WANEP conceptualized and designed the requirements for operationalizing the WARN system.
The system emerged as a platform for joint civil society and ECOWAS participation in peacebuilding activities. It became a means of involving community groups and civil society experts across the region in the monitoring
of indicators for the prevention of armed violence.[26]

The formal partnership on early warning between WANEP and ECOWAS
began in February 2004, based on a common approach to peace and security
that resonated well with the WANEP vision of promoting human security.
The resulting partnership was designated as ECOWARN, following the
recommendation of WANEP. The prefix of "ECO" to the WARN system
designed by WANEP was significant. It reflected underlying African cultural
traditions about the significance and meaning of names. It embodied a unique
symbolism and meaning of a civil society organization partnering with an
intergovernmental regional organization. The formal partnership agreement
specified that ECOWAS was the owner of the Early Warning System, with
the copyright belonging to both parties, and WANEP was given the title and
role of "implementing partner."[27]

The ECOWARN system operates as a partnership between ECOWAS and
a range of civil society actors. Data on incidents and situations is collected
by WANEP and other sources and input into the system. Reports are collected of incidents and situations that could escalate into armed conflict. The
system tracks sixty-six indicators in eleven thematic areas. Among the most
important predictors of armed conflict are indicators related to crime, corruption, and safety; governance, political action, and the law; and security and
the availability of arms. The data for incident and situation reports is collected
from open sources such as credible newspaper accounts, radio and television
broadcasts, and information provided from communities by trained monitors.
WANEP's Peace Monitoring Centre at the regional secretariat in Accra veri-
fies the reports from community monitors through follow-up telephone calls
and sourcing from other people located in the communities where the data is
collected.[28]

An online database reporting system captures reports submitted regularly
from the field by both WANEP's networks of monitors and ECOWAS'
member state monitors. The 15 member states of ECOWAS are clustered
into four zones, each of which maintains an interface with WANEP. The
civil society analysts working with WANEP are located in the offices of the
four ECOWAS zones and the WANEP central liaison office is colocated with
the offices of the ECOWAS Commission in Abuja. There, analysts of the
ECOWAS Early Warning Directorate and WANEP's Peace Monitoring Centre examine the country reports together and develop assessments, alerts, and
recommendations for action if needed. These state and civil society analysts

are also responsible for collating and analyzing early warning reports from all four zones for onward transmission, in digestible form, to the president of the ECOWAS Commission.[29] In addition to the collection, analysis, and input of data into the ECOWARN database, WANEP writes policy briefs on all major conflict issues, organizes briefing sessions for ECOWAS personal, and provides capacity-building support in programs related to peace and security. WANEP and ECOWAS also organize quarterly review meetings in which the challenges and opportunities of the previous quarter are assessed for the purpose of improving the quality of work.

A recent example of how the system works is the report by WANEP-Nigeria of an incident of armed attack in July 2015 in which eighteen people were killed and numerous civilians injured. Islamist insurgents belonging to Boko Haram launched a renewed attack on a small community in Borno State near the border with Adamawa State.[30] The incident indicated the lack of state capacity for protecting civilians. Another incident was reported by WANEP-Ghana on the same date of a 36-year-old man wielding a gun in a church where the president of Ghana and other prominent leaders often attend worship service. This second example identified a local threat of violence that could have national implications.[31]

In partnering with ECOWAS, WANEP also conducts strategic risk and opportunity assessments. A study was conducted of Guinea to explain why a country surrounded by neighboring states at war (Liberia, Sierra Leone, Côte d'Ivoire, Guinea-Bissau) managed to avoid violent conflict. The assessment identified key peace-generating factors. These include a deep sense of belonging to local communities, strong social ties through intermarriages, and the influence of religion in restraining violence. All provided strong social bridging linkages that have averted large-scale national violence. The ECOWARN system thus also includes assessments of factors that hold societies together and encourage peace.[32] Implicit in these assessments is a recognition of community-based efforts for mediation, women's empowerment, and peacebuilding that cumulatively offset threats of armed conflict.

At times, indicators of possible armed violence appear informally in unexpected ways. WANEP monitors learned, for example, that market behavior can be a sign of escalating conflict. Market women in Liberia recounted how they often observed during the fifteen-year Liberian war that the escalation of violence was always preceded by armed youths of the main insurgent groups buying large quantities of sugar and cigarettes from the markets. The stockpiling of such commodities was often the precursor of armed attacks in towns and villages. The women understood that preparations for an escalation of violence, as indicated by the visible stockpiling of essential commodities by armed youth, affected the markets. Such monitoring of threats, informed by indigenous cultural knowledge of the milieu of the region, was a significant asset for civil society in assessing the risk of conflict. It helped to make WANEP the right choice for ECOWAS in creating an appropriate and effective early warning and response mechanism.

The partnership between WANEP and ECOWAS has worked well because each partner gains from the other what neither can provide on its own. WANEP has access to a wide range of community monitors who have crucial firsthand information on local developments that could lead to conflict, while ECOWAS has a mandate from states in the region to take action and use security forces when needed to prevent the escalation of violence. This successful model of a civil society organization working with a regional institution on early warning and response is unique and innovative, and perhaps a useful reference for civil society actors and multilateral institutions in other regions.

As ECOWARN developed it became evident that a regional early warning system would be deficient without functional early warning systems at national and local levels. WANEP took on this challenge with a pilot experiment in Nigeria where a National Early Warning System (NEWS) was designed and developed, capturing the contextual issues in each of the thirty-six states in six geopolitical zones. The quality and quantity of data collected in Nigeria demonstrated a vast improvement in real time reporting. It also provided additional support for the national focal point feeding the relevant information into the regional ECOWARN system. Following the pilot effort in Nigeria, WANEP started to deploy civil society NEWS in other countries in the region.[33]

The WANEP-Nigeria experience of the NEWS and the expansion of this model in some of the national networks provided a good foundation for a policy decision at the level of ECOWAS to devolve ECOWARN to national levels. A study on ECOWAS member states' early warning mechanisms focused on Ghana, Niger, and Nigeria affirmed the relevance of such an effort.[34] An HLM of member states of ECOWAS in Abidjan made the policy decision and affirmed in a declaration that all member states should establish National Early Warning Mechanisms (NEWMs).[35] WANEP has partnered with ECOWAS in building these early warning systems at the national level, seeking to embed the national early systems in national infrastructures for peace. Such a shift conforms with the new ECOWAS vision of moving from an ECOWAS of states to an ECOWAS of people. Within the peace and security context, this represents a paradigm shift from unilateral state-centric action to multistakeholder intervention with civil society participation in joint responses to conflict.

Thanks to its partnership with ECOWAS, WANEP grew into the largest peacebuilding organization in the region, with national networks in all the countries in the region. The growth of the organization brought legitimacy and influence. WANEP national networks were involved with state institutions in the promotion of peace and stability throughout West Africa. Membership in the organization increased as more and more NGOs approached WANEP for registration to be part of the network. This was positive, as most organizations in peacebuilding at national levels preferred the option of working with and complementing one another rather than duplicating efforts. WANEP's influence also grew across the African continent as the ECOWARN system was integrated with the AU's CEWS. Growing interest in ECOWARN led to the development of new partnerships and exchanges with organizations like La Francophonie and the IGAD in East Africa.

As WANEP staff gained expertise, the organization was overwhelmed with invitations to facilitate trainings in peacebuilding in various thematic areas at regional and national levels. Invitations also came in for meetings, conferences, and symposia at regional and international levels. The professionalism of the organization and its strategic partnership with ECOWAS made it a leading organization for peacebuilding. This institutional growth led to greater international interest in WANEP and new opportunities for additional peacebuilding partnerships. Finland, Sweden, and other donor states began to enter into partnerships with WANEP for collaborative conflict prevention and crisis management programs in West Africa.[36]

FROM EARLY WARNING TO EFFECTIVE RESPONSE

More than sixteen years after the signing of the 1999 protocol that paved the way for the implementation of ECOWARN, the economic potential of the West Africa region remains vastly undermined by threats of instability and violent conflict. West African waters in the Gulf of Guinea have replaced the waters off Somalia as the leading area of maritime piracy and insecurity.[37] The region remains unstable with deep-seated resentments entrenched in the fabric of societies as a result of social, economic, and political inequalities. New threats of violent extremism have increased the vulnerability of the region. The end of the Gadhafi regime and the violent implosion in Libya accelerated the proliferation of weapons and created a major new security threat in the region.[38]

The insurgency and rebellion that erupted in Mali in 2012 provide a good example of how unaddressed conflicts create militarization of society with a potential to generate violent extremism and hatred. This danger was anticipated in a September 2011 ECOWAS report.[39] Previous Tuareg rebellions in Mali in the postcolonial period took place in 1963, the 1990s, and 2006–2008. Each eruption of conflict had different drivers but the core issues have remained related.[40] The regional consequences of the crisis following the collapse of Libya allowed the now well-equipped and trained Tuareg rebels to overrun the northern half of Mali. Extremist jihadists exploited the security vacuum that was created, expanding southward and easily recruiting Malian youths, mostly the unemployed, some of them former combatants. Even with a well-resourced UN Mission in Mali and ongoing mediation efforts to resolve the underlying conflict between the insurgent groups and the government of Mali, the crisis persists and further vulnerability of the Sahel region to promote violent extremists remains perceptible.[41]

This crisis and other dangers in the region posed the challenge of creating structures for preventive response and finding ways to react and respond to crises before destruction has already occurred. The focus of the WANEP-ECOWAS partnership has turned to building stronger response systems and creating national infrastructures for peace. Effective early warning depends upon requisite institutional frameworks around which the prevention of violent conflicts within states becomes plausible. Assessments of ECOWARN all pointed to the need for putting the emphasis on response-generation capacities. The evidence was overwhelming that there was little to show for the system's ability to respond to incipient threats of conflict.

From the outset, the creation of an effective early warning system was understood to include the mitigation of conflicts. It is unrealistic to assume that early warning capacities are sufficient for conflict prevention, or that conflicts can be fully prevented from escalating. The literature on early warning and conflict prevention is ambivalent on this point.[42] Good early warning systems should not be preoccupied with prevention. How these systems facilitate the mitigation of crises that could escalate further is probably more important as a tangible goal of early warning systems.

It was often misunderstood that response initiatives were limited to the authority of the heads of state of ECOWAS. WANEP made the argument in its presentations at various meetings in the region and beyond that because the disconcerting number and nature of conflicts in West Africa were happening at intranational levels and manifested as intrastate conflicts, effective response capacities were needed at the substate level to tackle these conflicts in their nascent stages where they spread. Response capacities within society can help to prevent such conflicts from assuming national dimensions and becoming fault lines of conflicts that could implode at national levels.

In September 2013 ECOWAS issued a declaration on strengthening national, regional, and continental coordination toward building national peace infrastructures for conflict prevention.[43] This declaration took cognizance of the existing initiatives, structures, and institutions for early warning and conflict prevention at various levels of maturity, harmonization, and coordination in the region. It also enjoined member states to take the primary responsibility to establish, develop, and sustain national peace infrastructures.

The result was the creation of an ECOWAS Conflict Prevention Framework (ECPF) to provide a more comprehensive response to conflict that includes addressing root causes in the medium- to long-term while also creating more effective responses to immediate crises of violence.[44] The September declaration recognized the active roles and engagement of civil society in this process. This reinforced the emphasis on building conflict prevention efforts within states. If armed conflicts in West Africa are occurring within the state, the logical response is to develop response capacities within states. This increased the importance of building peacebuilding capacities to promote national cohesion through dialogue and mediation and sustained intercommunal and intrastate reconciliation efforts.

In the context of the Mali crisis ECOWAS officials acknowledged the weakness of preventive diplomatic efforts at the regional and state level. The lethargy of collective responses to threats within states spurred ECOWAS to become more responsive and proactive. WANEP sought to partner with ECOWAS in this effort to improve response capacities. WANEP's support for dialogue and mediation efforts in local communities and within ECOWAS' member states provided impetus for more effective response mechanisms. Examples from several cases of responding to crises of conflict illustrate the challenges and opportunities for improving the effectiveness of mitigating armed conflict.

BRIDGING SOCIAL DIVIDES IN CÔTE D'IVOIRE AND JOS PLATEAU OF NIGERIA

When civil war and sectarian violence gripped Côte d'Ivoire from 2002 to 2006, the WANEP structure in the country sought to build peace by applying in practice Lederach's theory of combining a vertical capacity from the bottom up with a horizontal capacity with scope and latitude to move across social barriers that divided communities and caused conflict.[45] In Côte d'Ivoire, intercommunal violent conflicts over land rights were often left unaddressed. During the civil war these became the fault lines of conflicts between cocoa plantation farmers among predominantly Muslim communities in the north and indigenous land owners in the south who are mainly Christian. These divides also permeated the military and political structures of the country leading to a war fought along the north–south divide. WANEP-Côte d'Ivoire used its access and entry points among the various communities to engage in peacebuilding and conflict transformation.

In the sprawling commercial city of Abidjan, sectarian violence was often exacerbated by the patterns of settlements. Neighborhoods such as Treichville had concentrations of Muslims in the majority while areas such as Plateau had majority Christian settlements. This reinforced the sectarian divide in which Muslim neighborhoods were predominantly from the north of the country while Ivoirians from the southern regions mainly populated Christian areas. WANEP-Côte-d'Ivoire engaged in shuttle preventive initiatives through dialogue in which a horizontal capacity to move across these settlements was achieved through video recorded peace and goodwill messages. WANEP carried bridge-building messages from community leaders in Muslim settlements into Christian settlements where the videos were viewed around organized community town hall meetings followed by discussions on the messages articulated. Similarly, in Christian settlements, such as in Plateau area, they recorded messages from Christian leaders and played back the videos in town hall meetings in Muslim communities. These activities had the immediate and direct impact of dispelling the unsubstantiated rumors that demonized Muslims or Christians along the sectarian lines of politics, religion, and geographical region. More importantly, the messages served to counter ethnocentric politics that had heightened during the civil war. They contributed to reducing the scale of the violence.

A similar approach was employed in Nigeria in 2011. The Jos Plateau State of Nigeria is famous for its hospitality industry, but in recent years it has been gripped by a vicious cycle of violent conflicts. The conflict involves seven ethnic communities in the state including the Afizere, Anaguta, Berom, Hausa, Fulani, Igbo, and Yoruba. Critical issues revolve around contestation over land ownership, land tenure systems, the distinction between indigenous communities as against settler communities, perceptions about ethnic power relations at the state level, and a weak justice system.

Because of the political dynamics of state sovereignty and intervention in such local conflicts, ECOWAS was unable to convene the communities in Jos for dialogue. As a CSO, WANEP faced no such constraints and was able to lead in a process designed to facilitate dialogue, with behind-the-scenes support and observer status from ECOWAS. The process began with quiet consultations of different groups and leaders including chiefs and traditional and religious leaders. With endorsements from these leaders, a consultative meeting was organized by WANEP in Abuja in February 2011 at which key leaders from the different ethnic groups agreed to engage in facilitated dialogue. The consultative meeting sought to determine how many representatives of the seven ethnic groups should participate and what should be the composition of different stakeholders from each group. WANEP was able to lead a design process that included significant numbers of women in each delegation.

With these local communities committed to dialogue, WANEP leveraged its national network to engage in further consultations, including with a prominent former head of state, General Yakubu Gowon, who was asked to play a leading role in the dialogue. The Centre for Peace Advancement in Nigeria (CEPAN) in Jos, a lead member of WANEP-Nigeria, took on the role of ensuring efficient logistics arrangements for the dialogue sessions. WANEP further sought partnership with the Institute for Peace and Conflict Resolution (IPCR) in Nigeria, a state agency. Together these groups convened the main dialogue in Jos in March 2011. ECOWAS sent a representative but only in the capacity of observer. The state security agencies and state government were also represented.

This was the first time the seven communities in conflict on the Jos Plateau were able to sit in the same room and encounter one another with agreed ground rules in an honest and frank conversation. With diligent facilitation led by WANEP, the dialogue sessions were intense, frank, and introspective.[46] They allowed the participants to envision a future of interethnic peaceful coexistence in the Plateau State. All the representatives of the seven groups, fifty in total, agreed on a set of forward-looking recommendations with the commitment to work together for peace. The recommendations were clustered in six areas including the role of federal and state government, security and humanitarian needs, religion, peacebuilding and reconciliation, human rights and the media, and justice and reparations. They also agreed to form an interethnic working committee to pursue their collective efforts to sustain dialogue.

The outcomes of the Jos dialogue had an immediate impact in creating an enabling political environment for peaceful elections in the state during the 2011 general elections. While some of the contentious issues remained unaddressed, the initiative led by WANEP with indirect support from ECOWAS created a sense of ownership in the dialogue process that continues to inform the search for peace on the Plateau State. The process has been slow due largely to the absence of political will to legislate political reforms at the state level, but the scale of internecine violence in the local area has largely abated as community members are able to talk with one another and initiate preventive measures.

COORDINATING RESPONSES IN BURKINA FASO

The recent case of the crisis in Burkina Faso illustrates how early warning of danger combined with effective response can contain levels of violence. As instability spread in the region after 2011, agitation and political resistance increased in Burkina Faso. The focus was a planned revision to the constitution that would have allowed President Blaise Compaore to stand again for presidential elections after two decades in office. By January 2014, street protests in Burkina Faso signaled a growing crisis. WANEP became preoccupied with addressing the situation. Data from its field monitors and regular analyses of political developments flowed into the WANEP Peace Monitoring Centre at its regional office in Accra and into the Situation Room at the ECOWAS Commission in Abuja. This placed Burkina Faso on the radar screen as a country of potential emerging crisis. In March 2014, WANEP issued a policy brief providing an analysis of the political challenges and trends that could lead to violence.[47] The analysis noted the regional implications at a time of spreading violent extremism in the Sahel region. It offered options for collaborative engagements of civil society, ECOWAS, the international community, and the government of Burkina Faso.

In April 2014, ECOWAS and the United Nations Office for West Africa (UNOWA) conducted a joint mission to Burkina Faso to meet with the ruling and main opposition political parties as well as with civil society representatives. These meetings confirmed WANEP's warning of potential violence and political instability in Burkina Faso. The joint mission of ECOWAS and the UN was significant at two levels. It demonstrated how the UN could leverage and complement the leadership of the regional organization to confront crisis at an early stage before it escalated into violent destruction. It also showed how ECOWAS could leverage the involvement of the UN for a mission of preventive diplomacy. A concern was whether the president of the ECOWAS Commission, Kadré Désiré Ouédraogo, a former prime minister of Burkina Faso under President Compaore, could lead a mission that might have outcomes contrary to the interests of the president. As it turned out, Ouédraogo navigated the crisis skillfully and engaged in effective preventive efforts, supporting the efforts of ECOWAS, WANEP, and others to contribute to a peaceful political transition in his home country.[48]

President Compaore and his government ignored the recommendations of the initial intervention efforts and proceeded to amend the constitution, creating a volatile political environment ripe for explosion. These events led to the Burkinabè uprising in late October 2014 as demonstrations and riots spread to multiple cities. Political uncertainty and the risk of violence increased as the military dissolved parliament, President Compaore resigned and left the country, and Lieutenant Colonel Isaac Yacouba Zida installed himself as transitional leader. The risk for violence had been anticipated, due to consistent monitoring and engagement for prevention, and this time mitigation interventions were much faster, more efficient, and better coordinated.[49]

A second joint mission was quickly organized, now including the AU in addition to ECOWAS and the UN, with continued engagement with civil society, to work with the political parties and the military to mitigate violence.[50] Significant pressure was applied to prevent the military from taking over political power. The cumulative effect of the synergy of ECOWAS, the UN, and the AU prevailed, leading to an interim arrangement in which a transitional president was accepted by consensus and a transitional government was put in place for a period of one year that would end with a political transition following elections in October 2015. While some amount of destruction was reported and about twelve people were killed, the violence was contained and prevented from spiraling beyond control.

In yet another attempt to disrupt the transitional process, soldiers of the presidential guard and loyalists of former president Blaise Compaore staged another coup in September 2015. Because of the resolve of civil society groups and the momentum of concerted political will that had built up with ECOWAS leadership and AU and UN support, the coup could not be sustained. It was reversed and the transitional process reinvigorated, while the October elections were rescheduled for November. With regional and international support, the balloting was successful as Burkina Faso conducted the best democratic elections since its independence. The transitional period effectively ended with the investiture of the new president Roch Marc Christian Kabore on 29 December, 2015.[51]

These complementary early response efforts in Burkina Faso confirmed the WANEP argument that collaborative efforts between the UN and regional organizations, with support from civil society, could be effective in conflict prevention. The decisive and coordinated response in Burkina Faso was in sharp contrast to the uncertain and disjointed intervention in the Mali crisis. It showed the need for cooperative efforts to deal effectively with crisis, and also the need for civil society engagement. Without attributing the subsequent success solely to civil society, it is certainly the case that unlike in other crises within the region, Burkina Faso provided a good example of proactive preventive diplomacy through effective collaboration.

CONCLUSION

Ten years ago the world's largest gathering of heads of state at the 2005 World Summit endorsed the Responsibility to Protect principle, committing the world to the protection of civilian populations and the prevention of atrocities and crimes against humanity. The WANEP-ECOWAS partnership is a model for implementing these high ideals in practice on the ground in West Africa. This chapter has mapped the evolution of this partnership and its expansion of scope and operation. WANEP and ECOWAS have worked together to harness and coordinate civil society expertise and leadership in developing good practices in conflict prevention that are now a reference worldwide.

The WANEP peace architecture remains a work in progress. The process is a constant learning of lessons and meeting of challenges, with a forward-looking determination to leverage early warning into equally early and effective response. Peacebuilding capacity is evolving from regional to national levels, creating national infrastructures for bottom-up approaches to conflict prevention to combine with state and regional efforts. In reviewing these efforts this chapter identifies potential models for future practice that are inclusive of all critical stakeholders—civil society, member states, and ECOWAS—and that inform pathways for more robust peacebuilding practice throughout the region.

NOTES

1. Hassan A.R. Hamdy, "State and Civil Society in Africa: A North African Perspective," *African Journal of Political Science and International Relations* 3, no. 2 (February 2009): 66–76.

2. F. K. Buah, *A History of Ghana Revised and Updated* (London: Macmillan Education Ltd., 1998).

3. For details, refer to George Padmore, *The Gold Coast Revolution: The Struggle of an African People from Slavery to Freedom* (London: Dennis Dobson, 1953).

4. Ibid.

5. Helge Ronning, "Democracy, Civil Society and the Media in Africa in the Nineties: A Discussion of the Emergence and Relevance of Some Analytical Concepts for the Understanding of the Situation in Africa," *Innovation: The European Journal of Social Sciences* 8, no. 4 (December 1995): subsection titled "A historical perspective."

6. Joseph G. Amamoo, *Ghana: 50 Years of Independence* (Accra: Jafint Enterprise Publications, 2007).

7. Victor K. Ametewee, "Ethnicity and Ethnic Relations in Ghana," in *Ethnicity, Conflicts and Consensus in Ghana*, ed., Steve Tonah (Accra: Woelli Publishing Services, 2007).

8. United Nations Development Program, *Human Development Report 2004: Cultural Liberty in Today's Diverse World* (New York: United Nations Development Program, 2004), 281, http://hdr.undp.org/sites/default/files/reports/265/hdr_2004_complete.pdf.

9. For more on the abduction and forced participation of children in violent and armed conflicts in West Africa, refer to Myriam S. Denoy, *Child Soldiers: Sierra Leone's Revolutionary United Front* (Cambridge: Cambridge University Press, 2010).

10. Jim Wormington, "After Simone Gbagbo's Trial, What Next for Justice in Côte D'Ivoire," *Human Rights Watch*, April 8, 2015, http://www.hrw.org/news/2015/04/08/after-simone-gbagbo-s-trial-what-next-justice-cote-d-ivoire.

11. Monde Kingsley Nfor, "No Shortage of Recruits for Boko Haram in Cameroon's Far North," *IRIN*, March 5, 2015, http://www.irinnews.org/report/101198/no-shortage-of-recruits-for-boko-haram-in-cameroon-s-far-north.

12. For more on International Alert's work in Liberia, refer to their organizational website's briefing on Liberia at http://www.international-alert.org/liberia.

13. For more on the Centre's impressive history of racial mediation in South Africa and eventual expansion into broader peacebuilding efforts in the larger Southern African region, refer to their "History" page at http://ccr.org.za/index.php/about/history.

14. The history and goals of ACCORD and its peacebuilding work may be further explored at www.accord.org.za.

15. A brief history and explanation of the goals and mission of NPI-Africa may be found at www.npi-africa.org/aboutus.

16. John Paul Lederach, *Building Peace: Sustainable Reconciliation in Divided Societies* (Washington DC: United States Institute of Peace Press, 1997), 37–61.

17. The application of these operating principles and the concepts for peacebuilding principles and frameworks is outlined in Reina Neufeldt et al., *Peacebuilding: A Caritas Training Manual* (Vatican City: Caritas Internationalis, 2002), 101–102, http://dmeforpeace.org/sites/default/files/Neufeldt%20et%20al_Caritas%20Peacebuilding.pdf.

18. Lisa Schirch and Manjrika Sewak, "The Role of Women in Peacebuilding," European Centre for Conflict Prevention, January 2005, https://www.google.com/url?sa=t&rct=j&q=&esrc=s&source=web&cd=5&cad=rja&uact=8&ved=0ahUKEwjymKCFn6rKAhVFbR4KHWYgDfgQFgg4MAQ&url=http%3A%2F%2Fwww.conflictrecovery.org%2Fbin%2FIssue_paper_on_the_Role_of_Women_in_Peacebuilding_Jan2005.doc&usg=AFQjCNGzaAgpv_ESncIxgMycjdwUTu1PAQ&sig2=n_PjhzXDEA_GagyaeIgVMw&bvm=bv.111677986,d.dmo; see also Lisa Schirch, *Women in Peacebuilding: Resource and Training Manual* (West African Network for Peacebuilding and Conflict Transformation Program at Eastern Mennonite University, 2004), https://www.emu.edu/cjp/publications/faculty-staff/lisa-schirch/women-in-peacebuilding-pt1.pdf.

19. Ademola Abass, *Regional Organizations and the Development of Collective Security: Beyond Chapter VIII of the UN Charter* (Oxford: Hart Publishing, 2004).

20. ECOWAS Executive Secretariat, "Protocol Relating to the Mechanism for Conflict Prevention, Management, Resolution, Peacekeeping and Security," December 10, 1999, 11–13, http://www.afrimap.org/english/images/treaty/ECOWAS_Protocol_Conflicts.pdf.

21. "Constitutive Act of the African Union," July 2000, 1–4 and 6–7, http://www.au.int/en/sites/default/files/ConstitutiveAct_EN.pdf.

22. Ibid., 7.

23. "Panel of the Wise (PoW)," *African Union*, http://www.peaceau.org/en/page/29-panel-of-the-wise-pow.

24. "The Continental Early Warning System," *African Union*, http://www.peaceau.org/en/page/28-continental-early-warning-system-cews#sthash.yU3T0RHD.dpuf.

25. "Assembly of the African Union, First Ordinary Session: Protocol Relating to the Establishment of the Peace and Security Council of the African Union," *African Union*, July 9, 2002, http://www.au2002.gov.za/docs/summit_council/secprot.htm.

26. For a detailed overview of the ECOWAS-WANEP collaboration in the creation of ECOWARN and the way in which ECOWARN functions, see Birikit Terefe Tiruneh, "Establishing an Early Warning System in the African Peace and Security Architecture: Challenges and Prospects," KAIPTC Occasional Paper No. 29 (Accra: Kofi Annan International Peacekeeping Training Centre, September 2010), 15–20,

http://www.kaiptc.org/publications/occasional-papers/documents/occasional-paper-29-birikit.aspx.

27. For details on the agreement and division of tasks between WANEP and ECOWAS, see the official press release announcing the renewal of the Memorandum of Understanding between WANEP and ECOWAS from September 2014 at http://www.wanep.org/wanep/attachments/article/658/pr_sept_2014_WANEP-ECOWAS_mou.pdf.

28. Tiruneh, "Establishing an Early Warning System in the African Peace and Security Architecture: Challenges and Prospects," 15–20.

29. WANEP has a coordinator in each zone to interface with the ECOWAS'zonal bureaus. The four zonal bureaus are located in Banjul, Ouagadougou, Monrovia, and Cotonou for zones one through four, respectively.

30. WANEP-Nigeria, "National Early Warning System Weekly Highlight: 5–11 July 2015," 2–3.

31. "I wanted to kill Mahama—Gunman Confesses," *GhanaWeb*, July 28, 2015, http://www.ghanaweb.com/GhanaHomePage/NewsArchive/I-wanted-to-kill-Mahama-Gunman-confesses-371501.

32. Anna Matveeva, "Early Warning and Early Response: Conceptual and Empirical Dilemmas," *European Centre for Conflict Prevention* and *International Secretariat of the Global Partnership for the Prevention of Armed Conflict*, September 2006, 33, https://www.peaceportal.org/documents/127900679/127917167/Issue+paper+1+Early+Warning+and+Early+Response.pdf.

33. A fuller discussion of the success of the NEWS in Nigeria and WANEP's decision to expand the NEWS model to other places in West Africa is found in the "WANEP General Assembly's January 2011 Concept Paper," January 24, 2011, http://www.wanep.org/wanep/attachments/article/240/Concept%20Paper%20-%20 Media.pdf. This paragraph contains a close paraphrase from page 2.

34. "Policy Framework for the Establishment of Early Warning/Response Mechanisms in ECOWAS Member States," *ECOWAS Department of Political Affairs, Peacekeeping and Security (PAPS)*, November 2012 (Internal Document).

35. "ECOWAS Member States Hold Consultative Meeting on Establishing of National Early Warning Mechanism," October 2013, http://www.wanep.org/wanep/index.php?option=com_content&view=article&id=500:ecowas-member-states-hold-consultative-meeting-on-establishment-of-national-early-warning-mechanism-&catid=25:news-releases&Itemid=8.

36. This is an argument made in the Mid-Term Review by a researcher commissioned by SIDA regarding the growth, role, and importance of WANEP. SIDA is the Swedish International Development Cooperation Agency, the official government organ of the Swedish Ministry of Foreign Affairs charged with assisting the developing world. The Mid-Term Review led to a final report dated June 2013 and written by Mehari Taddele Maru. See Mehari Taddele Maru, *The Mid-Term Review of the West African Network for Peacebuilding (WANEP)*, (Stockholm: SIDA, 2013), http://www.sida.se/contentassets/b9003394b16e4d48b7246b0617b6f54f/ee420a49-911f-4a7e-b959-1df22fdcb4a5.pdf.

37. "Another Somalia: Piracy off West Africa Is on the Rise," *The Economist*, May 25, 2013, http://www.economist.com/news/middle-east-and-africa/21578409-piracy-west-africa-rise-another-somalia.

38. The UN Assessment Mission to the Sahel worked closely with ECOWAS in 2011 in order to examine the impact of the collapse of the Libyan government. See United Nations Security Council, "Report of the assessment mission on the impact of the Libyan crisis on the Sahel region: report of the Secretary General," S/2012/42, January 18, 2012, http://www.iom.int/sites/default/files/event/docs/Interagency-Assessment-Mission-Report-on-the-Impact-of-the-Libyan-Crisis-to-the-Sahel-Region-IA-7-23-December-201-English.pdf.

39. "The Impacts of the Libyan Crisis on the Sahel Region of ECOWAS," *Early Warning Directorate,* September 9, 2011 (Internal Document).

40. Shivit Bakrania, *Conflict Drivers, International Responses, and the Outlook for Peace in Mali: A Literature Review* (GSDRC Issues Paper, University of Birmingham, Birmingham, UK, 2013), http://www.gsdrc.org/docs/open/IP14.pdf.

41. The United Nations Multidimensional Integrated Stabilization Mission in Mali (MINUSMA) was established by the United Nations Security Council's Resolution 2100 on April 25, 2013. Its objectives were further clarified by Resolution 2164 on June 25, 2014. More information on MINUSMA may be found at http://www.un.org/en/peacekeeping/missions/minusma/background.shtml.

42. Kumar Rupesinghe, "A New Generation of Conflict Prevention: Early Warning, Early Action and Human Security" (paper presented at the Global Partnership for the Prevention of Armed Conflict Global Conference, "Role of Civil Society in the Prevention of Armed Conflict and Peacebuilding," New York, July 2015). See also Rupesinghe, "FCE Citizen-Based Early Warning and Early Response System: A New Tool for Civil Society to Prevent Violent Conflict," February 24, 2009, 6–12, https://earlywarning.files.wordpress.com/2009/03/fce-citizen-based-early-warning-and-early-response-system.pdf.

43. Government of Ghana, "Declaration on Strengthening National, Regional and Continental Co-ordination towards Building National Peace Infrastructures for Conflict Prevention," September 10, 2013, http://www.i4pinternational.org/files/514/declaration+accra+10-9-2013.pdf.

44. ECOWAS Commission, "The ECOWAS Conflict Prevention Framework," January 2008, 9–10, http://www.lawschool.cornell.edu/womenandjustice/upload/ECOWAS-Conflict-Prevention-Framework.pdf.

45. Lederach, *Building Peace,* 37–61.

46. "Report of 2nd Jos Dialogue Process: Sustaining the Search for Lasting Peace in the Home of Peace and Tourism," *WANEP and IPCR Report,* 2012, http://www.wanep.org/wanep/attachments/article/290/rp_2nd_jos_dialogue_process.pdf; "Democratic Transitions in West Africa: A Year of Elections," *WANEP Quarterly Highlights,* June 2011, 2–3, http://www.wanep.org/wanep/files/2011/qh_jan_mar_2011.pdf.

47. WANEP, "Burkina Faso's Test of Resilience and Democratic Stability—The 2015 Political Dynamics and Drifts," WARN Policy Brief, March 29, 2014, http://www.wanep.org/wanep/files/2014/mar/pb_burkina_faso_mar_2014.pdf.

48. United Nations Security Council, "Report of the Secretary-General on the Activities of the United Nations Office for West Africa," S/2014/945, December 24, 2014, 2, https://unowa.unmissions.org/Portals/UNOWA/Report/Report%20of%20the%20Secretary-General%20on%20the%20activities%20of%20the%20UNOWA.DOC.

Emmanuel Bombande

49. Ibid., 2–3.

50. The cooperation between ECOWAS, the AU, and the UN to resolve the political crisis in Burkina Faso is discussed in "Briefing on Burkina Faso," *What's In Blue*, November 4, 2014, http://whatsinblue.org/2014/11/briefing-on-burkina-faso.php.

51. United Nations Security Council, "Report of the Secretary-General on the Activities of the United Nations Office for West Africa," 2–3.

Chapter 7

The Role of Women in Regional Peace and Security

Experiences from the Pacific

Sharon Bhagwan-Rolls and Laurel Stone

Women peacebuilders in the Pacific Islands have been a powerful force for peace when conflicts in Bougainville, the Solomon Islands, and Fiji threatened to create instability across the entire region. Intervention by a participatory network of women during these crises helped broker a more peaceful Pacific by emphasizing a nonmilitarized view of security. Yet despite successes women remain marginalized and excluded from formal decision-making institutions, reflecting the patriarchal governance structures inherited from the colonial era.[1] The underrepresentation of women in leadership paired with some of the highest levels of violence against women in the world reveal the need for a regional effort to improve equality and safety for Pacific women.

The Pacific Islands have a long and vibrant history of civil society advocacy linking local issues of climate change, poor economic development practices, and gender inequality to regional-level policies surrounding peace and security. Prominent among these civil society groups is FemLINKPACIFIC, a nongovernmental organization based in Fiji with feminist media and advocacy networks spanning several countries in the Pacific Islands region. FemLINKPACIFIC's network focuses on how gender inequality generates insecurity and negatively impacts economic growth and development. Through media outreach and lobbying efforts at the national, regional, and international levels, FemLINKPACIFIC played a major role in the establishment of a Regional Action Plan (RAP) for Women, Peace and Security (WPS) in 2012 within the Pacific Islands Forum (PIF). In this case a strong civil society network partnered with a regional organization to institute a gendered plan for regional peace and security, thus providing a precedent for the institutional mainstreaming of UNSCR 1325.[2]

This chapter provides a brief history of women's peacebuilding organizations in the Pacific, followed by an overview of the PIF regional framework for security and its mechanisms for engagement with civil society. The chapter then reviews how UNSCR 1325 became a unifying agenda for women's networks and how FemLINKPACIFIC and its media network contributed to the development of a Pacific RAP for WPS. The chapter concludes with an assessment of the difficulties in coordinating at the regional level and a review of relevant lessons from the work of FemLINKPACIFIC.

A REGIONAL NETWORK OF WOMEN

The Pacific Islands have a rich history of women peacebuilding activism that stems back to the 1940s era when women led regional development programs for the South Pacific Commission and church congresses.[3] In the 1960s, local women's peacebuilding groups led protests against nuclear weapons testing in the Pacific.[4] Since the 1980s, women peacebuilders have turned their attention to the internal security problems of their own countries as conflict and unrest within Fiji, the Solomon Islands, and Bougainville began to increase.[5] This shift from focusing on external security threats to internal threats resulted in advocacy toward a gendered perspective to security. As a region with high rates of sexual violence and low numbers of female parliamentarians,[6] it was critical that women's voices and concerns transcended their local communities into regional and international realms of policymaking.

A number of organizations sought to fill this gap by uniting around a gendered security platform and approach for the Pacific. One of these groups was FemLINKPACIFIC, a nonprofit organization founded in September 2000 and based in Fiji. The organization was born during the Blue Ribbon Peace Vigil in May 2000 when a coup and hostage crisis in Fiji triggered a "chaotic rebel insurgency."[7] The Blue Ribbon Peace Vigil prompted women to take an urgent stand for peace and oppose the political and military crisis caused by the coup. The blue ribbon, the same color as the Fiji flag, symbolized the "collective call to action for peace and democracy as well as an affirmation of active nonviolence and inclusive and just reconciliation."[8] It was from this organization of female peace activists that FemLINKPACIFIC was born. The women active during the vigil established the NGO to ensure that gender issues and women's stories during the crisis would remain visible after the return to parliamentary democracy.[9] Since 2000, FemLINKPACIFIC has offered a variety of media strategies and tools for peacebuilders working to bring women's issues to the center of national policymaking.

This effort was facilitated by the adoption of UNSCR 1325, which also occurred in 2000. Pacific states committed to the new international agenda on WPS and praised the policy as progress for gender equality, yet there was much work to be accomplished in the region to improve the role of women in policy areas related to peace and security issues.[10] FemLINKPACIFIC and its sister organizations throughout the Pacific Islands saw UNSCR 1325 as an opportunity to unify the efforts and voices of Pacific women in support of the international agenda while also localizing the key themes to fit their own domestic context. The resolution in a sense "licensed" Pacific women peace-builders to demonstrate the relevance of their needs to the male-dominated political establishment.[11]

While UNSCR 1325 provided an opportunity for Pacific women to lobby for their interests, there was some criticism that the "UN-mandated language" seemed to be "directly at odds with local sociocultural values."[12] However, this resistance provided opportunities for female activists to frame and translate the goals of the resolution into a more relevant form that matched the local security priorities of the Pacific. This translation strategy helped women's peacebuilding networks to utilize the international agenda while creating local solutions to the problems identified in the resolution.

In order to reach their goals and create local solutions, FemLINKPACIFIC realized that the women's network needed to engage at the regional political level in order to gain support of the national governments. UNSCR 1325 had catalyzed several NAPs as UN member states adopted the resolution into their own governance architectures; however, these national plans were rarely properly resourced, especially in the Pacific. FemLINKPACIFIC calculated that if a plan was created at the regional level, national governments could receive assistance for the implementation of their national plans. FemLINK-PACIFIC therefore sought out PIF, the key regional institution in the Pacific, as the arena for advocacy because the forum had identified both civil society and gender equality as key political principles. By lobbying at the regional level, FemLINKPACIFIC could build bridges and mutual support at local, national, and international levels.

In 2006, several women's organizations came together to create a media and policy network with the specific intent to lobby the forum because of its commitment to dialogue and collaboration with civil society. The advocacy effort demonstrated by this network culminated in the adoption of an RAP for WPS at PIF in 2012. The gender policy adoption by the forum can offer key insights into the possibilities for RIGO collaboration with civil society but also the constraints that civil society can face at the regional level of policymaking. In order to understand these opportunities and challenges, a better understanding of the regional infrastructure of the Pacific Islands is necessary.

A REGIONAL FRAMEWORK FOR PEACE AND SECURITY IN THE PACIFIC ISLANDS

As a collection of island states, the governments of the Pacific Islands realized that strategic economic strength could increase by forming a coalition. In 1971 they founded the South Pacific Forum, later renamed in 1999 as PIF to reflect member states located in both the North and South Pacific.[13] The founding members of the forum were Australia, Cook Islands, Fiji, Nauru, New Zealand, Tonga, and Western Samoa (now Samoa). The membership now includes sixteen independent states, adding to the founding members: Federated States of Micronesia, Kiribati, Niue, Palau, Papua New Guinea, Republic of Marshall Islands, Solomon Islands, Tuvalu, and Vanuatu.

A major concern of the organization initially was nuclear testing and proliferation, which led PIF to release a communiqué in 1975, soon followed by the signing of the Treaty of Rarotonga establishing a South Pacific nuclear-free zone.[14] The focus of the organization went beyond hard security impacts of nuclear weapons, however, as PIF demonstrated an evolving and nuanced view of the links between environmental harm, poor development practices, and the security of states in the region.[15]

The forum's outlook reflected a holistic approach to security, recognizing that threats of conflict and instability in the region were internal and driven by increased migration due to problematic development practices and environmental threats.[16] Viewing these problems as the triggers to conflict rather than the result of conflict shifted the security perspective from one that viewed the national security architecture as dominant to one that recognized the importance of prevention, with an emphasis on people and community. Addressing the inequalities that created opportunities for violent conflict thus became the organization's main objective.

The forum noticed that internal political issues rooted in inequality, typically addressed by states internally, could grow into transnational security problems. These national threats to regional security convinced forum members that a regional architecture could provide a "progressive risk management strategy."[17] The Honiara Declaration signed in 1992 provided the first precedent, which was further developed and emphasized in the Biketawa Declaration in 2000.[18] The Biketawa Declaration signaled the evolution of PIF to perceiving security threats not solely confined to a particular member state, but as threats that could be transnational and needed an "enhanced regionalism" in response.[19] The Biketawa Declaration guaranteed the principle of noninterference in the affairs of its member states, but it also provided a list of possible actions the forum can take if crises become a threat to the region.[20] These two declarations in addition to other security declarations related to terrorism provided a foundation for the current regional security architecture of PIF.[21]

The present goals of the Forum are "to stimulate economic growth and enhance political governance and security for the region, through the provision of policy advice; and to strengthen regional cooperation and integration through coordinating, monitoring and evaluating implementation of Leaders' decisions."[22] The guiding principles to execute these goals reflect a human security lens that the PIF can use to ensure that conflict-inducing inequality is addressed. For instance, one of the guiding principles is "Address the priority needs and rights of our most vulnerable Members, communities and people (Special and Differential Treatment)," and another is "Embrace the cultural diversity of the region with tolerance and respect (The Pacific Way)."[23] Another excellent example of a human security approach is in their last guiding principle, "Embrace good governance and gender equality, and seek peak performance." The stated intention to address the needs of people and communities in the Pacific provides a unique approach for regional leadership.

The PIF structure includes a Secretariat and a Council of Regional Organisations in the Pacific (CROP). The Secretary-General of PIF leads the Forum Secretariat and reports to the Forum Officials' Committee which comprises representatives from each forum member.[24] The Secretariat is technically established as an international organization by treaty, so it has the mandate to work in each of its member states in order to fulfill the directives established in the forum's communiqués and high-level ministerial decisions.[25] The Secretary-General also holds the status of permanent chair of CROP, which works to improve coordination on regional agendas.[26]

These regional structures frame the mechanisms for engagement that can be used by member states to address threats to peace and security. Three threats in particular, rooted in inequality, have been identified as a necessary focus—economics, climate change, and gender—because they "reflect the experience of violence" in the Pacific.[27] The human security approach embedded within the regional security architecture therefore provides an opportunity for the field of peacebuilding that many other regions do not have. It is especially through the creation of mechanisms for increased dialogue with peacebuilding CSOs that PIF has been able to further its human security agenda. By gathering the concerns and opinions of civil society, the forum has found a way to implement at the local level its regional policy of dispelling the inequalities that could lead to destabilizing transnational threats.

PACIFIC ISLANDS FORUM ENGAGEMENT WITH CIVIL SOCIETY

The first official meeting between the forum and civil society representatives occurred in 2005, and its success resulted in an endorsement by the Forum

Regional Security Committee, which deliberates on security matters facing the Pacific.[28] The outcomes of this first meeting emphasized the importance of human security in strategies of conflict prevention. A subsequent paper on human security was commissioned from the Forum Secretariat in order to better understand what the concept of human security looked like in the Pacific Islands. The research for this paper was conducted through several consultations with civil society, demonstrating the forum's desire to learn from civil society knowledge and experience in order to develop a regional plan. The consultations revealed how much work would be needed to establish an early warning and prevention approach in the region and that the only way to make this happen would be to create "an integrated approach, linking community, national and regional efforts."[29] As a result of this consultation process and commissioned paper, PIF produced the *Pacific Plan for Strengthening Regional Cooperation and Integration (2005–2015)*, which outlined steps for strengthening regional cooperation on security matters.[30] Not only did the plan respond to the civil society consultation process, but it also acknowledged that cooperation with CSOs was vital to achieving these goals.

The Forum Regional Security Committee again emphasized the need for increased collaboration with civil society in a 2009 meeting and subsequently created a twice-annual dialogue workshop for CSOs, forum staff and member state leaders, intergovernmental organizations, and development partners.[31] This dialogue process was housed under the political division of PIF and created a channel allowing CSOs to have access to regional policymaking processes on security. This allowed civil society concerns to be heard directly by the leaders of the region. The forum viewed the dialogue process as a necessary tool for building networks of collaboration between multiple stakeholders dealing with conflict and security concerns.[32]

While this dialogue process opened a channel for CSO networks, the forum did not allow free access to all meetings. For instance, formal forum meetings could not be attended by CSO representatives unless forum members approved their participation. If a CSO was unable to attend, the organization could submit a paper for the Forum Regional Security Committee to consider and potentially endorse.[33] The early stages of the dialogue process and engagement with CSOs revealed that much more work was needed to ensure regular and engaged collaboration between PIF and civil society. Resource and time constraints made it difficult for small, local organizations to attend the dialogues, creating a low level of CSO participation. The Secretariat also acknowledged that its own members needed to be encouraged to take the opportunity to hear CSOs voice their concerns.[34] The creation of the twice annual dialogue process on regional peace and security nonetheless demonstrated significant strides by the Forum to engage with civil society.

The mechanisms established by PIF revealed a potential method for other RIGOs to establish in their own collaborative arrangements with civil society actors. Regular dialogues enabled CSOs to participate in the policymaking process on a routine basis as opposed to ad hoc attendance at meetings. CSOs also utilized these dialogues each year for their advocacy efforts around particular areas of interest, gaining a larger audience at the regional level. The dialogue process was unfortunately not sustained by PIF leadership, as discussed later in this chapter, but the example of FemLINKPACIFIC's regional advocacy offers lessons for engaging RIGOs.

A PACIFIC REGIONAL ACTION PLAN ON WOMEN, PEACE, AND SECURITY

Despite the strong human security approach articulated by PIF, the needs of women in particular have not been well represented in the history of the regional organization.[35] With the adoption of UNSCR 1325, Pacific women found an opportunity to unify their advocacy around the international agenda in order to influence the policies in their own countries. Engaging the Forum in particular offered a channel for women's CSOs to work with the forum's Political Division in order to create a gendered approach to regional peace and security. As previously mentioned, many of the Pacific governments had adopted gender NAPs, but these were often poorly resourced and therefore not well implemented. Women's organizations decided that national efforts for increasing gender equality were not sufficient as some national governments lacked the willpower or the capacity to create these gender plans. To overcome these problems of inadequate willpower and limited resources, FemLINKPACIFIC directed its attention to the regional organization by lobbying for an RAP on WPS.

Forming a Women's Media Network for Regional Advocacy

FemLINKPACIFIC was originally founded with a strong media component in order to broadcast the voices of Pacific women in the midst of the 2000 Fiji crisis. The 2006 PIF Secretariat meeting on "Gender, Conflict, Peace and Security" launched a FemLINKPACIFIC media initiative to bring UNSCR 1325 into the regional security architecture.[36] To achieve this goal, FemLINKPACIFIC created the media network with other local women's organizations including Ma'a Fafine mo e Famili (Tonga), Leitana Nehan Women's Development Agency of Bougainville (PNG), and Vois Blong Mere Solomon (Honiara).[37] In addition to these local organizations, Fem-LINKPACIFIC also networked with and was supported by international women's organizations like the Women's International League for Peace and Freedom (WILPF), the United Nations Development Fund for Women (UNIFEM), and the NGO Working Group on WPS,[38] and received funding from Australian Aid (AusAID).[39] These partnerships with other women's organizations enabled FemLINKPACIFIC to develop a regional media strategy to promote women's participation and create gender-inclusive content. This strategy also promoted awareness of women's human rights and UNSCR 1325 policy issues, especially reaching out to marginalized communities of women who would not otherwise have a voice in public spaces.

FemLINKPACIFIC used the PIF mechanisms for CSO engagement to begin lobbying for a regional policy agenda on UNSCR 1325 soon after the formation of this media network.[40] At first, the lobby effort largely focused on weaving UNSCR 1325 into security policies under review at PIF.[41] As the media network grew stronger, FemLINKPACIFIC was able to engage more directly with PIF. In 2007 and 2008, women were granted access to the forum's Track II Dialogues on regional security policy.[42] This was followed by an invitation to address the forum's annual Regional Security Committee meeting during the 2008 retreat.[43] FemLINKPACIFIC was also able to participate in the Fiji Peace Talks Dialogue between female NGO representatives and government officials.[44] This increased engagement with PIF offered women direct contact with government officials and allowed a clear channel for communicating their views on incorporating UNSCR 1325 into regional policy.

The release of a policy paper entitled, "Women, Peace and Security: Policy Responses and Solutions for our Pacific Region," summarized these advocacy efforts and launched the policy initiative for targeted lobbying to create an RAP on WPS.[45] The policy initiative acknowledged the reasons an RAP was important for the Pacific. UNSCR 1325 was identified as a framework and a tool that has begun to change how security is conceptualized and has increased the opportunity for collaboration between government and civil society.[46] Yet the benefits of UNSCR 1325 had not been fully realized or implemented, especially in the Pacific. In order to translate the ideals of UNSCR 1325 into actual policy, a mechanism for implementation and accountability measures would have to be created at both the national and regional levels. This concerted policy initiative led by the media network offered PIF much needed guidance on how to integrate women's concerns into a regional security agenda.

The Forum agreed to draft an RAP for WPS, and FemLINKPACIFIC's media network continued its advocacy and helped draft the document to ensure that standards from UNSCR 1325 were included.[47] While engaging PIF, the media network simultaneously continued to influence multiple realms of decision-making at the local and national levels. An example of engaging national governments was through the initiative called "Peace Talks" where various gender issues that were significantly impacting the country could be discussed between women's civil society representatives and government officials. [48] These national and regional initiatives were pursued in addition to the local-level programming that formed the heart of Fem-LINKPACIFIC's outreach. Regular radio programs like the "Suitcase Radio Initiative" in Fiji allowed rural women to express their opinions, which were directly fed into the policy goals of the media network.[49] Radio programs, social media outreach, and media events, like the 2008 "16 Days of Activism against Gender Violence," continued to ensure that local women felt connected to the regional outreach initiative by giving them a voice through the 1325 media network.[50]

The achievement of a gendered regional plan showed how a unified network of CSOs can target regional institutions through advocacy. In order to effectively reach this unity at the regional level, a great deal of effort was simultaneously focused at the local level so Pacific women across the region could participate. FemLINKPACIFIC's use of media advocacy in particular demonstrated how a communication network can be a vital link between local and regional levels.

Designing Inclusive Implementation Mechanisms

As a result of several years of advocacy for a Pacific policy on UNSCR 1325, PIF adopted an RAP on WPS for 2012–2015 on October 18, 2012. The Forum viewed the plan as complementary to any nationally adopted legislation on gender among its member states, which meant the regional plan could offer guidance to those states that had not yet developed a gendered approach to peace and security.[51] The RAP states that one of its purposes is to mainstream gender in the Pacific and "Strengthen civil society, women's groups, including young women and gender equality advocates, engagement with regional security and conflict prevention policy and decision making."[52] The emphasis on civil society in the plan demonstrated the forum's understanding that civil society voices were critical for establishing such a plan.

While the adoption of an RAP for WPS by PIF signaled a significant success for a decade of lobbying by women activists, a number of challenges for gender mainstreaming in the Pacific remain. The RAP concentrated on the role of women in conflict, but the text continued to define regional conflict and security issues in a militarized way without fully adopting the peace-building strategies the media network was emphasizing.[53] This resulted in a limitation of the ways women could collaborate in the implementation of the RAP, because regional officials were focused on increasing the role of women in places of active conflict, like the Melanesian countries, which completely sidelined approaches such as reducing inequality in which women could play a preventive role.[54] This in itself is a paradox given the holistic human security approach promoted by PIF. While focusing on the role of women in ongoing conflict is an important component of UNSCR 1325, FemLINKPA-CIFIC and its media network were lobbying for a much more holistic agenda which gives women a role in security institutions in all settings, especially for conflict prevention, not just in relation to violent conflict.[55]

The RAP's focus on active conflict scenarios also led to an absence of discussion on the structural barriers to women's equality in the Pacific. This could be considered a form of "slow violence" that escapes regional awareness because it is not linked to any direct security threat.[56] Instead, this structural form of violence permeates the institutions and leads to increasing inequality between men and women, which later becomes a trigger for violence when women are raped or assaulted during conflict. Neglecting these softer forms of discrimination during peacetime means failing to prevent crimes of gender-based violence during a period of crisis. Continued effort to ensure that structural barriers to gender equality are successfully articulated by regional and national political institutions remains an important priority for the Pacific Islands.

Another critical challenge for the gender RAP was how CSOs could partner in implementing the plan. CSO participation was instrumental in making the agenda reach the regional level, yet the RAP did not fully operationalize how CSOs could assist in implementing the goals. Budgeting for CSO assistance was also not included in the plan.[57] This created a great deal of difficulty for local organizations lacking the resources to add the RAP to their planned agenda of activities. The lack of operationalizing and budgeting resulted in both areas of significant overlap and areas of gaps because of the absence of a mechanism for coordination among the CSOs wanting to work on the RAP. If a regional plan is to succeed with the help of civil society, proper resource allocations must be considered in addition to an overarching mechanism for coordinating the work of organizations wanting to take part.[58]

The design process for the RAP on WPS showed inclusivity for CSOs, but this inclusion of women in the planning did not translate into a mechanism for the inclusion of women's civil society in the implementation. After lobbying for the regional plan for a decade, FemLINKPACIFIC and other women's organizations were not sure how to support it other than to continue their advocacy for its implementation. After the adoption of the RAP, channels of communication that the women had been able to use for the drafting process no longer seemed open for discussion of their possible role in the implementation of the plan. Unfortunately, this lack of communication did not occur solely in relation to the RAP. Peacebuilding CSOs at large began to face a changing regional security infrastructure that no longer offered a space for civil society engagement.

REGIONAL TRANSITIONS AND THE SUBSEQUENT CHALLENGES FOR CIVIL SOCIETY

As discussed in chapter 5, RIGOs are subject to transitions due to change in the leadership of its member states or even a change in the leadership of the organization itself. Priorities can wax or wane depending on the political climate of the RIGO, and this can create a complicated landscape for civil society as they seek a channel for engagement. PIF witnessed such a shift in the past five years as bureaucratic changes in the political division altered the structure that allowed civil society participation.

PIF collaboration with CSOs on security issues was institutionalized through a twice-annual dialogue series with the Forum Regional Security Committee, and these dialogues had offered FemLINKPACIFIC a platform for UNSCR 1325 advocacy. However, an organization-wide review process of PIF in 2011 surfaced forum officials' critique of the dialogues, and the mechanism for engagement was suspended. A change of leadership in the Political Division of the forum also occurred during this review process, ending previous relationships, so by the launch of the RAP the regional infrastructure FemLINKPACIFIC had engaged for years had completely changed.

Through the review process, PIF decided to create a larger dialogue process with civil society representatives from all fields, not just peace and security. This gathering of CSOs was titled the Non-State Actor (NSA) Working Group and was launched in 2013.[59] The Forum Secretariat decided it would be more effective to convene one large dialogue session with civil society and then channel relevant information into particular forum meetings. While the new format still offers a venue for engagement with civil society, the extent of openness previously experienced by FemLINKPACIFIC has now been drastically reduced. Rather than having an opportunity to engage directly with the Forum Regional Security Committee, peacebuilding CSOs now have to participate first in the broader dialogue and hope their recommendations will be channeled to the Regional Security Committee. This revised infrastructure and leadership change has forced FemLINKPACIFIC to renew its advocacy and outreach efforts.

The transition created an uncertain status regarding the implementation of the RAP. PIF made no statement about the RAP or what has been achieved and gave no indication whether the plan would be renewed or not. This generated concerns about whether the forum would continue this particular agenda. Other regional declarations on gender equality have been issued, for instance the Pacific Leaders Gender Equality Declaration signed in 2012. This will keep a regional mechanism in place for advancing the rights of women, but the declaration does not offer a clear path for increasing women's equality in the Pacific or focus on women's roles in peace and security.[60] The result of these changes has been a setback for the women's media network.

While the door for deeply engaging PIF has partially closed for the moment, opportunities for engaging with other Pacific regional institutions have offered FemLINKPACIFIC ways to continue advocating for women's participation in peace and security issues. Despite the regional changes, the women's media network is stronger than ever, and a growing number of women are participating in regional efforts to ensure a more peaceful Pacific. The lobby for WPS in the region remains vigorous.

The network is looking for other openings at PIF to engage through formal and informal processes. The new NSA Working Group offers some opportunity for civil society, although it is not as focused as the original CSO dialogues. Other regional organizations in the Pacific, like the Pacific Community, have welcomed FemLINKPACIFIC's advocacy, demonstrating another potential avenue to continue working at the regional level.

LESSONS FROM THE PACIFIC

FemLINKPACIFIC and its women's media network were able to engage PIF on women's equality and bring UNSCR 1325 into an RAP for the Pacific. Through more than a decade of work, the women's media network gained international recognition for advancing women's equality in the Pacific Islands. A number of observations can be made about this case that offer guidance on how civil society can collaborate with regional organizations on peace and security agendas.

One of the most significant lessons is the need to focus on local women, especially rural and marginalized populations. To ensure that women in the Pacific community felt connected to the UNSCR 1325 agenda, FemLINKPACIFIC and its sister organizations began translating UNSCR 1325 into the local languages of the Pacific. This allowed local women to access the document in their own language and connect with other women advocating gender equality. The media network provided multiple opportunities for local women to engage and feel that they could make a difference in their region. Special attention was given to young women and girls in order to strengthen the next generation of women peacebuilders. These efforts created a regional platform that FemLINKPACIFIC could use to bring the agenda of local women to the PIF.

While the connection to local women was a priority, FemLINKPACIFIC also found a key advantage in networking with international partners, especially international women's networks. By using the established 1325 agenda, the network sought to encourage local accountability to international gender frameworks.[61] FemLINKPACIFIC and its allies were able to receive support from UNIFEM, WILPF, and many other international networks looking to help support UNSCR 1325 in the Pacific. Connecting to UN Women's agenda also assisted coordination in the Pacific as the resolution became a unifying call for women's organizations in the region. Rather than experiencing extensive competition among women's organizations, the network used 1325 as a rallying call for women in their national and regional institutions.

FemLINKPACIFIC also partners with other international networks focused on peacebuilding, for instance GPPAC. This connection brought alliances with other Pacific CSOs focused on peacebuilding to create a regional platform for civil society engagement on peace and security. These international linkages allowed the network to expand and gain opportunities for strengthening civil society engagement at large with the PIF Regional Security Committee.

FemLINKPACIFIC learned that bureaucracies of regional institutions always change, and this can create both opportunities and challenges for civil society engagement. FemLINKPACIFIC and its network slowly made gains over the course of several years, and then experienced a number of gains beginning in 2008. After finally receiving recognition for the strength of its media network and support for the UNSCR 1325 agenda, it was able to capitalize on the openness of PIF to accelerate the development of an RAP for implementation.

Regardless of the region, persistence is required in a civil society-regional organization relationship. Changes in leadership, transitioning bureaucracies, and new international trends can create opportunities and challenges for civil society engagement. FemLINKPACIFIC and its network forged a channel to engage policymakers by creating a strong network of Pacific women voicing their desire for their inclusion in peace and security policy. Some small steps have been taken in that direction, but a long road lies ahead to achieve real progress. Advocacy persists for the voice of women to be heard and acted upon, from the local community to national governments and regional institutions. Despite past and current obstacles, Pacific women will continue to play a vital role in building and sustaining peace in the Pacific.

NOTES

1. NGO Working Group on Women, Peace and Security, "Sharon Bhagwan-Rolls," accessed March 28, 2016, http://womenpeacesecurity.org/programs-events/peacebuilders/sharon_bhagwan-rolls/.

2. United Nations Security Council Resolution 1325, S/RES/1325 (October 31, 2000), https://documents-dds-ny.un.org/doc/UNDOC/GEN/N00/720/18/PDF/N0072018.pdf?OpenElement.

3. Nicole George, "Pacific Women Building Peace: A Regional Perspective," *The Contemporary Pacific* 23, no. 1 (Spring 2011): 41.

4. FemLINKPACIFIC ENews Bulletin, "The Eights Years On Special," October 2008, http://www.femlinkpacific.org.fj/images/PDF/E-Bulletin/femTALK_ENews_October_2008.pdf, 5.

5. Nicole George, "Pacific Women Building Peace," 39.

6. UN Women Asia and the Pacific, "Fiji Multi-Country Office," accessed March 19, 2016, http://asiapacific.unwomen.org/en/countries/fiji.

7. Nicole George, "Promoting Women, Peace and Security in the Pacific Islands," *Australian Journal of International Affairs* 68, no. 3 (2014): 317.

8. FemLINKPACIFIC, "Blue Ribbon Peace Special," October 2006, http://www.peacewomen.org/content/blue-ribbon-peace-special.

9. NGO Working Group on Women, Peace and Security, "Biography of Sharon Bhagwan-Rolls, Coordinator, FemLINKPACIFIC, Fiji Pacific Islands," accessed March 19, 2016, http://womenpeacesecurity.org/programs-events/peacebuilders/sharon_bhagwan-rolls/.

10. Statement by Robert Guba Aisi (Papua New Guinea on behalf of the Pacific Islands Forum) in "Security Council, Recalling Resolution 1325 (2000), Seeks Measures to Strengthen Role of Women in Peacekeeping, Post-Conflict Situations," *United Nations Press*, October 26, 2006, http://www.un.org/press/en/2006/sc8858.doc.htm.

11. Nicole George, "Promoting Women, Peace and Security in the Pacific Islands," 318.

12. Ibid.

13. Pacific Islands Forum, "About Us," accessed March 9, 2016, http://www.forumsec.org/pages.cfm/about-us/.

14. P. Papadimitropoulos, "The Rarotonga Treaty: A Regional Approach to Non-Proliferation in the South Pacific," *International Atomic Energy Agency* Bulletin (1/1988), https://www.iaea.org/sites/default/files/30103472931.pdf.

15. Timothy Bryar, "Violence and Security in the Pacific" (presentation at the Geneva Declaration Regional Review Conference, Manila, Philippines, October 8–9, 2014), 3, http://www.genevadeclaration.org/fileadmin/docs/2014RRC/3._RRC_Manila/D114PP%20Timothy_Bryar_presentation.pdf.

16. Ibid., 2.

17. Nicole George, "Pacific Women Building Peace: A Regional Perspective," 40.

18. Andie Fong Toy, "Structured Cooperation between Civil Society and Regional Intergovernmental Organisations: Best Practices" (presentation at the International Conference Strengthening Global Peace and Security for Development, Madrid, Spain, November 15–16, 2011), 1, https://www.peaceportal.org/c/document_library/get_file?uuid=82fa17df-443d-4335-bc14-76b896f3edc9&groupId=125878116.

19. Ibid., 1.

20. Nicole George, "Pacific Women Building Peace: A Regional Perspective," 40.

21. Andie Fong Toy, "Structured Cooperation," 1.

22. Pacific Islands Forum, "Mission and Vision," accessed March 9, 2016, http://www.forumsec.org/pages.cfm/about-us/mission-goals-roles/.

23. Ibid.

24. Pacific Islands Forum, "About Us," accessed March 9, 2016, http://www.forumsec.org/pages.cfm/about-us/.

25. Ibid.

26. Pacific Islands Forum Secretariat, "Council of Regional Organisations in the Pacific (CROP)," accessed March 10, 2016, http://www.forumsec.org/pages.cfm/about-us/our-partners/crop/.

27. Timothy Bryar, "Violence and Security in the Pacific," 5.

28. Andie Fong Toy, "Structured Cooperation," 2.

29 Ibid.

30. Pacific Islands Forum Secretariat, "The Pacific Plan for Strengthening Regional Cooperation and Integration," November 2007, http://www.adb.org/sites/default/files/linked-documents/robp-pac-2010-2013-oth01.pdf.

31. Andie Fong Toy, "Structured Cooperation," 3.

32. Ibid., 4.

33. Ibid.

34. Ibid.

35. Nicole George, "Promoting Women, Peace and Security in the Pacific Islands," 316.

36 Pacific Islands News Association, "On the 8th Anniversary of UN Security Council Resolution 1325 (Women, Peace and Security) Pacific Peacewomen Offer Policy Responses and Solutions for our Pacific Region," October 31, 2008, http://www.pina.com.fj/?p=pina&m=events&o=156530706248fff9ff6ffb38e82786.

37. Ibid.

38. FemLINKPACIFIC ENews Bulletin, "The Eights Years On Special," October 2008, http://www.femlinkpacific.org.fj/images/PDF/E-Bulletin/femTALK_ENews_October_2008.pdf, 7.

39. Australian High Commission—Fiji, "Promoting Women's Leadership and Peace Building in the Pacific," October 31, 2008, http://fiji.highcommission.gov.au/suva/mrel31oct.html.

40. FemLINKPACIFIC ENews Bulletin, "The Eights Years On Special," 7.

41. FemLINKPACIFIC, "Regional Action Plans (RAPS), National Action Plans (NAPS) and 'Twinning' for Women, Peace and Security" (PowerPoint presentation), http://www.spc.int/hdp/index2.php?option=com_docman&task=doc_view&gid=249&Itemid=4, 11.

42. Nicole George, "Promoting Women, Peace and Security in the Pacific Islands," 319.

43. "Regional Action Plans (RAPS), National Action Plans (NAPS) and 'Twinning' for Women, Peace and Security," 11.

44. FemLINKPACIFIC ENews Bulletin, "The Eights Years On Special," 15.

45. Ibid.

46. Pacific Islands News Association, "On the 8th Anniversary."

47. FemLINKPACIFIC, "Policy for Peace: A FemLINKPACIFIC Policy Initiative," 2015, http://www.femlinkpacific.org.fj/images/PDF/Policy/PolicyForPeace_2015.pdf, 25.

48. Pacific Islands News Association, "On the 8th Anniversary."

49. "The Pacific: Women's Civil Society Engagement in Security Dialogue," in *Examples from the Ground: Civil Society Oversight of the Security Sector and Gender* (DCAF, 2011), 80–81, http://www.poa-iss.org/kit/Gender-SSR-E.pdf.

50. FemLINKPACIFIC ENews Bulletin, "The Eights Years On Special," 26.

51. Pacific Islands Forum Secretariat, "Pacific Regional Action Plan: Women, Peace and Security 2012–2015," 2012, http://www2.kobe-u.ac.jp/~alexroni/TR2015%20 readings/2015_8/Pacific%20Regional%20Action%20Plan%20on%20Women%20 Peace%20and%20Security%20Final%20and%20Approved.pdf, 3.

52. Ibid.

53. FemLINKPACIFIC, "Policy for Peace: A FemLINKPACIFIC Policy Initiative," 26.

54. Nicole George, "Promoting Women, Peace and Security in the Pacific Islands," 324.

55. FemLINKPACIFIC, "Policy for Peace: a FemLINKPACIFIC Policy Initiative," 26.

56. Nicole George, "Promoting Women, Peace and Security in the Pacific Islands," 320.

57. FemLINKPACIFIC, "Policy for Peace: a FemLINKPACIFIC Policy Initiative," 28.

58. Peace Women, "1325 at 15: Reflections on the Implementation of WPS from the Pacific Region," October 2015, http://www.peacewomen.org/e-news/ article/1325-15-reflections-implementation-wps-pacific-region.

59. Andie Fong Toy, "Structured Cooperation," 6.

60. "Annex 1: Pacific Leaders Gender Equality Declaration," in *Pacific Islands Forum Secretariat Forum Communique* (Rarotonga, Cook Islands: August 30, 2012), 13–15, http://www.forumsec.org/resources/uploads/attachments/documents/2012%20 Forum%20Communique,%20Rarotonga,%20Cook%20Islands%2028-30%20Aug1. pdf.

61. Nicole George, "Pacific Women Building Peace: A Regional Perspective," 46.

Section 3

ENGAGING THE MILITARY
FOR HUMAN SECURITY

Chapter 8

Civil Society's Peacebuilding Approach to Civil-Military-Police Coordination and Security Sector Reform

Lisa Schirch

Security is a public good, but all too often the public has little say in how security is defined or pursued. This needs to change. Easy access to weapons and media attention allows transnational nonstate armed groups and other illicit actors to multiply their harmful impacts and mobilize communities and nations to war. This "democratization of violence" requires a "democratization of peace and security" that harnesses civil society's capacities for conflict prevention and peacebuilding through mitigating the drivers of conflict and instability. If security is a public good, then the local people who are "consumers" of that service need to have a voice.

International organizations are calling for greater community engagement and local ownership of development assistance, security sector reform, and programs for countering violent extremism. This reflects a growing recognition that the state-society relationship is fundamental to both security and development. Military leaders also recognize the need for new approaches to relating to civilians and are using terms such as "human terrain" and "human aspects of military operations." They are adding courses in their educational programs on conflict prevention, negotiation, protection of civilians, civilian assistance, and human security. They increasingly acknowledge the limits of military solutions to problems that are fundamentally about political and economic governance. Police training programs are also focusing on community engagement, with some programs emphasizing community policing, problem-solving policing, and restorative justice.

At the same time, CSOs are moving from "protest" to "proposal" on security issues, not only opposing current national security policies, but also making concrete policy proposals on how to improve human security. Despite rhetoric supporting local ownership, local civil society groups often face significant challenges in asserting their expertise and taking part in assessing, designing, implementing, and evaluating security programs and strategies. Civil-military-police tensions have increased in many settings, along with a growing number of attacks against NGOs and CSOs. With the increase in military forces participating in civilian assistance efforts, civil society expresses caution and concern about blurring the lines between military and civilian staff and projects. Operational requirements for independence and impartiality are essential for CSOs to gain access and trust with populations in need and to assure the safety of their staffs and beneficiaries, who may be seen as "soft targets" by armed opposition groups who may also see them as collaborating with government or external military forces.

This chapter addresses these and other challenges in civil-military-police interaction and outlines a spectrum of relationships between the security sector and civil society. While historically states have sought to repress, silence, and exclude civil society, they have increasingly begun to recognize civil society's central role in peace and security. Initial efforts to coordinate or support civil society have missed the mark in the last two decades. New efforts to structure joint assessment, planning, implementation, and oversight of security programs offer fresh hope for making progress on human security.

THE GAP BETWEEN STATE SECURITY
AND HUMAN SECURITY

National security or state security refers to security of the national interests of the state, including for example protection of state territory, citizens, and political and economic interests. States define their national interests in different ways. Human security refers to the security of individuals and communities. The UN's Human Security Unit defines human security as

> protecting fundamental freedoms—freedoms that are the essence of life. It means protecting people from critical (severe) and pervasive (widespread) threats and situations. It means using processes that build on people's strengths and aspirations. It means creating political, social, environmental, economic, military and cultural systems that together give people the building blocks of survival, livelihood and dignity.[1]

Comprehensive human security includes three components: freedom from fear, freedom from want, and freedom to live in dignity. Human security is measured, at least in part, by the perceptions of civilians, including women, who experience different types of insecurity and threats of violence. Do men and women feel safer? Are they able to work, travel, and be in their homes without fear of violence?

A number of international trends gave birth to the concept of human security. At the end of the Cold War, the UN approach to human security emerged to articulate the need to focus on threats to individuals and communities and not just states.[2] UN Secretary-General Kofi Annan wrote that "we will not enjoy development without security, we will not enjoy security without development, and we will not enjoy either without respect for human rights."[3] The UN's MDGs set out expectations that some of the sources of human insecurity—such as poverty, lack of education, and health care—could be addressed through concerted effort. The mass atrocities in Rwanda and Srebrenica brought attention to the lack of political will to respond to mass violence against civilians. The concept of human security began as a strategic narrative to link human development, human dignity, state-society relations, governance, and peace and security issues.

The human security agenda is distinct from the national security paradigm in several ways. First, the protection of individuals and communities is critical to national and global security. Second, many security threats, such as government corruption, cheap access to weapons, religiously motivated violence, and climate change, do not have military solutions. Lastly, the security of individuals and communities depends on political, economic, and social factors and not just military approaches.

There are various approaches to human security. Some emphasize immediate threats and an operational approach to the protection of civilians; some believe human security is "complementary" to national security. While there may be times when human security overlaps with state security concerns related to pandemic illness or climate change, civil society tends to see national security strategies as more frequently undermining, not complementing, human security.

STATE-SOCIETY RELATIONS AND GOVERNANCE OF THE SECURITY SECTOR

State-society relations refer to the quality of relationships between state institutions and the public.[4] The state derives legitimacy from a social contract that defines what they will do to protect public interests and rights and what freedoms the public will give up in return. In a democratic regime, the state integrates the public into its decision-making processes and provides public services. Society agrees to give up some of its freedoms to follow the state's rule of law.

Historically, the state earned the right to rule by virtue of its "monopoly on the use of force." Today, the issue of state legitimacy is more complex. With the widespread availability of weapons to private individuals and nonstate groups, some governments take part in violent competitions with their own citizens and with other states to earn legitimacy to govern. A different approach sees states earning legitimacy through public engagement. Citizens support their government when they have opportunities to participate in decision-making, and when leaders make decisions that benefit all groups and do not disadvantage or persecute parts of the population. States win public support when they work to protect the human security of the whole population and not just the security of elite groups. A government's public legitimacy is a reflection of public perceptions of government performance in providing public goods, such as security. Elite-captured governments, especially those that use repression on civilians, are widely seen as illegitimate and unstable. Government legitimacy can be enhanced through democratic reforms that enable civil society to both hold the government to account and partner with the government to provide public goods.

Judging the degree of functional or "good" governance requires assessment of the degree to which people participate in decisions that affect their lives and the degree to which governance institutions serve all people. State formation aims to improve the state-society relationship. The goal is to improve the social contract between people and the government to ensure accountability, perceived legitimacy, and a system of checks and balances on state powers.[5] State formation seeks to coordinate governance approaches between formal institutions and the informal governance structures already operating at the provincial, district, and subdistrict levels. State formation recognizes that governance requires both formal and informal leadership by state, business, and society. It acknowledges that no government can fill all of the social roles needed to ensure human security.

In most societies today, informal, nonstate governance structures that predate the existence of the state continue to complement formal state governance. Informal governance exists in every country. Many different groups outside of government help to manage resources, address social problems, and meet human needs. For example, religious and community-based organizations in every country play a role in addressing people's basic needs. Tribal leaders carry out informal justice. In Ghana, traditional leaders still play a major role in the resolution of land disputes and the provision of health care or education.

Nonstate or informal governance can be abusive and corrupt, or it can be functional and cost-effective. The same is true for states. Abuses by state-run security forces are often an important root cause of violent conflict. The memory of past abuses by the state can shape negative attitudes and skepticism toward security forces, regardless of the current goals and tactics of those forces.[6]

Human security involves improving governance to make it more fair and responsive to all groups. Citizens can start this process by identifying shared values and collective interests to improve their lives and then working together to advocate change. This can include implementing reforms to foster equal treatment of identity groups, setting minimum levels for participation and access to public institutions, using redistributive or preferential treatment to redress historic grievances, and ensuring that institutions have mechanisms for setting standards of quality assurance for the public.

A "citizen-oriented" state serves the public interest and shares decision-making with society through representative structures such as parliaments. A state that orients its power and resources toward the needs and interests of its population is most likely to be seen as legitimate. In a citizen-oriented state, an active civil society both partners with the government to fill public services and holds the government to account and presses for equal access to government services for all people. In an "elite-captured" state, by contrast, the government serves elite interests, often those of a relatively small political, economic class, or a particular ethnic, cultural, or religious group. Elite-captured states use security forces to pacify and repress civil society's demands for human rights, democracy, and freedom. They adopt authoritarian approaches to security that rely on military and police force and deny civil society efforts to bring attention to the root causes of violence. Armed insurgencies and/or nonviolent social movements often develop in response to repression by elite-captured governments. Nonstate armed groups are able to take root and gain public support if the public distrusts the government.

THE EVOLUTION OF STATE SECURITY
APPROACHES TO CIVIL SOCIETY

There are several distinct approaches or stages in security sector relationships with society. As noted, some governments repress civil society, executing and torturing political opponents and social groups that challenge corrupt authority. These forms of "state-based terrorism" have been increasingly documented and as a consequence, international pressure has been building to expose and prevent such violent pacification tactics.[7] A legacy of this approach continues in the distrust that some governments and security actors have toward civil society, and the parallel civil society distrust of security forces.

A second concern is the rise of counterterrorism laws that restrict civil society and are criticized as a continuation of the pacification mind-set.[8] In this approach, counterterrorism legislation restricts civil society from contact with nonstate armed groups identified as "terrorists" even if they have legitimate political grievances and self-determination aims protected by international law. In many countries, counterterrorism laws also restrict funding for civil society, especially support from external donors. Counterterrorism "lawfare" (warfare by legal means) makes it difficult in many settings for civil society to offer humanitarian aid and development assistance or engage in peacebuilding programs that might have a moderating effect on nonstate armed groups.[9]

Over the last fifteen years, security actors have been adopting less repressive approaches toward civil society. Some aspects of the concept of pacification continue to be found in counterinsurgency literature, which takes a cautious approach toward civilians, viewing them as potential allies or potential enemies. Rather than intimidating civil society, counterinsurgency aims to pacify local populations by winning hearts and minds through establishing or reestablishing local government responses to and involving the participation of the people.[10] Rather than attacking civilians, military forces provide civilian assistance to local villages to gain acceptance and prevent local populations from supporting hostile nonstate armed actors.

A related approach emphasizes the priority of civilian safety in security sector-civil society relations. A number of states, regional organizations like the Africa Union, and the United Nations mandate security actors with the task of "protection of civilians." New military doctrines and training missions emphasize military and police roles in the protection of civilians as well as avoiding civilian casualties and mitigating harm against civilians during military or police operations. New frameworks for international action such as the Responsibility to Protect call for governments to refrain from violent repression of civilians and to protect them against violence from nonstate armed actors.

Another approach views civil society groups as service providers, contributing to peace and stability as contractors or "implementing partners." States, regional organizations, and international organizations fund CSOs to provide health care, food, water, and shelter to vulnerable populations such as the young, old, veterans, and disabled members of society; and to build the capacity of communities to govern effectively and maintain the rule of law, community safety, economic development, and efforts to "counter violent extremism." Many CSOs are wary of government funding and worry about losing the trust and legitimacy they have with local communities when they are seen as for-profit contractors working on behalf of governments. Civil society specifically opposes the use of the term "implementing partners," as it implies that CSOs implement rather than design programs.

A final approach, the one explored in this chapter, involves coordination between security forces and an empowered and independent civil society to address the root causes of insecurity and coordinate efforts to support human security. In the "coordination for human security" approach, conflict prevention and peacebuilding skills, values, and processes enable less antagonistic relationships and allow for joint problem solving. It is important to recognize how this multistakeholder coordination for human security approach contrasts with other security strategies. Unlike other approaches, a human security approach does not try to use civil society actors as "assets" to achieve national security goals. Instead it emphasizes the empowerment of civil society to participate in identifying human security challenges, designing and implementing human security programs, and overseeing the security sector's performance.

In some contexts, different security actors may each be using a different approach simultaneously. Some national or international military and police units may focus on protection of civilians while others are actively using violent pacification. A government's development agency may be funding programs to support civil-military-police coordination while other agencies use legal frameworks to prevent CSOs from talking to armed groups, or keep CSOs busy with lucrative contracts to provide public services.

THE EVOLUTION OF CIVIL SOCIETY APPROACHES TO SECURITY: FROM PROTEST TO PROPOSAL

Civil society does not take a uniform approach to the security sector. In some places, civil society actors view military and police forces as legitimate representatives of society and may also decide to voluntarily sign up for service. In such countries, a growing number of CSOs are also working as implementing partners providing public services to contribute to the security agenda of governments, regional organizations, and international organizations.

In countries where (a) security forces repress or violate human rights, (b) there is forced conscription into the military, or (c) military recruitment excludes certain racial, ethnic, or religious groups, civil-military relations can be contentious and there may be wide public opposition to security forces. In these countries, some CSOs—especially human rights organizations—adopt an adversarial approach to the security sector. These groups document human rights violations and publish reports to denounce and protest against abuses committed by security forces in an effort to seek accountability. Human rights organizations play an important role in holding governments to account for their duties to protect civilians. The "protest" approach relies mostly on "naming, blaming, and shaming" state security forces and nonstate armed groups for human rights abuses. Civil society protests play an important role in drawing attention to and disrupting corruption and injustice.[11] Many social movements have helped move unstable, authoritarian countries toward democratic openness all over the world.[12]

This chapter identifies a third civil society approach to the security sector. While sharing concerns about human rights violations and firmly supporting human security, civil society leaders in diverse corners of the world have come to the conclusion that they must go beyond protesting security policies.

The chapters in this book on the Philippines and Guatemala describe a new pattern of peacebuilding CSOs using direct dialogue, negotiation, and problem solving with the security sector. These peacebuilding skills and processes help civil society to move from a reliance on *protest* to an ability to make *proposals* to improve human security.

Multistakeholder Coordination on Human Security

No one group can achieve human security on its own. Civil society, civilian government, the military, and police forces are all stakeholders that need to coordinate to support human security. Coordination improves coherence and effectiveness. The military, the police, and the civil society are increasingly working in the same complex environments. They perform similar tasks such as assessing conflict; providing civilian assistance to provide food, water, and shelter in complex emergencies; monitoring elections; facilitating dialogue, negotiation, and mediation between groups to promote reconciliation; conducting demining, disarmament, demobilization, and reintegration (DDR) operations; and carrying out security and justice sector reform (SSR and JSSR).

When diverse stakeholders are operating in the same space, coordination is necessary to prevent unintended consequences harmful to other stakeholders' interests. Coordination can help to *de-conflict* activities to ensure that each group's goals and activities do not undermine other groups. For example, if a military is building a school in a community using military personnel, this may undermine a civilian organization's efforts to do community-based development with community volunteers and local ownership of school-building and other activities. Coordination can also help to determine how to maintain a distinction between civilians and combatants, and preserve the autonomy and independence necessary for all stakeholders. This is necessary since in some contexts, nonstate armed groups may view civilian organizations as soft targets, easier to attack than security forces. If civilians are cooperating with the military or the police, they may be seen as symbolic extensions of the security sector and may be wrongly perceived as legitimate targets.

Coordination means that diverse groups working in the same place communicate with each other at a minimum. It does not necessarily mean that these groups will cooperate or work together. Civil society and the security sector are able to coordinate effectively when they share goals related to human security. But often, the gap between national security and human security is wide. Coordination is more difficult when civil society suffers from and thus opposes national security strategies.[13]

Coordination is not easy. Government civilians and military members may be so busy coordinating with each other that they exclude local civil society and overlook internal stakeholders. Local civil society is often last on the list of coordination priorities. Yet in reality, they may be the most important stakeholders for building sustainable human security.

The UN, NATO, and intervening states use different terminology and approaches for civil-military coordination. The UN has taken several steps toward "civil-military integration," including the establishment of the Integrated Mission Task Force (IMTF) and Integrated Mission Planning Process (IMPP), with an Integrated Assessment and Planning Policy (IAP) and an IAP *Handbook* to foster coherence within the UN system and with relevant external partners. "Unity of command" is the military concept of a single commanding authority making decisions that others must implement. The term "unity of effort" refers to multiple organizations working toward the same objective, but under different command or decision-making structures. Military forces often prefer the latter approach and would like to have greater unity of effort with civilian organizations operating in their area that are not under their command.

The "comprehensive approach" is another term used to describe coordination between different stakeholders, although it has different interpretations. Some understand the term to mean that civilian agencies and security forces are brought together under one command structure. Others describe this comprehensive approach as a set of communication and coordination mechanisms on more neutral ground, without a command and control structure and allowing civilians to maintain an independent status. Civil-Military Interaction (CMI) is a NATO concept for efforts to foster coordination and cooperation between the military and civilians. Civil-Military Cooperation (CIMIC) is a related military concept that is defined in different ways by different countries and organizations. NATO CIMIC refers to coordination and cooperation in support of a mission between Alliance forces and the civil environment (both governmental and nongovernmental civilian groups). UN CIMIC refers to the interface between the military component of a UN peace operation and the political, humanitarian, developmental, human rights, and rule-of-law components of that mission. Some countries such as the United States establish Civil-Military Operation Centers (CMOC) for coordinating civil-military operations in an area of operations.

Government personnel—especially from foreign governments and international organizations—often lack direct accountability to local populations or local governments. External assistance may "undermine or destroy the capacity that exists in a society and replace it with a weak and dysfunctional new capacity."[14] External interveners are often oblivious to local perceptions of their legitimacy or presence in the country. While outsiders tend to see themselves as benevolent or even making sacrifices to help local populations, insiders are often suspicious of the motivations of interveners operating in their country, assuming they are working on behalf of foreign national interests and intelligence gathering rather than truly assisting and respecting the local context.

National governments, security forces, and donors seeking to coordinate with each other often assume there is "no local capacity." In reality, there are often local civil society groups that work to prevent conflict and support human security. In most situations, only a portion of civil society personnel belong to NGOs with identifiable logos, vehicles, or clothing. Security forces will only be able to identify those with logos, or those they meet in coordination forums. While military forces and large international humanitarian organizations may establish communication platforms for information sharing, coordination forums with smaller groups or informal local humanitarian responders are largely absent. Military forces may not have sufficient information on local civil society. Small CSOs may not know how to contact military forces and inform them about their presence. As a result, external interveners often do not have an adequate stakeholder map or skill set to understand how to identify diverse local voices inside and outside of the national government.

Coordination is also not easy for civil society. In complex environments and contexts of political conflict, civil society groups must navigate between state and nonstate armed groups to maintain their legitimacy among constituents and their safety amid armed actors. This requires adherence to operational requirements and guidelines that guarantee the independence of nongovernmental groups. The more empowered, independent, distinct, and accepted the CSOs are, the better they can coordinate with the government, the military, and the police to improve human security. Disempowered CSOs that are dependent on government funding, indistinguishable from security forces, and lacking operational freedom, will likely be rejected by local communities. Table 8.1 describes the key operational requirements for civil society coordination with security sector in contexts of complex environments.

DEMOCRATIC PRINCIPLES AND CIVILIAN OVERSIGHT OF SECURITY

Democratizing the security sector is essential to ensuring that human security priorities are in place in every country. The UN defines SSR as

> a process of assessment, review and implementation as well as monitoring and evaluation of the security sector, led by national authorities, and that has as its goal the enhancement of effective and accountable security for the State and its peoples, without discrimination and with full respect of human rights and the rule of law.[15]

Table 8.1

Operational Requirements for Civil Society Organizations (CSOs) in Complex Environments

Empowerment: CSOs need to have the power to influence public decisions. To acquire this power, they need to be able to organize, mobilize, and inspire communities to work together; gain access to information, education, and training; and receive funding or invitations (voluntary or donor-mandated) to participate in public decision-making processes.

Independence: CSOs need to be viewed as independent of explicit political and security interests tied to political parties or regimes. Independence enables CSOs to be accepted by all communities and armed groups that might otherwise threaten or attack them if they are viewed as a proxy for state interests. CSOs need to be able to independently assess the needs of local populations to identify local security priorities rather than following government or donor interests that might target specific groups to achieve political goals.

Distinction: CSOs depend on the distinction between unarmed civilians and armed groups encoded in International Humanitarian Law. This is to prevent attacks on the civilians they represent or on their own staff. Distinction can be achieved through clearly identifiable clothing, the demarcation of facilities, separate transportation, and housing of civilians and security forces in different locations.

Consent and Acceptance: CSOs depend on the consent and acceptance of local citizens and all state and nonstate actors controlling the territory on which they want to operate. In order to secure consent to facilitate dialogue or mediation, CSOs negotiate with a variety of actors including governments and nonstate armed groups, informal traditional governing bodies such as councils of tribal elders or religious authorities, or armed actors at checkpoints, airports, ports, or regions.

Access and Freedom: CSOs need to be able to speak and move around freely, unhindered by legal constrictions or security threats. In many countries, counterterrorism laws are restricting civil society's ability to contribute to human security by limiting their access to communities or organizations involved in armed conflict.

Source: Schirch, Lisa (editor). *Handbook on Human Security: A Civil-Military-Police Curriculum.* The Hague, The Netherlands: Alliance for Peacebuilding, GPPAC, Kroc Institute, March 2016.

SSR seeks to overcome the legacy of past abuses by reforming and professionalizing security forces. It aims to improve democratic state-society relations by raising public trust in the military and the police. It also applies to the wider security sector including intelligence, justice, security policymakers, and nonstate armed groups. SSR requires a transformation of a security system from one that protects the safety and economic and political interests of an elite group to one that protects all citizens—male and female—and all minority groups.

The concept of "democratic security" reflects the idea that governments should consult with and listen to the security interests of their own citizens. Democratic security also relates to how civilians voice their concerns about foreign military forces to civilian policymakers. When policymaking is democratic, civil society can participate with civilian government, military, and police leaders in open debate and dialogue on national priorities and strategies to achieve those interests, and the roles, authorities, and budgets of government agencies in pursuing those strategies. This form of participatory policymaking leads to democratic civil-military relations, where civil society helps to set and achieve human security goals together with the security sector.

In *Military Engagement: Influencing Armed Forces to Support Democratic Transitions,* Admiral Dennis Blair (US Navy ret.) argues that armed forces have a critical role to play in supporting society's move toward democracy. "The military heroes that history remembers have acted not to oppress their people but to defend them," he writes.[16] The development of democratic relations between security forces and civilians depends upon a recognition of how this new view departs from current and past realities.

Civilian oversight of the security sector is the most important indicator of democratic civil-military-police relations. But which civilians take part in oversight? It is important that military and police forces serve the interests and goals of all citizens, not just an elite group. There are three mechanisms of civilian oversight of the security sector: the executive branch of the government, an elected parliament or congress, and civil society, including an independent media. Examples of civil society oversight and collaboration with the security sector to improve human security are examined in the following chapters.

The traditional mechanism to assure the accountability of the security sector is the civilian government. The government's executive branch and representative bodies such as the parliament or congress hold effective oversight functions. They administer and control the budget and provide the authority and legal mandate to ensure that all security sector policies and programs represent and satisfy the needs of citizens. Civilian government oversight is not always sufficient to guarantee genuine human security for all, however. If a parliament is made up mostly of men, preventing violence against women will likely be less of a priority. If members of a congress are drawn primarily from one ethnic group, the government may be less concerned about ensuring diversity within police departments or stopping police violence against marginalized groups. Even in states with democratic electoral systems, an elite-captured government may make security decisions based exclusively on its own political and economic interests rather than broader public interests.

Additional participatory mechanisms are needed to offer opportunities for civil society and the wider public to have input into security sector policies and programs. The purpose of such mechanisms is to enable the full participation of all sectors of society, including women and marginalized social groups, in the shaping of security policies. This more inclusive and participatory approach asks critical questions related to the assessment, planning, implementation, and evaluation of security challenges and appropriate policy responses.

THE LOGIC OF LOCAL OWNERSHIP

Nearly every international assistance framework—at the UN, the World Bank, the OECD, and the recent Busan Principles of International Assistance and the New Deal for engagement in Fragile States—mandates the principle of "local ownership." Some donor governments recognize the necessity of this approach and push for greater democratic governance, but most foreign donors and interveners have a tendency to ignore or reject the principle of local ownership. Greater recognition is needed of the value of local ownership and community engagement in creating genuine human security.

Donor governments often focus on "train and equip" programs to meet urgent security threats or support fragile peace agreements in a timely manner. Train and equip programs will ultimately fail or cause even more violence, however, unless they are accompanied by mechanisms for assuring accountable security forces and preventing human rights abuses. To build legitimate state-society relationships with local ownership in security, "you have to go slow to go fast," as the saying goes. Local ownership takes time to construct, but it is ultimately the faster route to sustainable security. There is no avoiding the need for authentic local ownership.

By improving state-society relationships, local ownership increases government legitimacy and helps to create the public perception that security forces serve the people as a whole rather than a narrow elite. Legitimate, citizen-oriented states face fewer threats from nonstate armed groups.

Local ownership is especially important to ensure that security policies protect the safety of both women and men. Security needs to be gender-sensitive to ensure that everyone has equal access to justice and security, including protection from sexual and gender-based violence (SGBV). The government needs to include women and men equally in the planning, oversight, and implementation of security policies. Women and men of different ages, regions, languages, religions, and ethnicities as a diverse set of representatives of distinct civil society groups should all participate in security sector policymaking and programming.

Sometimes, INGOs act as intermediaries between the security sector and local civil society. They provide support structures such as forums, dialogues, and capacity building to strengthen the ability of civil society to oversee security sector policies and programs. At times INGOs engage and hand over functions to national CSOs, which in turn draw in traditional CSOs such as tribal leaders. But this chain of engagement does not always proceed without tensions. INGOs have been effective in applying models and lessons they have learned elsewhere, as is evident in the work of international peacebuilding NGOs including Saferworld, International Alert, Conciliation Resources, Search for Common Ground, and Partners Global. Other INGOs have faced criticism for holding onto neocolonial attitudes toward local civil society groups, underestimating their capacities and tending to speak for local people, and sometimes taking over the role and funding of local groups. INGOs and elite local civil society representatives should not be gatekeepers, but instead should step back and open doors to more diverse individuals and groups that truly represent aspects of society.

Local ownership should be broad, including as many diverse stakeholders as possible. Involving just a handful of local elite men in a consultation cannot yield an accurate picture of the interests or needs of local society. True local ownership includes mechanisms to engage all parts of the affected population, from every sector of society, with different levels of education, religious beliefs, economic status, and with diverse gender, ethnic, racial, and linguistic identities. Meaningful local ownership is not only about *whom* to engage but also about *how* to engage, through meaningful and sustainable ties with all elements of local communities. It involves oversight and engagement mechanisms that provide citizens the ability to contribute, influence, and control security sector policies and programming.

It is also important to deepen local ownership, so that civil society engagement evolves from isolated, project-based efforts toward platforms for joint implementation and institutional oversight. There are a great variety of institutions and activities that enable civil society to contribute to security sector policies and programs. Not all of them are effective in creating sustainable relationships between civil society and security forces. To strengthen their ties, civil society and security forces need to build long-term relationships and trust. They need to come together, discuss their respective interests, and find joint solutions that optimize their respective outcomes.

Civil society and the security sector can coordinate in five areas. The first is joint capacity building, which includes joint training, coaching, and support to build relationships and develop a common set of skills, concepts, and processes for working together to support human security. Second is joint assessment, which includes jointly designing research questions and data collection methods and jointly analyzing data to identify factors driving conflict and supporting peace. Third is joint planning, which includes jointly determining appropriate programs and strategies to support human security, and determining relevant theories of change. This can include coordination to plan civilian assistance, protection of civilians, conflict assessment, and peacebuilding efforts. The fourth is joint implementation, which involves coordinated efforts such as increasing the gender sensitivity of the police, developing a civilian harm mitigation plan, or addressing trauma in local communities. The last is joint monitoring and evaluation of security sector performance. This includes combined efforts to identify the baselines, benchmarks, and indicators for assessment of security sector performance and discussing the outputs, outcomes, and impacts of security strategies.

LEVELS OF LOCAL OWNERSHIP

In order to deepen local ownership, it is important to increase and institutionalize the functions of civil society in relation to the security sector. Levels of local ownership relate to at least two factors: the number of joint activities that civil society and the security sector perform together and the level of civil society empowerment within those activities. The most robust levels of local ownership are those in which civil society is involved in multiple activities and holds institutionalized power to monitor and evaluate the security sector's performance.

For example, sharing information with civil society or setting up a dialogue to listen to civil society indicates less local ownership than setting up joint implementation of human security programming with civil society or institutionalizing a joint oversight mechanism. A community policing dialogue where the police just listen to citizen complaints is less robust than a community policing program that involves local neighborhood watch committees where citizens work with the police to manage community conflicts. A permanent citizen oversight committee where the community can assess threats to its human security, and report and take action to address incidents of civilian harm illustrates even greater local ownership. Institutionalized oversight forums that give civil society a seat at the table to monitor and evaluate the security sector indicate that state-society relationships are seen as legitimate, democratic, and citizen-oriented.

Each level of local ownership should build on the prior levels of engagement. Often there is an initial dialogue to assess human security threats and/or pilot capacity-building efforts. Joint implementation and institutional oversight mechanisms are more likely to grow out of these lighter forms of engagement. There is an approximate progression from modest forms of information sharing to more meaningful types of engagement where civil society plays an active role in implementation and oversight of security.

Information sharing is a minimum requirement for local ownership. It means governments sharing security information with the public, and opportunities for civil society groups to share information with the government. Some governments publish information and reports about their security policies to increase transparency. They also encourage the public to provide information about security threats through such mechanisms as hotline phone numbers, a complaints desk, or a web form. These can be portals where citizens share information about security problems or register grievances and complaints regarding the performance of specific security members or units.

Civil society groups can use information sharing channels when advocating improvements to human security policies. A common approach is the publication and dissemination of reports that are critical of security policies and that include recommendations for change. Independent research projects on security issues may create an opportunity for civil society advocates to build relationships with people in the government and the security sector. Civil society groups have become adept at using this approach to facilitate public dialogue on security issues.[17] CSOs often seek to play a watchdog role and serve as "an index of public contentment."[18] They play an important role in ensuring that the security sector respects human rights and serves the public.

Watchdog mechanisms are an important means of holding the security sector accountable. If they are successful, they force police or military services to change their policies or to apply punitive measures to perpetrators of abuses. These mechanisms are valuable but they do not create long-term relationships and trust between civilians and the military. Indeed, because of their one-way direction and adversarial nature, critical reports and watchdog efforts may make it more difficult to build the relationships with security stakeholders that are necessary to reorient the security sector toward human security.

As noted at the outset, civil society is moving from relying solely on one-way information sharing and "protest" methods toward developing relationships with security sector officials and offering "proposals" for two-way communication and joint efforts to create human security. This does not mean neglecting accountability and civilian oversight, but rather achieving accountability by creating meaningful long-term institutional relationships and mutual trust. Permanent, institutionalized civil society-security sector coordination mechanisms—on as many levels and as many security issues as possible—provide the most effective guarantee for meaningful security.

Dialogue and consultation processes allow civil society actors to engage directly with the security sector in joint threat assessments and planning to improve human security. They are a step beyond mere information exchange and can serve as a basis for the formation of relationships and mutual partnerships. Successful dialogue and consultation forums—like all coordination mechanisms—require professional facilitation to foster effective cross-cultural communication and enable stakeholders to hear and understand each other's interests and perspectives.

Security professionals in many countries are open to engaging in dialogue and consultations with civil society representatives. They recognize that civil society leaders may have information and insights needed to achieve national security priorities. Military forces receive training on civil-military coordination in humanitarian operations, knowing that they will need to communicate with civilian humanitarian organizations operating in the midst of emergency crises. CIMIC centers and other mechanisms to support a "comprehensive approach" are examples of this. However, few military forces receive training on how to interact with civil society groups involved in long-term development projects, human rights defense, or peacebuilding efforts. This limits their possibility to engage effectively, as many security forces are not even aware that other civil society groups exist and are working to support human security. Coordination is not possible without a thorough mapping of this local capacity.

Where national security overlaps with civil society's human security priorities, dialogue, consultation, and coordination forums may be productive. There are different types of dialogue. Some, such as the POLSEDE (Towards a Security Policy for Democracy) initiative in Guatemala and the Bantay Bayanihan process in Mindanao, the Philippines, are initiated and organized by local civil society groups to foster exchange and understanding between security forces and civil society around specific challenges or needs. In other instances, INGOs may convene national consultations at which civil society has a seat at the table in defining the national security agenda.

In Yemen and Guinea, for example, Partners Global helped to facilitate a series of national dialogue forums that enabled joint analysis of human security challenges and strategies. In Nepal, civil society conducted comprehensive joint security assessments on the district level including 80 focus groups with more than 800 individuals participating in efforts to develop community policing approaches. In Tanzania, Search for Common Ground gathered security forces, civil society groups, and representatives of private companies to discuss the security of mining operations. These dialogues usually happen ad hoc, that is, only for a particular purpose and duration, and rarely include national leadership.

Dialogue and consultation has its limits unless it is institutionalized and accompanied by accountability mechanisms. Governments may seek to understand and review the community's point of view on an ad hoc basis only when the political climate makes it convenient or necessary. They may acknowledge civil society perspectives without having to commit to actually include them in their strategies and programs.

A step beyond dialogue and consultation is "joint implementation," which involves civil society participating with the security sector in the development and/or implementation of human security strategies. Civil society not only provides input but may also take on certain programmatic functions, such as participating in neighborhood patrols. Civil society and the security sector can carry out joint implementation in a wide range of efforts in diverse sectors, including community policing, restorative justice, criminal justice reform, transitional justice, SSR, preventing sexual and gender-based violence, and many more. It can also mean that civil society groups play a role in dialogue and mediation with nonstate armed groups.

Joint implementation can take place at the local and national level. An example at the local level would be community policing projects bringing together local communities and the police to dialogue with each other. Some countries have national peace infrastructures that provide permanent institutionalized mechanisms enabling civil society and security sector actors at all levels to work together in preventing and responding to violence. The National Peace Councils in Ghana provide a good example of such an "infrastructure for peace." They show how local peace committees work to provide early warnings and address local tensions. In case of escalation, the infrastructure provides recourse mechanisms at the regional, national, and also military level. The National Peace Council in Kenya is another example of a peace infrastructure that played a role in reducing the scale of election-related violence in the country's 2013 national vote.

Joint institutional oversight mechanisms are the most advanced form of civil society involvement in the monitoring and evaluation of the security sector. These official institutional platforms represent a new generation of oversight mechanisms for civil society involvement in assuring the accountability of the security sector. They complement the watchdog and protest functions mentioned earlier by enabling civil society and security forces to build long-term institutional relationships and trust.

Most states are still reluctant to set up permanent institutional structures to enable civil society oversight. Dialogue, coordination, and joint implementation are thus second-best options that enable civil society to contribute to security sector policies and programs and complement civilian government oversight in order to ensure local ownership in the security sector.

Case studies of civil society oversight of the security sector are few and far between. However the Guatemala case examined in chapter 10 illustrates how a UN-brokered peace plan provided an opportunity and need for civil society accountability mechanisms to provide oversight in all areas of the security sector, including intelligence, military, police, criminal justice, and national security policy formulation. In the Philippines (chapter 9), a permanent civil society oversight platform has led to regular meetings and trainings with members of the security forces at the national and regional level to identify security challenges, formulate joint strategies, and monitor and evaluate the performance of the security sector. This type of institutional engagement between civil society and security sectors creates a foundation for more accountable state responses to violence and embodies a "whole of society" approach to human security. More recent attempts indicate growing interest in civil society oversight of SSR processes. In Burundi, two civil society representatives participated in the National Defence Review, serving as official representatives to help monitor and evaluate the reform process.[19]

Capacity building for both the security sector and civil society is necessary to enable each to reach these levels of local ownership. A lack of capacity can often represent a major obstacle to building an effective working relationship. When civil society representatives and security sector actors are gathered in the same classroom, they may often experience the very first institutional opportunity to meet. Training curricula that favor discussions and interactive exercises will enable the participants to start building common ground and increase their understanding and appreciation for each other. This can be the basis for building relationships and working together in joint problem-solving missions.

A PEACEBUILDING APPROACH TO LOCAL OWNERSHIP

Peacebuilding analytical tools, values, skills, and processes help to support all the ideas discussed in this chapter: legitimate state-society relations, human security, SSR, local ownership, civil society oversight of the security sector, and civil society-military-police coordination. Peacebuilding organizations work to advocate and support more robust levels of local ownership. The case studies in this book illustrate how peacebuilding CSOs are playing a mediating role to engage with governments, police, military, and local communities in order to achieve dialogue and consultation, joint implementation, and, in some cases, joint institutional oversight to improve human security.

Peacebuilding includes a wide range of efforts by diverse actors in government and civil society at the community, national, and international levels to address the immediate impacts and root causes of violent conflict before, during, and after it occurs. Peacebuilding values, skills, and processes such as dialogue, negotiation, and mediation support human security. The prevention of violent conflict involves addressing structural and proximate causes of violence, promoting sustainable peace, employing dispute resolution strategies, building peacemaking capacity within society, and reducing vulnerability to triggers of violence.[20] From the various case studies in this book, some common principles of peacebuilding emerge as critical to SSR, local ownership, and human security.[21]

Peacebuilding stands apart from other approaches to armed conflict because it focuses on the lack of legitimate, democratic governance as a root cause of violence. Other approaches focus less on structures and more on individuals or groups as the cause of violence. Conflict assessment frameworks emerging out of the field of peacebuilding can help to improve shared understanding of security challenges.[22] Such a shared analysis of violence between diverse stakeholders in the security sector as well as civil society is necessary to enable multistakeholder coordination for human security.

Security forces and civil society can jointly advance human security when both groups respect each other as human beings, even though they may distrust or disagree with each other on issues. Mutual respect is a fundamental peacebuilding value. Focusing on relationships does not mean accepting or accommodating adversarial interests. A peacebuilding approach does not back away from differences or tensions. It is "hard on the problems, but soft on the people."[23] It encourages individuals to distinguish between opinions and the persons who hold the opinion; to criticize ideas or reject types of behavior, while maintaining an appreciation for the person behind them. Such an attitude is the prerequisite for building strong and sustainable relationships and trust.

Peacebuilding skills and processes enable women and men in civil society and the security sector to understand each other's interests. Peacebuilding forums for dialogue and consultation and joint implementation and oversight enable both civil society groups and security sector representatives to solve problems. Trained facilitators keep a dialogue focused, help participants consider a variety of views, and summarize group discussions. They model active listening and respectful speaking. Facilitators and mediators help groups explore similarities and differences of opinion. Peacebuilding facilitates dialogue processes and builds consensus to help diverse stakeholders through a dialogue process to ensure that all stakeholders' interests and perspectives are heard.

One last unique characteristic of a peacebuilding approach is its ability to measure changes in attitudes as well as behaviors and knowledge. Civil society measures human security, at least in part, by the perceptions of safety held by civilians, including women who might experience different types of threats and violence. A common indicator of human security is whether the public perceives security forces as protectors rather than predators.

CONCLUSION

While civil society has made significant strides in reaching out to policymakers to influence policy in a wide range of areas, the security sector is perhaps the last arena still off limits to civil society in many societies. A history of tension and sometimes trauma makes it seem impossible for civil society to even attempt to build relationships with security sector leaders. At the same time, disdain for civil society is often pronounced in the security sector. This chapter identifies a way forward. The case studies in this book from Guatemala and the Philippines provide hope that real progress is possible.

In recent decades there is growing appreciation of the role of civil society in fostering peace, security, and recognition that "local ownership" of security is critical. This chapter outlines how to move beyond just informing the public to actually involving civil society in active dialogues, from local-level community policing forums to high-level national security dialogues. Local ownership means including diverse stakeholders in many different activities, such as conflict assessment, jointly implementing security strategies, civilian protection and assistance, conflict prevention, and jointly monitoring and evaluating security sector governance, accountability, and performance. Local ownership is most robust when civil society is empowered, independent, distinct, accepted, and free to advocate on behalf of broad civil society interests.

Peacebuilding analysis, concepts, skills, and processes are not just useful in structuring macro-level transitions to a just peace. They are also necessary and useful for micro-level interactions between civil society and the security sector. By applying peacebuilding methods in interaction with the security sector, innovative peacebuilding CSOs are providing a compelling vision for a future in which civil society and the security sector sit down together and jointly assess the causes of conflict and design a world where human security prevails.

NOTES

1. Human Security Unit of the United Nations, *Human Security in Theory and Practice: An Overview of the Human Security Concept and the United Nations Trust Fund for Human Security* (New York: United Nations, 2009), http://www.un.org/humansecurity/sites/www.un.org.humansecurity/files/human_security_in_theory_and_practice_english.pdf.

2. United Nations Development Program, *Human Security Report 1994* (New York: Oxford University Press, 1994).

3. United Nations Secretary-General Kofi Annan, "In Larger Freedom: Towards Development, Security and Human Rights for All," A/59/2005, 55.

4. Elisabeth Jay Friedman, Kathryn Hochstetler, and Ann Marie Clark, *Sovereignty, Democracy, and Global Civil Society: State-Society Relations at UN World Conferences* (New York: SUNY Press, 2005).

5. OECD Development Assistance Committee, "Concepts and Dilemmas of State Building in Fragile Situations: From Fragility to Resilience," OECD/DAC Discussion Paper, http://www.oecd.org/dac/governance-peace/conflictandfragility/docs/41100930.pdf, 8.

6. Alexander Mayer-Rieckh and Serge Rumin, "Confronting an Abusive Past in Security Sector Reform after Conflict: Guidelines for Practitioners," Initiative for Peacebuilding, 2010.

7. For a complete set of correlates of attacks by nonstate armed groups, refer to *Global Terrorism Index 2014: Measuring and Understanding the Impact of Terrorism* (New York: Institute for Economics and Peace, 2014), http://www.visionofhumanity.org/sites/default/files/Global%20Terrorism%20Index%20Report%202014_0.pdf.

8. See, for example, Louise Boon-Kuo, Ben Hayes, Vicki Sentas, and Gavin Sullivan, *Building Peace in Permanent War: Terrorist Listing and Conflict Transformation* (London: International State Crime Initiative—Transnational Institute, 2015).

9. John Paul Lederach, "Addressing Terrorism: A Theory of Change Approach," in *Somalia: Creating Space for Fresh Approaches to Peacebuilding* (Uppsala: Life and Peace Institute, 2011).

10. Major Louis J. Ruscetta, *Education for Philippine Pacification: How the U.S. Used Education as Part of Its Counterinsurgency Strategy in the Philippines from 1898 to 1909* (Damascus, MD: Pennyhill Press, 2013).

11. Erin McCandless, *Polarization and Transformation in Zimbabwe: Social Movements, Strategy Dilemmas, and Change* (Durban: University of Kwazulu-Natal Press, 2011).

12. Erica Chenoweth and Maria J. Stephan, *Why Civil Resistance Works: The Strategic Logic of Nonviolent Conflict* (New York: Columbia University Press, 2011); Dennis Blair, *Military Engagement: Influencing Armed Forces to Support Democratic Transitions* (Washington DC: Brookings Institution Press, 2013).

13. For clarification on the distinction between "coordination" and "cooperation," refer to Edwina Thompson, *Principled Pragmatism: NGO Engagement with Armed Actors* (Monrovia, CA: WorldVision International, 2008).

14. Cedric De Coning, "Clarity, Coherence, and Context: Three Priorities for Sustainable Peacebuilding," Working Paper: The Future of the Peacebuilding Architecture Project, Norwegian Institute of International Affairs and Centre for International Policy Studies, University of Ottawa, 2010, http://www.betterpeace.org/files/CIPS_NUPI_Clarity_Coherence_and_Context_deConing_Feb2010.pdf, 26.

15. Security Sector Reform Unit of the Office of Rule of Law and Security Operations of the Department of Peacekeeping Operations of the United Nations, "The United Nations SSR Perspective," 2012, http://www.un.org/en/peacekeeping/publications/ssr/ssr_perspective_2012.pdf, 2.

16. Blair, *Military Engagement*.

17. Duncan Hiscock, "Research and Information," in *Public Oversight of the Security Sector: A Handbook for Civil Society Organisations*, eds., Eden Cole, Kerstin

Eppert, and Katrin Kinzelbach (Valeur, Slovakia: United Nations Development Program, 2008), 49.

18. Maria Caparini and Eden Cole, "The Case for Public Oversight of the Security Sector: Concepts and Strategies," in *Public Oversight of the Security Sector: A Handbook for Civil Society Organisations*, eds., Eden Cole, Kerstin Eppert, and Katrin Kinzelbach (Valeur, Slovakia: United Nations Development Program, 2008), 19.

19. Lisa Schirch and Deborah Mancini-Griffoli, *Local Ownership in Security: Peacebuilding Approaches to Civil-Military-Police Coordination* (The Hague: Alliance for Peacebuilding, GPPAC, and the Kroc Institute, 2015).

20. Daniel Serwer and Patricia Thomson, "A Framework for Success: International Intervention in Societies Emerging from Conflict," in *Leashing the Dogs of War*, eds., Chester Crocker, Fen Osler Hampson, and Pamela Aall (Washington DC: United States Institute for Peace, 2007); Luc Reychler and Thania Paffenholz, *Peacebuilding: A Field Guide* (Boulder: Lynne Rienner Publishers, 2001); Lisa Schirch, *Strategic Peacebuilding* (Intercourse, PA: Good Books, 2004).

21. Schirch and Mancini-Griffoli, *Local Ownership in Security*.

22. For a comparison of different types of conflict assessment frameworks used by peacebuilding organizations, refer to Lisa Schirch, *Conflict Assessment and Peacebuilding Planning: Toward a Participatory Approach to Human Security* (Boulder: Kumarian Press, 2013).

23. Roger Fisher and William Ury, *Getting to Yes. Negotiating Agreement Without Giving In* (New York: Penguin, 1983).

Chapter 9

Unlikely Partners for Conflict Transformation

Engaging the Military as Stakeholders for Peace in Mindanao

Myla Leguro and Hyunjin Deborah Kwak

In this chapter, we discuss civil society work in peacebuilding and emphasize the importance of actively engaging the military as a key stakeholder in
working toward peace. In the context of the Mindanao conflict, we argue that
a reframing process is necessary for civil society and military actors to collaborate in peacebuilding—a reframing that defines the military as a crucial
stakeholder for peace. This kind of reframing in the context of peacebuilding
is what John Paul Lederach describes as moral imagination:

> The moral imagination requires the capacity to imagine ourselves in a web
> of relationships that includes our enemies; the ability to sustain a paradoxical
> curiosity that embraces complexity without reliance on dualistic polarity; the
> fundamental belief in and pursuit of the creative act; and the acceptance of the
> inherent risk of stepping into the mystery of the unknown that lies beyond the
> far too familiar landscape of violence.[1]

The moral imagination in partnerships between civil society and military
actors may be a long and difficult process, especially in conflict contexts in
which the military has in the past, as an instrument of the state, engaged in
acts of violence in communities or repressed civilians and ethnic minorities.
The moral imagination requires a transformation of frames on both sides.
On the one hand, the military should be able to imagine the possibility of
fulfilling their role and responsibility in achieving human security[2] and contributing to peacebuilding and community development. On the other hand,
civil society actors should be able to imagine the potential of military actors
to work for human security as well as how they can engage the military as a
stakeholder in local peace efforts. The case of Basilan[3] in this chapter suggests that these framing processes allow trust and strong relationships to

develop between civil society groups and military actors, in turn enabling them to initiate joint efforts of conflict transformation and peacebuilding in local communities.

We proceed by providing a brief historical and contextual analysis of civil-military relations in the Philippines. Next, we discuss specific developments at the institutional level and in bottom-up efforts by civil society groups that encouraged both sides to reimagine the military as an important stakeholder in the peace process and partner in local peacebuilding. We show how the military's participation and position as a stakeholder in peacebuilding efforts developed through two specific initiatives. First, the Armed Forces of the Philippines (AFP) adopted a top-down, human security and human development approach at the institutional level in order to guide their operations in and engagement with local communities. Second, civil society groups organized efforts to provide high-ranking military officers and soldiers with training in conflict transformation as well as to engage them in opportunities for community development and peacebuilding. Based on in-depth interviews and focus group discussions with civil society and military actors in Basilan, we describe how members of the military were able to build trust and participate in peace efforts in communities, employing social and peacebuilding skills in their daily interactions with civilians. Finally, we discuss the challenges and policy implications of sustaining a collaborative relationship between civil society and military actors.

THE CHANGING ROLE OF THE PHILIPPINE MILITARY

The military sector holds a strategic position within a conflict society. Lederach identifies military leaders in his framework of peacebuilding actors as part of the top-level leadership often involved in top-down peace negotiations.[4] The cooperation of the military can be a significant factor in contexts where peacebuilding is taken as a strategy for social change and conflict transformation. However, this recognition does not negate the reality that while the military possesses the potential and capacity for constructive change, it has often served as the pillar for, or perpetrator of, unjust regimes and/or violent conflict. In the context of the Philippines, the military as a political force in society became crucial during the period of Ferdinand Marcos's dictatorial rule from 1972 to 1986. It was a key pillar that supported martial law in the country. Revolutionaries, nonviolent activists, and community people during this reign of terror experienced military abuse and brutality. Despite the military's role in sustaining Marcos's rule, defections among Marcos's trusted military officials and staff significantly contributed to the success of the first People Power Revolution in 1986. The military's support of the second People Power Revolution in response to the calls of business, church, and political opposition leaders to oust President Estrada also resulted in a regime change in 2001. The events of 1986 and 2001 thus create a legacy of participation in social change movements and nonviolent campaigns on the part of the military.

The Philippine military today continues to wield significant influence over the politics and governance of the country. While functioning as a primary government agency that combats the different armed rebel groups in the Philippines, the military has also been given a meaningful role in the government's peace process efforts.[5] In view of the military's important function in peace and conflict issues, civil society groups and community peacebuilders have increased direct engagement with the military in the last ten years in both the formal peace process and the peacebuilding efforts in local communities.

The persistence of armed conflict and violence plaguing the country highlights the need for a deeper understanding of the unlikely partnership between civil society and the military. While the nonviolent movements were successful in overthrowing an authoritarian regime in 1986 and a corrupt administration in 2001, injustice and structural violence continue to fuel the grievances of the Moro separatist armed groups and the communist revolutionary armed movement. To address and resolve the root causes of armed conflict, civil society groups and the military have learned to collaborate in applying effective practices and skills of peacebuilding in dialogue, negotiation, and vertical and horizontal relationship-building.

After the 1986 People Power Revolution, the Philippine peace movement evolved from government efforts to negotiate with the various armed rebel groups, starting with the administration of Cory Aquino in 1986 and continuing under president Benigno Aquino. CSOs are now engaged in various peacebuilding interventions, including peace constituency building, conflict reduction efforts, conflict settlement efforts, peace research and training programs, and social development work.[6] These efforts complement top-level peace process interventions, which involve peace negotiations but also interreligious dialogue among high-level religious leaders. Grassroots efforts mostly involve the establishment of zones of peace and efforts that integrate peace and development initiatives.

In this array of endeavors at various levels of society, CSOs' strategic ability to engage in vertical and horizontal networking facilitates a process of harmonization of formal and informal peace processes. In her assessment of initiatives of "peace CSOs," Miriam Ferrer reports a "phenomenal growth of Moro and Mindanao CSOs."[7] The peacebuilding efforts in Mindanao correspond to the specific conflict context of structural injustice related to ethnic and religious identities. The conflict situation is shaped by systemic concerns in relation to political, economic, and social exclusion and marginalization of the Muslim and indigenous populations. Thus, a key part of the peace-building approach among civil society groups is strengthening relationships horizontally at the community level. Relationship-building between Muslims, Christians, and indigenous peoples in Mindanao has been nurtured through peace education and interreligious dialogue efforts.

Civil society efforts to engage the military have been long and difficult. The euphoric solidarity created between members of the military and civil society actors during the 1986 People Power Revolution did not automatically translate into a collaborative partnership for nation-building. Although the armed forces had played a critical role in the country's return to democracy, during the period of martial law and authoritarianism NGOs and the military often found themselves on opposite sides of the barricades.[8] Various programs were initiated to bridge this trust gap between military and civil society groups during the presidency of Corazon Aquino (1986–1992). This paved the way toward establishing important links and some degree of understanding and mutual confidence.[9] It was during this period that the military adopted the Military Values Education program, which aimed to professionalize the AFP through the formation of values that were defined as being God-centered, nation-centered, and people-centered. Human rights education also became part of military training, later including certification from the Philippine Human Rights Commission as a criterion for promotion.[10] During the presidency of Fidel Ramos (1992–1996), the government institutionalized the "left hand approach" of socioeconomic development and peace negotiations. The peace program opened up political and social space for civil society participation in formal peace negotiations, and the military adopted a dual approach in addressing insurgency and armed rebellion. The Arroyo administration issued an executive order mandating the military to abide by the "primacy of the peace process."[11] The order prioritized the peace process over and above other strategies. This served as a policy guide for CSOs to engage the military as a stakeholder for the peace process and peacebuilding, particularly in Mindanao. Under the Benigno Aquino administration, the AFP adopted an Internal Peace and Security Plan (IPSP) "guided by multistakeholder approach and people-centered human security."[12] This security plan emphasized the need to engage national government agencies, the Philippine National Police (PNP), the local government, CSOs, and the broader public in sustainably addressing peace and security concerns. According to the plan "the AFP, as an able partner in peace and development, believes in the importance of shared responsibility with the various peace and security stakeholders in addressing the peace and security concerns of the country."[13] Four areas of engagement for the AFP are identified: "governance, delivery of basic services, economic reconstruction and sustainable development, and security sector reform."[14] Through the IPSP, the military has mainstreamed the approach of positive engagement with civil society and communities in addressing peace and security issues on the ground.[15]

LOCAL EFFORTS TO ENGAGE THE MILITARY IN MINDANAO

Although the process of bridging the divide between the military and civil society groups began after 1986, it was only recently that CSOs in Mindanao were able to establish concrete efforts of direct engagement with the military within their respective peace programs. The policy development on the "primacy of the peace process" and the expanding role of former and active military officials and staff in formal peace structures paved the way for the active engagement of the military. Efforts of civil society groups include peace education and training, peace advocacy, follow-up and accompaniment, peace constituency building, and peace policy development. Civil society groups employ conflict transformation strategies aimed at increasing awareness and participation of the military in peacebuilding initiatives. The positive engagement with the military is guided by theories of change at the individual, personal, and relational level and in sociopolitical or structural dimensions.

The personal change approach is based on the premise of nurturing individual peace champions who will become change agents within the military hierarchy. Civil society seeks to reframe the perspective of the military from an enemy to a partner. This has been quite a difficult process for a number of peace advocates given their personal experience of military atrocities and abuse during the martial law and postmartial law years. Civil society actors expressed such sentiments during a focus group session in Basilan. A local Moro CSO leader explained, "I was hesitant to work with the military before because of the human rights concerns … we have pointed out that the military was the number one violator of human rights in previous years [the crackdown from 2001 to 2003]."[16] Another Moro civil society member described how personal experiences of violence in relation to the military had strongly affected his view of the military in general: "I am a victim of human rights abuse. My father was killed by a soldier so I became a human rights defender. My brother was killed, then my cousin. This was [in] a massacre killing of 11 people. This happened in 1997."[17] In this same focus group, participants were asked about the process of engaging the military in peacebuilding. A woman in the group explained that this was possible because of the paradigm shift in the Philippine military about what it means to be a soldier: "Because of the paradigm shift through [IPSP] now we can approach and talk to them. Before there was a wall, now they are friendly to us, so we entered into partnership with them."[18] Other participants from civil society groups recounted that over time they were able to change their perceptions of the military due to the sincerity of individual soldiers in their daily interactions with them. One member described it this way, "[When] I look at the person, I can build trust if I see the sincerity [in them]. Then I am also transformed."[19] Thus, the institutional changes in the military significantly affected the military's regular interactions as well as their long-term relationship with civil society actors.

Civil society actors in Basilan further shared that their perceptions about the military changed when they observed how the military responded to human rights violation cases brought against them. For instance, a focus group member shared that with the IPSP approach guiding the military's activities, he saw significant change in the way cases were addressed:

> [The] military now plays a vital role as protector of civilians. This lessened human rights violations because the military has learned that they have to connect with the community. Before, they were hard to get or they were very sensitive and defensive, especially when we brought cases of rape to the sessions.[20]

In this way, civil society actors acknowledged the significant change in their perceptions regarding the military based on important institutional changes that were occurring within the military.

To facilitate the process of change on a personal level, Fr. Bert Layson, a prominent peacebuilder in Central Mindanao, mainstreamed the principle of "recognizing the goodness in each person."[21] The values of engaging the military actor as a person can be likened to the approaches outlined by Dr. Martin Luther King in his speech, "How Long, Not Long." King espoused the Gospel principle of recognizing the elements of goodness in one's enemies and further explained the importance of not seeking the defeat or humiliation of the enemy but to "win his friendship and understanding."[22] Similarly, as explained by Veronique Duduoet, Gandhi promoted the process of nonviolent conversion, "whereby it [nonviolence] moves the adversaries to embrace the point of view of the challengers."[23]

The reframing of the military actor through a personal approach in turn facilitates developments at the relational level. Civil society groups see this as an opportunity to connect military peace champions with grassroots activists, Muslim NGOs, and religious leaders through networks and relationships. The relational approach is aimed at expanding the network of connections for the military peace champions so that their level of influence can be mutually maximized for the collective vision of peace. As a peacebuilding strategy, the relationship-building component concretely strengthens the vertical and horizontal networks of the military, civil society, and communities to help connect efforts from the grassroots to the top level.

PEACE FORMATION AND TRAINING

A number of civil society groups have provided peace formation and training for military officials, staff, and civilian reserve forces in Central, Western, and Northern Mindanao. Workshops have presented on cultures of peace, conflict transformation, nonviolent communication, active nonviolence, peacebuilding, and peace advocacy. For example, in 2006 some local NGOs partnered with a military commander to conduct culture of peace workshops for 2,400 paramilitary men in Western Mindanao.[24] In Central Mindanao, two NGOs collaborated to conduct a conflict resolution workshop for military officers in one brigade. The same military officers had a two-week study session on conflict transformation led by their brigade commander who was trained in the Mindanao Peacebuilding Institute in 2007.[25] Some of the workshops were conducted in the military camps but the more effective and transformative trainings were the ones in which the military attended together with participants from other sectors. These mixed workshops were opportunities for the military to interact with civilian groups they do not usually engage, such as Muslim peace advocates, grassroots peace leaders, and young peace activists. The workshops also provided deliberative spaces in which the military learned about peace and nonviolent approaches to social change, thus facilitating the creation of formal and informal networks of civil and military actors.

A battalion commander formerly stationed in Central Mindanao and trained in the Mindanao Peacebuilding Institute in 2007 shared his personal reflections on the impact of the workshop:

> The importance of being exposed to the different groups and sectors widened my perspective on peace. The value of intent listening to sharing among classmates and participants was apparent as we not only focused on the military point of view. The art of listening must likewise be taught in passing before the start of each seminar or workshop in order to have optimum assimilation. Most important ... is how to effectively apply it, which was a big challenge on my part as a commander [with responsibility for] ... the whole of Central Mindanao.[26]

Similarly, the following reflection from a young military officer represents the kind of change that often occurs in terms of reframing of identity as more than being a soldier to include the identity of also being a peacebuilder:

> As a young lieutenant, I was able to start founding [*sic*] my niche where I should grow as a leader in my own league, that I am more of a "soldier" when peacebuilding became my perspective. I would rather volunteer to mediate and resolve things in a peaceful manner as long as I can and as [the] situation

permits rather than immediately throw myself in the battle zone and cry out that I'm a warrior.[27]

Many personal reflections such as these confirm that training and formation were crucial in nurturing personal transformation among the military participants.

The strategic targeting of influential military officials in Mindanao was critical for civil society to gain entry into the military structure. Despite apprehensions in the beginning, the auspicious decision to accept the first military officer to the training at the Mindanao Peacebuilding Institute in 2005 became crucial in restarting the process of engaging the military. The first military officer trained in the institute was later promoted to general and over time gained considerable clout and influence among his peers as well as in other sectors. He has served as an active peace advocate since and has been heavily involved in mainstreaming peacebuilding within the military sector. With strong support for his leadership among civil society groups, he was recently promoted to commander of the Eastern Mindanao Command which covers half of the island of Mindanao. Other leaders within the military hierarchy in Mindanao have been recruited. Civil society groups have maintained connections not only with senior officials but also junior officials on the ground. The strategy is to build relationships through formal and informal mechanisms. Civil society actors have tried to maximize and strengthen their military connections. For example, a church worker involved in justice and peace work sought the help of a military official to locate the whereabouts of a youth activist who was allegedly picked up by the military in her area. The military official made inquiries on her behalf and the youth activist was safely released. Because of this incident, the trust and friendship strengthened between the young church worker and the military official.

Some CSOs engage the military in policy issues in relation to the formal peace negotiations. Policy dialogues on the role of the military in the peace process have been conducted in order to expand the peace constituency within the military hierarchy. High-level dialogues between the military and key Muslim and Christian religious leaders have also helped to nurture collaborative partnerships for peacebuilding. The dialogues paved the way for mainstreaming the theme of the military and the police as peace partners during the annual celebration for the Mindanao Week of Peace in 2006.

Civil society also organized a series of dialogue sessions between the Philippine military and the leadership of the Moro Islamic Liberation Front (MILF) in order to strengthen the commitment of both parties to the peace negotiations. This engagement contributed to solidifying peace process structures such as the joint ceasefire committee of the government (predominantly represented by the military) and the MILF. Top-level government efforts have been supplemented by numerous local-level initiatives between military commanders, local leaders, and communities. The military has participated in various community-based peacebuilding efforts such as local zones of peace, local dialogues between warring parties in communities, and community development projects.

In order to sustain the personal and relational changes experienced through these dialogues and training workshops, various CSOs established follow-up structures to provide support to the trained military men and women. The support mechanism is mostly informal such as follow-up conversations, phone calls, and texts. Formal strategies include regular meetings, integration of the trained military into local peace networks, and visits to military camps. This posttraining support is crucial because trained military peace champions often face opposition within the hierarchy. For example, a young military official described that there is "a strong opposition among top military officials on the basic concepts of peace because it diminishes their roles as defenders of the state into mere 'peace advocates.'"[28] In response, civil society groups use formal and informal strategies to continue accompanying these military peace champions. One peace mentor sends out daily text messages to military officials that she has trained in order to maintain the connection. This line of communication became crucial when the trained military officers entered situations in which they had to put their peacebuilding skills into practice. On a number of occasions, the virtual accompaniment provided opportunities for the military to creatively expand options to prevent violence in managing local conflicts in Mindanao.[29]

A number of the trained military are involved in concrete peacebuilding efforts often through the integration of peace values and principles in their community development work. Some are practicing skills in conflict resolution in areas where military officers are seen to be credible as mediators. One military official shared his experience: "I have seen how my learnings from the Mindanao Peacebuilding Institute worked effectively in trying to settle disputes among feuding Muslim clans."[30] Later he also shared,

> My MPI experience helped me to transform my thinking in dealing with conflicts … [and] that soldiers can be peacebuilders without necessarily abandoning the core competencies of soldiery. It is just adding more lenses through which one could view the various factors that contribute to the occurrence of conflicts. Having better appreciation of conflict situations allows one to formulate more courses of action than when just having a very limited perspective of what is really happening around.[31]

This reflection shows how trained soldiers practice peacebuilding by expanding their understanding, and embracing the complexity of their identity and roles in the military. The peacebuilding training experiences also enable military officers to serve as resource persons for peace training in their respective units.

The different civil society groups accompanying the military have developed innovative platforms to ensure that the military officers are integrated within the Mindanao peace constituency. For instance, Balay Mindanao, an NGO based in Northern Mindanao, established a regular forum in which top-level military officials in Mindanao participate. Moreover, the Mindanao Peacebuilding Institute has encouraged the military officials trained there to become members of province-based networks of peacebuilders. Key members of the military peace champions are invited to join civil society groups on various mobilization and solidarity activities to ensure that they continue to maintain their connection to and representation as stakeholders for peace.

BANTAY BAYANIHAN IN BASILAN

The case study of Bantay Bayanihan[32] in Basilan demonstrates the process of how relations between civil society and local military forces have developed. We briefly explain the context of the conflict dynamics in Basilan, an island province of the Philippines within the Autonomous Region in Muslim Mindanao. Next, based on data collected from focus group discussions and interviews, we describe the process of reframing undergone by both civil society groups and the military. We show how through this process civil-military interactions developed into concrete peace efforts in local communities in Basilan. We also discuss the challenges of sustaining civil-military relationships, obstacles to collaborative peace efforts, and lessons and policy implications drawn from this case.

Basilan is home to three main ethnic groups—the Yakans, Tausugs, and Chavacanos. The Yakans and Tausugs are predominantly Muslim, while the Chavacanos are mainly Christian. Basilan has been ravaged by conflict and violence for more than forty years. In the 1970s, the island became a battleground between the Moro National Liberation Front (MNLF) and the armed forces and the Philippine Constabulary. In the early 1990s, Basilan became a haven for terrorists with the formation of the Abu Sayyaf Group (ASG). The group was responsible for atrocities within and outside of Basilan—including kidnappings, beheadings, rape, and other violent acts that targeted civilians. Their kidnap-for-ransom operations soared in 2000 and 2001, which included kidnappings of foreign tourists.

While the threats of the ASG and other loose armed groups remain a serious cause of violence and insecurity in the communities, other factors exacerbate the situation, including: proliferation of armed groups, intertribal and interethnic conflict, clan warfare, local election disputes, extreme poverty, and social exclusion and marginalization. The Bangsamoro Conflict Monitoring database confirms that "political violence, shadow economies and clan feuding were the dominant causes of violent conflicts in the province."[33] Moreover, the same database indicates that "Basilan outpaced the other Bangsamoro provinces with an annual average of 78 violent incidents per 100,000 persons during 2011–2013."[34]

To address the recurrence of conflict and violence in the province, major stakeholders including local government units, civil society, religious leaders, and the military formally established a convergence platform in 2012. However, civil society and military engagement in peace and security started much earlier around 2004–2005. One of the critical challenges to the convergence platform was civil society actors' suspicion of and lack of trust in the military. According to a civil society actor, "Muslim CSOs were at first hesitant to work with the military because of past human rights abuses."[35] These CSOs pointed out that the military was the number one violator of human rights in Basilan, especially during the crackdown on communities from 2001 to 2003. The military forces committed many human rights violations, and civilians were hit by military airstrikes in areas like Tipo-tipo, Al Barka, and Tuburan. In our conversations with military officials, they acknowledged that past abuses of the military have resulted in negative perceptions and fear among local communities.[36]

Despite experiences of violence, CSO actors were compelled to engage with the military because of their own security needs as well as that of their constituents in the communities. Moreover, the paradigm shift within the military encouraged CSOs to build collaborative relationships with the military. "They were the ones that opened first before we opened too," said a local civil society leader. "Through the Bantay Bayanihan platform, CSOs can now approach and talk with military forces in our area. There is no wall and they are friendly with us. But still we do not rely on them because we have our own programs in the community where they also engage with us."[37]

More importantly, the building of trust and relationships between CSOs and the military was founded on concrete results that were observed in the communities. For example, one CSO member shared that:

> There have been changes too in Moro communities. Back in 2008, people were fearful of the military—when they see the soldiers, they hide in their houses. In 2012, if people see the military they greet them, they shake hands with the military. People have increased their trust with the military.[38]

For the military, the process of transformation started with the recognition that war operations would not solve the security problem and that they needed to seek a better way of addressing it. This approach involves establishing trust with the community and engaging with various stakeholders. One military official shared during a focus group discussion, "The military has evolved its primary function beyond war fighting–now it is also stakeholder engagement."[39]

Through the convergence platform in Basilan, the military and local government units have launched various peace and development efforts to address the needs and problems of communities in the province. The initiatives include joint activities undertaken by members of the platform. Some are CSO-led development activities that involve the military as partners offering logistics and security support, while other activities are led by the military, which in turn engages the support and participation of CSOs and local governments. The diversity of actors initiating the different activities demonstrates the balance of power in the relationships among various stakeholders of the convergence platform.

Beyond strengthening the collaboration of the different stakeholders, joint initiatives of Team Basilan have helped address human security issues in the communities. For example, the platform worked together to settle clan feuds, facilitated dialogues to address the concerns of agrarian reform cooperatives, and facilitated psychosocial debriefings for women and children in conflict-affected communities. Civil society and the military also collaborated in development programs, particularly in communities that are difficult to reach due to security concerns. Military forces provided personnel and logistics support to CSOs, thus enabling them to deliver services. CSOs also often engaged soldiers to become mentors and counselors to youth participants for community programs.

Military forces in Basilan have engaged significantly with civilian communities. They have organized medical missions, set up a children's library, provided schools with supplies, and facilitated support to empower young people through education and employment. One battalion organized an acoustic band contest which was held inside the military camp. The friendly competition attracted groups of young musicians from different communities. For most of the youth, it was their first time to step inside a military camp, and their experience changed their perspective of the military.

When asked about the outcomes of civil society and military engagement in Basilan, CSO members report that there was a marked reduction in conflicts in the communities. Human rights violations have decreased because the military has formed strong relationships with the communities and now functions as a protector of civilians. Furthermore, the military is now more open to discussing the concerns of communities.[40] Due to the convergence platform, CSOs are able to freely bring their concerns to the stakeholder meetings. In these meetings CSOs are given information about military operations and activities. CSO members of Bantay Bayanihan have also been able to bring issues to national-level meetings, which high-ranking military officials attend. This accountability mechanism increases pressure on military personnel on the ground to act accordingly.

For the military, the new approach has also redefined their standards of success. One military official discussed what would it mean to win peace: "If I am the commander for two years and am able to encourage people from outside to bring development, if children are able to go to school and do not see their parents carrying guns, meaning there is no war, then I would win peace as a military commander."[41] Another officer said he wants to help people understand that soldiers have transformed from being violent human rights violators to now being protectors of the people.[42] Equally important is the increased sense of accountability, as shared by one military official: "The negative perspective of the military has changed with the continuous engagement with the community. One effect is that we don't tolerate wrongdoings of the soldiers because if soldiers commit a mistake, they will immediately be investigated and a case will be filed against them."[43]

CONDITIONS THAT MOBILIZE STAKEHOLDERS

In analyzing the experiences of civil society and military actors in Basilan, we identify certain conditions that have contributed to the success of Bantay Bayanihan. These conditions have cultivated an environment conducive for both civil society and military actors to undergo the process of changing their attitudes about the "Other" and expanding the paradigm of the military's potential role and responsibility in peacebuilding. The conditions have also encouraged stakeholders to collaborate in violence prevention, peacebuilding, and development efforts.

The first step in the process was a conscious effort of civil society actors in Basilan to incorporate the military into their peacebuilding agenda. This was accompanied by innovative peace efforts in the larger context of Mindanao and a strong belief among mainstream peace groups that the peace process should include *all* stakeholders of the conflict. This encouraged the cultivation of civil-military partnerships.

Second was the AFP's adoption of a strong peace policy that upholds human security and human development. This stimulated a top-down process in which the Philippine Army's approach to peace slowly but surely began to change. Because it is a particularly hierarchical institution, the military's formal adoption of a new peace policy in 2010 was necessary in order for both top-level military leaders and rank-and-file soldiers to undergo a significant paradigm shift. Consequently, this encouraged high-ranking military officers to initiate collaborative efforts with civil society actors in their respective geographic areas of assignment as well as to train soldiers to engage in peace-building. Creating important peace structures at the policy level gave way to peace education and training opportunities for military officers and soldiers serving at the community level, although such opportunities and processes emerged inconsistently depending on the military personnel in charge and the relational dynamics between civic and military actors in specific geographic areas in the Philippines.

Third was the role of senior officers at the battalion level who believed in the military's responsibility for peacebuilding and were influential in changing the views of lower-ranking soldiers in their units. The role of these officers is critical in promoting human security and development approaches. They play the role of the "critical yeast," as Lederach puts it.[44] In our focus group discussions and interviews with officers in Basilan, a significant minority of military officers in high ranks were vocal advocates and practitioners of the IPSP approach in their battalions and communities. One officer said:

> As commander I urge my soldiers to build trust through small gestures such as a smile, a greeting, shaking hands. The immediate effect is an impression that soldiers are kind, and [we] are able to gain trust of the civilians. Respect the children, the elderly, and the religious leaders. Soldiers should be disciplined, and when they go into the communities, they should connect with them by speaking the local dialect, in Yakan, for example.[45]

The senior officers also serve as examples for their soldiers in practices of cultural sensitivity and community engagement.

A fourth step was civilian assistance for the military that contributes to the success of security operations. This is an important reason why the military needs to cultivate trust in their relations with communities. A military officer described the role that communities play in helping the military prevent and respond to violence:

> There will be peace if the Abu Sayyaf group is not able to plant bombs in the communities. Now it is the people who can inform us [the military] if the group has planted bombs. ... If people are united [against extremist groups] then the Abu Sayyaf cannot enter [their communities]. ... When I assumed the position, there had been many bombings in my area. What I did was to conduct face-to-face dialogues in the barangays and then I established outposts in each barangay for the civilians to take the lead role in guarding the barangay. Then one-two months after, [there were] no bombings. The communities also report [to us] about incidents of suspicious individuals in the community.[46]

This officer's experience is evidence for the claim that the military needs the cooperation of communities in order to safeguard peace.

Fifth was the willingness of civil society actors in Basilan to play the role of mediator between the military and communities. This mostly happened in regular meetings where representatives of civil society groups had the time and opportunity to raise the specific needs and problems of communities with the military. In our focus group discussions, civil society leaders described how they openly share with high-ranking officers their security and development concerns in specific communities and appeal for the military's help. As experienced community organizers and often as residents of the communities themselves, they can give advice to the military about community attitudes and culturally sensitive responses in particular situations. In these discursive spaces, the military is also able to share with civil society leaders important information about security or emergency situations so that they can inform their community members. A military officer described the relationship this way:

> I learned a lot from them [civil society]. By engaging with them, I could feel the pulse of the people. If we are the only ones talking [directly] to the people [in the communities]—they will hold back because we are military. They have stereotyped the military. [But] If we engage with CSOs, we can discuss freely without holding back. They can criticize and I am open to suggestions and advice.[47]

A civil society leader also shared with us that she personally contacts a high-ranking officer when she receives complaints from community members about indecent behaviors of soldiers.

Finally, our interviews and focus group discussions with civil society leaders and military officers revealed that an active and ongoing peace process motivates stakeholders to engage in peacebuilding efforts and collaborate with other actors. The recognition of the primacy of the peace process by civil society groups, the military, and the MILF rebel group is crucial because it creates an environment conducive to collaboration. Stakeholders sense the importance and urgency of preventing incidents of violence that may disrupt the peace process. They recognize that they need to collaborate and build relations with the "Other" to prevent violent incidents. A civil society leader highlighted the importance of the peace process: "Now it is different. With the peace process ... there is already change in terms of conflict in remote areas. Before there was conflict recurring three to four times [a month], now only one or even none. ... So there is reduction in violence."[48] The MILF rebel group is also cooperating with government forces to ensure security, according to civil society leaders. "MILF is helping the military to drive away the Abu Sayyaf. They don't want the Abu Sayyaf in their areas because of the peace process. ... Although MILF and Abu Sayyaf are relatives, the MILF does not allow it to be near their camps. MILF is sincere in their negotiations."[49] The MILF and the Philippine Army have also collaborated in settling family feuds over land with the help of the current regional governor of the autonomous region of Muslims.

CHALLENGES AND POLICY IMPLICATIONS

Both civil society and military actors recognize several challenges that need to be addressed in order to sustain civil-military relations and collaborative efforts. First, weak capacity and governance in local government units can hamper the institutionalization of the process. Civil society groups have found that capacity building of local government structures is crucial for good governance and in turn for effective collaboration on development and peace-building efforts. One local leader argued that low levels of education and lack of civic skills among local government officials are significant obstacles to the active participation of local government units in Bantay Bayaihan. She pointed out that CSOs contribute much more in terms of material, organizational, and human resources to collaborative efforts in communities than local government units, despite the resources that municipal governments are allocated for "peace and order."[50] A military officer during a focus group discussion emphasized the connection between bad governance and security concerns:

> I see malgovernance [in local government units] as the problem. For example, the local chief executives at the barangay level—they are not able to control their areas of jurisdictions because most of them are staying in the city and not in their barangays. We look for the local executives, but they are not in their offices. [So] they are not able to address the issues and concerns of their constituents.[51]

Local government leaders are often not accountable for their decisions and because of security concerns live in cities far away from their communities. People living in barangays that are strongholds of extremist groups like the Abu Sayyaf often do not get access to basic services.

Second, civil society leaders observe that the frequent turnover of military leadership (every two years) in a particular region is a significant challenge. It means that civil society actors have to rebuild trust with new, high-ranking military officers quite often. The civil social leaders recommend that the military orient new officers about Bantay Bayanihan and its civil society partners during the transition process of leadership in order to sustain civil-military relationships and collaborative efforts.

Third, civil society actors need to strengthen relations with military actors in their respective regions. This will allow them to collaborate with the military in peacebuilding efforts yet maintain a healthy distance that permits a critical voice when necessary regarding the military's actions and policies. In our focus group discussions, civil society leaders emphasized the need to be self-critical of their role and identity as civil society so that they can effectively carry out their responsibilities as mediators between the military and the communities they serve.[52] In order to play both roles, partner and critic of the military, civil society leaders should not hesitate to point out soldiers' lack of discipline, cultural insensitivities, and harmful behaviors in communities. A healthy relationship with the military is one that serves as leverage to achieve human security.

Fourth, our conversations with military officers and civil society groups in Basilan revealed that the military's top-down, institutional approach on adopting human security and human development approaches often fails to permeate micro-relational dynamics on the ground. In certain areas of the Philippines, especially in strongholds of the New People's Army (NPA),[53] the military exercises power and authority like they did during the time of martial law. Communities often experience harassment and abuse by government soldiers and are considered NPA members or sympathizers. Government soldiers constantly interrupt daily life by interrogating barangay leaders, teachers, and children. Thus, there is significant variation in the extent to which civil society and military actors collaborate depending on the military officer in charge as well as the local conflict dynamics in a particular geographic region.[54]

Fifth, recent incidents of violence in Mindanao suggest that the human security approach should be adopted more consistently throughout the institutions of both the Philippine Army and the Philippine Police. This is illustrated in the tragic incident that occurred in January 2015 in Mamasapano. The PNP/Special Action Force (SAF) led an operation to capture a wanted Malaysian terrorist and bomb-maker Zulkifli Abdhir and members of the extremist group, Bangsamoro Islamic Freedom Fighters (BIFF). MILF forces were stationed in the same community where the operations occurred, and the MILF coordinated with the Philippine Army through the ceasefire committee of the local peace process. However, the PNP/SAF did not coordinate with the army and the MILF as they were supposed to do based on the ceasefire agreement and the Ad Hoc Joint Action Group (AHJAG). This led to an unplanned military encounter in which civilians and soldiers on both sides were killed. This violent clash also disrupted the peace process as public opinion leaned heavily against the MILF. This incident confirms the need for both the military and the police to adopt a unified, human security approach in conflict-affected areas.

CONCLUSION

In most literature on nonviolence, the military is often depicted as a direct opponent to civil society. More specifically, it is considered to be a support base for authoritarian regimes, an actor that needs to be converted as an ally in order to weaken the power of the "establishment." The Philippines' experiences of nonviolence in the People Power Revolutions confirmed this assessment. The emerging peacebuilding praxis in Mindanao, however, presents a transformative reframing of the military as an important actor potentially involved in peacebuilding. This reframing depicts the military as an important stakeholder for peace. It requires moral imagination on both sides—for the military, an ability to perceive themselves as stakeholders for peace; for civil society, a willingness to engage military officials and other security stakeholders in various peace efforts.

Civil society peacebuilders and community leaders have approached this reframing process through their own experiences with the military. Their initial encounters were wrought with fear and suspicion but over time this has led to trust and friendships. For instance, a woman activist who suffered from abuses during the height of the martial law has developed a strong friendship with one of the military officials. The friendship was developed during their dialogues and interactions in a peacebuilding workshop and cemented through participation in a collaborative peace effort in their area. In a focus group of civil society leaders in Basilan, many participants shared examples of how the relationship between the military and their communities has been transformed. One civil society member shared that the military's approach to dealing with members of the rebel groups has changed:

> Instead of taking the combat way of eliminating the lawless elements, they are looking for ways of winning the hearts and minds of people in the community. Lawless elements are [often] relatives of members of the communities; even MILF and ASG [Abu Sayyaf] are relatives also.[55]

These significant changes in the military's security paradigm have in turn changed the perceptions and actions of people in the communities, many of whom have transformed their negative perceptions of the military. Local peacebuilders have developed a mantra in their encounters with the military that emphasizes a belief in the goodness in each person. Civil society actors continue to supplement changes at the personal level with efforts to achieve relational and structural changes.

The reframing on the military side is best explained by one of the leading military peace champions in Mindanao, former major general Raymundo Ferrer. He states, "You cannot be part of the solution if you are not part of the problem."[56] This statement is based on his understanding of the history of abuses by the military, acknowledging the fact that the fear of the soldier permeates civilian society, and the feeling among Muslims that the military is an occupying force in their territories. At the same time, the statement hinges on the claim that the military should be a stakeholder for peace, thus reflecting its desire to be part of the solution. This understanding as articulated by Ferrer is now being mainstreamed among the military peace champions and guides the efforts of the military to address their contribution to the problem. This is indeed a big leap from the traditional militaristic approach of addressing the armed conflict in Mindanao. This vision of military transformation involves the transition "from fear of the soldier to respect for the soldier; from mistrust to mutual trust; from an image of oppressor to protector; from plain warriors to peacebuilders."[57] Ferrer further explains that this can be done by developing the capacity of the military to do peacebuilding, to engage all armed groups in dialogue, and to participate in multisectoral initiatives for peace.[58] The articulation of this peace agenda signifies the military's commitment not only to the peace process but also to fundamental values of peace.

While personal relationships are important, lessons in Mindanao point to the need for nurturing strategic connections vertically. Civil society is now using its unique position to serve as a facilitating channel in dialogues between the military and grassroots communities as well as interactions between the military and nonstate armed groups. Local military leaders, for their part, serve as a connection between civil society and top-level commanders who are in charge of the security agenda of the country. The military provides information to civil society actors on security policies and military operations and efforts in various areas. The goal is to maximize these connections and increase dialogue and interactions among key actors on fundamental issues of conflict.

The military's peace agenda and commitment to becoming part of the solution in Mindanao symbolizes a key achievement of civil society groups. Yet the current peace process in Mindanao remains fragile due to unexpected problems in the implementation stage of the peace agreement. It is critical for civil society groups to focus on bridging relationships not only between the Philippine military and the MILF but also with other rebel groups. Together military and civilian stakeholders for peace need to continuously address the root causes of the Moro armed struggle as well as tackle the underlying conditions of injustice that lead to insurgency.

NOTES

1. John Paul Lederach, *The Moral Imagination: The Art and Soul of Building Peace* (New York: Oxford University Press, 2005), 5.

2. Our definition of "human security" focuses on the safety of individuals and communities. At minimum, human security refers to safety from direct threats of violence. A comprehensive approach to human security includes three components: freedom from fear, freedom from want, and freedom to live in dignity.

3. Basilan is an island province in Western Mindanao that has experienced extensive armed conflict.

4. John Paul Lederach, *Building Peace: Sustainable Reconciliation in Divided Societies* (Washington, DC: United States Institute of Peace, 1997), 39.

5. Former and active military officials are holding key positions in the government peace process infrastructure. The peace process office of the government has been headed by former military officials. Today it is headed by the former head of the Philippine National Police. Active military personnel are part of peace process structures (e.g. ceasefire committee).

6. Miriam Coronel-Ferrer, "Institutional Response: Civil Society," background paper submitted for the Philippine Human Development Report, 2005, http://hdn.org.ph/wp-content/uploads/2005_PHDR/2005%20Civil_Society_Assessment.pdf, 1–6.

7. Ibid., 21.

8. Carolina Hernandez, "Restoring Democratic Civilian Control over the Philippine Military: Challenges and Prospects," *Journal of International Cooperation Studies* 10, no. 1 (2002): 34.

9. Ibid., 35.

10. Ibid.

11. President Gloria Macapagal-Arroyo, *Executive Order No. 3, s. 2001*, www.gov.ph/2001/02/28/executive-order-no-3-s-2001.

12. Armed Forces of the Philippines (AFP), *Internal Peace and Security Plan* (Manila: Government of the Philippines, 2010), http://www.army.mil.ph/pdf_files/bayanihan.pdf, 9.

13. Ibid.

14. AFP, *Internal Peace and Security Plan*, 27.

15. Major General Carlito C. Galvez, interview with authors, Davao City, Philippines, September 18, 2015.

16. Focus group discussions with seven civil society group leaders in Basilan, Mindanao, September 23, 2015.

17. Ibid.

18. Ibid.

19. Ibid.

20. Ibid.

21. Fr. Bert Layson, conversation with author.

22. Martin Luther King Jr., "How Long, Not Long (Our God is Marching On)" (speech, Montgomery, AL, March 25, 1965), King Institute at Stanford University, https://kinginstitute.stanford.edu/our-god-marching.

23. Veronique Duduoet, *Nonviolent Resistance and Conflict Transformation in Power Asymmetries* (Berlin: Berghof Research Center for Constructive Conflict Management, 2008), 15.

24. Maryann Cusimano Love, "Partnering for Peace in the Philippines: Military and Religious Engagement," *Georgetown University Institute for the Study of Diplomacy Pew Case Study Center*, Case 550, 2005, http://www.uscirf.gov/sites/default/files/resources/stories/pdf/maryann%20love%20philippines%20case%20study.pdf, 5.

25. The commander referred to is General Pedro Soria II of the Philippine Army. Details of his training initiatives may be found in the Catholic Relief Services, Philippines Peace and Reconciliation program archives.

26. The officer quoted here is Battalion Commander Lieutenant Colonel Paul Atal of the Philippine Army. The quote is cited in *Security Sector Monograph* (Davao City: Mindanao Peacebuilding Institute and Catholic Relief Services Mindanao Regional Program Office Peace and Reconciliation Program, November 17, 2008), 7.

27. The officer quoted here is First Lieutenant Melanie Sibayan of the Philippine Army. The quote is cited in *Security Sector Monograph*, 9.

28 Ibid., 8.

29. The trained military sometimes use these lines to ask for advice from their peace mentors, such as when they are asked to mediate conflicts and/or when they are asked to neutralize local situations involving politicians in their areas.

30. The officer quoted here is General Soria II. The quote is cited in *Security Sector Monograph*, 8.

31. General Soria II, oral testimony found in the Catholic Relief Services archive.

32. Bantay Bayanihan is a network of civil society organizations engaged in peacebuilding in the Philippines. The military has adopted the term *Bayanihan*, meaning "working together," for its Internal Peace and Security Plan. *Bantay Bayanihan* means "to guard the Bayanihan/the IPSP process."

33. International Alert, "Rebellion, Political Violence and Shadow Crimes in the Bangsamoro: The Bangsamoro Conflict Monitoring System (BCMS), 2011–2013," August 2014, http://bcms-philippines.info/vers1/sites/default/files/BCMS%20General%20Paper.pdf, 21.

34. Ibid.

35. Focus group with civil society group leaders.

36. Focus group discussions with five military leaders in Basilan, Mindanao, September 24, 2015.

37. Focus group with civil society group leaders.

38. Ibid.

39. Focus group with military leaders.

40. Focus group with civil society group leaders.

41. Focus group with military leaders.

42. Ibid.

43. Ibid.

44. Lederach, *The Moral Imagination*, 91.

45. Focus group with military leaders.

46. Ibid.

47. Ibid.

48. Focus group with civil society group leaders.

49. Ibid.

50. Ibid.

51. Focus group with military leaders.

52. Focus group with civil society group leaders.

53. The NPA is the armed wing of the Communist Party of the Philippines.

54. Focus group with civil society group leaders; and focus group with military leaders.

55. Focus group with civil society group leaders.

56. Major General Raymundo Ferrer, Untitled Presentation, Agong Peace Network General Assembly, Davao City, Philippines, 2005.

57. Ibid.

58. Ibid.

Chapter 10

POLSEDE, Civil Society, and Security Sector Reform in Guatemala

Bernardo Arévalo de León and Ana Glenda Táger

As part of the Guatemalan Peace Accords signed in 1996, an agreement was reached on the need to adapt security sector institutions to the goals and necessities of a democratic system. This was the Agreement on the Strengthening of Civilian Power and on the Role of the Military in a Democratic Society (AFPC, its Spanish acronym). Implementation of the agreement initially faltered, however, as the result of a resistant military, a distracted government, a polarized political atmosphere, and an uninformed public. To overcome these problems an initiative was launched in 1999 by the Guatemalan branch of the Latin American Faculty of Social Sciences (FLACSO) and other civil society groups that became known as Toward a Security Policy for Democracy (POLSEDE, its Spanish acronym).[1] This research and dialogue process was able to bring all the concerned parties in state and society together around a collective effort to achieve the goal of converting the military to democratic principles in the spirit of the peace accords.

The POLSEDE process was supported by the War-torn Societies Project (WSP) International—currently known as Interpeace—and the UNDP.[2] The initiative gathered CSOs, academic institutions, and relevant government agencies, including the military, into a three-year process that involved more than 200 meetings in six technical working groups, a high-level plenary, and a range of ad hoc events such as public conferences and workshops. The project issued twelve documents with specific recommendations that were integrated into a conceptual framework document on civil-military relations. It also produced concrete reform proposals for restructuring the security system, the intelligence services, and the functioning of the military.

This chapter examines the development of POLSEDE and its successor initiatives while also determining their impact on the partial transformation of the Guatemalan armed forces in the implementation of the postconflict peace process. It traces the development of multistakeholder consultative processes in the aftermath of the peace agreement that identified concepts and proposals for helping to implement the security provisions of the accord. These efforts helped to forge a political consensus within state and society, and also within the military, for significant steps toward democratic security policies. The processes evolved into direct consulting and lobbying efforts that had real impacts on national legislation and policy. Beyond these concrete results, POLSEDE and its successors instilled in participants the attitudes and skills that enabled them to pursue cooperative engagement in a range of initiatives that furthered the collaborative interaction between state and society while strengthening civil society capacities for advancing the democratization process. The result has been an empowered civil society, which has played important roles in security sector policymaking through technical advice, advocacy, and lobbying.

The process of democratizing the military that began in the 1990s helps to explain the remarkable restraint of the military in 2015 when social protests against corruption forced the resignation and arrest of Guatemala's president, vice-president, and other senior government officials. The fact that the armed forces remained in the barracks despite the sacking of these former leading generals was a testament to the influence of new structures of governance and changing attitudes in and toward the military. While these transformations remain tentative in the context of new threats today from violent crime and limited state capacity, they illustrate the potential of civil society engagement to achieve progress toward human security.

CONTEXT AND CHALLENGES FOR MILITARY REFORM

On December 31, 1996, thirty-six years of internal armed conflict between an authoritarian state and leftist guerrillas—leaving more than 250,000 victims, 63 massacres, and other crimes against humanity—ended in Guatemala. The conflict originated when all avenues for political reform were closed in the early sixties, and the military took over direct control of the state under the mantle of the National Security Doctrine developed by the United States in the context of the Cold War.[3] The development of an exclusionary and discriminatory political system that attended to the interests of a minority elite in the face of widening social protest condemned the state to a deep crisis of legitimacy that threatened its capacity to reproduce itself as political order. Its chronic inability to deal with this situation through noncoercive methods, negotiations, and dialogue resulted in a spiral of violence: the appearance of armed insurgent movements that were met with even more violence by the state apparatus. Repression and violence were exerted not only against the actual political groups that had resorted to armed struggle, but against the ever-widening concentric circles of 'active' and 'potential' threats, from nonviolent political dissent to civilian populations in the areas of insurgent activity.[4]

The military developed a web of formal and informal institutions—that is, networks of civilian informants, forcibly recruited paramilitary forces, and institutional coordinating units subordinated to the military at every level of the state—to ensure full control over the population and political institutions. The result was a pattern of civil-military relations characterized by the politicization of the armed forces, the militarization of state and society, the alienation of the population from political institutions, and the routinization of violence in social life. By the early eighties, the counterinsurgent state entered a deep political crisis. Widespread corruption among the military high command, a growing military threat by insurgent groups, and loss of international legitimacy as an effect of mounting international criticism for human rights violations led to a coup d'état by junior officers with a plan to liberalize politics as a strategy to relegitimize the counterinsurgency effort. The military would no longer directly run the government in order to concentrate on the military campaign, while democratically elected authorities would assume all nonsecurity government responsibilities thus providing a mantle of political legitimacy to their effort.[5]

It was democracy as a counterinsurgency strategy, with the intention of leaving executive office in the hands of elected civilians while enabling the military to retain political control. But the series of democratically elected governments that took office between 1985 and 1996 gradually wrestled political power away from the military. Initial decisions by civilian authorities to ignore the military veto on political contacts with the insurgency led to informal interaction with the guerrilla movements that evolved into formal peace negotiations between 1990 and 1996, a period during which three successive civilian governments sent political-military delegations to negotiate with the guerrilla commanders to reach a political settlement to the conflict.

A Blueprint for Reform

The peace process dealt not only with the end of the armed confrontation and its effects on society, but addressed a wide range of social and economic issues—from women's rights to socioeconomic policy—effectively becoming an agenda for social reform. This spirit of reforming institutions was reflected in the AFPC, the part of the agreement that dealt with issues of military reform and demilitarization of society. Out of eight sections of the peace agreement, only one—section VII—dealt with operative issues of demobilization, disarmament, and reintegration directly derived from the end of armed confrontation. Another one—the largest section, number IV—focused on the transformation of security sector institutions in order to guarantee control by democratic authorities. The rest included commitments on other necessary components for the strengthening of what is called "civilian" democratic power which includes the nature of the state (section I), the legislative branch (section II), the judicial branch (section III), establishment of a professional civil service (section IV, chapter F), social participation with explicit reference to the role of women (sections V and VI), and UN verification mechanisms (section VIII).

It is evident that the AFPC dealt not so much with the necessary redefinition of military functions as a result of the end of armed conflict and the disappearance of the subversive military threat to the state, as with the need to ensure the development of a military institution that responds to the security needs of a democratic political community. In this regard, it built upon the Central American Democratic Security Framework Treaty (TMSD, its Spanish acronym), which had been signed by the presidents of the Central American countries in 1995 with the explicit intention to eradicate the authoritarian regional security structures and concepts inherited from the Cold War.[6] Even if it did not adopt the "Democratic Security" terminology, the AFPC proposed an integral transformation of the security apparatus of the state—military services, public security, intelligence services, and presidential security—that included functional, organizational, and legal provisions for democratic control. While some of the proposed reforms were sketchy or ambiguous, like the establishment of the congressional committee for intelligence activities or the creation of the new presidential security apparatus, the AFPC managed to establish a basic agenda for democratic institutional reform that, if fully implemented and subsequently developed, would effectively transform the way in which the state thinks about and performs its security functions.[7]

CHALLENGES IN THE IMPLEMENTATION OF THE AFPC ACCORD

The first months after the signing of the Peace Accords, under the administration of President Alvaro Arzú Irigoyen (1996–2000) of the *Partido de Avanzada Nacional* (PAN), were a period of concrete and evident progress. Commitments on demilitarization, disarmament, and reintegration adopted under part VII began to be effectively implemented. Demobilization of specific military units, such as the Ambulatory Military Police, and paramilitary groups, such as the Voluntary Committees for Civilian Self-Defense and the Military Commissioners, were successfully concluded. But personal confrontations between key high-ranking military officers that were advancing the process of reform led President Arzú in 1997 to an abrupt decision: to replace them with a group of military officers that had developed good political links with the presidential entourage. The decision implied the displacement of the cadre of military officers that had taken active part in the peace process that publicly professed commitment toward implementation of the Peace Accords in general and the AFPC in particular, and that were perceived by the military as comprising legitimate institutional representatives of the armed forces. This action demonstrated favor to a group of officers that had little institutional legitimacy and, as their actions would evidence, little commitment to the peace process in general or to the implementation of the AFPC in particular.[8]

Between 1997 and 2000, these new military authorities developed a level of resistance toward implementation of the AFPC beyond what had already been achieved, with a procrastinating strategy that included an uncooperative attitude toward the United Nations Verification Mission (MINUGUA, its Spanish acronym). Implementation of the AFPC commitments began to falter. While the 33 percent reduction in the military budget was effectively achieved by 1999, the parallel reduction in personnel was achieved only formally. The demobilization affected mostly lower-ranking soldiers while maintaining the officer corps basically intact, and in doing so the military capacity could "grow back" with little effort. A disproportionate number of officers remained in service creating an imbalance in the hierarchical structure of the army.

After initially demobilizing some military units and outposts without altering the basic strategy of territorial control developed for counterinsurgency, the military authorities attempted to rename and dress it up in an unsuccessful attempt to convince military experts in MINUGUA that it was responding to external defense needs. The revised Military Doctrine presented by the Ministry of Defense at the very end of the Arzú administration was a confused collection of texts developed almost in secret by a military ad hoc command in an attempt to formally comply with the Peace Accords' commitment. It gave lip service to the idea of reform, while in fact justifying the role the military played during the armed conflict. The civilian affairs unit of the army continued conducting political surveillance activities at the local level, issuing regular reports on activities of social and political actors. Through systematic resistance to grant access to military archives to outspoken accusations of political bias, the army assumed a completely uncooperative attitude toward the work of the Historical Clarification Commission that was mandated in the Peace Accords to investigate the record of violence and human rights violations during the armed confrontation.[9]

The reluctance of the military was also evident in the absence of a new security policy clearly formulated by civilian authorities that would redefine the role of the armed forces. President Arzú and his government quickly

212   *Bernardo Arévalo de León and Ana Glenda Táger*

became indifferent to institutional military transformation and left the task of defining a new policy in the hands of appointed military officers—the minister of defense and his entourage. The few civilians within the government who understood the need to pursue institutional change in the military were not able to muster enough political power to confront a minister of defense who had become very close to the president.

As a result, the scope of progress in two critical areas of reform was limited. In terms of the redefinition of the military function and the corresponding institutional conversion, governmental action remained at the level of formalities avoiding any substantive transformation. As for the development of a democratic security policy that would break away from the conceptual and operational underpinnings of the authoritarian National Security Doctrine, no concrete steps were being undertaken to ensure a process of collective reflection involving the military and civilians in state and society. The resulting glaring contradiction between governmental policy and the letter of the AFPC introduced confusion and disorientation within the military rank and file and skepticism in civil society.[10]

During this period, resistance to implementation of the Peace Accords became entrenched in the armed forces and the military through the personalized leadership of Minister of Defense Marco Tulio Espinoza, who seemed to have retained a degree of autonomy from and political influence over civilian authorities. The situation of the postconflict scenario at that point could be summarized in the following factors: (1) a weak civilian political leadership—government officials, political parties—without the necessary capacities nor political will to design, negotiate, and implement the policies needed to reform the state security sector as per the commitments of the AFPC; (2) mistrust, misinformation, confusion, and different levels of resistance to transformation within a military establishment still entrenched in a National Security Doctrine mentality; (3) difficulties in cross-sectoral, civilian-military dialogue derived from deep social mistrust, political factionalism and polarization, and the weakness of political parties; and (4) asymmetry in the substantive knowledge the different actors in state and society had over the issues at stake, for instance civilians' very limited technical information on security sector issues and the military's conceptual and operational knowledge anchored on authoritarian frameworks.

BUILDING A MULTISTAKEHOLDER PROCESS TO BRIDGE DIVIDES

It was against this background that in 1999 two local institutions—the Guatemala office of FLACSO and the Guatemalan Institute for Development and Peace (IGEDEP, its Spanish acronym)—joined with an international initiative, WSP International, to design a multistakeholder dialogue project. The project aimed at gathering the different social and political actors involved in security sector reform issues around a collaborative effort to overcome the stalemate in the implementation of the AFPC and foster the development of the conceptual and operational frameworks for the security function of the state.

FLACSO, IGEDEP, and WSP International had already participated in the implementation of a multistakeholder dialogue in Guatemala immediately after the signing of the Peace Accords. This dialogue brought together actors in state and society around an effort to foster consensus on critical postconflict priorities for the operationalization of the Peace Accords.[11] In that process the Participatory Action Research (PAR) approach, developed by WSP for use in postconflict settings, enabled a diverse and polarized community of actors in state and society to engage in an inclusive evidence-based collaborative analysis and decision-making process. It consisted of the establishment of a local coordinating team capable of designing and managing a "research and dialogue" platform and of convening an inclusive and participatory multistakeholder forum that would cut across sociopolitical divides and work upon the principle of consensus. This effort implied two critical functions. Politically, it needed to guarantee the neutrality of the space, convening all relevant actors and ensuring representative and inclusive participation while navigating the usually agitated political waters of polarized postconflict settings. Methodologically, it required the effective implementation of a process combining research and dialogue methods, ensuring the development of sound policy recommendations that were both technically sound and politically legitimate.

Strategy

The intended result of the PAR method is an integrated approach which provides analytical clarity, a holistic perspective, access to information, and better responsiveness on the part of the concerned stakeholders, which enhances the impact of research products. A research and dialogue strategy, developed over several months in an atmosphere of neutrality and transparency, constitutes simultaneously a confidence-building process, a knowledge-generation initiative and—beyond the specific policy recommendations achieved—a capacity-building strategy addressing both the specific substantive issue approached and the capacities for collaborative interaction in society.

The goal in Guatemala was to facilitate the adoption of collaborative attitudes by undertaking the dialogue as an academic exercise instead of relying on adversarial "negotiation" formats. The "evidence based" nature of the process would prevent actors from engaging in discussions based upon predefined, often ideologically anchored notions of what the problems and the solutions were, allowing time for the establishment of sound, evidence-based parameters for the discussion. The consensus rule reduced concerns that the exercise could be politically manipulated in favor of one side or the other and eased resistance to participation from hardliners by guaranteeing they would not be "ambushed" by numbers.

Through a thorough consultation with different sectors in civil society and the state, FLACSO and IGEDEP were able to identify the existence of sufficient conditions of viability for an exercise of this nature. Government authorities expressed their support for the initiative, clearly identifying the value of consensus-based policies in such a polarized subject and specifically the potential contribution to the implementation of lagging AFPC commitments. CSOs expressed their interest in a space that would allow them to interact with civilian and military actors in government on a topic hitherto monopolized by security institutions, and that was clearly key for any progress toward democratization. Although some recalcitrant military elements expressed reservations about opening the process of security reform to civil society involvement, the military as an institution was interested in legitimizing itself in the new political context and therefore expressed its willingness to join a research-based effort that stood apart from the adversarial dynamics that characterized civil-military relations in the postconflict context.

Implementation

Critical for the viability of the project was the establishment and accreditation of a space that would be perceived by participant stakeholders as safe, neutral, and effective. The organizational set-up of the initiative included a dedicated team that operated as a UN-supported project independent from the sponsoring local institutions. The development of clear rules of procedure that were discussed with stakeholders in personal meetings enabled the establishment of a basic framework of trust sufficient for all to accept the invitation. It was the effective implementation of these rules along the whole process that enabled participants to accrue trust as they progressed into the discussion of more sensitive and complex issues. The prospect for effectiveness, demonstrated by whether the results of the process would effectively influence policy, was provided by the proactive engagement of governmental agencies with executive responsibility over the matters being discussed. This provided participants with a direct link to the policy-formulation processes even if the project was not an "official" forum with binding results.

The plenary platform of the process included high-level officials of five government agencies: the military, representatives of sixteen CSOs, and ten civilian and experts invited on a personal basis. The plenary convened ten times during the period of the project. It had a clear multisectoral character involving active and retired military officers, former guerrilla operatives active in political parties and CSOs, civilian government officials, human rights organizations, scholars from academic research centers, and members of the business sector. The realization of such a balanced group became one of the main tools accrediting the exercise as neutral and autonomous.

Several working groups were formed to involve technical-level representatives of participant institutions and others whose presence was considered necessary. They developed a research agenda that included the conceptual framework for the role of the state, society, and the armed forces in political transitions; issues of democratic security and civilian control; and operational strategies for the functioning of military forces and intelligence. The groups held dozens of working sessions ranging from three-hour meetings to seminars that lasted several days. Through this process, the topics identified by the plenary were explored in a slow, consensus-building process that started by developing a shared understanding of what the issue was, followed by the development of joint definitions of the problem and the goals, leading to the discussion of concrete technical proposals addressing the key issues identified through the PAR process.

The perception of political balance in the composition of this group became an important element. The coordinating team for the process took care to appoint researchers from institutions with different ideological affiliations including the military. Some researchers came from institutions perceived as belonging to the "Left," while others were more to the "Right" on the political spectrum, but the overall composition of the research team was balanced. In addition, each working group was requested to select by consensus one of their participants to serve as "facilitator," who also doubled as the working group's interface with researchers.

In addition, four large events were organized by the project coordinating team in order to provide important input to participant stakeholders at critical moments of the process: an international conference on military function and democratic control, a seminar on intelligence reform experiences, a three-week course on defense policy for military personnel and civilians, and an international conference on security sector reform in fragile democracies. The number of topics identified in these events and the many meetings and seminars produced a full agenda and led to an intense process. By generating several important research and policy analyses, the project created necessary relationships and extensive webs of formal and informal interaction, resulting in multiplied contacts on civil-military issues between civilians and the military and between government officials and civil society.

Results

At the end of the process, two different types of results were evident. First, concrete policy recommendations addressing critical gaps in the implementation of the AFPC were issued, reflecting both a political consensus that seemed difficult to achieve beforehand and greater technical command of AFPC terms by state and civil society actors. The products included conceptual parameters for anchoring state security norms and practices in functional democratic principles, a proposal for the establishment of a national intelligence system, and detailed operational structures and mechanisms for democratic oversight. A total of twelve documents were approved by the plenary on the basis of the work of the six working groups.[12]

In addition to producing policy recommendations, the project contributed to the strengthening of necessary social capacities for addressing similar challenges in the future. This included a better understanding of the technical issues at stake and greater capacities for research and policy analysis across the state-society divide and a network of actors—civilian and military, state and society. The project also helped participants develop the skills and self-confidence to continue constructive interaction around issues of common interest, on the basis of the shared understandings and goals developed through it.

Obviously, this transformative effect was obtained in a gradual and progressive fashion, in the logic of a confidence-building mechanism. The mistrust and suspicion that characterized the social and political environment of postconflict society ceded only gradually, and only after the realization that intersectoral collaboration strategies were not only possible but also necessary and effective. As a result, extreme positions that initially dominated the tone of the conversations gradually lost relevance and, paradoxically, facilitated the emergence of a new consensus. The fact that participants were able to achieve consensual policy recommendations in a political context marked by polarization and mistrust became a source of confidence and self-satisfaction. It was also a motivation to sustain the effort, materialized in decisions to continue the collaboration beyond the project dynamics in what would be the nucleus of an emerging civil-military security community.[13]

In terms of the factors that contributed to the effectiveness of the process, the following stand out as most salient. First, the academic character of the project, its intentionally low public profile and its orientation toward medium- and long-term policies created a conducive framework enabling participants to overcome a priori ideological or political positions and engage in a rational analysis of the issues. Second, the neutrality and autonomy of the project from institutional interests, the balancing of political ideologies in the project group, and the use of a methodology of gradual consensus-building sustained over several months enabled the achievement of significant sectoral consensus on sensitive issues like intelligence reform.

Third, using a participatory action research methodology involved "training in the process" for both civilian and military actors which allowed them to renew, validate, and disseminate relevant technical knowledge, and raised the proactive capacity of the members of the groups. Fourth, the involvement of representatives of state institutions in the working groups facilitated the integration of academic capacities into public policy processes, and generated the interest of political actors seeking to contribute to governance needs. Finally, the combined effect of building trust and recognition of the existence of shared interests from which to build consensus helped to reduce the level of distrust, polarization, and resistance, which facilitated the emergence of cross-sectoral partnerships built from the subject under study and not from political or ideological positions and prejudices.

The Aftermath

The POLSEDE process led to a number of follow-up initiatives that continued the multisectoral dialogue approach to public security issues. These efforts included policy dialogues launched by the state institutions with the participation of civil society, the establishment of a coordinating body of CSOs working on security sector issues—which is still active—and the signing of an agreement between CSOs and Congress to provide technical assistance to congressional commissions working on security sector legislation.[14] These efforts have sustained and amplified the original intent of the POLSEDE project, with concrete influences felt even today.

Among the most relevant of these efforts is POLSEC: Toward a Citizen's Security Policy (2002–2004). This was a direct follow-up project, implemented by FLACSO-Guatemala, the Association for Security in Democracy (SEDEM), and WSP International, with operational support from the UNDP. POLSEC applied the same research and dialogue approach to the design of a citizen security policy. The initiative lobbied Congress for implementation of the conceptual and operational parameters for the public security function defined in the POLSEDE process. Its agenda focused on three critical areas with a working group assigned to each: a democratic, legal, and institutional framework for citizen security, a preventive approach to security, and a criminal investigations framework respectful of human rights. The initiative crafted several specific proposals for institutional reform of the public security system.

Another significant effort was the Guatemalan Democratic Security Network (2002–2003). Voluntarily created by POLSEDE participants with the intention of sustaining the multisectoral dialogue around democratic security issues, "La Red"—the network—was created as a collaborative space open to individuals and institutions supportive of the principles and goals developed through POLSEDE. Its goals included fostering the implementation of recommendations in the emerging legal and operational security frameworks, as well as the development of technical know-how on security and defense issues. A number of state officials, both civilian and military, were able to remain engaged on a personal basis even when not officially representing their agency. Although La Red was not legally incorporated or institutionally anchored, it functioned through periodic meetings for two years as a reference point and reservoir of expertise on technical aspects of democratic security norms and practice.

State-convened policy dialogues were also a notable attempt in which the military developed its own multistakeholder dialogue effort on defense and security issues. The trust developed across the state-society and civil-military divides made viable the implementation of dialogic processes convened by state institutions, which would not have been attended by the more serious academic and nongovernmental organizations beforehand. The first initiative was the White Paper on National Defense Dialogue, convened by the Ministry of Defense in 2003. Four of POLSEDE's Policy Recommendations were among the documents introduced by the military as official input to the process, further validating their importance and value as policy guidance.[15] In the following years, and until today, the military has continued convening participatory dialogue processes on issues such as Military Doctrine (2004), revision of the initiative on Military Law (2009), and Defense Strategy (2014). Not every organization that participated in the POLSEDE effort has participated in these dialogues. The results of these processes—not bound by the consensus rules implemented in POLSEDE—have not had the same degree of civil society input and support. Nevertheless, the possibility of influencing the proceedings and the determination to keep open the channels of communication with the government, have led some organizations and institutions to sustain their participation and regularly engage in the exchange of ideas.

A fourth major effort was conducted through the Civil Society Security Forum (FOSS, 2003–present). FOSS—the Spanish acronym for Strengthening of Civil Society Organizations Specialized in Security—was established as a follow-up to POLSEDE by IGEDEP and WSP International, with the support of the United States Agency for International Development (USAID) and the United Nations Office for Project Services (UNOPS). The goal has been to strengthen civil society capacities to sustain their engagement with the state in security sector issues. This has included the strengthening of the technical capacities of participant organizations on key issues in the security sector agenda (such as civilian oversight, community policing, and intelligence reform), as well as their capacities to engage in the public policy cycle at different phases and through different strategies (provision of technical assistance to government, advocacy or lobbying, and social auditing). At its inception FOSS included thirteen nongovernmental institutions, including civil society groups, universities, think tanks, and NGOs with diverse political and ideological affiliations.

Over the years FOSS has matured and evolved from a project that initially included opportunities to get funding for organizational development to a forum that, even without the 'carrot' of funding, provides a space for the collective consideration of key issues for addressing security sector transformation.[16] In its first phase, FOSS focused on the development of a series of studies and proposals on issues of democratic security and the establishment of an operational framework to sustain civil society's engagement with the government. It focused on one of the commitments of the AFPC that had not been implemented—the establishment of a Governmental Security Advisory Council (CAS) through which civil society could provide assistance to the government. Fifteen CSOs and the national authorities agreed to set up a Preparatory Commission charged with designing the functional and organizational profile of CAS. The resulting commission had a strengthened role beyond the one originally defined in the Peace Accords, and it was established as an advisory group attached to the Presidency of the Republic, whose members were selected by the president from a list proposed by civil society.[17]

Subsequently FOSS's strategy, collectively designed by the participant institutions, focused on strengthening the convergence between state institutions and social organizations in support of an agenda for security sector transformation that responded to the democratic security paradigm. The goal was the development of a National Security System (SNS, its Spanish acronym) that in its legislative, organizational, doctrinal, and operational frameworks would conform to the new security paradigm. With supporting funds from a multidonor basket, it established two strands of work: influencing congressional commissions working on the development of the normative framework for security and the promotion of interinstitutional collaboration across the state-society divide. The momentum generated through this process led eight of the participant organizations to sustain intersectoral collaboration even though funding from the international community ceased. The groups formed the Civil Society Forum—keeping the original acronym—to provide continued pressure and support to national authorities for the implementation of the SNS, which was formally approved by Congress in December 2008.

The last major effort assessed in this chapter is the FOSS Liaison Office in Congress (2004–2009). The growing recognition of the technical capacities and collaborative attitudes developed by CSOs through POLSEDE, POLSEC, and FOSS enabled other CSOs to strengthen their engagement in the security policy formulation process, enhancing their ability to exercise civilian oversight over the security sector and demand accountability from state institutions. In 2004 the Congress of the Republic and FOSS-Interpeace signed an official agreement enabling CSOs to actively support congressional commissions working on security sector legislation and oversight functions. The agreement established a Liaison Office through which civil society was able to engage directly with the Presidency of Congress and congressional commissions working on security sector and justice issues as technical advisors, a highly unique arrangement. The Liaison Office focused on three tasks: promoting the legislative agenda for implementing security sector commitments in the Peace Accords, later extended to human rights commitments as well; improving the technical capacity of national and international civil society networks by strengthening collaboration among social actors; and monitoring and analyzing congressional work on justice and security issues.

The objective presentation of information, analyses, and proposals, including appropriate cross-references of relevant comparative legislation, national and international, mitigated ideological and political differences and allowed the discussion to focus on technical questions and options. The Liaison Office fostered informal dialogues in which parliamentarians and their policy advisors could informally meet and discuss the issues at stake with CSOs and among themselves, free from the formal trappings and commitments implicit to congressional proceedings, thus enabling them to access alternative perspectives and insights. For CSOs, the Liaison Office provided privileged access to, and influence in, the policy formulation process, enabling the effective monitoring of parliamentary agendas and schedules, keeping them abreast of the dynamics of the Congress, which allowed them to prioritize and synchronize their efforts. It became a clear win-win formula.[18] An external evaluation carried out in 2009 reported that twelve different pieces of human rights and security legislation approved by the Congress had been influenced by CSOs working through the Liaison Office.[19]

The Liaison Office also had an important impact in preventing negative pieces of legislation from being approved, such as repressive 'iron fist/zero tolerance' legislation similar to what El Salvador and Honduras adopted in response to the surge of criminal activity by youth gangs (*maras*). Such legislation relies on authoritarian security concepts and frameworks, which threaten to undermine democratic and human rights gains achieved through the peace and democratization processes, often without any actual reduction in crime or violence.[20] In Guatemala, political actors outside and inside the Congress proposed the implementation of similar repressive legislation, an attempt that failed given the fact that it contradicted basic democratic security principles which were already ingrained in the security sector debate in which civil society played a key role. The evolution of the different initiatives for

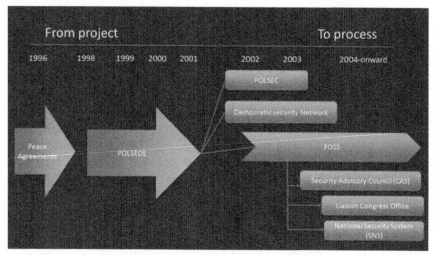

Figure 10.1 From Project to Process: The Evolution of POLSEDE.

democratic security over recent years is depicted in the following timeline of POLSEDE and derived initiatives.

The Current State of Civil-Military Affairs: Catalytic Effects and Contextual Limitations

To understand the extent of the influence POLSEDE and its follow-up initiatives have had in the texture of civil-military relations in Guatemala, the role of the military in the state, and the capacity of civil society to engage constructively with the state in these issues, we turn our attention to two political events that have marked Guatemalan society recently.

The first event is the wave of political unrest that took over the country between April and October of 2015, which ended with the imprisonment of the sitting president, vice-president and several members of their government. For over six months, citizens occupied streets and squares of the main cities in a movement that cut across ethnic and socioeconomic categories, demanding the resignation of all political officials involved in a series of corruption scandals that were being investigated by the judicial authorities with the support of the International Commission against Impunity in Guatemala (CICIG, its Spanish acronym).[21] These events, which ended with the resignation and indictment of the vice-president, the president and several other officials, were underscored by an unprecedented feature: in a country known as one of the most violent in the planet in terms of homicide rates, both sides—citizens and national authorities—succeeded in preventing the spread of violence along the process.

The civil society groups that loosely coordinated the protest invested significant efforts to ensure civic and peaceful behavior, and the government did not try to resort to violent repression or provocation. Security forces kept a low profile and avoided interfering with the civic protest. This was the first serious national political crisis since the establishment of the national army in 1871 in which the military was not an actor, remaining out of the fray even though the now ex-president and several in his entourage were retired military officers. Neither civilians in government nor the citizen opposition appealed for military intervention. The military did not attempt to intervene to guarantee "public order" or "stabilize" the situation, typical excuses for intervention in years past. This clearly indicates the scope of the transformation of the conceptual and institutional frameworks of the role of the military in the country. Nobody, civilian or military, expected the military to intervene in a political matter. No state security policy or military doctrine contemplated military intervention in what was a nonmilitary problem. The omnipresent ghost of a coup d'état was no longer hovering over the country.

This stands in contrast with the second event: the decision of the Chief of Staff of the army in January 2016 to intervene, against current military policy and without consulting with civilian authorities, in a judicial case brought by the state Prosecutor's Office against a large group of retired military officers for human rights violations committed during the internal armed conflict. The Chief of Staff, acting as an individual and jointly with an association of retired military officers, asked the Constitutional Court to void the provision of the National Reconciliation Law of 1996, which established that crimes of genocide and forced disappearance are not covered by the general amnesty for crimes committed during the internal armed conflict.[22] Though the demand was not presented on behalf of the military institution but as an individual, it is evident that the second highest-ranking officer in the armed forces acted in contradiction to the state's position in this matter as represented by the State Prosecutor.

The matter was complicated by its timing. The action by the Prosecutor's Office and the subsequent arrest of the accused military officers took place less than a week before the inauguration of the new government that emerged from the general elections of October 2015. This meant that the country was in a de facto power void created by the process of transition between the weak transitional administration that took over after the resignation of the president and vice-president, and the inauguration of political outsider Jimmy Morales, who won the 2015 presidential election thanks to the wave of popular protest against corruption in politics.

The demand of the Chief of Staff was a calculated risk. He acted in defiance of norms and regulations and in violation of fundamental principles of military subordination to political authority and noninterference in politics, calculating that the political context of the transition would prevent effective institutional response. The gamble worked initially. The outgoing transitional president brushed the issue aside as a "personal decision" that did not represent institutional interests or positions, leaving the Chief of Staff in his position. The new government acted more decisively. Possibly under the pressure of public debate and concerns about the dangerous precedent being established by this case, President Morales decided to fire the Chief of Staff without any explicit reason. Rumors of an emerging rift between the minister of defense and the outgoing Chief of State over this matter suggest the reemergence of a cleavage within the military between "institutionalist" and "recalcitrant" officers that dominated institutional politics during the peace process and its aftermath. The affair indicates that attitudes of military resistance to political authority still exist among serving military officers and reveals the difficulties civilian authorities still face to rein in such attitudes.

It is evident that the model of military domination that characterized political relations in Guatemala at the apex of the armed confrontation has been long left behind. Guatemala is no longer a militarized state; the armed forces do not enjoy political control over the system. Their presence in society does not have the scope that developed during the conflict. The structure and organization of the military no longer corresponds to the counterinsurgency strategies developed through the years of conflict. The military has gradually opened up to substantive interactions with other political and social actors, and in this process has begun to overcome ideological and attitudinal barriers that blocked effective transformation. The absence of the military as a political actor during the 2015 political crisis was historic evidence of the scope of this change, the first time in its history that the army remained on the sidelines. But the actions of the former Chief of Staff and the existence of internal cleavages between the reformers and the recalcitrant officers indicate that the changes in the military are still insufficient. The army might accept the need for institutional adaptation to the new security environment and to presidential executive authority, but there is still reluctance to submit to other institutionalized forms of civilian democratic control, such as parliamentary and judicial supervision. It is a situation that can be described as "relative autonomy."

Effective military subordination to civilian authority in Guatemala has to be understood in the context of the general process of the democratization of the state and the challenges for the establishment of effective democratic governance in a country marked by the exercise of authoritarian practices throughout most of its history. The process is also affected by the development of a postconflict political culture marked by clientelism and patrimonialism. Subordination of the military requires the development of a professional, politically neutral military institution, which submits to structures of civilian authority capable of providing policy guidance and control as well as effective political and technical supervision. Both institutional dimensions have to be transformed, the military apparatus and civilian political structures. Problems have emerged along both axes in the development of a professional, thoroughly apolitical military and in the development of adequate political control and supervision structures.

In the twenty years since the signing of the Peace Accords, military accommodation to a redefinition of their role in state and society has gradually progressed from high to low levels of resistance. Ebbs and flows of resistance can be explained by the internal competition between different military cliques within successive civilian presidencies and the absence of a national civilian policy to guide the process of military transformation. On the other hand, the gradual retirement of military personnel who were active during the conflict and the arrival of a new cadre of officers without that experience of internal armed conflict, along with the disappearance of the "security threat" to the state brought by peace, have facilitated a change in outlook and attitudes. Although there have been many instances of military resistance to the transformation of legal and institutional frameworks, these have lasted only until civilian authorities expressed their determination to act. Critical decisions such as the 50 percent reduction in the army's budget decided by the Berger administration or the decision for early retirement of generals enforced by the Portillo administration were obediently implemented, even if fiercely opposed.[23]

Most of the limitations in the scope of the security system transformation have come from deficiencies in the quality of the guidance, control, and supervision of the process provided by civilian authorities. Civilian politicians have lacked the necessary political will to embark on the full, integral, and sustained process of transformation implicit in the redefinition of the role of the military in society. Different reasons might explain such attitudes: identification with the military and its historical role, usually due to ideological or pragmatic alliances; lack of understanding the scope of the necessary transformations (i.e., confusing a return to the barracks with the end of military intervention in politics); an unwillingness to assume the political or personal cost of reforms; or sheer lack of interest in the issue.

An additional problem has been the low level of conceptual and technical command of the issues, with few civilian politicians and bureaucrats having the knowledge or preparation needed to establish a comprehensive institutional platform for civilian control. A major factor has been the lack of institutional governance capacity for policy implementation and supervision, particularly when policy execution takes place in the complex and shifting political environment of a transition to democracy. The result has been a situation of incomplete transformation. On the one hand, concrete legal and institutional outcomes such as the development of civilian intelligence structures, a citizen security strategy in which military support is transitory, and a military force deployment that follows external defense hypotheses instead of the "internal enemy" hypothesis of the National Security Doctrine demonstrate positive developments. On the other hand, there are continued shortcomings, especially the lack of effective democratic control mechanisms in the executive and legislative branches and budgetary opacity. It is in this context that the impact of the POLSEDE process and its follow-up initiatives has to be understood. The implementation of the security reform process and the broader peace agreement has been limited by the weakness of the Guatemalan state and inadequate civilian capacity for coherent policy formulation and implementation.

Overall, the POLSEDE, POLSEC, and FOSS initiatives generated a systemic synergy that transformed the nature of state-society relations around security sector issues and produced concrete results that showed the potential of collaborative strategies bridging the state-society and civil-military divides. Building upon institutional frameworks achieved at the international level—the Framework Treaty for Democratic Security—and at the national level—the Peace Accords—these collaborative, multisectoral approaches energized the positive agency that existed in Guatemalan society to promote the transformation of security sector institutions according to a democratic paradigm, overcoming considerable obstacles at the conceptual and operational level. The determination and capacity of WSP, WSP International, and Interpeace—successive identities of the same entity—was critical in sustaining the support for the process unleashed by the original POLSEDE project and identifying at each juncture the opportunities through which this could be pursued.

The synergy among the different results—"hard" outputs such as policy proposals and coordination mechanisms, and "soft" outcomes such as transformed knowledge, attitudes, and relationships—generated a substantive difference in the quality of the interaction between state and society around policymaking processes. The identification and strengthening of technical skills in CSOs and the development of a political strategy for constructive interaction enabled civil society to play an important role in a technical area usually left to state institutions. The milestones that were achieved in this process reinforced the collaborative dynamic and expanded the scope of impact. The determination to sustain the interaction across the state-society divide was also shown through initiatives such as La Red and FOSS and the establishment of CAS as a state organ upon a proposal presented by civil society. Other milestones in this process include the invitation for civil society to participate in the official "White Paper" Defense Policy and Military Doctrine processes and the adoption of POLSEDE recommendations as official input to the process. Another milestone was the government's interest in creating POLSEC as a forum that would play a role similar to POLSEDE on citizen security issues and the adoption of several of its recommendations as the basis for institutional development in this area. Furthermore, the agreement assigning CSOs the status of technical advisors to parliamentary commissions (functioning between 2004 and 2009) and the government's establishment of intersectoral working groups to discuss intelligence reform upon the basis of civil society proposals demonstrated an active integration of civil society's recommendations into government outputs. All of these were progressive achievements enabled by the development of a long-term strategy and a capacity to sustain the engagement through changing times.

Indeed, the political context in which the projects and processes were implemented by WSP, WSP International, and then Interpeace changed substantially between 1999 and 2016 with the shift of the overall political agenda and the specific security agenda. From a transformation whose rationale was the need to ensure the anchoring of the state security function on democratic principles, the new priorities are marked by the need to strengthen state capacity to confront threats such as transnational organized crime and the emergence of new violence phenomena undermining the security of society.

The situation is far from being rosy. The new threats from criminal violence undermine the well-being of the population and challenge the legitimacy of governance. The institutionalization of patrimonialism and corruption in the state prevents the development of effective institutional responses that curtail the scope of violent crime and its damage to society. Moreover, the combination of a weak state still incapable of effectively performing its security, development, and political functions with a military institution still in a situation of relative autonomy does not preclude the possibility of a regression to a politicized military or a militarized state. In this challenging context one thing is certain and different: Guatemalan civil society can play a critical role by creatively combining civic protest and constructive advocacy into a strategy that strengthens principles of democracy in the functioning of the state security apparatus. If POLSEDE can make any claims of impact, it is in reference to the development of an emerging and empowered policy community,[24] which has since grown and evolved, influencing in many different ways the transformation of the conceptual and institutional frameworks of state and society. As recent events have demonstrated, it is this empowered and capable civil society, in a context of only partial transformation at the political and institutional level that can make the difference between sustained reform and stalemate.

NOTES

1. POLSEDE is the Spanish acronym for *Hacia una Política de Seguridad para la Democracia* (Toward a Security Policy for Democracy).

2. The organization that is today called Interpeace was founded in 1994 as the War-torn Societies Project with support from the United Nations Research Institute for Social Development and the Programme for Strategic and International Security Studies of the Graduate Institute of International Studies in Geneva, Switzerland.

3. Comisión de Esclarecimiento Histórico (Historical Clarification Commission), *Guatemala: Memoria del Silencio* (Guatemala City: CEH, 1999).

4. Bernardo Arévalo de León, "Del Estado Violento al Ejército Político: Violencia, Formación Estatal y Ejército en Guatemala 1500–1963" (Ph.D. diss., University of Utrecht, 2015); James Dunkerley, *Power in the Isthmus: A Political History of Modern Central America* (Verso: London, 1988).

5. Jennifer Schirmer, *Las Intimidades del proyecto político de los militares en Guatemala* (Guatemala City: FLACSO, 1999); Bernardo Arévalo de León, *Sobre Arenas Movedizas: Sociedad, estado y ejército en Guatemala, 1997* (Guatemala City: FLACSO, 1998).

6. Bernardo Arévalo de León, "Democratic Security in Guatemala: Reflections on Building a Concept of Security in and for Democracy," in *Human Security, Conflict Prevention and Peace in Latin America and the Caribbean*, eds., Moufida Goucha and Francisco Rojas Aravena (Santiago: UNESCO-FLACSO Chile, 2003).

7. Bernardo Arévalo de León, "Civil-Military Relations in Post-Conflict Guatemala: Military Transformation in the Light of the 1996 Agreement on the Strengthening of Civilian Power and the Role of the Armed Forces in a Democratic Society," in *Democratic Governance of the Security Sector beyond the OSCE Region: Regional Approaches in Africa and the Americas*, eds., Victor Ghebali and Alexander Lambert (Munster: DCAF—Lit Verlag, 2007).

8. Arévalo de León, *Sobre Arenas Movedizas.*

9. United Nations General Assembly, 59th assembly, Resolution 746, "United Nations Verification Mission in Guatemala: Report of the Secretary-General," March 18, 2005, https://documents-dds-ny.un.org/doc/UNDOC/GEN/N05/277/50/PDF/N0527750.pdf?OpenElement.

10. Arévalo de León, "Civil-Military Relations in Post-Conflict Guatemala."

11. Edelberto Torres Rivas and Bernardo Arévalo de León, *The WSP Guatemala Way* (Guatemala City: UNRISD-FLACSO, 1999).

12. These documents were: *Bases for the Consideration of the Military Question*— a conceptual framework for the analysis of civil-military relations in democratic transitions; *State, Society and the Military at the Dawn of the Twenty-First Century*—a balance of civil-military relations in the aftermath of conflict with an agenda for the future; *Security Concept and Agenda*—a proposal developing the democratic security paradigm to substitute authoritarian security configurations and guide institutional and operational implementation of state security policies; *Military Doctrine: Approach to constitutive elements and considerations for a new doctrinaire vision*—a set of recommendations for the general guidelines underpinning the axiological part

of the military's new military doctrine; *The Security System of Guatemala: Notes for a Reform*—a proposal for the institutional integration of the different security sector institutions within a new legal and functional framework; *Intelligence Reform*—a set of six detailed documents (*Contribution to the Study of State Intelligence; General Criteria for Intelligence System Reform; Guatemala: Foundations of the Intelligence System; Organic Structure and Career of the Intelligence System; Democratic Control of the Intelligence System; Civilian Intelligence Sub-System at the Interior Ministry*) proposing a thorough reorganization of the intelligence services, ranging from conceptual considerations underpinning intelligence operations in a democracy, to democratic oversight mechanisms and sanctions; *Military Functions in a Democratic Society. A definition of the internal and international security roles the military should assume in the new democratic security context*; and a draft proposal for the *General Law of the Intelligence System*.

13. Bernardo Arévalo de León, "Investigación-Acción Participativa (IAP) como herramienta para la reforma del sector seguridad: El proyecto Hacia Una Política de Seguridad para Democracia en Guatemala," in *Hacia una Política de Seguridad para la Democracia en Guatemala: Investigación Acción Participativa (IAP) y Reforma del Sector Seguridad*, eds., Bernardo Arévalo de León et al. (Munster: DCAF—Lit Verlag, 2005).

14. Ana Glenda Táger Rosado, "El Proyecto Hacia una Política de Seguridad para la Democracia dos años después," in *Hacia una Política de Seguridad para la Democracia en Guatemala: Investigación Acción Participativa (IAP) y Reforma del Sector Seguridad*, eds., Bernardo Arévalo de León et al. (Munster: DCAF—Lit Verlag, 2005).

15. The official government "White Paper on National Defense" which emerged from these talks is available online. The online publication includes a link to a list of all contributing parties to the process of producing the document. For more, see Ministerio de la Defensa Nacional, República de Guatemala, *Guatemala: Libro de la Defensa Nacional*, published online by Red de Seguridad y Defensa de América Latina, 2003, http://www.resdal.org.ar/Archivo/d00001f8.htm.

16. The organizations in FOSS are recognized as possessing outstanding capacities in different security areas in which they have been specializing. Such breadth and depth of knowledge enables them to function within the forum under the principle of complementarity and synergy: CEG specializes in legislative procedures and lobbying; ASIES, in research and drafting of legislative content; IDEM in civil-military relations; FMM in civil intelligence and defense issues; SEDEM in democratic controls and local community-level-security; ICCPG in the security and justice interface; and IEPADES in institutional development and democratic culture.

17. Government of Guatemala, Government Accord 115–2004, passed on March 16, 2004.

18. Thorbjörn Waagstein and Claus Thure Hastrup, "Proyecto de Modernización y Agenda Legislativa del Congreso 2005-2008," *SIDA Review* 22 (2009): 1–54, http://www.sida.se/contentassets/07804173eb5f41c68484e5398 776bbc8/proyecto-de-modernizaci243n-y-agenda-legislativa-del-congreso-en-guatemala-200582112008_2932.pdf.

19. These pieces of legislation were: Law of the National Security System (2008); Law for the Public Access to Information (2008); Law against Sexual Violence, Exploitation and Smuggling of Persons (2009); Law Against Femicide and Other Forms of Violence Against Women (2008); Ratification of the Facultative Protocol of the Convention against Torture (2007); Ratification of the Agreement of the International Commission Against Impunity (2007); Law of the Penitentiary System (2006); Organic Law of the National Institute of Forensic Sciences—INACIF (2006); Law against Organized Crime (2006); and Law of the General Directorate of Civil Intelligence—DIGICI (2005). CSOs were contributing to ongoing discussions for other pieces of legislation that were approved later: the Law of Private Security Services (approved 2010); Law of Firearms and Ammunition (approved 2012); Law of Criminal Investigation Police (approved 2012); and other pieces of legislation pertaining to the implementation of the National Security System.

20. Isabel Aguilar Umaña, Bernardo Arévalo de León, and Ana Glenda Táger, "El Salvador: Negotiating with Gangs" in *Legitimacy and Peace Processes: From Coercion to Consent*, eds., Alexander Ramsbotham and Achim Wenneman, special issue, *Accord* 25 (2014): 95–99, http://www.c-r.org/downloads/Accord25WEB.pdf; Bernardo Arévalo de León and Ana Glenda Táger, "Central America Regional Perspectives," Geneva Peacebuilding Platform, White Paper for Peacebuilding Series, no. 5, 2015.

21. For an informative collection of blogs and essays published during the civic campaign, see Nómada, *140 días de primavera* (Guatemala City: Editorial Rara, 2015).

22. "Jefe del Estado Mayor de la Defensa busca Amnistía por Crímenes de Guerra," *Prensa Libre*, January 12, 2016, http://www.prensalibre.com/guatemala/justicia/jefe-del-emd-busca-amnistia-por-crimenes-de-guerra.

23. Arévalo de León, "Civil-Military Relations in Post-Conflict Guatemala."

24. Jenny Pearce, "Case Study of IDRC-Supported Research on Security Sector Reform in Guatemala," International Development Research Centre, Peace, Conflict, and Development Program Final Report, February 2006, http://idl-bnc.idrc.ca/dspace/bitstream/10625/27529/1/122103.pdf.

Conclusion

Civil Society Empowerment for Human Security

David Cortright, Melanie Greenberg, Laurel Stone, and Anna Milovanovic

Each of the chapters in this volume highlights creative ways in which civil society organizations have engaged with political or military actors and sought to transform the relationship between state and society. No matter how fractured or polarized the governance or conflict settings in which they operate, civil society groups have played a role in bridging political divides, connecting local voices with the policy realm, and creating significant social change. On a small scale and in often unrecognized and subtle ways, civil society action has helped to shape the parameters of political power.

The primary feat of civil society across all these cases has been its role in increasing human security in settings where the dignity, safety, and voice of ordinary citizens are severely compromised or threatened. In a number of chapters we refer to the concept of human security as an alternative to traditional state-centric approaches to security. The human security framework incorporates human rights, democracy, and development into a new paradigm that focuses on protecting the safety and well-being of communities and individuals, not just the security of the state. It is a term that encompasses the diverse array of threats that people face in their daily lives and offers a new way of understanding the need for safety from all forms of violence, direct and indirect. It is a reframing of the security discourse for an age in which the nation state is no longer the exclusive source of political authority, a world in which the problems of armed conflict are predominantly within states and regions rather than between warring nations.

The idea of human security was popularized by Mahbub ul Haq, special advisor to the UNDP, and was proposed initially in the *Human Development Report 1994*.[1] The report identified economic deprivations, inadequate health and nutrition, and the lack of personal and political freedom as fundamental sources of insecurity. The 2003 report *Human Security Now* links security to development and human rights.[2] It defines peace as the protection of civilians and the empowerment of people to develop their potential and participate in public decision-making. Human security provides a framework for understanding and overcoming the insecurities that threaten the safety and dignity of daily life.[3] It is a people-centered approach that addresses the underlying causes of armed conflict and the requirements for sustainable peace.

The concept of human security is not without its critics. Roland Paris argues that the term lacks precise definition and is too vague and muddled to provide guidance to international policymakers and scholars.[4] The concept is "normatively attractive but analytically weak," writes Edward Newman.[5] By encompassing so many dimensions of human insecurity it attempts to address everything and risks becoming overly generalized. Andrew Mack agrees that the concept aspires to explain too much, but he emphasizes the importance of the term as "a signifier of shared political and moral values."[6]

To be concerned about human security is to be concerned about threats to peace from human rights abuse and economic deprivation as well as from military attack. From this perspective, human security's importance lies less in its explanatory power than its role as a broad category of research and policymaking that encompasses nonmilitary threats to people and communities, in contrast to traditional security approaches that focus narrowly on threats to the state.[7]

Mary Kaldor has done pioneering work in defining and attempting to operationalize the meaning of human security. She identifies six core principles for these purposes:

1. The primacy of human rights, with the focus on civilian protection rather than defeating enemies;
2. Legitimate political authority, which emphasizes the importance of enabling local communities to establish effective local governance;
3. A bottom-up approach, which requires an inclusive approach in which affected populations have an active role;
4. Effective multilateralism, within the framework of international law and ideally under UN mandate;
5. Regional focus, recognizing that the roots and consequences of conflict cross borders and must be addressed comprehensively; and
6. Civilian command, guaranteeing civil supremacy and establishing rules of engagement more suitable to police work than armed combat.[8]

These principles provide guidelines for policies that can enhance the security of people and communities and build a long-term foundation for peace. They overlap significantly with the standards of good governance. They reflect the need for multifaceted approaches that address the myriad sources of insecurity and the social, economic, and political conditions that are necessary for sustainable peace.[9] They are the inspiration for, and theoretical foundation of, much of the civil society action for peace, development, and human rights in the world today.

CIVIL SOCIETY'S ROLES IN BOLSTERING HUMAN SECURITY

In the opening chapters to this volume, John Paul Lederach and Peter van Tuijl describe key functions of civil society in peacebuilding, reconciliation, and human security. These functions can be seen as falling across two broad categories, some having to do with *creativity and resilience* and others with *power and leverage. Creativity and resilience* describe the ability of civil society to envision and bring to light potential solutions to complex problems, to help define new pathways of resilience, to describe and map turbulent conflict systems, and to build improbable relationships across ideological and social divides. *Power and leverage* refer to civil society's role in overcoming lack of political will, institutionalizing partnerships, creating inclusive frameworks for building peace, and leading advocacy around contentious issues. There is fluidity between these two roles, as together they portray a holistic picture of civil society helping to create human security.

As Darynell Rodriguez Torres suggests in chapter 5, CSOs can play a range of functions across the conflict cycle—infusing creativity and resilience into violent conflict systems as well as developing new webs of relationships and nascent institutions. CSOs can address root causes of structural violence and promote human security through diverse development and human rights processes. They can use their skills in monitoring and conflict analysis to provide early warning and can mobilize "zones of peace." During violent conflict, they can enable communication, develop Track II processes, negotiate local ceasefires, and facilitate mediation processes. After peace agreements, CSOs can facilitate action on issues of implementation, transitional justice, DDR programs, and ongoing conflict prevention.

Creativity and Resilience

Some of the most important functions of civil society in conflict settings are to generate new ideas, create novel forms of relationship-building, and test innovative frameworks for sustainable peace. To paraphrase Einstein, no problem can be solved from the same level of consciousness that created it. Civil society has the ability to move conflict actors into new levels of awareness and action, through innovative thinking and linked relationships, in order to resolve problems and create new frameworks that tackle the drivers

of conflict and fragility, often in unforeseen ways. This requires moral imagination, to use Lederach's term, an ability to envision the transformation of
relationships between warring parties, and to elicit this vision among those
who are presently blinded by their enmity.[10] In this sense creative thinking is
highly practical, manifesting itself in fresh approaches to understanding the
drivers of conflict and new forums for peacebuilding.

At the heart of civil society power lies the ability to build creative relationships within society and between civil society actors and policymakers.
These relationships can unlock entrenched patterns of conflict, crossing
social and ideological divides to create new platforms and institutions for
sustainable peace. Whereas civil society might have been viewed at one
time solely as either a watchdog or service provider for the government, the
kind of transformational shifts described in this volume allow civil society
actors to work alongside government officials in creative and collaborative
ways. Efforts to forge relationships within society can help to create higher
levels of social cohesion in situations of polarization and fragmentation,
empowering affected communities to find ways of cooperating for peace.
The case studies in this volume highlight multiple examples of creativity on the part of civil society across a number of different purposes and
dimensions.

Gender integration in societies where women were previously voiceless
and disenfranchised emerges as another creative theme in this volume. In the
Pacific Islands, FemLINKPACIFIC operated community radio stations in
Fiji, Tonga, and the Marshall Islands, highlighting feminist voices and creating important platforms for women of diverse backgrounds. Radio was able
to reach a wide range of citizens, and to change dominant narratives in an
entertaining, nonthreatening way. FemLINKPACIFIC was also able to use
these creative media platforms to establish relationships with a regional organization in order to create a Pacific RAP for WPS.

In Afghanistan, women have used media channels to raise awareness of
women's rights, while advocating generally for stronger institutions of governance in the country and a reduction in endemic corruption. In some instances
CSOs have been asked to join government processes in highly charged political matters. For example, the government of Afghanistan asked civil society
representatives to serve as fact-finders to investigate the inflammatory case of
the murder of Farkhunda Malikzada, a 27-year-old Afghan woman accused
of burning a copy of the Qur'an. Even the Taliban—while notorious for sup-
pressing women's freedoms—has negotiated with women's groups in some
instances, perceiving them as less corrupt than government officials. This is
a rather extreme example of an unlikely relationship emerging creatively in
the interest of peace.

The building of creative relationships for human security has been especially striking in civil society dialogues with security sector forces. In the Philippines and Guatemala, military professionals and civil society actors have developed new frameworks for cooperation, finding significant intersections between human and national security. These cases are creative not only in the way the military has been able to reimagine its role as a protector, but also in the transformational nature of the relationships—with the military in some cases becoming a stakeholder in local peace processes. These transformed relationships necessitate a high level of personal reflection on both sides and can lead to the creation of new institutions and the emergence of new conceptions of security. The success so far in safeguarding mutual trust between civil society and military actors in these two countries has been truly remarkable, given the level of structural and actual violence in both societies before the beginning of the peace process. As Lisa Schirch observes, a key element of success in renegotiating the relationship between civil society and the security sector is the development of *joint platforms*—not simply discrete projects—in which civil society and security sector actors can continue to innovate and resolve conflict.

An example of institutionalized civil-military cooperation, in this case through engagement with a regional organization, is the ECOWAS and WANEP early warning system in West Africa—ECOWARN. Although more of a "top down" approach than the examples in Guatemala and the Philippines, the ECOWAS-WANEP partnership has proven to be a highly creative model for building regional security, one that has motivated efforts to build similar systems in East Africa and elsewhere. While early warning systems are no panacea for peace, especially in the absence of institutionalized response mechanisms, they provide opportunities for preventing incidents of violence from cascading into full-scale civil conflict. The ECOWARN system is also important, to apply Schirch's analysis, in establishing an institutionalized platform for ongoing interaction and communication between civil society actors and the military.

Creative engagement and relationship-building were also at the heart of civil society efforts to participate in the IDPS New Deal and to advocate the inclusion of peacebuilding goals in the SDG process. As examined in section one, the New Deal was predicated upon a novel partnership among donors, fragile state governments, and civil society. Notwithstanding attempts to make this sector-spanning collaboration a reality, the results were incomplete in some countries. The New Deal process nonetheless established important international precedents in linking development and peacebuilding and engaging civil society in this approach. The process also helped in the creation of new relationships that remain important for civil society participation in development and peacebuilding dialogues, internationally and in conflict-affected countries.

In the run-up to the creation of the 2030 Agenda for Sustainable Development, civil society united across a range of sectors—from peacebuilding to good governance, democracy, rule of law, and the responsibility to protect—to define a framework for peace that would be acceptable in the highly polarized and politicized environment of the United Nations. It took intensive creativity to negotiate a series of targets and indicators for peace that incorporated governance, security, and inclusion while not overstepping the development mandate of the SDGs. This creativity continues in the development of indicators for Goal 16, where civil society is devising complementary indicators—perceptual and objective—to accompany the official ones developed internationally and by individual governments.

Power and Leverage

Moisés Naím has written of the devolution of power worldwide, specifically about how globalization and cultural liberalization are weakening the previous mechanisms of government control.[11] The cases in this book show how civil society is attempting to fill the governance gap left in the wake of decentralization. CSOs, social movements, and new cultural identities have emerged as "micropowers," to use Naím's term. Civil society has become a new actor on the global stage, setting agendas, shaping social preferences and norms, and building innovative and unexpected partnerships to influence policy and exercise political power.

The shift in civil-military relations described in section three illustrates these patterns. There is a growing realization that traditional uses of military force are not effective in addressing the new security threats posed by nonstate armed groups and that coercive force means little if these groups lack social capacity and legitimacy. In Guatemala and the Philippines, civil society groups stepped up to help implement peace agreements and a new agenda of social reform by engaging the military in novel ways by essentially democratizing it and creating new civil-military capacities for addressing potential threats to peace.

When leveraging power internally has been ineffective, CSOs have engaged at the regional level and advocated that regional organizations take action on peacebuilding issues. The WANEP and ECOWAS partnership in West Africa exemplifies the ability of civil society to work with a regional organization for conflict prevention. In Burkina Faso, CSOs were able to overcome the government's lack of political will by connecting with other regional actors to reverse a military coup and prevent large-scale armed conflict. CSOs in the Pacific have constructed networks that bring the voice of their collective needs to the regional level. They have leveraged their power and created a platform from which to have a top-down influence on national policy.

In fragile states, CSOs have had less success in shaping development outcomes and preventing armed conflict. In some countries, CSOs reflect political or identity divisions within society or are not able to work to their full potential due to resource limitations or operational constraints imposed by the government. The initial energy of the New Deal has dissipated, leaving CSOs without a formally institutionalized role and more vulnerable for having asserted themselves.

Schirch emphasizes the importance of institutionalizing partnerships and building long-term relationships in civil-military interaction, but the same principle applies in other areas of civil society engagement. In the Philippines and Guatemala, civilian peacebuilders and security officers developed formal and informal partnerships that helped to enhance human security.

In West Africa, WANEP developed an institutionalized role with ECOWAS in the development and implementation of ECOWARN, which gave civil society greater authority and influence in the region. In the Pacific, Fem-LINKPACIFIC was able to directly assist in the development of an RAP for WPS, but it did not become an implementing partner despite its decade-long advocacy for the plan.

Whereas WANEP was able to gain access as a key implementer of early warning, the role of FemLINKPACIFIC in implementing the RAP for WPS remains undefined. Having a role in the decision-making process is important, but it is also vital to have an institutionalized role to help shape the implementation effort. This distinction is crucial to the discussion of civil society power. The ability to lobby for policy change is important, but institutionalized partnerships for implementing policies within society are vital to maintaining influence and building momentum for human security.

FUTURE CHALLENGES AND OPPORTUNITIES FOR CIVIL SOCIETY ACTION

The world is facing humanitarian crises on a scale that is almost unimaginable. The December 2015 report on humanitarian financing asserted that, if all the victims of war, conflict, and natural disaster were to come together, they would form the 11th most populous country in the world:

> Imagine a country of 125 million people ...: its citizens are without employment or shelter and do not have the means to feed themselves or provide for their loved ones. Too many of their women die giving birth and too few children are lucky enough to live until their 5th birthday. For those who do, especially girls, they do not attend school. They have been deprived of their dignity and live in insecurity ... [and] rely upon charity to survive.[12]

From war in the Middle East and Afghanistan, to refugee crises across Europe, outbreaks of disease (Ebola, Zika), rising homicide rates in Latin America, and the threat of terrorist violence spreading at a frightening rate, humanity faces problems that are too large for governments to solve alone. At a time when these crises require dynamic, systems-based thinking, as well as unified and effective action, international politics remain fractured and divided. The European Union is fraying at the seams, China is experiencing an economic slowdown, the United States is mired in partisanship, and Central America is struggling with criminal violence that has driven the homicide rate up to staggering levels.

Bright spots remain, however, and civil society can help capitalize on these. The adoption of the SDGs—and especially Goal 16—represents the most important chance in a generation to blend peacebuilding, development, and security around the world. UN Security Council Resolution 2250 (2015) gives youth a voice as peacebuilders, creating possibilities for a powerful new force for change. The private sector is branching out beyond corporate social responsibility to take a proactive role in mitigating conflict. Peace tech is creating new tools for communication, analysis, and social mobilization—with the possibility of revolutionizing elements of peacebuilding. Science is revealing the neurological and epigenetic elements of conflict, allowing us to design peacebuilding programs that work at the most basic human level.

A New Focus on Prevention

At the opening plenary of the recent World Bank Forum on Fragility, Conflict and Violence, Dr. Jim Kim (president of the World Bank), Jan Eliasson (deputy Secretary-General of the United Nations), and Nancy Lindborg (president of the US Institute of Peace) each underscored the need to put *peacebuilding and conflict prevention* at the heart of humanitarian assistance, development, and poverty reduction efforts. This reflects a major change in policy, which until recently separated issues of peace and security from the economic and social aspects of development aid. With the evolution of Goal 16, and the recognition that conflict is "development in reverse," peacebuilding is now seen to be central to a wide range of social change processes, including development, governance, and humanitarian assistance.

Three influential reports issued in 2015 underline this deeper conception of peacebuilding, with strong civil society components, as necessary for development and human security. The independent review of the United Nations Peacebuilding Architecture emphasized the need to include civil society in all peacebuilding efforts.[13] It also widened the definition of peacebuilding from a strictly postconflict perspective to encompass efforts for peace through the full spectrum of the conflict cycle and in all the integrated fields that come together in attempting to sustain peace.

The report of the Independent High Level Panel on UN Peace Operations called for conflict prevention to be placed at the center of peacekeeping policy:

> The avoidance of war rather than its resolution should be at the centre of national, regional and international effort and investment. We know that conflict prevention saves lives and averts social, economic and physical devastation. As the Panel heard in its consultations across four continents, there is an unassailable logic in investing early and adequately to prevent the onset of an armed conflict. Such investment would prevent the need for much larger investments in the ambulances and triage at the bottom of the cliff after many thousands of lives, even hundreds of thousands of lives, have been lost and billions of dollars spent on, and lost to, war.[14]

The report urged peacekeeping forces to recognize mediation efforts at national and local levels and to support local development actors as resources for early warning, local peacebuilding, and stabilization.[15]

Finally, the report on humanitarian financing prepared for the United Nations World Humanitarian Summit in May 2016 emphasized that without conflict prevention, the scope of humanitarian disasters will continue to grow exponentially:

> The most effective way to bring down the cost of humanitarian aid is to reduce the necessity to resort to it. ... The world needs strong determination at the highest level of global political leadership to prevent and resolve conflicts. This applies to the wars actively covered by the media and even more so to "forgotten crises," all giving rise to seemingly intractable situations of misery and suffering. In the absence of determined and persistent political and diplomatic efforts to resolve conflicts, humanitarians are forced to assume a burden that should not be their responsibility. Unfortunately it is easier to deliver humanitarian assistance than it is to invest in political solutions.[16]

These and other reports reflect growing recognition that conflict prevention is necessary to build peace and reduce the scale of humanitarian disaster. Unless the global community addresses the drivers of violence, we will never be able to stem the tide of human suffering. Civil society can play a critical role in helping to mitigate the effects of humanitarian and development failures, and also to build integrated frameworks for addressing the key drivers of violence and war. One of the `most important areas for proactive civil society conflict prevention is in the area of violent extremism, explored below.

Meeting the Challenges of Violent Extremism

By any measure, terrorism and violent extremism are on the rise, and threaten to undermine the very nature of open, democratic societies.[17] Violent extremism undercuts human security in a multitude of ways—not only through the violence itself, but also from governmental counterreaction leading to restricted civil liberties and a shrinking of space for civil society action. Understanding and defeating terrorism is a complex issue that does not lend itself to linear solutions from any single sector. A Countering Violent Extremism (CVE) strategy requires addressing fundamental social problems and political drivers through a whole-of-society comprehensive approach that cannot be dictated by fear. In spite of the tremendous resources that national governments have invested in rooting out and preventing terrorism, extremist movements are growing. ISIS, while attempting to form a state, is also simultaneously selling Yazidi women into slavery, trafficking in artifacts and oil, using social media to attract support and recruit fighters from around the world, and inspire attacks in Europe, the United States, and beyond. Boko Haram continues to terrorize Northern Nigeria, while Al-Shabaab makes violent incursions into Kenya, and Al-Qaeda plots large-scale attacks on the West, despite its reduced powers.

The kinetic counterterrorism strategies that have dominated international security policy since 9/11 have not been effective in reducing the extremist threat, and the rate of terrorism continues to rise dramatically. A peacebuilding approach to countering violent extremism uses the civil society tools demonstrated so effectively in the chapters in this volume. The peacebuilding community has an important role to play in ensuring that the military takes a "do no harm" approach and does not inadvertently exacerbate conflict dynamics. Civil society actors emphasize that military action should not work at cross-purposes with development and peacebuilding approaches, and that the space for civilian action must not be compromised by overly repressive counterterrorism measures.

The development community has long been involved in addressing the social, economic, and governance factors that drive violent extremism. USAID and other donors have invested significant resources in CVE programming in Africa, the Middle East, and Asia, recognizing that good development and peacebuilding are necessary to counter extremism. Policymakers debate how much emphasis to place on local action versus addressing drivers at the national level. Research shows that corruption, human rights violations, and predatory security forces drive young people, especially, to extremist groups.[18] These are issues that need to be addressed at a *national* level. However, many CVE programs are focusing at a hyper-local level, on strategies such as youth programs and counternarrative programs. A much stronger connection between local-level and national-level strategies is pivotal for effective action, in conjunction with the role that local communities can play in mobilizing around national-level drivers of conflict. Security assistance programs aim to give national governments a monopoly on the legitimate use of force, but CVE programs also need to give governments a monopoly on political legitimacy. Purely local approaches that do not address governmental issues of legitimacy and corruption are bound to fail.

Much more research and dialogue are needed to determine the links between development, peacebuilding, and CVE, and to develop a more holistic and integrated model of countering violent extremism. This moment is reminiscent of the struggle in the mid-1990s to define "ethnic conflict," and craft appropriate responses. It took several years, and a great deal of research, to identify different patterns of "ethnic conflict" and to balance military and peacebuilding responses. It turned out that ethnicity was only the surface manifestation of deeper drivers of conflict such as economic and political inequality, historical grievances, government repression, and the regional dynamics and spillover effects of conflicts in neighboring countries.

A similar process of analysis is necessary to inform effective CVE strategy: a far more nuanced view of the different faces of extremism (controlling territory versus lightning strikes such as the Shabaab attacks in Kenya), a greater focus on addressing tactics used by extremists, and more fine-grained local-level knowledge about what drives different forms of violent extremism in different kinds of communities. An example of a fundamental policy mistake is the idea that the West can "counter the messages" and reduce the push factors while the United States and other governments continue to support repressive regimes and conduct extralegal military operations beyond their borders without international authorization.

Civil society has a crucial role to play in working with governments to develop whole-of-society approaches to violent extremism that reinforce *human security* and address the underlying drivers of extremism. All of the modalities discussed in this volume are relevant to preventing and countering violent extremism: the role women play in building peace; early warning and response systems; civil society engagement in security sector reform; campaigns against corruption; and cooperation with local, national, and regional organizations to develop new platforms for integrated development and peacebuilding.

Shrinking Space for Civil Society Action

One of the great ironies and challenges of counterterrorism policy is that at a time when the engagement of citizens is critically necessary, waves of repressive legislation and human rights reversals are shrinking the space in which civil society can operate. In dozens of countries, governments have adopted laws and regulations that widen police and intelligence powers and narrow the political freedoms and human rights protections that are essential to civil society. Often these restrictive measures are adopted in the name of fighting terrorism. In some countries they reflect the strengthening of authoritarian tendencies and pushback by entrenched political leaders against demands for democracy and human rights. As a result of this closing of political space, CSOs that attempt to address the root causes of violent extremism are facing constraints on their ability to operate.[19]

Counterterrorism measures in each country vary, but collectively they reinforce existing provisions that increase the power of police officials to investigate, detain, and arrest suspects; reduce due process rights and limit judicial review; restrict financial transactions and remittances to individuals and entities abroad, especially in Muslim-majority countries; require Internet companies to provide personal communication information to state officials; and increase government authority to control Internet content.[20] States have also sought to place limits on the ability of civil society groups to receive foreign assistance.

Restrictive measures such as these can have a chilling effect on the exercise of civil and human rights and may impede efforts by independent civil society groups to defend human rights and address political grievances. They make it difficult to engage in peacebuilding dialogue with people in marginalized communities about the political, social, and religious issues that drive people toward extremist ideologies. A Human Rights Watch report warns that such measures also risk alienating specific ethnic communities.[21] They can generate resentment and erode public trust in law enforcement among the very communities whose cooperation is needed in the fight against terrorism.

The rise of restrictive measures around the world has been accompanied by a significant erosion of global political freedom. In its 2015 annual survey, Freedom House stated that the condition of global political rights and civil liberties declined for the ninth consecutive year.[22] It described developments in 2014 as "exceptionally grim," with nearly twice as many countries showing declines in freedoms compared to those experiencing gains. A number of countries lost ground due to increases in state surveillance, restrictions on Internet communications, and curbs on personal autonomy. The most notable reversals were in the areas of freedom of expression, the rights of civil society, and the rule of law. According to Freedom House, the past nine years have witnessed the longest continuous period of decline for global freedom in its more than forty years of publishing annual ratings. Freedom House does not attribute the observed decline in freedom directly to counterterrorist legislation, but the effect of such laws is typically to reduce rather than expand personal freedoms. Such measures are weighted toward increasing the authority of security forces and the executive branch of government, usually at the expense of judicial independence, legislative oversight, personal privacy, and the rights of civil society.

Especially challenging for NGOs and civil society groups have been measures that limit access to external funding. As Thomas Carothers and Saskia Brechenmacher observe in their report *Closing Space*, restrictions on financing have multiplied in many countries, particularly in less democratic states that are prone to armed conflict.[23] Governments often vilify local organizations that accept external funding, seeking to undercut their domestic legitimacy. In semiauthoritarian regimes, governments allow some degree of foreign support for NGOs but try to channel it into functions such as public service delivery rather than advocacy. In fully authoritarian states, governments have long restricted independent civil society efforts but have "further tightened the screws" recently by dissolving some NGOs and requiring prior approval for foreign support.[24] Even some relatively democratic countries have adopted measures to limit external funding for domestic NGOs. In many cases these actions are part of a broader crackdown on independent civil society and a shrinking of political space for activism and dissent.

Major studies and research reports have drawn attention to the problem of dwindling democratic space.[25] Civil society groups, donor governments, and international organizations are pushing back against the trend. A broad network of national and international NGOs is pressing the Financial Action Task Force to revise counterterrorism guidelines to allow unimpeded funding of credible development and peacebuilding organizations.[26] USAID, the European External Action Service, the UN Human Rights Council, and other national and international bodies have criticized restrictions on foreign assistance and have urged a strengthening of norms and legal frameworks for democracy and human rights.[27] The fight for democratic political space is an important arena of political contestation between state and society and is vital to preserving and strengthening the emerging power of civil society.

CHALLENGES FOR FUTURE RESEARCH

The cases and examples examined in this volume offer important insights and lessons on the role of civil society peacebuilding organizations in three distinct arenas of policy: international development, cooperation with regional organizations, and civil-military interaction for human security. The case studies and analyses offer fresh insights into these approaches and present new information and perspectives on recent developments that are not well known and so far have attracted relatively little scholarly and practitioner literature.

The chapters take us to the frontiers of new knowledge, but they also raise challenging questions and expose significant gaps in our knowledge about peacebuilding challenges in the three arenas of inquiry. Several major questions for future scholarly research and practitioner evaluation arise from the analyses in this volume. The following are a few of the most important.

How does peacebuilding contribute to the broader international development agenda? What specific forms of peacebuilding practice are most strongly associated with higher rates of economic growth and reduced levels of poverty, hunger, and disease? Ample research confirms a robust linkage between high levels of economic growth and reduced conflict risk, making this one of the most robust relationships in all of social science.[28] As Paul Collier and his colleagues conclude, "The key root cause of conflict is the failure of economic development."[29] Knowledge of these relationships does not settle questions about the direction of causality, nor does it tell us how peacebuilding policies advance development outcomes. More refined analysis is needed to trace the effects of specific peacebuilding actions and policies, and how they contribute to improved economic conditions for affected communities.

A related question is how to define "statebuilding" in relation to SDG Goal 16 of the 2030 Agenda, which reads, "Promote peaceful and inclusive societies for sustainable development, provide access to justice for all and build effective, accountable and inclusive institutions at all levels."[30] What is the theory of change explaining how specific forms of institutional development lead to more peaceful and prosperous societies? Substantial analysis exists in the literature on the relationship between institutional performance and peaceful outcomes, but the findings are at a high level of generality and do not tell us much about the effects of specific statebuilding policies and actions.[31] Much depends on the type of regime and whether the institutions in question are inclusive and accountable. Clearer guidance is needed on which institutions to support and also on what kinds of activities are most likely to generate more peaceful and prosperous states.

More knowledge and additional case studies are needed on the peacebuilding policies of regional organizations and civil society engagement with these policies. The case studies in this volume offer examples of the relationship between civil society and regional organizations, but there are many other models and examples to consider. The ECOWARN early warning system described in chapter 6 illustrates the rich potential that exists for civil society partnerships with regional organizations and security forces in identifying and preventing the sources of armed conflict. Locally based conflict monitoring programs also exist in Indonesia and southern Thailand, funded by the World Bank, and have also emerged in East Africa. Research and practitioner exchanges are needed to learn lessons from these and related programs and to identify if and how they prevent deadly conflict. More knowledge is also needed on the strategies to engage regional organizations over an extended period of time when leadership and bureaucratic transitions in the organization limit extended collaboration, as experienced in the case of FemLINK-PACIFIC in chapter 7.

Similar research and practitioner exchanges are needed to study additional examples of civil society interaction with security forces. Chapters 9 and 10 describe significant cases of civil society engagement with security forces in the Philippines and Guatemala, but many other examples exist. Some of these are available in the *Local Ownership in Security* guide accompanying the *Handbook on Human Security* produced by the Alliance for Peacebuilding.[32] Other studies on civil-military interaction have been published over the years, some with specific attention to conflict prevention and democracy-building goals, but fewer studies are available on bottom-up approaches.[33] Additional work to identify patterns and draw lessons from these experiences could yield important guidelines for constructive policy and practice in advancing human security.

More research and practitioner assessment is needed on relationships among the different types of civil society actors and between civil society and the business sector. Many different types of organizations and networks exist within civil society, including professional nongovernment organizations, informal social networks, social movements, and professional associations. The dynamics within and among these actors vary greatly and create either possibilities or obstacles to collaborative action for conflict prevention. A better understanding of these dynamics would help greatly in shaping civil society peacebuilding strategies. Especially important is the relationship between secular civil society groups and religious and faith-based organizations. As Appleby and other scholars have observed, religion can serve as either a motivation for violence or a foundation for constructive peacebuilding.[34] Identifying religious groups that embody the latter approach and developing forms of collaborative or parallel action could be important for advancing peacebuilding knowledge and practice.

Last is the need for a deeper understanding of the role of civil society in relation to theories of political power. Civil society influences are usually considered outside the realm of realist theory, which focuses on the nation state as the dominant actor and emphasizes military means as the supreme power, the *ultima ratio regis*. States are not unitary rational actors, however, as liberal theory reminds us. They are subject to a range of influences, including pressures from society, as the chapters in this volume attest. Civil society fits best within Kenneth Boulding's theory of integrative power—the ability to achieve results through voluntary cooperation and high levels of social support and political legitimacy.[35] Power is expressed in this model through relationships and the desire of people to be part of a community or network that brings mutual benefits and reinforces shared values. This is the power of civil society, the collective power of people and communities working together to achieve human security. Understanding this concept and how it is manifest in the peacebuilding challenges of our time has been the purpose of this volume, and remains a central challenge for future research and action.

NOTES

1. United Nations Development Programme, *Human Security Report 1994* (New York: Oxford University Press, 1994).

2. Commission on Human Security, "Outline of the Report of the Commission on Human Security," 2003, http://www.unocha.org/humansecurity/chs/finalreport/Outlines/outline.html.

3. Commission on Human Rights, *Human Security Now: Protecting and Empowering People* (New York: Commission on Human Security, 2003), 8–9.

4. Roland Paris, "Human Security: Paradigm Shift or Hot Air," *International Security* 26, no. 2 (2001): 88–89.

5. Edward Newman, "Critical Human Security Studies," *Review of International Studies* 36, no. 1 (2010): 82.

6. Andrew Mack, "A Signifier of Shared Values," *Security Dialogue* 35, no. 3 (2004): 367.

7. Paris, "Human Security," 96.

8. Shannon D. Beebe and Mary Kaldor, *The Ultimate Weapon Is No Weapon: Human Security and the New Rules of War and Peace* (New York: Public Affairs, 2010), 8–9.

9. Mary Kaldor, *Human Security: Reflections on Globalization and Intervention* (Cambridge, UK: Polity Press, 2007).

10. John Paul Lederach, *The Moral Imagination: The Art and Soul of Building Peace* (New York: Oxford University Press, 2005).

11. Moisés Naím, *The End of Power: From Boardrooms to Battlefields and Churches to States, Why Being in Charge Isn't What It Used to Be* (New York: Basic Books, 2013).

12. High-Level Panel on Humanitarian Financing Report to the Secretary-General, "Too Important to Fail—Addressing the Humanitarian Financing Gap," December 2015, 1, http://www.un.org/news/WEB-1521765-E-OCHA-Report-on-Humanitarian-Financing.pdf.

13. "A second critical determinant of success is fostering 'inclusive national ownership.' In the aftermath of violence, neither a cohesive nation state nor an inclusive system of governance can be taken as givens. The national responsibility to drive efforts to sustain peace must therefore be broadly shared across all key social strata and divides. A wide spectrum of political opinions and domestic actors must be heard—particularly women and youth." *The Challenge of Sustaining Peace*, Report of the Advisory Group of Experts for the 2015 Review of the United Nations

Peacebuilding Architecture, June 29, 2015, 8, http://www.un.org/pga/wp-content/uploads/sites/3/2015/07/300615_The-Challenge-of-Sustaining-Peace.pdf.

14. United Nations General Assembly, "Report of the High-Level Independent Panel on Peace Operations on Uniting Our Strengths for Peace: Politics, Partnership and People," 70th session, A/70/95, June 17, 2015, 30, http://www.un.org/sg/pdf/HIPPO_Report_1_June_2015.pdf.

15. United Nations General Assembly, "Report of the High-Level Independent Panel on Peace Operations on Uniting Our Strengths for Peace," 34.

16. High-Level Panel on Humanitarian Financing Report to the Secretary-General, "Too Important to Fail," 5.

17. In 2014 the total number of deaths from terrorism increased by 80 percent when compared to the prior year. This is the largest yearly increase in the last 15 years. Since the beginning of the twenty-first century, there has been over a nine-fold increase in the number of deaths from terrorism, rising from 3,329 in 2000 to 32,685 in 2014. Institute for Economics and Peace, *Global Terrorism Index* (Sydney: Institute for Economics and Peace, 2015).

18. Mercy Corps, *Youth and Consequences: Unemployment, Injustice and Violence* (Portland: Mercy Corps, 2015), https://www.mercycorps.org/research-resources/youth-consequences-unemployment-injustice-and-violence.

19. David Cortright et al., "Friend Not Foe: Opening Spaces for Civil Society Engagement to Prevent Violent Extremism," Report to Cordaid from the Fourth Freedom Forum and the Kroc Institute for International Peace Studies at the University of Notre Dame, 2nd edn., May 2011, http://www.hscollective.org/wp-content/uploads/2013/09/Friend-not-Foe-2.pdf.

20. David Cortright, "Could New Laws to Fight Terrorism Actually Help Fuel It?" International Peace Institute, *Global Observatory*, March 31, 2015, https://theglobalobservatory.org/2015/03/terrorism-financing-civil-liberties/.

21. Human Rights Watch, *Preempting Justice: Counterterrorism Laws and Procedures in France* (New York: Human Rights Watch, 2008), https://www.hrw.org/sites/default/files/reports/france0708_1.pdf.

22. Arch Puddington, "Discarding Democracy: A Return to the Iron Fist," article of highlights from Freedom House 2015 Report, https://freedomhouse.org/sites/default/files/01152015_FIW_2015_final.pdf.

23. Thomas Carothers and Saskia Brechenmacher, *Closing Space: Democracy and Human Rights under Fire* (Washington DC: Carnegie Endowment for International Peace, 2014), 5–6, http://carnegieendowment.org/files/closing_space.pdf.

24. Ibid., 6–7.

25. Examples include Larry Diamond, "The Democratic Rollback: The Resurgence of the Predatory State," *Foreign Affairs* 87, no. 2 (March/April 2008); Human Rights Watch, *In the Name of Security: Counterterrorism Laws Worldwide Since September 11* (New York: Human Rights Watch, 2012); Ben Hayes, "Counter-Terrorism, 'Policy Laundering,' and the FATF: Legalizing Surveillance, Regulating Civil Society," *The International Journal of Not-for-Profit Law* 14, nos. 1–2 (April 2012).

26. See, for example, the Charity and Security Network in the US, http://www.charityandsecurity.org/, or the International Civil Society Platform on the FATF, http://fatfplatform.org/.

27. Carothers and Brechenmacher, *Closing Space*, 32.

28. Edward Miguel, "Economic Shocks, Weather and Civil War," *The National Bureau of Economic Research: NBER Reporter 2011*, no. 3: Research Summary, 1; Lael Brainard, Derek Chollet, and Nica LaFluer, "The Tangled Web: The Poverty-Insecurity Nexus," in *Too Poor for Peace? Global Poverty, Conflict, and Security in the 21st Century*, eds., Lael Brainard and Derek Chollet (Washington, DC: The Brookings Institution, 2007).

29. Paul Collier et al., *Breaking the Conflict Trap: Civil War and Development Policy* (Washington, DC: World Bank and Oxford University Press, 2003), 53.

30. United Nations, Department of Economic and Social Affairs, "Sustainable Development Knowledge Platform," Goal 16 webpage, https://sustainabledevelopment. un.org/sdg16.

31. Pippa Norris, *Making Democratic Governance Work: How Regimes Shape Prosperity, Welfare, and Peace* (Cambridge: Cambridge University Press, 2012); World Bank, *World Development Report 2011: Conflict, Security, and Development* (Washington, DC: The World Bank, 2011).

32. Lisa Schirch, ed., *Handbook on Human Security: A Civil-Military-Police Curriculum* (The Hague: Alliance for Peacebuilding, GPPAC, Kroc Institute, 2015), https://www.peaceportal.org/documents/130617663/0/ FINAL+HANDBOOK+November+30+1154.pdf/25025a3b-3247-4714-b1b4-d1530d84b0f1; Lisa Schirch with Deborah Mancini-Griffoli, *Local Ownership in Security: Case Studies of Peacebuilding Approaches* (The Hague: Alliance for Peacebuilding, GPPAC, Kroc Institute, 2015).

33. Dennis Blair, ed., *Military Engagement: Influencing Armed Forces to Support Democratic Transitions*, Vol. 2 (Washington DC: Brookings Institution Press, 2013).

34. R. Scott Appleby, *The Ambivalence of the Sacred: Religion, Violence, and Peacebuilding* (Lanham, MD: Rowman and Littlefield, 2000).

35. Kenneth Boulding, *Three Faces of Power* (Newbury Park, CA: Sage Publications, 1989).

Bibliography

CHAPTER 1

Boulding, Kenneth. *Three Faces of Power.* Newbury Park, CA: Sage Publications, 1989.

Christie, Ryerson. *Peacebuilding and NGOs: State-Civil Society Interactions.* New York: Routledge, 2013.

Cortright, David, with Alistair Millar, Linda Gerber-Stellingwerf, George A. Lopez, Eliot Fackler, and Joshua Weaver. "Friend not Foe: Opening Spaces for Civil Society Engagement to Prevent Violent Extremism." Report to Cordaid from the Fourth Freedom Forum and the Kroc Institute for International Peace Studies at the University of Notre Dame. 2nd edn. May 2011. http://www.hscollective.org/wp-content/uploads/2013/09/Friend-not-Foe-2.pdf.

Dudouet, Veronique. "Rezensionen." *Die Friedens-Warte* 85, no. 4 (2010): 114.

Edwards, Michael. *Civil Society.* 2nd edn. Cambridge, MA: Polity Press, 2009.

Edwards, Michael, eds. "Introduction: Civil Society and the Geometry of Human Relations." In *The Oxford Handbook of Civil Society*, 3–14. Oxford: Oxford University Press, 2011.

Edwards, Michael. *NGO Rights and Responsibilities: A New Deal for Global Governance.* London: The Foreign Policy Centre, 2000.

Francis, Diana. "New Thoughts on Power: Closing the Gaps between Theory and Action." In *Advancing Conflict Transformation: The Berghoff Handbook II*, edited by Beatrix Austin, Martina Fischer, and Hans-Joachim Giessmann, 505–25. Farmington Hills, MI: Barbara Budrich Publishers, 2011.

Gaventa, John. "Civil Society and Power." In *The Oxford Handbook of Civil Society*, edited by Michael Edwards, 416–27. Oxford: Oxford University Press, 2011.

The Geneva Declaration on Armed Violence and Development. 2006. http://www.genevadeclaration.org/fileadmin/docs/GD-Declaration-091020-EN.pdf.

Goldstein, Joshua S. *Winning the War on War: The Decline of Armed Conflict Worldwide.* London: Penguin, 2011.

Haspeslagh, Sophie and Zahbia Yousuf, eds., "Local Engagement with Armed Groups in the Midst of Violence." *ACCORD: An International Review of Peace Initiatives* Insights 2 (May 2015). http://www.c-r.org/downloads/CONJ2670_Accord_new_paper_for_January_06.05.15_WEB_2.pdf.

Hayes, Ben. "Counter-Terrorism, 'Policy Laundering,' and the FATF: Legalizing Surveillance, Regulating Civil Society." *The International Journal of Not-for-Profit Law* 14, nos. 1–2 (April 2012): 5–48.

Hayes, Ben. "Terrorising the Rule of Law: The Policy and Practice of Proscription." Statewatch Analysis and the Policy Laundering Project, 2005. http://www.statewatch.org/terrorlists/terrorlists.pdf.

Hofmann, Claudia and Ulrich Schneckener. "NGOs and Nonstate Armed Actors, Improving Compliance with International Norms." Special Report 284. Washington, DC: United States Institute for Peace, 2011.

Hopgood, Stephen. *The Endtimes of Human Rights*. Ithaca, NY: Cornell University Press, 2013.

Hudson, Valerie M., Bonnie Baliff-Spanvill, Mary Caprioli, and Chad F. Emmet. *Sex and World Peace*. New York: Columbia University Press, 2012.

Jordan, Lisa. "Global Civil Society." In *The Oxford Handbook of Civil Society*, edited by Michael Edwards, 93–108. Oxford: Oxford University Press, 2011.

Jordan, Lisa and Peter van Tuijl. "Political Responsibility in Transnational NGO Advocacy." *World Development* 28, no. 12 (2000): 2051–65.

Keck, Margaret and Kathryn Sikkink. *Activists beyond Borders: Advocacy Networks in International Politics*. Ithaca, NY: Cornell University Press, 1998.

Keohane, Robert O. "The Contingent Legitimacy of Multilateralism." GARNET Working Paper No. 09/06. University of Warwick, September 2006. http://www2.warwick.ac.uk/fac/soc/pais/research/researchcentres/csgr/garnet/workingpapers/0906.pdf.

Lederach, John Paul. *The Little Book of Conflict Transformation*. Intercourse, PA: Good Books, 2003.

Lederach, John Paul. *Preparing for Peace: Conflict Transformation Across Cultures*. Syracuse: Syracuse University Press, 1995.

Marchetti, Raffaele and Nathalie Tocci, eds. *Conflict Society and Peacebuilding: Comparative Perspectives*. New Delhi: Routledge, 2011.

Marchetti, Raffaele and Nathalie Tocci, eds. "Conflict Society in Conflict and Peace." In *Conflict Society and Peacebuilding: Comparative Perspectives*. New Delhi: Routledge, 2011.

McCandless, Erin. *Polarization and Transformation in Zimbabwe: Social Movements, Strategy Dilemmas and Change*. Lanham, MD: Lexington Books, 2011.

McMinn, Karen. "Candid Voices from the Field: Obstacles to a Transformative Women, Peace and Security Agenda and to Women's Meaningful Participation in Building Peace and Security." Action Research Report sponsored by Cordaid, Global Partnership for the Prevention of Armed Conflict, and Women Peacemakers Program, 2015. https://www.womenpeacemakersprogram.org/assets/CMS/Action-Research/WPP-15-01-WPP-publicatie-LRPages.pdf.

Naím, Moisés. *The End of Power: From Boardrooms to Battlefields and Churches to States, Why Being in Charge Isn't What It Used to Be*. New York: Basic Books, 2013.

Nilsson, Desirée. "Anchoring the Peace: Civil Society Actors in Peace Accords and Durable Peace." *International Relations* 38, no. 2 (2012): 243–66.

Nye, Joseph S. *Soft Power: The Means to Success in World Politics.* New York: Public Affairs, 2004.

Nye, Joseph S. *Understanding International Conflicts: An Introduction to Theory and History.* 4th edn. New York: Longman, 2003.

O'Reilly, Marie, Andrea Ó Súilleabháin, and Thania Paffenholz. "Reimagining Peacemaking: Women's Roles in Peace Processes." New York: International Peace Institute, 2015. https://www.ipinst.org/wp-content/uploads/2015/06/IPI-E-pub-Reimagining-Peacemaking-rev.pdf.

Paffenholz, Thania. "Civil Society and Peace Negotiations: Beyond the Inclusion-Exclusion Dichotomy." *Negotiation Journal* 30, no. 1 (2014): 69–91.

Paffenholz, Thania. "Civil Society and Peacebuilding." *Development Dialogue* 63 (December 2015): 108–18.

Paffenholz, Thania, ed. "Conclusion." In *Civil Society and Peacebuilding: A Critical Assessment*, 425–30. Boulder: Lynne Riener, 2010.

Paffenholz, Thania, ed. "Preface." In *Civil Society and Peacebuilding: A Critical Assessment.* Boulder: Lynne Riener, 2010.

Paffenholz, Thania, ed. *Civil Society and Peacebuilding: A Critical Assessment.* Boulder: Lynne Riener, 2010.

Paffenholz, Thania and Christoph Spurk. "A Comprehensive Analytical Framework." In *Civil Society and Peacebuilding: A Critical Assessment*, edited by Thania Paffenholz, 65–78. Boulder: Lynne Riener, 2010.

Peruzzotti, Enrique. "Civil Society, Representation and Accountability: Restating Current Debates on the Representativeness and Accountability of Civic Associations." In *NGO Accountability: Politics, Principles and Innovations*, edited by Lisa Jordan and Peter van Tuijl, 43–58. London: Earthscan, 2006.

Petterson, Thérése and Peter Wallensteen. "Armed Conflicts, 1946–2014." *Journal of Peace Research* 52, no. 4 (2015): 536–50.

Schirch, Lisa, ed. *Handbook on Human Security: A Civil-Military-Police Curriculum.* The Hague: Alliance for Peacebuilding, GPPAC, Kroc Institute, 2015. https://www.peaceportal.org/documents/130617663/0/FINAL+HANDBOOK+November+30+1154.pdf/25025a3b-3247-4714-b1b4-d1530d84b0f1.

Shank, Michael and Elizabeth Beavers. "The Militarization of U.S. Police Forces." *Chicago Tribune*, October 22, 2013.

Spurk, Christoph. "Understanding Civil Society." In *Civil Society and Peacebuilding: A Critical Assessment*, edited by Thania Paffenholz, 3–28. Boulder: Lynne Riener, 2010.

Turner, Nicholas. "Testimony to President's Task Force on 21st Century Policing." Written testimony on behalf of Vera Institute of Justice, New York, January 9, 2015. http://www.vera.org/sites/default/files/resources/downloads/nick-turner-testimony-presidents-task-force-21st-century-policing.pdf.

United Nations. "Transforming Our World: The 2030 Agenda for Global Action." A/RES/70/1. https://sustainabledevelopment.un.org/content/documents/21252030%20Agenda%20for%20Sustainable%20Development%20web.pdf.

Waddell, Steve. *Global Action Networks: Creating Our Future Together*. Basingstoke, England: Palgrave MacMillan, 2011.

Wallensteen, Peter and Anders Bjurner, eds. *Regional Organizations and Peacemaking: Challengers to the UN?* London: Routledge, 2015.

Wanis-St. John, Anthony and Darren Kew. "Civil Society and Peace Negotiations: Confronting Exclusion." *International Negotiation* 13, no. 1 (2008): 11–36.

CHAPTER 2

African Charter for Popular Participation in Development and Transformation (Arusha 1990)," *ISS Africa*, 1990, https://www.issafrica.org/uploads/POPULARPPARTCHARTER.PDF.

Alvazzi del Frate, Anna, Keith Krause and Matthias Nowak, eds. *The Global Burden of Armed Violence 2015*. Geneva: Small Arms Survey of Geneva Declaration on Armed Violence and Development, 2015.

Anderson, Mary B. and Lara Olson. *Confronting War: Critical Lessons for Peace Practitioners*. Cambridge, MA: CDA, 2003.

Beckman, Björn, Hannson, Eva, and Anders Sjögren, eds. *Civil Society and Authoritarianism in the Third World: A Conference Book*. Stockholm: Department of Political Science, Stockholm University, 2001.

"Bringing Peace into the Post-2015 Development Framework: A Joint Statement by Civil Society Organizations." September 21, 2012. http://www.cspps.org/documents/130616042/130626578/2012_09_28_CSO_Joint_Statement_Post-2015_ENG.pdf/a187d69f-3a87-46b1-82d1-90e24768424d.

Ernstorfer, Anita, Diana Chigas and Hannah Vaughan-Lee. "From Little to Large: When Does Peacebuilding Add Up?" In "Vertical Integration in Peacebuilding." *Journal for Peacebuilding and Development* 10, no. 1 (Special Issue 2015).

Gamson, William A. *The Strategy of Social Protest*, 2nd edn. Belmont, CA: Wadsworth Publishing, 1990.

Goldstone, Jack A., ed. "Introduction: Bridging Institutionalized and Noninstitutionalized Politics." In *States, Parties, and Social Movements*. Cambridge: Cambridge University Press, 2003.

Gumah, Awudu Ahmed. "Prospects for Poverty Reduction in Ghana: A Critical Analysis of the PRSP Process and Outcomes." Harare: *AFRODAD PRSP Series*, 2003.

IDPS. "Peacebuilding and Statebuilding Indicators: Progress, Interim List and next steps." IDPS Global Meeting, Washington, DC, April 19, 2013.

International Dialogue on Peacebuilding and Statebuilding. "New Deal Principles," http://www.pbsbdialogue.org/en/new-deal/new-deal-principles/.

International Peace Institute. "Conflict, Violence, and Instability in the Post-2015 Development Agenda." Meeting Note. October 2013. https://www.ipinst.org/wp-content/uploads/publications/ipi_e_pub_post_2015.pdf.

Keck, Margaret and Kathryn Sikkink. "Transnational Advocacy Networks in International and Regional Politics." *International Social Science Journal* 51, no. 159 (1999): 89–101.

McAdam, Doug. "Freedom Summer Project, Mississippi, 1964." In *Protest, Power, and Change: An Encyclopedia of Nonviolent Action from ACT-UP to Women's Suffrage*, eds. Roger S. Powers and William B. Voegele. New York: Garland Publishing, 1997.

McAdam, Doug and David Snow, eds. *Social Movements: Reader on Their Emergence, Mobilization, and Dynamics*. Los Angeles: Roxbury, 1997.

McCandless, Erin. "In Pursuit of Peacebuilding for Perpetual Peace: Where the UN's Peacebuilding Architecture Needs to Go." Working Paper for the Future of the Peacebuilding Architecture Project, Center for International Policy Studies, University of Ottawa and the Norwegian Institute of International Affairs, 2010. http://www.cips-cepi.ca/wp-content/uploads/2015/01/McCandless.pdf.

McCandless, Erin. *Polarization and Transformation in Zimbabwe: Social Movements, Strategy Dilemmas and Change*. Maryland: Lexington Books, 2011.

McCandless, Erin. "Wicked Problems in Peacebuilding and Statebuilding: Making Progress in Measuring Progress in Peacebuilding and Statebuilding." *Global Governance* 19, no. 2 (2013): 227–248.

McCandless, Erin, Tim Donais and Eric Abitbol. "Vertical Integration: A Dynamic Practice Promoting Transformative Peacebuilding." In "Vertical Integration in Peacebuilding." *Journal for Peacebuilding and Development* 10, no. 1 (Special Issue 2015): 1–9.

OECD-DAC. *States of Fragility 2015: Meeting Post-2015 Ambitions*, Revised edition Paris: OECD, 2015. http://www.keepeek.com/Digital-Asset-Management/oecd/development/states-of-fragility-2015_9789264227699-en#page1.

Paffenholz, Thania. "Results on Women and Gender from the 'Broader Participation' and 'Civil Society and Peacebuilding' Projects." Briefing Paper. Centre on Conflict, Development, and Peacebuilding Geneva: The Graduate Institute of International and Development Studies. 2015. http://graduateinstitute.ch/files/live/sites/iheid/files/sites/ccdp/shared/Docs/Publications/briefingpaperwomen%20gender.pdf.

Painter, Genevieve. *Quality Participation in Poverty Reduction Strategies: Experiences from Malawi, Bolivia, and Rwanda*. London: Eurodad, 2002.

"Putting Sustainable Peace and Safe Societies at the Heart of the Development Agenda: Priorities for post-2015." CSPPS and QUNO. September 2013. http://tinyurl.com/j2l86ar.

Quaker United Nations Office. "Funding for Peace: Lessons Learned." Meeting Note. June 2015. http://cic.nyu.edu/sites/default/files/quno_cic_ffd_meeting_note_final_june_2_2015.pdf.

Quaker United Nations Office. "QUNO Co-Hosts a High Level Side Event in the Opening Week of the 68th General Assembly on Stability and Peace." September 2013. http://quno.org/timeline/2013/9/quno-co-hosts-high-level-side-event-opening-week-68th-general-assembly-stability-and.

Quaker United Nations Office. "QUNO Participated in Open Working Group 8 on the Sustainable Development Goals." March 2014. http://quno.org/timeline/2014/3/quno-participated-open-working-group-8-sustainable-development-goals.

Sachikonye, Lloyd M. "Civil Society, Social Movements, and Democracy in Southern Africa." *Innovation: The European Journal of Social Science Research* 8, no. 4 (1995): 399–411.

Sztompka, Piotr. *The Sociology of Social Change.* Oxford: Blackwell, 1993.

The World We Want. "Visualizing People's Voices," http://millionvoices-data. worldwewant2015.org/.

Uhlin, Anders. "The Transnational Dimension of Civil Society: Migration and Independence Movements in Southeast Asia." In *Civil Society and Authoritarianism in the Third World.* eds. B. Beckman, E. Hansson and A. Sjögren. Stockholm: PODSU, Stockholm University, 2001.

UNICEF, PBSO, UNDP. *Report of the Expert Meeting on an Accountability Framework for Conflict, Violence, Governance and Disaster in the Post-2015 Development Agenda.* Glen Cove, NY: June 18–19, 2013.

United Nations, *Transforming Our World: The 2030 Agenda for Sustainable Development.* New York: UN, 2015. http://www.un.org/ga/search/view_doc. asp?symbol=A/RES/70/1&Lang=E.

United Nations Peacebuilding Fund. "What is Peacebuilding?" http://www.unpbf. org/application-guidelines/what-is-peacebuilding/.

van Tuijl, Peter. Statement during "Strengthening Peacebuilding Policy through Civil Society Empowerment" Conference. University of Notre Dame. October 25–27, 2015.

Wheeler, Thomas. "Peace Finds Its Place at the Heart of the New Global Development Framework." Saferworld. August 3, 2015. http://www.saferworld.org. uk/news-and-views/comment/182-peace-finds-its-place-at-the-heart-of-the-new-global-development-framework.

World Bank. *World Development Report 2011: Conflict, Security, and Development.* Washington, DC: World Bank, 2011. http://web.worldbank.org/WBSITE/EXTER-NAL/EXTDEC/EXTRESEARCH/EXTWDRS/0,,contentMDK:23256432~pageP K:478093~piPK:477627~theSitePK:477624,00.html.

CHAPTER 3

Barnes Robinson, Karen on behalf of Cordaid. "Integrating Gender into the New Deal for Engagement in Fragile States." Policy Paper. September 2012. https://www. cordaid.org/media/publications/Cordaid-7247-02-PP-Gender_into_the_New_ Deal-DEFHR-web.pdf.

"Bringing Peace into the Post-2015 Development Framework: A Joint Statement by Civil Society Organisations." September 21, 2012. http://www.cspps.org/document s/130616042/130626578/2012_09_28_CSO_Joint_Statement_Post-2015_ENG. pdf/a187d69f-3a87-46b1-82d1-90e24768424d.

CIVICUS. "CIVICUS' 2013 Enabling Environment Index." 2013. http://www. civicus.org/downloads/2013EEI%20REPORT.pdf.

Civil Society Platform for Peacebuilding and Statebuilding. "2030 Agenda and the New Deal—Where Next." November 2015. http://www.cspps.org/ documents/130616042/130793247/From+New+Deal+to+the+2030+Agenda+FI NAL-3-2.pdf/2146ea87-5f55-4c41-bf04-08fb8b80a91d.

Civil Society Platform for Peacebuilding and Statebuilding. "About the CSPPS." http://www.cspps.org/about-us.

Civil Society Platform for Peacebuilding and Statebuilding. "Post 2015, Goal 16 and Lessons on Indicators: Civil Society Perspectives from the New Deal Work on Indicators." February 25, 2015. http://www.cspps.org/documents/130616042/130793247/CSPPS+statement+post-2015+indicators+and+New+Deal+Lessons+-+25+Feb+2015.pdf.

CSPPS CSO Working Group. "The New Deal Implementation in South Sudan: A South Sudanese Civil Society Perspective Paper." March 2015. http://www.cspps.org/documents/130616042/130793247/New+Deal+Perspective+Paper++Final+2015.pdf/449c693d-61de-4d67-b3ef-4de932d6d788.

Department for International Development. "Building Peaceful States and Societies." DFID Practice Paper. 2010. https://www.gov.uk/government/publications/building-peaceful-states-and-societies-a-dfid-practice-paper.

Department for International Development. "UK Aid: Tackling Global Challenges in the National Interest." November 2015.

Global Partnership for the Prevention of Armed Conflict. "Promoting Peaceful and Inclusive Societies for Sustainable Development in the New Global Development Agenda: Beijing Seminar Report." March 24, 2015. http://www.gppac.net/news/-/asset_publisher/fHv91YcOz0CI/content/promoting-peaceful-and-inclusive-societies-in-new-post-2015-goals/.

de Weijer, Frauke and Ulrike Kilnes. "Strengthening Civil Society?: Reflections on International Engagement in Fragile States." European Centre for Development Policy Management (ECDPM) Discussion Paper 135. October 2012. www.ecdpm.org/dp135.

Hughes, Jacob, Ted Hooley, Siafa Hage, and George Ingram. "Implementing the New Deal for Fragile States." Brookings Institution. July 2014. http://www.brookings.edu/research/papers/2014/07/implementing-new-deal-fragile-states.

International Dialogue on Peacebuilding and Statebuilding. "A New Deal for Engagement in Fragile States." December 2011. http://www.pbsbdialogue.org/media/filer_public/07/69/07692de0-3557-494e-918e-18df00e9ef73/the_new_deal.pdf/.

International Dialogue on Peacebuilding and Statebuilding, Working Group on New Deal Implementation. *New Deal Monitoring Report 2014*. November 2014.

Interpeace. "CSOs and the IDPS." Policy Brief 1. August 2011. http://www.interpeace.org/index.php/documents/international-dialogue/168-policy-brief-1-an-introduction-to-the-international-dialogue-on-peacebuilding-and-statebuilding/file.

Interpeace. "CSOs and the IDPS." Policy Brief 4: Core Civil Society Messages to the International Dialogue on Peacebuilding and Statebuilding. August 2011. http://www.interpeace.org/wp-content/uploads/2011/08/2011_08_CSOs_An,d_IDPS_Policy_Brief_4_en_v2.pdf.

Interpeace. "Peacebuilding and Statebuilding - Interpeace Brings the Voices of 50 Civil Society Organizations." April 12, 2010. http://www.interpeace.org/2010/04/peacebuilding-and-statebuilding-interpeace-brings-the-voices-of-50-civil-society-organizations.

Manuel, Marcus. "Implementing the New Development Framework in Countries Affected by Conflict and Fragility." Overseas Development Institute Briefing Note. September 28, 2015. http://www.pbsbdialogue.org/media/filer_public/c4/6d/ c46dc18d-52bb-4635-9ea5-dfb2d5ecced7/odi_briefing_paper_idps_side_event. pdf.

McCandless, Erin and Nicholas Bouchet. "Tackling and Preventing Ebola while Building Peace and Societal Resilience: Lessons and Priorities for Action from Civil Society in Ebola-Affected New Deal Countries." CSPPS Policy Report. May 2015. http://www.cspps.org/news/-/asset_publisher/2nEICmeFS2z2/content/ tackling-and-preventing-ebola-while-building-peace-and-societal-resilience-lessons-and-priorities-for-action-from-civil-society-in-ebola-affected-new-/.

OECD. *States of Fragility 2015: Meeting Post-2015 Ambitions*. Paris: OECD Publishing, 2015.

OECD-DAC Fragile States Group. "Statebuilding in Situations of Fragility." April 2008. http://www.oecd.org/dac/governance-peace/conflictandfragility/ docs/41212290.pdf.

Okumu, Paul. "State-Society Relations: The Prospects for the New Deal Engagement in Addressing an Enabling Environment in Conflict-affected and Fragile States." In *State of Civil Society 2013*, edited by CIVICUS, 200-208. http://socs.civicus. org/?page_id=4289.

Paffenholz, Thania. "Inclusive Politics: Lessons from and for the New Deal." *Journal of Peacebuilding and Development* 10, no. 1 (2015): 84–89.

Smits, Rosan and Deborah Wright. "Engagement with Non-State Actors in Fragile States: Narrowing Definitions, Broadening Scope." Clingendael Netherlands Institute of International Relations, CRU Report. 2012. http://www.clingendael. nl/sites/default/files/20121200_cru_engagement_with_nsa_in_fragile_states.pdf.

United Nations General Assembly 68th session. "Report of the Open Working Group of the General Assembly on Sustainable Development Goals." A/68/970. August 12, 2014. http://www.un.org/ga/search/view_doc.asp?symbol=A/68/970.

Voluntary Action Network India. "Civil Society Engagement in Aid Effectiveness Discourse." 2013. http://www.vaniindia.org/publicationpdf/Primer%20Inside%20 -Civil%20Society%20Engagement.pdf.

Wall, Kristen and Rachel Fairhurst. *Assessing Civil Society Engagement in the New Deal: Opportunities and Challenges*. Kroc Institute for International Peace Studies. March 2014. http://kroc.nd.edu/sites/default/files/Assessing_Civil_Society_1.pdf.

World Bank. *World Development Report 2011: Conflict, Security and Development*. 2011. http://siteresources.worldbank.org/INTWDRS/Resources/WDR2011_Full_ Text.pdf.

CHAPTER 4

Afshar, Haleh and Deborah Eade, eds. *Development, Women, and War: Feminist Perspectives*. Oxford: Oxfam GB, 2004.

Barnes, Karen and Peter Albrecht. *Civil Society Oversight of the Security Sector and Gender*. Geneva: DCAF/OSCE, 2008.

Castillejo, Clare. "Building a State That Works for Women: Integrating Gender into Post-Conflict State Building." Working Paper no. 107. Madrid: FRIDE, 2011. http://fride.org/download/WP107_Building_state.pdf.

Chade, Jamil. "The Conflict and Fragility Agenda Post-Busan: Directions, Opportunities, Challenges." Geneva Peacebuilding Platform, Brief No. 2, 2012.

Clark, Cindy, Ellen Sprenger, and Lisa VeneKlasen. *Where is the Money for Women's Rights?: Assessing Resources and the Role of Donors in the Promotion of Women's Rights and the Support of Women's Organizations.* Toronto: AWID, 2006.

Cordaid. *Integrating Gender into the New Deal for Engagement in Fragile States.* The Hague: Cordaid, 2012. https://www.cordaid.org/media/publications/Cordaid-7247-02-PP-Gender_into_the_New_Deal-DEFHR-web.pdf.

Cueva-Beteta, Hanny, Christopher Kuonqui, and Limon B. Rodriguez. *What Women Want: Planning and Financing for Gender-Responsive Peacebuilding.* New York: UN, 2010.

GNWP. *Security Council Resolution 1325: Civil Society Monitoring Report 2014.* New York: GNWP, 2014. http://www.gnwp.org/sites/default/files/resource-field_media/2014Global%20Report_Aug13_2015HiRes_Jim.pdf.

Hedman, Jenny with Patti O'Neill and Catherine Gaynor. "Findings from the Gender Equality Module of the 2011 Paris Declaration Monitoring Survey." Prepared on behalf of the OECD, Development Co-Operation Directorate. http://www.oecd.org/dac/gender-development/49014760.pdf.

Hudson, Valerie M., Mary Caprioli, Bonnie Ballif-Spanvill, Rose McDermott, and Chad F. Emmett. "The Heart of the Matter: The Security of Women and the Security of States." *International Security* 33, no. 3 (Winter 2008/09): 7–45.

Hudson, Valerie M., Mary Caprioli, Bonnie Ballif-Spanvill, Rose McDermott, and Chad F. Emmett. *Sex and World Peace.* New York: Columbia University Press, 2012.

International Dialogue on Peacebuilding and Statebuilding. "Draft Concept Note for 'Road Testing' the Fragility Spectrum and Menu of Indicators." Room Document 8, June 2012. http://cso-effectiveness.org/IMG/pdf/rd8_en_concept_note_roadtesting_fragility_spectrum_and_menu_of.pdf.

International Dialogue on Peacebuilding and Statebuilding. "Integrating Gender into the Future of the International Dialogue and New Deal Implementation." International Dialogue Steering Group Meeting, November 2015. http://www.pbsbdialogue.org/media/filer_public/5e/54/5e542b5c-300d-4f22-af87-68a1567d2815/rd_9_gender_and_the_new_deal.pdf.

International Dialogue on Peacebuilding and Statebuilding. "New Deal Implementation Progress Overview." Seventh International Dialogue Working Group Meeting on New Deal Implementation, 2015. http://www.pbsbdialogue.org/media/filer_public/00/52/00527062-ddc0-418a-9e55-eee78312ff4d/rd_2_nd_implementation_progress_overview_feb_2015.pdf.

"International Peacebuilding and Statebuilding Indicators: CSO Joint Submission." Saferworld, January 2013. Summary and full article accessible at http://www.saferworld.org.uk/resources/view-resource/717-international-peacebuilding-and-statebuilding-indicators-a-cso-joint-statement.

Justino, Patricia, Ivan Cardona, Rebecca Mitchell, and Catherine Müller. "Quantifying the Impact of Women's Participation in Post-Conflict Economic Recovery." Households in Conflict Network Working Paper 131, November 2012.

Moser, Caroline O.N. and Fiona C. Clark, eds. *Victims, Perpetrators or Actors?: Gender, Armed Conflict and Political Violence.* London: Zed Books, 2001.

OECD. "Supporting Coherent and Sustainable Transition from Conflict to Peace." Draft Guidance, November 4, 2011.

OECD-DAC. *Financing UN Security Council Resolution 1325: Aid in Support of Gender Equality and Women's Rights in Fragile Contexts.* Paris: OECD, 2015.

O'Gorman, Eleanor. "Independent Thematic Review on Gender for the UN Peacebuilding Support Office: Final Report." March 2014. http://www.un.org/en/peacebuilding/pbso/pdf/Final%20Report_Thematic%20Review%20on%20Gender%20&%20Peacebuilding.pdf.

Olonisakin, Funmi, Karen Barnes, and Eka Ikpe. Women, Peace and Security: Translating Policy into Practice. London: Routledge, 2012.

Paffenholz, Thania. "Results on Women and Gender." Briefing Paper, Centre on Conflict, Development and Peacebuilding and University of Geneva, Graduate Institute of International and Development Studies, 2015. http://graduateinstitute.ch/files/live/sites/iheid/files/sites/ccdp/shared/Docs/Publications/briefingpaperbroader%20participation.pdf.

Suralaga, Dewi and Mavic Cabrera-Balleza, eds. *Financing for the Implementation of National Action Plans on UNSCR 1325: Critical for Advancing Women's Human Rights, Peace and Security.* The Hague: Cordaid and the Global Network of Women Peacebuilders, 2014. https://www.cordaid.org/media/medialibrary/2014/10/FinancingUNSCR1325_2014_27oct.pdf.

United Nations. "Tracking Progress: Seven Point Action Plan." A/65/354–S/2010/466, Report of the Secretary-General on Women's Participation in Peacebuilding. http://www.un.org/en/peacebuilding/pbso/pdf/seven_point_action_plan.pdf.

United Nations Security Council. Resolution 1889, "Women, Peace, and Security." S/RES/1889, October 5, 2009. http://womenpeacesecurity.org/media/pdfscr1889.pdf.

United Nations Security Council. "Women and Peace and Security: Report of the Secretary-General." S/2004/814, October 13, 2004. https://documents-dds-ny.un.org/doc/UNDOC/GEN/N04/534/14/PDF/N0453414.pdf?OpenElement.

United Nations Security Council. "Women, Peace and Security: Report of the Secretary-General." S/2010/173, 2010.

UN Women. *Preventing Conflict Transforming Justice Securing the Peace: A Global Study on the Implementation of United Nations Security Council Resolution 1325.* New York: UN Women, 2015. http://wps.unwomen.org/en.

UN Women. *Sourcebook on Women, Peace, and Security.* New York: UN Women, 2012.

UN Women *Women's Participation in Peace Negotiations: Connections between Presence and Influence.* New York: UN Women, 2012. http://www.unwomen.org/~/media/headquarters/attachments/sections/library/publications/2012/10/wps-sourcebook-03a-womenpeacenegotiations-en.pdf.

World Bank. *2012 World Development Report on Gender Equality and Development.* Washington DC: World Bank, 2012.

CHAPTER 5

Barnes, Catherine. *Agents for Change: Civil Society Roles in Preventing War and Building Peace*. The Hague: Global Partnership for the Prevention of Armed Conflict, 2006.

Buzan, Barry, Ole Wæver, and Jaap de Wilde. *Security: A New Framework for Analysis*. Boulder, CO: Lynne Rienner, 1997.

Campisi, Camila and Laura Ribeiro Rodrigues Pereira. *Filling the Gap: How Civil Society Engagement Can Help the UN's Peacebuilding Architecture Meet its Purpose*. The Hague: Global Partnership for the Prevention of Armed Conflict, 2015. http://www.peaceportal.org/documents/130492842/131164610/Filling+the+Gap. pdf/ebc53edd-5265-4b9a-806f-bd9d9786dd63.

Cedric De Coning, "Regional Approaches to Peacebuilding," *United Nations University Centre for Policy Research*, 2015, http://i.unu.edu/media/cpr.unu.edu/attachment/1007/Regional-Approaches-to-Peacebuilding.pdf.

Chenoweth, Erica and Maria Stephan. *Why Civil Resistance Works: The Strategic Logic of Nonviolent Conflict*. New York: Columbia University Press, 2011.

Collins, Craig, Erik Friberg, and John Packer. *Overview of Conflict Prevention Capacities of Regional, Sub-Regional and Other Inter-Governmental Organizations*. The Hague: European Centre for Conflict Prevention, 2006. http://www.i4pinternational.org/files/203/8.+overview+of+conflict+prev+capacities.pdf.

Constructive Engagement - Building a People-Oriented Community. Jakarta: ASEAN Secretariat, 2010. https://www.peaceportal.org/documents/130225323/130275120/ConstructiveEngagement-Building+a+People-Oriented+Community.pdf.

De Coning, Cedric. "Regional Approaches to Peacebuilding." Bruges: United Nations University, Centre for Policy Research, 2015. http://i.unu.edu/media/cpr.unu.edu/attachment/1007/Regional-Approaches-to-Peacebuilding.pdf.

Græger, Nina and Alexandra Novosseloff. "The Role of the OSCE and the EU." In *The United Nations and Regional Security: Europe and Beyond*, edited by Michael C. Pugh and W.P.S. Sidhu, 75–94. Boulder: Lynne Rienner, 2003.

Kaldor, Mary. *New and Old Wars: Organised Violence in a Global Era*. 3rd ed. Cambridge: Polity Press, 2012.

Ki-moon, Ban. "Preventive Diplomacy: Delivering Results." Report of the Secretary-General. New York: United Nations, 2011. http://www.un.org/wcm/webdav/site/undpa/shared/undpa/pdf/SG%20Report%20on%20Preventive%20Diplomacy.pdf.

Klabbers, Jan. "Two Concepts of International Organization." *International Organizations Law Review* 2, no. 2 (2005): 277–293.

Konrad, Katherine. "Appendix III: UN and Regional Arrangements since 1990: Doctrine, Developments, Current Thinking." In *Regional Organizations and Peacemaking, Challengers to the UN?* edited by Peter Wallensteen and Anders Bjurner, 255–263. London: Routledge, 2015.

Nathan, Laurie. "The Peacemaking Effectiveness of Regional Organisations." Crisis States Working Papers Series No.2, London School of Economics, Development Studies Institute, 2010. http://www.lse.ac.uk/internationalDevelopment/research/crisisStates/download/wp/wpSeries2/WP812.pdf

Paffenholz, Thania. "Can Inclusive Peace Processes Work? New Evidence from a Multi-Year Research Project." Policy Brief published online by the University of Geneva Graduate Institute of International and Development Studies' Centre on Conflict, Development, and Peacebuilding, April 2015. http://graduatein-stitute.ch/files/live/sites/iheid/files/sites/ccdp/shared/Docs/Publications/Can%20 Inclusive%20Peace%20Processes%20Work.pdf.

Ramcharan, Bertrand G. *Preventive Diplomacy at the UN*. Bloomington: Indiana University Press, 2008.

Smiles Persinger, Sarah. "Regional Organizations and Peacebuilding: The Role of Civil Society." Policy Brief commissioned by the Kroc Institute for International Peace Studies, University of Notre Dame, October 2014. http://www.gppac.net/documents/130492842/131146243/Regional+Organizations+and+Peacebuilding+The+Role+of+Civil+Society+(1).pdf/9f716c8f-267c-4533-ae7d-6dd3a9a0f4e8.

Tavarez, Rodrigo. *Regional Security: The Capacity of International Organizations*. New York: Routledge, 2010.

United Nations General Assembly. 65th session, Resolution 283. "Strengthening the Role of Mediation in the Peaceful Settlement of Disputes, Conflict Prevention and Resolution." June 22, 2011. http://www.un.org/en/ga/search/view_doc.asp?symbol=A/RES/65/283.

Van Langenhove, Luk. "Chapter VIII of the UN Charter: What It Is and Why It Matters." Published online by the United Nations University, August 26, 2014. http://unu.edu/publications/articles/chapter-viii-of-the-un-charter-what-it-is-and-why-it-matters.html.

Van Langenhove, Luk. *Multilateralism 2.0*. EU-GRASP Working Papers No. 21. Bruges: UNU-CRIS, 2010.

Van Langenhove, Luk. "The UN Security Council and Regional Organisations: A Difficult Partnership." In *Belgium in the UN Security Council: Reflections on the 2007–2008 Membership*, edited by Jan Wouters, Edith Drieskens and Sven Biscop, 165–174. Antwerp: Intersentia, 2009.

Van Langenhove, Luk, Anna Sophie Selzer, and Josh Gartland. 2015. "Strengthening the Global Peacebuilding Architecture through Chapter VIII." (Working paper presented at the "Conference on Strengthening Peace and Security Cooperation towards Democracy and Development, Vienna, Austria, April 29–30 2015).

Wallensteen, Peter and Anders Bjurner. "The Challenge of Regional Organizations: An Introduction." In *Regional Organizations and Peacemaking, Challengers to the UN?* edited by Peter Wallensteen and Anders Bjurner, 239-245. London: Routledge, 2015.

Wallensteen, Peter. "International Conflict Resolution, UN and Regional Organizations: The Balance Sheet." In *Regional Organizations and Peacemaking, Challengers to the UN?*, edited by Peter Wallensteen and Anders Bjurner, 13–27. London: Routledge, 2015.

CHAPTER 6

Abass, Ademola. *Regional Organizations and the Development of Collective Security: Beyond Chapter VIII of the UN Charter.* Oxford: Hart Publishing, 2004.

Amamoo, Joseph G. *Ghana: 50 Years of Independence.* Accra: Jafint Enterprise Publications, 2007.

Ametewee, Victor K. "Ethnicity and Ethnic Relations in Ghana." In *Ethnicity, Conflicts and Consensus in Ghana,* edited by Steve Tonah, 25–41. Accra: Woelli Publishing Services, 2007.

"Another Somalia: Piracy off West Africa Is on the Rise." *The Economist,* May 25, 2013. http://www.economist.com/news/middle-east-and-africa/21578409-piracy-west-africa-rise-another-somalia.

"Assembly of the African Union, First Ordinary Session: Protocol Relating to the Establishment of the Peace and Security Council of the African Union." *African Union,* July 9, 2002. http://www.au2002.gov.za/docs/summit_council/secprot.htm.

Bakrania, Shivit. *Conflict Drivers, International Responses, and the Outlook for Peace in Mali: A Literature Review.* GSDRC Issues Paper, University of Birmingham, Birmingham, UK, 2013. http://www.gsdrc.org/docs/open/IP14.pdf.

"Briefing on Burkina Faso." *What's In Blue,* November 4, 2014. http://whatsinblue.org/2014/11/briefing-on-burkina-faso.php.

Buah, F. K. *A History of Ghana Revised and Updated.* London: Macmillan Education Ltd., 1998.

"Constitutive Act of the African Union." July 2000. http://www.au.int/en/sites/default/files/ConstitutiveAct_EN.pdf.

"The Continental Early Warning System." *African Union.* http://www.peaceau.org/en/page/28-continental-early-warning-system-cews#sthash.yU3T0RHD.dpuf.

"Democratic Transitions in West Africa: A Year of Elections." *WANEP Quarterly Highlights.* June 2011. http://www.wanep.org/wanep/files/2011/qh_jan_mar_2011.pdf.

Denoy, Myriam S. *Child Soldiers: Sierra Leone's Revolutionary United Front.* Cambridge: Cambridge University Press, 2010.

ECOWAS Commission. "The ECOWAS Conflict Prevention Framework." January 2008. http://www.lawschool.cornell.edu/womenandjustice/upload/ECOWAS-Conflict-Prevention-Framework.pdf.

ECOWAS Department of Political Affairs, Peacekeeping and Security (PAPS). "Policy Framework for the Establishment of Early Warning/Response Mechanisms in ECOWAS Member States." November 2012 (Internal Document).

ECOWAS Executive Secretariat. "Protocol Relating to the Mechanism for Conflict Prevention, Management, Resolution, Peacekeeping and Security." December 10, 1999. http://www.afrimap.org/english/images/treaty/ECOWAS_Protocol_Conflicts.pdf.

"ECOWAS Member States Hold Consultative Meeting on Establishing of National Early Warning Mechanism." October 2013. http://www.wanep.org/wanep/index.php?option=com_content&view=article&id=500:ecowas-member-states-hold-consultative-meeting-on-establishment-of-national-early-warning-mechanism-&catid=25:news-releases&Itemid=8.

Government of Ghana. "Declaration on Strengthening National, Regional and Continental Co-ordination towards Building National Peace Infrastructures for Conflict Prevention." September 10, 2013. http://www.i4pinternational.org/files/514/declaration+accra+10-9-2013.pdf

Hamdy, Hassan A.R. "State and Civil Society in Africa: A North African Perspective." *African Journal of Political Science and International Relations* 3, no. 2 (February 2009): 66–76.

"The Impacts of the Libyan Crisis on the Sahel Region of ECOWAS." *Early Warning Directorate.* September 9, 2011 (Internal Document).

"I wanted to kill Mahama—Gunman Confesses." *GhanaWeb*, July 28, 2015. http://www.ghanaweb.com/GhanaHomePage/NewsArchive/I-wanted-to-kill-Mahama-Gunman-confesses-371501.

Lederach, John Paul. *Building Peace: Sustainable Reconciliation in Divided Societies.* Washington DC: United States Institute of Peace Press, 1997.

Maru, Mehari Taddele. *The Mid-Term Review of the West African Network for Peace-building (WANEP).* Stockholm: SIDA, 2013. http://www.sida.se/contentassets/b9003394b16e4d48b7246b0617b6f54f/ee420a49-911f-4a7e-b959-1df22fdcb4a5.pdf.

Matveeva, Anna, "Early Warning and Early Response: Conceptual and Empirical Dilemmas," *European Centre for Conflict Prevention* and *International Secretariat of the Global Partnership for the Prevention of Armed Conflict*, September 2006, https://www.peaceportal.org/documents/127900679/127917167/Issue+paper+1+Early+Warning+and+Early+Response.pdf.

Neufeldt, Reina, Larissa Fast, Robert Schreiter, Brian Starken, Duncan MacLaren, Jaco Cilliers, and John Paul Lederach. *Peacebuilding: A Caritas Training Manual.* Vatican City: Caritas Internationalis, 2002. http://dmeforpeace.org/sites/default/files/Neufeldt%20et%20al_Caritas%20Peacebuilding.pdf.

Nfor, Monde Kingsley. "No Shortage of Recruits for Boko Haram in Cameroon's Far North." *IRIN*, March 5, 2015. http://www.irinnews.org/report/101198/no-shortage-of-recruits-for-boko-haram-in-cameroon-s-far-north.

Padmore, George. *The Gold Coast Revolution: The Struggle of an African People from Slavery to Freedom.* London: Dennis Dobson, 1953.

"Panel of the Wise (PoW)." *African Union.* http://www.peaceau.org/en/page/29-panel-of-the-wise-pow.

"Report of 2nd Jos Dialogue Process: Sustaining the Search for Lasting Peace in the Home of Peace and Tourism," *WANEP and IPCR Report*, 2012, http://www.wanep.org/wanep/attachments/article/290/rp_2nd_jos_dialogue_process.pdf.

Ronning, Helge. "Democracy, Civil Society and the Media in Africa in the Nineties: A Discussion of the Emergence and Relevance of Some Analytical Concepts for the Understanding of the Situation in Africa." *Innovation: The European Journal of Social Sciences* 8, no. 4 (December 1995): 335–352.

Rupesinghe, Kumar. "A New Generation of Conflict Prevention: Early Warning, Early Action and Human Security." Paper presented at the Global Partnership for the Prevention of Armed Conflict Global Conference, "Role of Civil Society in the Prevention of Armed Conflict and Peacebuilding," New York, July 2015.

Rupesinghe, Kumar. "FCE Citizen-Based Early Warning and Early Response System: A New Tool for Civil Society to Prevent Violent Conflict." February 24, 2009. https://earlywarning.files.wordpress.com/2009/03/fce-citizen-based-early-warning-and-early-response-system.pdf.

Schirch, Lisa and Manjrika Sewak. "The Role of Women in Peacebuilding." European Centre for Conflict Prevention, January 2005. https://www.google.com/url?sa=t&rct=j&q=&esrc=s&source=web&cd=5&cad=rja&uact=8&ved=0ahUKEwjymKCFn6rKAhVFbR4KHWYgDfgQFgg4MAQ&url=http%3A%2F%2Fwww.conflictrecovery.org%2Fbin%2FIssue_paper_on_the_Role_of_Women_in_Peacebuilding_Jan2005.doc&usg=AFQjCNGzaAgpv_ESncIxgMycjdwUTu1PAQ&sig2=n_PjhzXDEA_GagyaeIgVMw&bvm=bv.111677986,d.dmo.

Schirch, Lisa. *Women in Peacebuilding: Resource and Training Manual.* West African Network for Peacebuilding and Conflict Transformation Program at Eastern Mennonite University, 2004. https://www.emu.edu/cjp/publications/faculty-staff/lisa-schirch/women-in-peacebuilding-pt1.pdf.

Tiruneh, Birikit Terefe. "Establishing an Early Warning System in the African Peace and Security Architecture: Challenges and Prospects." KAIPTC Occasional Paper No. 29. Accra: Kofi Annan International Peacekeeping Training Centre, September 2010. http://www.kaiptc.org/publications/occasional-papers/documents/occasional-paper-29-birikit.aspx.

United Nations Development Program. *Human Development Report 2004: Cultural Liberty in Today's Diverse World.* New York: United Nations Development Program, 2004. http://hdr.undp.org/sites/default/files/reports/265/hdr_2004_complete.pdf.

United Nations Security Council. "Report of the Assessment Mission on the Impact of the Libyan Crisis on the Sahel Region: Report of the Secretary General." S/2012/42, January 18, 2012. http://www.iom.int/sites/default/files/event/docs/Interagency-Assessment-Mission-Report-on-the-Impact-of-the-Libyan-Crisis-to-the-Sahel-Region-IA-7-23-December-201-English.pdf.

United Nations Security Council. "Report of the Secretary-General on the Activities of the United Nations Office for West Africa." S/2014/945, December 24, 2014. https://unowa.unmissions.org/Portals/UNOWA/Report/Report%20of%20the%20Secretary-General%20on%20the%20activities%20of%20the%20UNOWA.DOC.

WANEP. "Burkina Faso's Test of Resilience and Democratic Stability—The 2015 Political Dynamics and Drifts." WARN Policy Brief, March 29, 2014. http://www.wanep.org/wanep/files/2014/mar/pb_burkina_faso_mar_2014.pdf.

"WANEP General Assembly's January 2011 Concept Paper." January 24, 2011. http://www.wanep.org/wanep/attachments/article/240/Concept%20Paper%20-%20Media.pdf

WANEP-Nigeria. "National Early Warning System Weekly Highlight: 5–11 July 2015."

Wormington, Jim. "After Simone Gbagbo's Trial, What Next for Justice in Cote D'Ivoire." *Human Rights Watch*, April 8, 2015. http://www.hrw.org/news/2015/04/08/after-simone-gbagbo-s-trial-what-next-justice-cote-d-ivoire.

CHAPTER 7

Australian High Commission—Fiji. "Promoting Women's Leadership and Peace Building in the Pacific." October 31, 2008. http://fiji.highcommission.gov.au/suva/mrel31oct.html.

Bryar, Timothy. "Violence and Security in the Pacific." (presentation at the Geneva Declaration Regional Review Conference, Manila, Philippines, October 8–9, 2014), 3. http://www.genevadeclaration.org/fileadmin/docs/2014RRC/3._RRC_Manila/D114PP%20Timothy_Bryar_presentation.pdf.

FemLINKPACIFIC ENews Bulletin. "The Eights Years on Special." October 2008. http://www.femlinkpacific.org.fj/images/PDF/E-Bulletin/femTALK_ENews_October_2008.pdf.

FemLINKPACIFIC. "Policy for Peace: A FemLINKPACIFIC Policy Initiative." 2015. http://www.femlinkpacific.org.fj/images/PDF/Policy/PolicyForPeace_2015.pdf.

FemLINKPACIFIC. "Blue Ribbon Peace Special." October 2006. http://www.peace-women.org/content/blue-ribbon-peace-special.

FemLINKPACIFIC. "Regional Action Plans (RAPS), National Action Plans (NAPS) and 'Twinning' for Women, Peace and Security." (powerpoint presentation). http://www.spc.int/hdp/index2.php?option=com_docman&task=doc_view&gid=249&Itemid=4.

Fong Toy, Andie. "Structured Cooperation Between Civil Society and Regional Inter-governmental Organisations: Best Practices." (presentation at the International Conference Strengthening Global Peace and Security for Development, Madrid, Spain, November 15–16, 2011), 1. https://www.peaceportal.org/c/document_library/get_file?uuid=82fa17df-443d-4335-bc14-76b896f3edc9&groupId=125878116.

George, Nicole. "Pacific Women Building Peace: A Regional Perspective." *The Contemporary Pacific* 23, no. 1 (Spring 2011): 37–71.

George, Nicole. "Promoting Women, Peace and Security in the Pacific Islands." *Australian Journal of International Affairs* 68, no. 3 (2014): 314–332.

NGO Working Group on Women, Peace and Security. "Biography of Sharon Bhagwan-Rolls, Coordinator, FemLINKPACIFIC, Fiji Pacific Islands." (accessed March 19, 2016). http://womenpeacesecurity.org/programs-events/peacebuilders/sharon_bhagwan-rolls/.

Pacific Islands Forum. "About Us." (accessed March 9, 2016). http://www.forumsec.org/pages.cfm/about-us/.

Pacific Islands Forum. "Mission and Vision." (accessed March 9, 2016). http://www.forumsec.org/pages.cfm/about-us/mission-goals-roles/.

Pacific Islands Forum Secretariat. "Council of Regional Organisations in the Pacific (CROP)." (accessed March 10, 2016). http://www.forumsec.org/pages.cfm/about-us/our-partners/crop/.

Pacific Islands Forum Secretariat. "The Pacific Plan for Strengthening Regional Cooperation and Integration." November 2007. http://www.adb.org/sites/default/files/linked-documents/robp-pac-2010-2013-oth01.pdf.

Pacific Islands Forum Secretariat. "Pacific Regional Action Plan: Women, Peace and Security 2012–2015." 2012. http://www2.kobe-u.ac.jp/~alexroni/TR2015%20

readings/2015_8/Pacific%20Regional%20Action%20Plan%20on%20Women%20 Peace%20and%20Security%20Final%20and%20Approved.pdf.

Pacific Islands Forum Secretariat. "Annex 1: Pacific Leaders Gender Equality Declaration." In *Forum Communique*. (Rarotonga, Cook Islands: August 30, 2012). http://www.forumsec.org/resources/uploads/attachments/documents/2012%20 Forum%20Communique,%20Rarotonga,%20Cook%20Islands%2028-30%20 Aug1.pdf.

Pacific Islands News Association. "On the 8th Anniversary of UN Security Council Resolution 1325 (Women, Peace and Security) Pacific Peacewomen Offer Policy Responses and Solutions for our Pacific Region." October 31, 2008. http://www. pina.com.fj/?p=pina&m=events&o=156530706248fff9ff6ffb38e82786.

Papadimitropoulos, P. "The Rarotonga Treaty: A regional approach to non-proliferation in the South Pacific." *International Atomic Energy Agency* Bulletin (1/1988). https://www.iaea.org/sites/default/files/30103472931.pdf.

Peace Women. "1325 at 15: Reflections on the Implementation of WPS from the Pacific Region." October 2015. http://www.peacewomen.org/e-news/ article/1325-15-reflections-implementation-wps-pacific-region.

"The Pacific: Women's civil Society Engagement in Security Dialogue." in *Examples from the Ground: Civil Society Oversight of the Security Sector and Gender* (DCAF, 2011). http://www.poa-iss.org/kit/Gender-SSR-E.pdf.

United Nations Press. "Security Council, Recalling Resolution 1325 (2000), Seeks Measures to Strengthen Role of Women in Peacekeeping, Post-Conflict Situations." October 26, 2006. http://www.un.org/press/en/2006/sc8858.doc.htm.

United Nations Security Council Resolution 1325. S/RES/1325, October 31, 2000. https://documents-dds-ny.un.org/doc/UNDOC/GEN/N00/720/18/PDF/N0072018. pdf?OpenElement.

UN Women Asia and the Pacific. "Fiji Multi-Country Office." (accessed March 19, 2016). http://asiapacific.unwomen.org/en/countries/fiji.

CHAPTER 8

Blair, Dennis. *Military Engagement: Influencing Armed Forces to Support Democratic Transitions*. Washington DC: Brookings Institution Press, 2013.

Boon-Kuo, Louise, Ben Hayes, Vicki Sentas, and Gavin Sullivan. *Building Peace in Permanent War: Terrorist Listing and Conflict Transformation*. London: International State Crime Initiative—Transnational Institute, 2015.

Caparini, Maria and Eden Cole. "The Case for Public Oversight of the Security Sector: Concepts and Strategies." In *Public Oversight of the Security Sector: A Handbook for Civil Society Organisations*, edited by Eden Cole, Kerstin Eppert, and Katrin Kinzelbach, 11–30. Valeur, Slovakia: United Nations Development Program, 2008.

Chenoweth, Erica and Maria J. Stephan. *Why Civil Resistance Works: The Strategic Logic of Nonviolent Conflict*. New York: Columbia University Press, 2011.

De Coning, Cedric. "Clarity, Coherence, and Context: Three Priorities for Sustainable Peacebuilding," Working Paper: The Future of the Peacebuilding Architecture

Project. Norwegian Institute of International Affairs and Centre for International Policy Studies and University of Ottawa, 2010. http://www.betterpeace.org/files/ CIPS_NUPI_Clarity_Coherence_and_Context_deConing_Feb2010.pdf.

Fisher, Roger and William Ury. *Getting to Yes. Negotiating Agreement Without Giving In.* New York: Penguin, 1983.

Friedman, Elisabeth Jay, Kathryn Hochstetler, and Ann Marie Clark. *Sovereignty, Democracy, and Global Civil Society: State-Society Relations at UN World Conferences.* New York: SUNY Press, 2005.

Global Terrorism Index 2014: Measuring and Understanding the Impact of Terrorism. New York: Institute for Economics and Peace, 2014. http://www. visionofhumanity.org/sites/default/files/Global%20Terrorism%20Index%20 Report%202014_0.pdf.

Hiscock, Duncan. "Research and Information." In *Public Oversight of the Security Sector: A Handbook for Civil Society Organisations,* edited by Eden Cole, Kerstin Eppert, and Katrin Kinzelbach, 53–74. Valeur, Slovakia: United Nations Development Program, 2008.

Human Security Unit of the United Nations. *Human Security in Theory and Practice: An Overview of the Human Security Concept and the United Nations Trust Fund for Human Security.* New York: United Nations, 2009. http://www.un.org/ humansecurity/sites/www.un.org.humansecurity/files/human_security_in_theory_ and_practice_english.pdf.

Lederach, John Paul. "Addressing Terrorism: A Theory of Change Approach." In *Somalia: Creating Space for Fresh Approaches to Peacebuilding,* 7–19. Uppsala: Life and Peace Institute, 2011.

Mayer-Rieckh, Alexander and Serge Rumin. "Confronting an Abusive Past in Security Sector Reform after Conflict: Guidelines for Practitioners." Initiative for Peacebuilding, 2010.

McCandless, Erin. *Polarization and Transformation in Zimbabwe: Social Movements, Strategy Dilemmas, and Change.* Durban: University of Kwazulu-Natal Press, 2011.

OECD Development Assistance Committee. "Concepts and Dilemmas of State Building in Fragile Situations: From Fragility to Resilience." OECD/DAC Discussion Paper. http://www.oecd.org/dac/governance-peace/conflictandfragility/ docs/41100930.pdf.

Reychler, Luc and Thania Paffenholz. *Peacebuilding: A Field Guide.* Boulder: Lynne Rienner Publishers, 2001.

Ruscetta, Major Louis J. *Education for Philippine Pacification: How the U.S. Used Education as Part of Its Counterinsurgency Strategy in the Philippines from 1898 to 1909.* Damascus, MD: Pennyhill Press, 2013.

Schirch, Lisa. *Conflict Assessment and Peacebuilding Planning: Toward a Participatory Approach to Human Security.* Boulder: Kumarian Press, 2013.

Schirch, Lisa. *Strategic Peacebuilding.* Intercourse, PA: Good Books, 2004.

Schirch, Lisa and Deborah Mancini-Griffoli. *Local Ownership in Security: Peacebuilding Approaches to Civil-Military-Police Coordination.* The Hague: Alliance for Peacebuilding, GPPAC, and the Kroc Institute, 2015.

Security Sector Reform Unit of the Office of Rule of Law and Security Operations of the Department of Peacekeeping Operations of the United Nations. "The United Nations SSR Perspective." 2012. http://www.un.org/en/peacekeeping/publications/ssr/ssr_perspective_2012.pdf.

Serwer, Daniel and Patricia Thomson. "A Framework for Success: International Intervention in Societies Emerging from Conflict." In *Leashing the Dogs of War*, edited by Chester Crocker, Fen Osler Hampson, and Pamela Aall, 369–388. Washington DC: United States Institute for Peace, 2007.

Thompson, Edwina. *Principled Pragmatism: NGO Engagement with Armed Actors*. Monrovia, CA: WorldVision International, 2008.

United Nations Development Program. *Human Security Report 1994*. New York: Oxford University Press, 1994.

United Nations Secretary-General Kofi Annan. "In Larger Freedom: Towards Development, Security and Human Rights for All." A/59/2005.

CHAPTER 9

Armed Forces of the Philippines. *Internal Peace and Security Plan*. Manila: Government of the Philippines, 2010.

Cusimano Love, Maryann. "Partnering for Peace in the Philippines: Military and Religious Engagement." *Georgetown University Institute for the Study of Diplomacy Pew Case Study Center*, Case 550, 2005. http://www.uscirf.gov/sites/default/files/resources/stories/pdf/maryann%20love%20philippines%20case%20study.pdf.

Duduoet, Veronique. *Nonviolent Resistance and Conflict Transformation in Power Asymmetries*. Berlin: Berghof Research Center for Constructive Conflict Management, 2008.

Ferrer, Miriam Coronel. "Institutional Response: Civil Society." Background paper submitted for the Philippine Human Development Report, 2005. http://hdn.org.ph/wp-content/uploads/2005_PHDR/2005%20Civil_Society_Assessment.pdf.

Hernandez, Carolina. "Restoring Democratic Civilian Control over the Philippine Military: Challenges and Prospects." *Journal of International Cooperation Studies* 10, no. 1 (2002): 25–48.

International Alert. "Rebellion, Political Violence and Shadow Crimes in the Bangsamoro: The Bangsamoro Conflict Monitoring System (BCMS), 2011–2013." August 2014. http://bcms-philippines.info/vers1/sites/default/files/BCMS%20General%20Paper.pdf.

King Jr., Martin Luther. "How Long, Not Long (Our God is Marching On)." Speech, Montgomery, AL, March 25, 1965. Published online by the King Institute at Stanford University. https://kinginstitute.stanford.edu/our-god-marching.

Lederach, John Paul. *Building Peace: Sustainable Reconciliation in Divided Societies*. Washington, DC: United States Institute of Peace, 1997.

Lederach, John Paul. *The Moral Imagination: The Art and Soul of Building Peace*. New York: Oxford University Press, 2005.

Macapagal-Arroyo, President Gloria. *Executive Order* No. 3, s. 2001. www.gov. ph/2001/02/28/executive-order-no-3-s-2001.

Security Sector Monograph. Davao City: Mindanao Peacebuilding Institute and Catholic Relief Services Mindanao Regional Program Office Peace and Reconciliation Program, 2008.

CHAPTER 10

Aguilar Umaña, Isabel, Bernardo Arévalo de León, and Ana Glenda Táger Rosado. "El Salvador: Negotiating with Gangs." In *Legitimacy and Peace Processes: From Coercion to Consent*, edited by Alexander Ramsbotham and Achim Wenneman, special issue, *Accord* 25, (2014): 95–99. http://www.c-r.org/downloads/Accord-25WEB.pdf.

Arévalo de León, Bernardo. "Civil-Military Relations in Post-Conflict Guatemala: Military Transformation in the Light of the 1996 Agreement on the Strengthening of Civilian Power and the Role of the Armed Forces in a Democratic Society." In *Democratic Governance of the Security Sector beyond the OSCE Region: Regional Approaches in Africa and the Americas*, edited by Victor Ghebali and Alexander Lambert, 155–191. Munster: DCAF—Lit Verlag, 2007.

Arévalo de León, Bernardo. "Del Estado Violento al Ejército Político: Violencia, Formación Estatal y Ejército en Guatemala 1500–1963." PhD diss., University of Utrecht, 2015.

Arévalo de León, Bernardo. "Democratic Security in Guatemala: Reflections on Building a Concept of Security in and for Democracy." In *Human Security, Conflict Prevention and Peace in Latin America and the Caribbean*, edited by Moufida Goucha and Francisco Rojas Aravena, 141–156. Santiago: UNESCO-FLACSO Chile, 2003.

Arévalo de León, Bernardo. "Investigación-Acción Participativa (IAP) como herramienta para la reforma del sector seguridad: El proyecto Hacia Una Política de Seguridad para Democracia en Guatemala." In *Hacia una Política de Seguridad para la Democracia en Guatemala: Investigación Acción Participativa (IAP) y Reforma del Sector Seguridad*, edited by Bernardo Arévalo de León, José Beltrán Doña, and Philipp H. Fluri. Munster: Lit Verlag—DCAF, 2005.

Arévalo de León, Bernardo. *Sobre Arenas Movedizas: Sociedad, estado y ejército en Guatemala, 1997*. Guatemala City: FLACSO, 1998.

Arévalo de León, Bernardo and Ana Glenda Táger Rosado. "Central America Regional Perspectives." Geneva Peacebuilding Platform, White Paper for Peacebuilding Series, no. 5, 2015.

Comisión de Esclarecimiento Histórico. *Guatemala: Memoria del Silencio*. Guatemala City: CEH, 1999.

Dunkerley, James. *Power in the Isthmus: A Political History of Modern Central America*. Verso: London, 1988.

Government of Guatemala. Government Accord 115–2004. Passed on March 16, 2004.

"Jefe del Estado Mayor de la Defensa busca Amnistía por Crímenes de Guerra." *Prensa Libre*, January 12, 2016. http://www.prensalibre.com/guatemala/justicia/jefe-del-emd-busca-amnistia-por-crimenes-de-guerra.

Ministerio de la Defensa Nacional, República de Guatemala. *Guatemala: Libro de la Defensa Nacional*. Published online by Red de Seguridad y Defensa de América Latina, 2003. http://www.resdal.org.ar/Archivo/d00001f8.htm.

Nómada. *140 días de primavera*. Guatemala City: Editorial Rara, 2015.

Pearce, Jenny. "Case Study of IDRC-Supported Research on Security Sector Reform in Guatemala." *International Development Research Centre, Peace, Conflict, and Development Program*, Final Report, February 2006. http://idl-bnc.idrc.ca/dspace/bitstream/10625/27529/1/122103.pdf.

Schirmer, Jennifer. *Las Intimidades del proyecto político de los militares en Guatemala*. Guatemala City: FLACSO, 1999.

Táger Rosado, Ana Glenda. "El Proyecto Hacia una Política de Seguridad para la Democracia dos años después." In *Hacia una Política de Seguridad para la Democracia en Guatemala: Investigación Acción Participativa (IAP) y Reforma del Sector Seguridad*, edited by Bernardo Arévalo de León, José Beltrán Doña, and Philipp H. Fluri. Munster: Lit Verlag—DCAF, 2005.

Torres Rivas, Edelberto and Bernardo Arévalo de León. *The WSP Guatemala Way*. Guatemala City: UNRISD-FLACSO, 1999.

United Nations General Assembly. 59th assembly, Resolution 746. "United Nations Verification Mission in Guatemala: Report of the Secretary-General." March 18, 2005. https://documents-dds-ny.un.org/doc/UNDOC/GEN/N05/277/50/PDF/N0527750.pdf?OpenElement.

Waagstein, Thorbjörn and Claus Thure Hastrup. "Proyecto de Modernización y Agenda Legislativa del Congreso 2005-2008." *SIDA Review* 22 (2009): 1–54. http://www.sida.se/contentassets/07804173eb5f41c68484e5398776bbc8/proyecto-de-modernizaci243n-y-agenda-legislativa-del-congreso-en-guatemala-200582112008_2932.pdf.

CHAPTER 11

Appleby, R. Scott. *The Ambivalence of the Sacred: Religion, Violence, and Peacebuilding*. Lanham, MD: Rowman and Littlefield, 2000.

Beebe, Shannon D. and Mary Kaldor. *The Ultimate Weapon is No Weapon: Human Security and the New Rules of War and Peace*. New York: Public Affairs, 2010.

Blair, Dennis, ed. *Military Engagement: Influencing Armed Forces to Support Democratic Transitions*. Vol. 2. Washington DC: Brookings Institution Press, 2013.

Boulding, Kenneth. *Three Faces of Power*. Newbury Park, CA: Sage Publications, 1989.

Brainard, Lael, Derek Chollet, and Nica LaFluer. "The Tangled Web: The Poverty-Insecurity Nexus." In *Too Poor for Peace? Global Poverty, Conflict, and Security in the 21st Century*, edited by Lael Brainard and Derek Chollet, 1–30. Washington, DC: The Brookings Institution, 2007.

Carothers, Thomas and Saskia Brechenmacher. *Closing Space: Democracy and Human Rights under Fire*. Washington DC: Carnegie Endowment for International Peace, 2014. http://carnegieendowment.org/files/closing_space.pdf.

The Challenge of Sustaining Peace. Report of the Advisory Group of Experts for the 2015 Review of the United Nations Peacebuilding Architecture, June 29, 2015, http://www.un.org/pga/wp-content/uploads/sites/3/2015/07/300615_The-Challenge-of-Sustaining-Peace.pdf.

Collier, Paul, V. L. Elliot, Havard Hegre, Anke Hoeffler, Marta Reynol-Querol, and Nicholas Sambonis. *Breaking the Conflict Trap: Civil War and Development Policy*. Washington, DC: World Bank and Oxford University Press, 2003.

Commission on Human Rights. *Human Security Now: Protecting and Empowering People*. New York: Commission on Human Security, 2003.

Commission on Human Security. "Outline of the Report of the Commission on Human Security." 2003. http://www.unocha.org/humansecurity/chs/finalreport/Outlines/outline.html.

Cortright, David. "Could New Laws to Fight Terrorism Actually Help Fuel It?" International Peace Institute, *Global Observatory*, March 31, 2015. https://theglobalobservatory.org/2015/03/terrorism-financing-civil-liberties/.

Cortright, David, with Alistair Millar, Linda Gerber-Stellingwerf, George A. Lopez, Eliot Fackler, and Joshua Weaver. "Friend not Foe: Opening Spaces for Civil Society Engagement to Prevent Violent Extremism." Report to Cordaid from the Fourth Freedom Forum and the Kroc Institute for International Peace Studies at the University of Notre Dame. 2nd edn. May 2011. http://www.hscollective.org/wp-content/uploads/2013/09/Friend-not-Foe-2.pdf.

Diamond, Larry. "The Democratic Rollback: The Resurgence of the Predatory State." *Foreign Affairs* 87, no. 2 (March/April 2008): 36–48.

Hayes, Ben. "Counter-Terrorism, 'Policy Laundering,' and the FATF: Legalizing Surveillance, Regulating Civil Society." *The International Journal of Not-for-Profit Law* 14, nos. 1–2 (April 2012): 5–48.

High-Level Panel on Humanitarian Financing Report to the Secretary-General. "Too Important to Fail—Addressing the Humanitarian Financing Gap." December 2015. http://www.un.org/news/WEB-1521765-E-OCHA-Report-on-Humanitarian-Financing.pdf.

Human Rights Watch. *In the Name of Security: Counterterrorism Laws Worldwide Since September 11*. New York: Human Rights Watch, 2012.

Human Rights Watch. *Preempting Justice: Counterterrorism Laws and Procedures in France*. New York: Human Rights Watch, 2008. https://www.hrw.org/sites/default/files/reports/france0708_1.pdf.

Institute for Economics and Peace. *Global Terrorism Index*. Sydney: Institute for Economics and Peace, 2015.

Kaldor, Mary. *Human Security: Reflections on Globalization and Intervention*. Cambridge, UK: Polity Press, 2007.

Lederach, John Paul. *The Moral Imagination: The Art and Soul of Building Peace*. New York: Oxford University Press, 2005.

Mack, Andrew. "A Signifier of Shared Values." *Security Dialogue* 35, no. 3 (2004): 366–7.

Mercy Corps. *Youth and Consequences: Unemployment, Injustice and Violence.* Portland: Mercy Corps, 2015. https://www.mercycorps.org/research-resources/youth-consequences-unemployment-injustice-and-violence.

Miguel, Edward. "Economic Shocks, Weather and Civil War." *The National Bureau of Economic Research: NBER Reporter 2011*, no. 3: Research Summary.

Naím, Moisés. *The End of Power: From Boardrooms to Battlefields and Churches to States, Why Being In Charge Isn't What It Used to Be* (New York: Basic Books, 2013).

Newman, Edward. "Critical Human Security Studies." *Review of International Studies* 36, no. 1 (2010): 77–94.

Norris, Pippa. *Making Democratic Governance Work: How Regimes Shape Prosperity, Welfare, and Peace.* Cambridge: Cambridge University Press, 2012.

Paris, Roland. "Human Security: Paradigm Shift or Hot Air." *International Security* 26, no. 2 (2001): 87–102.

Puddington, Arch. "Discarding Democracy: A Return to the Iron Fist." Article of highlights from Freedom House 2015 Report. https://freedomhouse.org/sites/default/files/01152015_FIW_2015_final.pdf.

Schirch, Lisa, ed. *Handbook on Human Security: A Civil-Military-Police Curriculum.* The Hague: Alliance for Peacebuilding, GPPAC, Kroc Institute, 2015. https://www.peace-portal.org/documents/130617663/0/FINAL+HANDBOOK+November+30+1154.pdf/25025a3b-3247-4714-b1b4-d1530d84b0f1.

Schirch, Lisa with Deborah Mancini-Griffoli. *Local Ownership in Security: Case Studies of Peacebuilding Approaches.* The Hague: Alliance for Peacebuilding, GPPAC, Kroc Institute, 2015.

United Nations, Department of Economic and Social Affairs. "Sustainable Development Knowledge Platform." Goal 16 webpage: https://sustainabledevelopment.un.org/sdg16.

United Nations Development Programme. *Human Security Report 1994.* New York: Oxford University Press, 1994.

United Nations General Assembly. "Report of the High-Level Independent Panel on Peace Operations on Uniting Our Strengths for Peace: Politics, Partnership and People." 70th session. A/70/95, June 17, 2015. http://www.un.org/sg/pdf/HIPPO_Report_1_June_2015.pdf.

World Bank. *World Development Report 2011: Conflict, Security, and Development.* Washington, DC: The World Bank, 2011.

Index

About the Contributors

EDITORS

David Cortright is director of policy studies at the Kroc Institute for International Peace Studies at the University of Notre Dame's Keough School of Global Affairs. He has a long history of public advocacy for disarmament and the prevention of war. As an active duty soldier during the Vietnam War he spoke against that conflict. In 1978 David was named executive director of SANE, the National Committee for a Sane Nuclear Policy, which under his leadership became the largest disarmament organization in the United States. In November 2002 he helped create Win Without War, a coalition of national organizations opposing the invasion and occupation of Iraq. He is the author or editor of 18 books, the most recent including *Drones and the Future of Armed Conflict* (University of Chicago Press, forthcoming), *Ending Obama's War* (Paradigm, 2011), and *Towards Nuclear Zero* (Routledge, IISS, 2010). He has also published books with Cambridge University Press, MIT Press, Rowman & Littlefield, and Lynne Rienner.

Melanie Greenberg is president and CEO of the Alliance for Peacebuilding (AfP). Before joining AfP, she was the president and founder of the Cypress Fund for Peace and Security, a foundation making grants in the areas of peacebuilding and nuclear nonproliferation. In her work on international conflict resolution, she has helped design and facilitate public peace processes in the Middle East, Northern Ireland, and the Caucasus. Her publications include *Words over War: Mediation and Arbitration to Prevent Deadly Conflict* (Rowman & Littlefield, 2000). Her articles also appear in

International Negotiation Journal, Dispute Resolution Magazine, and the *Ohio State Journal on Dispute Resolution.*

Laurel Stone is program manager for policy studies at the Kroc Institute for International Peace Studies at the University of Notre Dame's Keough School of Global Affairs. She manages several research, editing and grant projects for both the Policy Studies Program and the Peace Accords Matrix Project. She earned a master's degree from the Seton Hall School of Diplomacy and International Relations, where she specialized in conflict resolution and international security. Her graduate thesis analyzed the role of women in peace process agreements, with excerpts published in *The Guardian* and a policy report by the International Peace Institute.

CONTRIBUTORS

Sharon Bhagwan-Rolls is a Fiji Islander and executive director and cofounder of FemLINKPACIFIC. In 2000, she served as coordinator of the Blue Ribbon Peace Vigil for the National Council of Women in Fiji during the coup, during which she cofounded FemLINKPACIFIC. In 2006, she was a cofacilitator with the Pacific Islands Forum Secretariat. She also was a member of the Fiji government delegation to the UN Fourth World Conference on Women. Between 2010–2012 she coordinated civil society input into the development of the Pacific Regional Action Plan on Women, Peace and Security (2012–2015). She was subsequently appointed as a civil society organization (CSO) member of the Pacific Islands Forum's Regional Working Group on Women, Peace and Security tasked with overseeing the implementation of the action plan. In 2014, she was appointed to the UN high-level advisory group for the global study on the United Nations Security Council Resolution (UNSCR)1325.

Emmanuel Bombande is cofounder of the West Africa Network for Peacebuilding (WANEP) and its former executive director. He recently was appointed as the Special Adviser to the UN Secretary-General's Special Representative to West Africa, acting as head of the UN office for West Africa. He has been a lead mediator in many community-based mediation efforts in West Africa, served as a member of the UN Advisory Team in Ghana, and advised the government of Ghana on various conflict-prevention strategies. He has presented his research and practical experiences to the policymakers at the OECD, UN General Assembly, Dutch Ministry of Foreign Affairs, and the Economic Community of West African States (ECOWAS). He contributed chapters to *Ethnicity, Conflicts and Consensus in Ghana* (Woeli Publishing Services, 2007) and *A Handbook of International Peacebuilding: Into the Eye of a Storm* (Jossey-Bass Publications, 2002).

Rachel Fairhurst is programme services coordinator of Oxfam New Zealand. She previously worked as an international programs coordinator at the International Women's Development Agency (IWDA) in Melbourne, Australia, and as a research associate for the Kroc Institute of International Peace Studies. As a Fulbright Graduate Award recipient, Rachel worked as a research associate for the National Center for Peace and Conflict Studies and at a sustainable development organization in the West Bank. She is coeditor of *Drones and the Future of Armed Conflict* (University of Chicago Press, 2015).

Hyunjin Deborah Kwak is a PhD candidate in sociology and peace studies at the University of Notre Dame. Her research interests include social movements, emotion, interaction, small groups, and religion. Deborah's dissertation, "Building and Burning Bridges: Contention and Solidarity among Civil Society Groups in Mindanao," examines how civil society groups in a post conflict society interact in deliberative spaces and how they go about or fail to reconcile differences in group identity, interaction style, and mobilization efforts.

John Paul Lederach is professor of international peacebuilding at the Kroc Institute for International Peace Studies and senior fellow of Humanity United. Widely known for his pioneering work in conflict transformation, he is involved in conciliation work in Colombia, the Philippines, and Nepal in addition to countries in East and West Africa. He is the author of twenty-two books, including *The Moral Imagination: The Art and Soul of Building Peace* (Oxford University Press, 2005), *When Blood and Bones Cry Out* (University of Queensland Press, 2010), and *Building Peace: Sustainable Reconciliation in Divided Societies* (USIP, 1997).

Myla Leguro holds an MA in peace studies from the Kroc Institute for International Peace Studies at the University of Notre Dame. She has worked for Catholic Relief Services (CRS) since 1991 on peace and development projects in Mindanao. As program manager of the Peace and Reconciliation Program of CRS-Philippines, Myla organized two major peacebuilding institutions: the Mindanao Peacebuilding Institute in 2000 and the Grassroots Peace Learning Center in 2003. She has worked as an international trainer in Timor-Leste and Nepal, and has served as a resource person in various peacebuilding conferences in Colombia, Thailand, and the United States.

Bernardo Arévalo de León is senior peacebuilding advisor for Interpeace's International Peacebuilding Advisory Team in Geneva. He previously worked as an ambassador of Guatemala, as director of the Joint Programme Unit for United Nations/Interpeace Initiatives (JPU-UNOPS), and deputy director general—research and development for Interpeace. Bernardo specializes in the design, management, and facilitation of inclusive, participatory, multi stakeholder processes in policy; research in conflict-affected contexts; and has long-standing expertise in democracy, security, and participatory research.

Erin McCandless is a tenured part-time professor at the New School's Graduate Program in International Affairs and cofounder and chief editor of the international, refereed *Journal of Peacebuilding and Development*. She is the author and/or editor of *Polarization and Transformation in Zimbabwe: Social Movements, Strategy Dilemmas and Change* (Lexington Press, 2011) and *Conflict, Peacebuilding and Development: A Critical Reader and Compendium* (UN University for Peace, 2011). She has contributed to *Peace Review* and *Global Governance*, in addition to writing several policy papers and reports for Interpeace, the United Nations Children's Emergency Fund (UNICEF), the United Nations Development Programme (UNDP), the UN Peacebuilding Support Office, the Department for Peacekeeping Operations (DPKO), the Institute for Security Studies, and the United States Institute for Peace (USIP).

Anna Milovanovic-Fazliu is program associate at the AfP and the communications and office manager at Mediators Beyond Borders International. She holds an LLM from the University of Kent at Brussels and has worked on research and in advocacy in Washington, DC—focusing on minority rights in the Balkans and North Africa. She is cofounder of the Macedonian chapter of 5th Pillar—an Indian initiative to counter petty corruption and empower citizens from the grassroots.

Karen Robinson is research associate at the Oversees Development Institute (ODI). She has research and policy-related expertise in the gender dimensions of peacebuilding and statebuilding. Her interests include justice and security sector reform, violence against women, and governance reform in fragile states. She has written several policy publications for the Organisation for Economic Co-operation and Development (OECD), the Democratic Control of Armed Forces (DCAF), and Cordaid. Karen holds a PhD in international relations from the London School of Economics.

Darynell Rodriguez Torres is programme manager for policy and advocacy at the GPPAC. His work is focused on strengthening cooperation between

GPPAC members and policymakers from governments, regional international organizations, and the United Nations to provide inputs for shaping conflict prevention and peacebuilding strategies. He has held different positions in the public, private, and not-for-profit sectors including government, regional organizations, and private firms specialized in political risk and public affairs.

Lisa Schirch is senior advisor on policy at the Alliance for Peacebuilding where she connects policymakers with global civil society networks, facilitates civil-military dialogue, and provides a conflict prevention and peacebuilding lens on current policy issues. Lisa is also research professor at the Center for Justice and Peacebuilding at Eastern Mennonite University. As a former Fulbright Fellow in East and West Africa, she conducted conflict assessments and participated in peacebuilding planning in addition to working in Afghanistan, Pakistan, Iraq, Sri Lanka, Indonesia, and Fiji. She has published five books and dozens of chapters and articles with Routledge, UN University Press, and the US Institute of Peace Press. Her most recent book is *Conflict Assessment and Peacebuilding Planning: Toward a Participatory Approach to Human Security* (Kumarian/Lynne Reinner Press, 2013).

Mahbouba Seraj is founder and director of Soraya Mashal Consulting in Afghanistan where she works with civil society to research, implement, and monitor programs that empower Afghan women and girls. She has been an advocate for women's inclusion in national reconstruction and reconciliation and successfully pushed for women's participation in the 2010 Peace Jirga as well as in the High Peace Council, both formed by the government to hold talks with the Taliban. She also was part of a delegation that promoted women's priorities during the December 2011 Bonn Conference.

Dewi Suralaga is the Indonesia National Coordinator for the Climate and Land Use Alliance (CLUA). She previously was policy advisor at Cordaid, where she wrote several policy papers, including *Gender Inequality and Fragility in the Post-MDG Framework, Financing for the Implementation of National Action Plans on UNSCR 1325*, and *Integrating Gender into the New Deal for Engagement in Fragile States*. She previously worked as the director of the Regional Office—Southeast Asia for Hivos and a conversation/programme director for the World Wide Fund for Nature (WWF) Indonesia.

Ana Glenda Táger has served as the Latin American regional director of Interpeace since 2005. Prior to her appointment as regional director, Ana Glenda worked with War-Torn Societies Project (WSP) International as a programme officer. In this capacity she supported the development of the "Toward a Policy in Citizenship Security" (POLSEC) programme, the Guatemalan Network for Democratic Security, and "Strengthening the Capacities of Civil Society on Security Issues" (FOSS) programme. She also helped to create a platform for dialogue between civil society and the military for the Latin American Faculty of Social Sciences (FLACSO–Guatemala) and other groups. She specializes in security and defense issues, and has published several articles on security, intelligence, and terrorism.

Peter van Tuijl is senior advisor to the Partnership for Governance Reform in Indonesia. From 2007–2016, he was executive director of the Global Partnership for the Prevention of Armed Conflict (GPPAC) Global Secretariat in The Hague. Between 2000 and 2007, he lived in Jakarta, Indonesia, and worked as a civil society expert with the UNDP-led Partnership for Governance Reform and as a senior technical advisor for a project to combat corruption in the Indonesian National Police, under the International Criminal Investigative Training Assistance Program (ICITAP), United States Department of Justice. He previously worked as a senior advisor with OxfamNovib, focusing on NGO advocacy capacity building. He coedited the book *NGO Accountability: Politics, Principles and Innovations* (Routledge, 2006). He has also published academic articles with the *Journal of International Affairs*, *World Development*, and *Third World Quarterly*.

Kristen Wall is former senior program officer for the Kosovo Project at the National Democratic Institute (NDI). Prior to working at NDI, Kristen was the program manager for the policy studies program at the Kroc Institute for International Peace Studies. She has taught nonviolent communication, trauma healing, restorative justice, and conflict transformation in prisons, religious congregations, and graduate programs. She is coeditor of *Drones and the Future of Armed Conflict* (University of Chicago Press, 2015).

CPSIA information can be obtained at www.ICGtesting.com
Printed in the USA
BVOW08s0022071016

464346BV00001B/2/P